RCC Pilotage Foundation
North Biscay
Ouessant to La Gironde

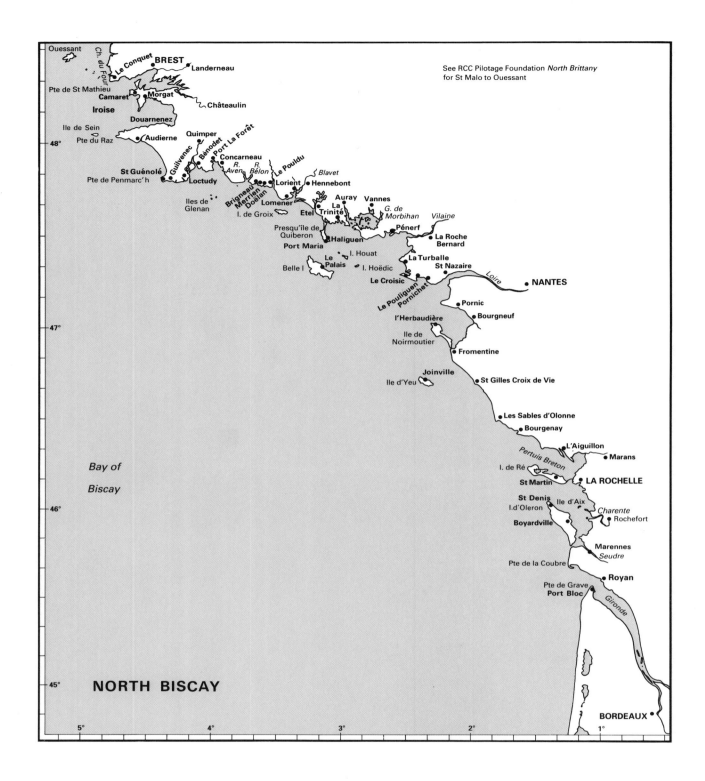

Ouessant

Le Conquet
BREST
● Landerneau

Ch. du Four

Pte de St Mathieu
Camaret ● Morgat
● Châteaulin

Iroise
Douarnenez

Ile de Sein
Pte du Raz ● **Audierne**
Quimper
● Bénodet
Port La Forêt
● **St Guénolé**
Guilvenec ● Concarneau
Pte de Penmarc'h **Loctudy**
R. R.
Aven Bélon
Le Pouldu
● Lorient ● Hennebont
Blavet
Brigneau
Merrien
Doëlan
Lomener
Iles de
Glenan
I. de Groix
Etel
La
Trinité
Auray
Vannes
G. de
Morbihan
Vilaine
Pénerf
Presqu'île de
Quiberon
Haliguen
La Roche
Bernard
Port Maria
I. Houat
La Turballe
Belle I
Le
Palais
I. Hoëdic
St Nazaire
Le Croisic
Loire
NANTES
Le Pouliguen
Pornichet
Pornic ●
l'Herbaudière
● Bourgneuf
Ile de
Noirmoutier
● Fromentine
Joinville
St Gilles Croix de Vie
Ile d'Yeu
● Les Sables d'Olonne
● Bourgenay
L'Aiguillon
Pertuis Breton
● Marans
I. de Ré
LA ROCHELLE
St Martin
St Denis   Ile d'Aix
I.d'Oleron   Charente
● Rochefort
Boyardville
Marennes
Seudre
Pte de la Coubre
● **Royan**
Pte de Grave
Port Bloc
Gironde

Bay of

Biscay

NORTH BISCAY

BORDEAUX ●

See RCC Pilotage Foundation *North Brittany*
for St Malo to Ouessant

48°

47°

46°

45°

5°   4°   3°   2°   1°

North Biscay

Ouessant to La Gironde

RCC PILOTAGE FOUNDATION

K. Adlard Coles
Revised by Nick Heath

Imray Laurie Norie & Wilson Ltd
St Ives Cambridgeshire England

Published by
Imray Laurie Norie & Wilson Ltd
Wych House, St Ives, Huntingdon
Cambridgeshire PE17 4BT England
☎ 0480 462114 *Fax* 0480 496109
1994

Partly based on
Biscay Harbours and Anchorages, Vols I and II
by K. Adlard Coles, first published in 1959 and 1960

As *North Biscay Pilot* published by Adlard Coles Ltd
Revised by Professor A. N. Black
Second edition 1977
Reprinted with amendments 1978
Third edition 1982
Revised by the RCC Pilotage Foundation
Reprinted with amendments 1985
Reprinted with amendments 1987
Fourth edition 1990
Fifth edition 1994

ISBN 0 85288 245 9

British Library Cataloguing in Publication Data
A catalogue record for this title is available from the British Library.

CAUTION

Every effort has been made to ensure the accuracy of this book. It contains selected information and thus is not definitive and does not include all known information on the subject in hand; this is particularly relevant to the plans, which should not be used for navigation. The Pilotage Foundation believes that its selection is a useful aid to prudent navigation, but the safety of a vessel depends ultimately on the judgement of the navigator, who should assess all information, published or unpublished.

PLANS

The plans in this guide are not to be used for navigation. They are designed to support the text and should always be used with navigational charts.

CORRECTIONS

The editors would be glad to receive any corrections, information or suggestions which readers may consider would improve the book, as new impressions will be required from time to time. Letters should be addressed to the Editor, *North Biscay*, care of the publishers. The more precise the information the better, but even partial or doubtful information is helpful, if it is made clear what the doubts are.

CORRECTIONAL SUPPLEMENTS

Imray pilot books are amended at intervals by the issue of correctional supplements. Supplements, if available, are supplied free of charge with the books when they are purchased. Further supplements are available from the publishers. The following should be quoted:

1. Name of book
2. Date of edition (above)
3. Date of last supplement (if applicable)
4. Name and address to which supplement should be sent on a stamped addressed A4 envelope.

The last input of technical information was April 1994.

Printed in Great Britain by The Bath Press, Avon.

Contents

Foreword

5th edition

The RCC Pilotage Foundation, a registered charity, is based on a very generous benefaction by an American member of the Royal Cruising Club, Dr Fred Ellis, and has been established to encourage the aspiring sailor to extend his cruising range with confidence. It edits and updates existing pilot books and guides and initiates its own where a need is recognised. The first works undertaken were new editions of *North Brittany Pilot*, by Adlard Coles, a member of the Club who gave his copyright to the Foundation, and *North Biscay Pilot*, which he wrote in collaboration with Professor Black. Its other works include *Atlantic Crossing Guide, Atlantic Spain and Portugal, Atlantic Islands (Azores, Madeira, Canary and Cape Verde Islands), Lesser Antilles* (in collaboration with the Service Hydrographique et Océanographique de la Marine), *The Baltic Sea* and *North Africa*.

As with the previous edition, the work of preparing this 5th edition of *North Biscay* was undertaken by Nick Heath, who again sailed the area. He was helped by contributions from other members of the RCC and many others interested in the project, noted elsewhere. The Pilotage Foundation is very grateful to all contributors, especially Nick Heath, for their work. Amendments to and comments on this or other volumes are very welcome, however large or small; they may be forwarded through Imray. Contributions are carefully considered and collated in annual amendments which may be obtained for no cost except that of a stamped addressed envelope sent to Imray with a request specifying the amendment required.

O. H. Robinson
Director
RCC Pilotage Foundation
1994

Acknowledgements

Although, in preparing the present edition, the editor was able to visit and photograph the many harbours and anchorages by sea, it would have been impossible to complete the work without the valuable assistance of harbourmasters, local yachtsmen, members of the RCC and of many other British yacht clubs.

He is particularly grateful to the British and French hydrographic offices for the help and co-operation that they provided, and to Michael Bonham Cozens (RCC), who flew the Director, Oz Robinson, along the coast to photograph the harbours from the air.

Among the many others who provided information there is space to mention only a very few:

Docteur Joseph Girad, President of the Association Nautique de l'Anse de Virly, an admirer of the late Adlard Coles and his books, went to great trouble in helping me to locate the elusive 'transformer' at the entrance to Le Lay river and to provide information about La Faute and L'Aiguillon.

Mr John Hinde pinpointed a rocky spur that can be a hazard, in a creek off the Odet. Paul Dane (RCC) has continued to provide information, particularly on the Vilaine and the Ile et Rance canal. Dr John Fabricus (RCC) was among those who corresponded on Royan. Captain Jake Backus RN (RCC) wrote about Audierne and La Rochelle, and drew attention to changes in the buoyage of the river at Etel. Miss Gillian Watson (RCC) made a comprehensive study of the harbours on Ile d'Oléron.

Finally, the family of Robert Beard spent a weekend measuring the heights of the power cables over the river Aulne, and he also reported a cable crossing the Vilaine and gave its height.

In order to maintain the accuracy of the edition it is essential that crews of yachts visiting the area continue to take note of changes and corrections and to report them by writing to the Pilotage Foundation, care of the publishers.

N. E. Heath
1994

Also by the RCC Pilotage Foundation
North Brittany
Atlantic Spain and Portugal
Atlantic Islands
North Africa
Lesser Antilles (with SHOM)
The Baltic Sea
Faeroe, Iceland & Greenland
Atlantic Crossing Guide (A. & C. Black Ltd)

Introduction

Cruising in south Brittany and Biscay

A small yacht heading for the Bay of Biscay will pass Ouessant, usually passing inside through the Chenal du Four. After she has rounded Pointe de St Mathieu, the Rade de Brest lies to the east, providing a magnificent cruising ground. Next comes the Baie de Douarnenez, a fine big bay, having however only two secure harbours.

Bound south, a vessel will next pass through the Raz de Sein. Here, as in the Chenal du Four, the tidal streams are strong and in bad weather the seas are dangerous, but once through the channel the Bay of Biscay is entered. The tidal streams are weaker and the weather becomes progressively warmer the further south one sails. Between Penmarc'h and La Rochelle there are three granite islands, Ile de Groix, Belle Ile and Ile d'Yeu, each of which has a harbour and minor anchorages. To the north and east of these islands, the mainland coast offers the variety of harbours and anchorages which makes it so attractive to the cruising man. There are anchorages in deep water and shallow, fishing harbours, busy ports, sophisticated holiday resorts, yachting centres, estuaries and rivers with peaceful reaches.

The first busy sailing area to be reached is the large bay from Loctudy to Concarneau, sheltered by the Iles de Glénan with their famous sailing school. Thence some passage-making leads to the Baie de Quiberon, another sheltered area, very popular with French yachtsmen. Here, between the yachting centres of La Trinité and Le Croisic, there lie all the anchorages in the Morbihan ('the little sea'), Pénerf and the beautiful river La Vilaine. To seaward there are the little islands of Houat and Hoëdic, and to the west Belle Ile with the crowded harbour of Le Palais and another, less active, at Sauzon. In this area one could spend a month exploring and sailing in shelter even in bad weather.

Shallow-draught yachts which do not wish to make the passage down Channel and through the rough waters of Four and Sein can come through the Breton Canals. The usual exit from these is to La Vilaine, but it is also possible to go on to Nantes and come down the Loire. The real canal enthusiast, if his draught is small enough, can turn aside at Redon, where he is almost at sea, and after another hundred locks, emerge at Lorient.

Beyond Le Croisic is the Loire, the southern boundary of Brittany. The coastal scene changes, rock reluctantly, but never entirely, giving place to sandy shores. The character of the harbours changes too; there are not so many harbours in which a yacht can lie afloat and come and go freely at any state of the tide. For this reason the best time for cruising in this region is when the tides are taking off from springs to neaps. It is then possible to leave near the morning high water and arrive in time for the evening one. On this part of the coast there are two large islands, Noirmoutier and Ile d'Yeu. Noirmoutier offers interesting anchorages, and one marina. Port Joinville is the only good harbour on Ile d'Yeu.

Another passage leads to the area around Ile de Ré and La Rochelle. La Rochelle is an historic city with two fine old towers guarding the entrance to one harbour and a vast marina. Ile de Ré is low and sandy. St Martin, the capital, has a secure harbour with a wet dock. This area is the end of the popular cruising ground, but a few ports down to the entrance to the Gironde have been included for the benefit of those using the Canal du Midi, which connects with the Mediterranean.

The cruising area which this book covers is a fascinating and varied one. For many British yachtsmen, the difficulty lies in the time taken to get there and return within the span of a summer holiday. A good plan is to work the yacht down Channel in weekends before the real holiday begins. Then make a direct passage from there to the South Brittany coast. The English Channel is fairly wide here, say 120 miles to Ouessant, and it is about the same distance on to Belle Ile.

Ouessant is not a nice landfall in bad weather and in fog it is unpleasant; in thick weather it is better to keep offshore, outside all the dangers. However, in summer really bad weather is uncommon.

Winds

Winds in the north of Biscay are variable, but westerly winds (SW to NW) are most frequent in the summer months, especially in July and August. In spring, early summer and late autumn, winds between N and E are also common. There is some indication that the climate is changing; the strong westerlies of the last few decades seem to be dying away. The Bay of Biscay has a reputation for gales, but in summer from May to September winds of force 7 and over are recorded only about once in 25 days. Most summer gales are associated with depressions passing to the northward, with backing winds followed by a veer to the W or NW. At intervals of several years, very severe short storms may occur, which may be missed by the forecasters. Beware of a sudden fall in the barometer in muggy, thundery weather, with poor visibility.

Land and sea breezes near the coast are common in settled summer weather. Especially in the southern part of the area they result in the *vent solaire*. After a noonday calm a westerly sea breeze sets in. This goes round to NW and by evening to N, and finally about midnight, or a little later, it settles in the NE, when it sometimes blows very freshly, causing quite a rough sea, and continues until 0800.

Another feature of this part of the Bay of Biscay is that if a NE wind starts to veer to S in the morning, and only goes as far as S and backs to the NE, the NE wind may be accompanied by strong squalls.

Visibility

Fog, mist or haze is quite frequent during the summer. There is visibility of under 5 miles on about one day in five, but real fog, reducing visibility to less than ½ mile, averages only one day in twenty. The coast is so well marked by beacons and towers that navigation in poor visibility is possible, but thick fog is very unpleasant if it occurs when one is sailing in narrow tidal waters.

Currents and tides

When navigating in light weather and fog, the tidal streams are of great significance. Small-scale tidal charts only show the main streams, but in coastal waters there are local variations and eddies. The local set can be estimated by examination of pot buoys, which are numerous on the coast.

Swell

Swell is a factor which sometimes has to be reckoned with on the NW and W coasts of France. It appears to run higher in some parts than others, and is notable in the vicinity of Ouessant and NE of Le Four. In the Bay of Biscay itself swell seems to be less frequent as the weather is better, and the swell ranges from gentle undulations to waves of considerable height, though it is rarely so uncomfortable as between Ile Vierge and Ouessant, where the strong tidal streams are an added complication.

A large swell will break heavily on bars and in shallow water, with the result that the approaches to some of the harbours, such as Bélon, Le Pouldu and Etel, are dangerous even in fine weather if there is a ground swell. Swell can break intermittently and

dangerously on rocks rising from deep water, even when there is apparently a safe depth over them.

Another characteristic of swell is that when it enters a narrowing inlet it tends to increase in height and steepness. It funnels up the entrance and will surge into anchorages which one would expect to be sheltered from the direction of the swell. For this reason, anchorages open to the Atlantic, such as those on the west side of Ile de Groix, Belle Ile and Ile d'Yeu, should be used only with caution, in settled weather, with an offshore wind and in the absence of swell. Furthermore, if ground swell manifests itself in calm weather (and it can arrive with little warning, originating in disturbances far out in the ocean), a vessel should leave the open anchorage before it builds up to possibly formidable dimensions, when no anchor will hold. French fishermen take swell seriously, and none should know better. The French weather forecasts for shipping include forecasts of swell (*la houle*).

Type of yacht - draught and drying out

The North Biscay coast suits all types of yacht, large or small, deep-keeled or shallow-draught.

For large yachts there are plenty of deep-water anchorages; most of the shallower harbours can be entered near high water, and the yacht can dry out against a quay. Before doing so it is best to make local enquiries, as the bottom in parts of some harbours is rough or rocky.

To ensure taking the bottom with the yacht at the correct angle against the quay, which need not be great, it is usual to put all movable weights on the landward side of the yacht. In addition it is a wise precaution to shackle the main halyard to a bollard on the quayside and set it up as the tide falls. By this means the mast is stayed to the quay and the yacht cannot fall outwards, but do not forget to release the halyard when the tide rises. Good fenders are needed, as quay walls are often very rough; they should be hard and not squashy or they will be squeezed flat and the yacht will lean heavily inwards.

The yacht *Cohoe III*, in which Adlard Coles carried out his many surveys, had a draught of 1·8m (6ft). She had a fairly long straight keel, which was an advantage when drying out alongside a quay. Yachts with very cut-away forefoots rest bow down at a considerable angle, which is not necessarily dangerous, but decidedly uncomfortable. The modern racing yacht with short fin keel and separate skeg does not usually lie comfortably against a quay. However, there are now many marinas along the coast in which a deep-draught vessel may find a berth.

French fishing vessels and most small French yachts are equipped with legs. Not only can they dry out against a quay more safely, but they can dry out anywhere in any sheltered anchorage if the bottom is smooth and hard. Legs are a great asset to cruising on the Biscay coast. Best of all is a bilge-keel yacht that can take the ground. She can explore many parts that are impossible for keel yachts, and can often find a snug berth inside the local moorings while her deep-keeled sister is rolling farther out.

Where reference is made in the text to a 'yacht which can take the ground', it is implied that she does not need the outside support of a quay wall.

A very large number of French yachtsmen sail dinghies or small yachts that are launched from trailers and the launching facilities are good nearly everywhere. It is quite easy, therefore, to trail a boat out and spend a happy holiday on this coast exploring its nooks and crannies, rocks and sands.

Navigating among rocks

The coast of Brittany and North Biscay is famous for its rocks, which to a stranger may cause some apprehension. This will be especially the case if he is accustomed to mud pilotage, as on the east coast of England. He will soon come to realise that although it is much more important to avoid hitting the bottom, the many landmarks, natural and man-made, make it easy to know exactly where one is; if one knows exactly where one is, one has no reason to run aground. It is usually easy, by sliding a ruler over the chart, to find your own transits to keep out of trouble.

Beacons and towers are permanent, although occasionally damaged by gales, but complete reliance should not be placed on buoys, which may drag their moorings during gales, though in practice I have never found one out of position. Many of the rocks and shoals shown on the charts are not dangerous to moderate-draught yachts, except in bad weather, when they cause the seas to break. Much depends upon the state of the tide.

A useful tip is to estimate the rise of tide at the time when a harbour is to be approached, and then to put a pencilled circle on the chart round each rock or shoal which will not have a safe depth of water over it, remembering that tides do not always rise exactly as predicted. It is often surprising to find how few they are, so that pilotage is simplified by concentrating on the rocks which may be dangerous.

A common feature of a rocky coast is the extension of a pronounced headland in the form of a reef continuing seaward under water. For this reason, when approaching an inlet between two promontories, never cut across one of the promontories to the entrance, unless the chart indicates clear water. Approach from seaward with the middle of the inlet well open, allowing for the probable extension of the promontory under water.

If there is a big swell the seas will probably break over sunken rocks which are dangerous, and it may be necessary to avoid rocks which are covered by water of a depth equal to several times the yacht's draught. In strong streams the presence of rocks may be indicated by rips, or in smooth water by circles of oily-looking water. Even in deep water an uneven bottom causes a disturbance on the surface if the current is strong, so the oily circles do not always denote danger. In parts of Brittany the water is very clear, and if a member of the crew stands forward he can often see underwater rocks.

Rocks can be dangerous in light weather to yachts not equipped with reliable auxiliary power. In such circumstances the danger is greater than in rough conditions, if the tide is setting towards them. There is a theory that if a yacht is drifting becalmed, the stream will set her safely past rocks on one side or the other. This may be true of steep isolated above-water rocks, but it is certainly not true of under-water ledges. Great care must be exercised when navigating in calm weather near rocks; a good kedge with a very long warp must be ready for use.

Some harbours, such as the Ile de Sein and St Guénolé, have many rocks in the approaches. These present no great difficulty to the experienced cruising man, but as a mistake could have serious consequences, a newcomer to these coasts may prefer to limit his cruising on the first occasion to the better known and more easily accessible harbours. The more difficult anchorages should only be attempted in settled weather with clear visibility and preferably at neaps. The transits and landmarks should be identified with certainty before the yacht enters the danger area of rocks.

It is a good idea to check the yacht's position regularly by reference to natural features. New beacons can be built, or one mistaken for another, the large white building can be rendered inconspicuous by a larger whiter building, but nobody replaces or removes headlands or islands. Above all keep the identifications going well ahead of the yacht; not only does this give more time if things do not 'add up', but minor headlands may be quite prominent when looked at along the coast, but insignificant and unidentifiable when seen from directly offshore.

It cannot be sufficiently emphasised that electronic position indicators such as DECCA and GPS are aids to the navigator of a vessel, who must be aware of their failings and should be continually developing his, or her, own skills in pilotage from the immediate experiences of a passage.

The editor is convinced that all waypoints should be taken by the navigator off the on-board chart and never from an almanac or other reference book.

Harbours

In artificial harbours formed by breakwaters, it is inadvisable to cross close off the end of a breakwater, as these are often built on rocks, or have rocks at their bases. When entering a strange harbour it is best to approach about midway between the jetties with the inner harbour open.

Unless using a mooring or a berth at a marina there is generally no need to seek out the authorities on entering a port. They will often visit a yacht after she is berthed. Stay away from areas assigned to the fishing fleets.

Mooring

It may be worth mentioning some methods of mooring which are more common in France than in England. The first is lying closely packed, side by side, with a mooring anchor ahead and the stern pulled in to a quay or pontoon. If it is necessary to lay out an anchor ahead, one must note the direction in which the chains of those already berthed lead, and lay the anchor accordingly. Sometimes there is a line of buoys to which to secure the bow. Sometimes the pick-up rope for the bow mooring is led back to the pontoon; this can be tricky, as one has to back into the pontoon before getting the mooring on board, unless one sends out a dinghy.

Another unfamiliar method of mooring uses a big-ship buoy or tonne. Each new arrival takes a bow rope to the buoy and a cluster forms. When this is full a second circle is sometimes formed, by anchoring and taking a line to the buoy.

Both of these methods call for a good supply of fenders. Both methods, and also more familiar methods, are made less comfortable than they might be because many French yachtsmen are unfamiliar with the use of springs in circumstances in which the English regard their use as normal. I have, indeed, been positively asked not to use them by my neighbour when we were moored ahead and stern to buoys.

Provisions

Ordinary provisions can be bought in all towns, most of which have a supermarket, and even in small villages there are shops which supply necessities and are nearly always open. Very small communities sometimes rely on a travelling shop, which is less convenient. Milk should be bought pasteurised, or it will not keep long. *Stérilisé* is similar to 'long-life'. Groceries and meat are similarly priced to the UK, but it is wise to stock up with nonperishables before starting the cruise. Seafood such as mussels, crabs and prawns is good and reasonably priced when bought in the market, though lobsters, alas, command their price anywhere. Mackerel can be caught, though less easily than in the English Channel; they seem more sluggish and will not come if the yacht is travelling fast. French bread is delicious, but does not keep. A *baguette* can sometimes be given a second life after 24 hours if placed in a hot oven for a short time. If bread is required to remain edible for several days, ask for *pain complet*, which is similar to a wholemeal loaf. Where there is a baker, bread will be available early, but there may be a delay where it comes by van to a *dépôt de pain*.

In the text, under Facilities, 'all shops' implies at least bread, grocer, butcher, cooked meats and usually ironmonger and *droguerie* (paraffin, paints, etc.) as well.

Telephone cards

These can be purchased from a post office or tobacconist/newsagent and from some café/bars. Most of the public telephones now require cards.

Water

There is a tradition that French water is suspect. The installation of a central piped water supply almost everywhere has changed this and brought other changes too. The water towers which have appeared in great numbers are conspicuous marks for the navigator, but piped supplies everywhere mean that the taps in the streets which used to be so convenient have now gone.

The availability of convenient watering points is given in the text under the heading Facilities. Only rarely is the absence of a watering point specifically mentioned; if water is not mentioned under this heading it should be assumed that water may be difficult to find, except by courtesy from shops or cafés.

Fuel

It is no longer permitted for yachtsmen to buy the tax-free fuel available to fishermen, or the red-tinted diesel oil sold for domestic heating as *fuel oil domestique* (FOD). It is, however, exceptional for the numerous marinas not to offer both petrol and diesel oil from quayside pumps, though not all will operate outside the French holiday season. Where there is no marina, fuel may be available from pumps, though the presence of a pump does not guarantee this; it may be for fishermen's supply only. In some ports it may be necessary to fill by can from roadside garages.

Petrol (*essence*) comes in two grades, 'super' and 'normal'. Prices are rather above those in the UK, with a rather higher differential between grades. Diesel (*gasoil*, pronounced 'gazwahl') costs as much as that obtained from roadside filling stations in the UK.

In marinas it is now common for pumps to be card operated. They cannot take UK cards, but a marina attendant can usually be persuaded to operate the pump for cash.

Formalities

As the European Union becomes established the regulations presently in force will no doubt be altered and skippers are advised to keep abreast of the changes. The situation at the start of 1994 appears to be as follows:

EU countries, including the UK but not the Channel Islands, no longer require yachts, when travelling from one EU country to another, to report their departure or arrival, unless dutiable or prohibited goods are carried, or non-EU nationals are on board.

It is advisable to carry on board evidence that VAT has been paid on the vessel, and all yachts visiting France must carry a Certificate of Registry. Heavy fines are imposed on defaulters. The British Certificate can be that of the Board of Trade or the Small Ships Register, administered by DVLA, Swansea, SA99 1BX ☎ (0792) 783355.

The status of yachts registered elsewhere should be established in advance.

Personal passports should be carried by all members of the ship's company. In practice they are likely to be required only for cashing cheques, for independent return to the UK by public transport and, in the case of the owner, for dealing with the Customs.

Yachts arriving in French waters with goods on board that are dutiable in France must enter a port where they can be cleared by Customs, flying the 'Q' flag. Yachts arriving from another EU country without dutiable goods can enter any harbour but must not fly a 'Q'. During its stay in French waters a yacht may be boarded on several occasions by Customs and the onus is on the skipper to prove that no regulations are being broken. During the first visit ask for *une fiche*; if the officers are satisfied, you will be given one to show that the vessel has been cleared. Should you be approached at a later date, it is only necessary to show *la fiche* to satisfy the intending boarders.

Few officials, except in marinas, speak English. To enforce the ownership regulations Customs visit yachts, even under way. A *fiche* from them will simplify later visits.

From 1994 it is no longer forbidden for one skipper to hand over to another in French waters, but owners must be aware of and abide by European VAT regulations and the French regulations for chartering.

Inland waterways

In January 1994 the French Inland Waterways Authority introduced a new regulation concerning any person helming a vessel with an engine of more than 6hp on an inland waterway.

There are three categories of certificate required for helming French-registered vessels. The present minimum requirement (1994) for all persons helming a powered vessel of less than 15 metres, registered in the UK, is that they should possess an RYA Helmsman's Overseas Certificate of Competence.

An inland waterway is defined as commencing above the first port on a waterway controlled by the Authority, but it is not yet clear whether the Rance above the Barrage, and other Brittany rivers and canals, are included. Until the RYA has been able to clarify the position with the French it is probably advisable to obtain the HOCC for helming in these waters.

Search and rescue

The French search and rescue organisations (CROSS CORSEN, N of Pointe du Raz; CROSS ETEL, S of Pointe du Raz) operate an excellent passage-surveillance service. Some harbourmasters require a form to be completed showing 'where from' and 'where to'. This information is passed on to CROSS CORSEN/CROSS ETEL. It is important that, if a yacht does not go to where she has said she is going, the information should be reported quickly. Otherwise a futile search may be instituted.

Yacht clubs

There are yacht clubs and sailing schools in most French harbours; they are invariably hospitable to visitors. Assistance or advice is always given readily, and showers are often available.

Laying up

In order to spend more time on the Biscay coast, it may be convenient to take a holiday late in the summer and leave the yacht in France for the winter. By taking an early holiday in the following year, the cruise can be continued and the yacht brought home again in time for the remainder of the season.

A number of British yachts are now wintered in such marinas as La Forêt, enabling their owners to cruise in these attractive waters and, at the same time, to save considerably on the fees charged in UK marinas.

Fishermen

There are many fishermen's dan buoys round the coast and sometimes well out to sea. They present a hazard, especially at night when under power, and a constant lookout is necessary. The buoys are usually in pairs, flying the owner's particular flag. If the pair can be identified, it is advisable not to pass between them when north of the Loire.

South from Lorient a line of very small floats may be seen running between the larger dans. Their presence can be indicated on French charts by the legend *Attention aux Orins des Casiers*. Do not pass between these pairs of dans!

Japanese seaweed (*Sargassum muticum*)

Some years ago, seaweed used for packing in a Japanese commercial vessel was deposited in the Solent. This spread rapidly and caused problems by blocking the water intakes for marine engine cooling systems.

This weed, floating on the surface, spread rapidly south and became more of a menace as it toughened in warmer waters. By 1988 it was found to cover the bottom in the harbour on Ile de Sein.

In 1992 it had spread as far as Ile d'Oléron, where the propellers of the yachts in the marina at St Denis appeared like mop heads and were useless for propulsion!

Patches of the weed seen floating on the surface must be avoided, especially when under power, and it is advisable to carry on board a two-metre length of plastic tubing, fitted at one end with a Perspex window, with which to inspect the propeller from dinghy or pontoon. A strong knife is necessary to clear the weed.

Charts, tides and navigation

In this edition metres have replaced feet, fathoms and cables. Larger distances remain in nautical miles.

Chart datum

Datum in the sailing directions and in the plans reproduced in this book is the same as on French charts; soundings are reduced to the approximate level of the lowest predicted tides. This level is referred to as LAT (lowest astronomical tide). Although the actual lowest predicted tide can only occur near the equinox and will not, therefore, affect most yachtsmen, predicted tides nearly down to LAT can occur at any time. At such times exceptional meteorological conditions could result in tides falling below chart datum.

This datum is of the utmost importance when navigating in the Bay of Biscay, for it means, especially in Brittany, that at mean low water springs there may be 0·6m (2ft) more water than is shown on the chart, and at mean low water neaps even greater depth. The height of MLWS and MLWN above datum at the Bélon river entrance is shown at the head of each chapter, so that the appropriate figure can be added to the soundings shown on the plan or given in the text. British charts of the French coast adopt the same datum as the French charts on which they are based.

Heights

In the plans and sailing instructions in this book the French method of measurement, which differs in some respects from British practice, has been followed.

Rocks that uncover and drying patches

The heights are given above chart datum, being shown in underlined figures. In the text the word 'dries' is used. This is the same as British practice. On modern French charts, but not in this book, these figures are in italics.

Rocks that never cover

The heights are given above chart datum, being shown in underlined figures. In the text the word 'high' is used. British practice is to give these heights above MHWS.

At present French practice is to give the height above mean tide level. This can lead to confusion. For instance, on the useful French chart *7138 Ports et Mouillages en Bretagne Sud* a group of rocks (all but one of which cover at HW) named Le Roc'h is shown as an islet some 100m long!

On older French charts rocks that never cover are marked with the symbol 'T' over them; this must not be misread as representing a beacon. This convention is not used in this book.

Land heights

Heights on land, not underlined, are above mean tide level where this does not lead to the confusion noted above. British practice is to give these heights above MHWS.

Lighthouses

The elevation of the lights (not the actual heights of the structures) is given above MHWS. This is the same as British practice.

Sailing directions

The description of each port is set out in the same form, so that the reader will come to know where to look for the information he wants. It is written from the point of view of the master of a sailing yacht of normal size. If there is more than 3m (10ft) of water, the channel is described as deep, on the assumption that users of this book will not have a greater draught than this. Low bridges are treated as blocking navigation; although many motor yachts will be able to pass them unhindered, the upper reaches beyond them have not been inspected.

Beacons

The offshore marks on this coast are subject to damage in bad weather which may not be repaired for some months. Beacons and beacon towers can lose their topmarks or even be totally destroyed. In this case a small buoy with the appropriate marking may be positioned close by until a repair is effected.

There are many kinds of beacon and it is hard to find a descriptive terminology. British charts use 'Bn' or 'Bn Tr' to cover this wide range. The scheme which has been followed as far as possible in this book can be set out thus:

Description on French charts	Appearance	Description in this book
Balise	A wood or iron pole beacon, usually on ground which covers and uncovers, or	*Beacon*
	A modern version of the above, made of concrete, usually about 1m in diameter, on a wider base. They resemble thin *tourelles*; or	*Concrete beacon*
	A built-up beacon on shore, often of iron or masonry in the shape of a pillar.	*Masonry beacon*
Tourelle	A stone or concrete beacon, usually on ground which covers with the tide. Cylindrical or slightly tapered in shape.	*Beacon tower*
Amer	A built-up beacon on shore, which may be of any shape, often painted white.	*Masonry beacon*
Mur blanchi	A wall painted white (sometimes specially built as a beacon).	*Wall beacon*
Pyramide	A slender conical beacon painted white (not a mathematical pyramid).	*Pyramid*

Beacons, concrete beacons and towers are commonly painted to conform with the buoyage systems (cardinal or lateral) and have the appropriate topmarks; the others are not. The word 'tower' is also used in a less restricted sense on occasion; there should be no confusion, since when it refers to a *tourelle* it will be followed by a note on the colour. The heads of breakwaters, forming a harbour entrance, are often marked with white paint, with a green triangle or red square indicating the side on which to pass them. When passing under a bridge there are similar marks to indicate the appropriate arch for the channel.

Key to plans

The cardinal system of buoyage is now well established and needs little explanation. Cardinal lights are all quick or very quick flashing white, memorable from a clock face: three flashes at 3 o'clock for E, six, with one long flash, for S, nine for W, and continuous, which may be thought of as twelve, for N. The conventional lateral system is used for marking a channel, with red for port hand and green for starboard, marked from the entrance without regard to the tidal stream.

Occasionally, as in the entrance to L'Aulne river, the red port-hand buoys are conical instead of can-shaped.

Isolated dangers with navigable water all round are marked by BRB beacons or buoys. Wrecks are now marked by lateral or cardinal warnings in the same way as any other obstacle to navigation. Fairway, landfall or safe-water buoys are painted with red and white vertical stripes, with white lights and a single red spherical topmark, to show navigable water. The key shows the topmarks, which are significant in a poor light when the colours cannot be identified. The French describe their buoys as *pylone* (pillar), *espar* (spar), *cylindrique* (can) and *conique* (conical).

Each plan has been subdivided along the left-hand and bottom margins into tenths of a minute of latitude and longitude. The use of identical units in each plan should give an immediate indication of the scale. In a large-scale plan, a scale of metres is shown on the plan and the left-hand margin can be used to measure off in cables if desired. One division on each edge is numbered so that references to other charts, notices to mariners, etc., are easily made.

Dry land is tinted grey, drying areas are blue/grey. In most cases, areas where the depth is less than 2 metres are shown blue and deep water is left white. A 2-metre contour is not available on some charts, and in this case the blue tinting is extended to the 3 or 5-metre contour, giving an extra margin of safety. When first entering an area, for safety, keep in the white if possible. In a plan where the division between blue and white does not define the 2m contour, this will be indicated in the caption below.

Beacons

Beacon towers (tourelles) Masonry towers, painted in appropriate IALA colours, otherwise white, e.g. ⨅

Beacons (balises) Iron, masonry or wooden pole-like structures painted in IALA colours and usually with the appropriate topmark, e.g. ⌁

Pyramids (pyramides) Conical beacon towers, usually white and quite narrow for their height, like obelisks with flat tops. Mainly used for leading and clearing marks e.g. △

Buoys (bouées)

Pillar Usually lattice structures. The colours on the latticework are not always easy to distinguish and from a distance the shape is considerably distorted when solar panels are fitted. Where a radar reflector is mounted, it is often larger than the topmark shown e.g. ⟁ ⟁ ⟁ ⟁ BY BYB YB YBY

Spindle Basically can-shaped cylindrical, but much higher in relation to its diameter. Invariably a lateral port mark, e.g. ⟋

Spar A narrow steel cylinder mounted on a float. Usually painted in IALA colours, with appropriate topmark. Not always conspicuous, e.g. ⟋

Can Generally used only as lateral and safe water marks e.g. ⌐

Conical Generally used as lateral starboard marks but occasionally as lateral port marks. △

In relation to all buoys:

Those fitted with lights are shown: 🔆

Those fitted with bells are noted 'Bell'

Those fitted with whistles are noted 'Whis'

Symbols used on plans

Fuel	⛽
Customs	⊖
Water	⊥
Harbourmaster	⊕
Lifeboat	✦
Slip	⌐
Yacht harbour	⛵

Bearings

Bearings are expressed in degrees true, but in the text magnetic bearings in points are occasionally given to indicate the approximate direction of a course or object. Variation is at present approximately 5°W in the north and 3°W in the south of the area.

Lights

The descriptions of all the lights to be used in entering a port are collected into one tabulation to assist in identification. The heights are given in metres (m), and the range of visibility is given in miles (M). Where a light has sectors the limits of the sectors are shown only on the plan and the range given refers to the light of maximum range (white, or intensified sector).

The light from a lighthouse may become invisible at long range for one of two reasons: the light may not be sufficiently bright, or it may disappear below the horizon (geographical range). The geographical range normally quoted is for a height of eye of 4·5m. From a typical yachting height of eye of, say, 1·5m the actual visible range is about 2 miles less than the geographical range.

The distance at which a light is bright enough to be seen varies with the haze in the atmosphere; the term nominal range is used for this distance when the meteorological visibility is 10 miles, though a light may of course be seen at a greater distance. It is this nominal range (quoted in Admiralty and French light lists) which is quoted in this book. If the nominal range quoted is 15M or more it is likely that it will exceed the geographical range. Lights with a nominal range of 10M or less are relatively weak and may be difficult to identify among other lights on the shore.

The characteristics referred to in the text are for 1994, and are liable to alterations which will be shown on chart corrections and in the current Admiralty *List of Lights Volumes A* and *D* (for shore lights) and *Pilot* (for buoys).

Although the general practice is for coloured sectors to indicate dangers and white sectors the clear passages, this is not universal, and it should not be assumed that the white sectors indicate deep water over the whole sector at all distances from the light. Generally, if a light shows a white safe sector with red and green sectors on each side, the green sector is to starboard and the red to port, at least in the principal channel. To return to the white sector, show your green to a green light and your red to a red light, a variant of 'green to green or red to red, perfect safety'. *This rule is not universal and should be checked for each light.* Also, narrow intensified sectors usually, but not always, fall within the safe width of the channel.

The French make considerable use of rhythmic lights, such as:

Fl(2+1), on French charts F.2é.1é.
or Oc(1+2), F.10.20.
or Oc(1+3), F.10.30.

Lights are often 'directional'; that is, they show brightly over a very narrow sector and sometimes faintly outside the sector.

Radiobeacons

The descriptions of the radiobeacons are given with the lights; they comprise:

1. The call sign.
2. The frequency in kHz, formerly called kc/s.
3. The range in nautical miles.

Tides

Tidal streams

The Biscay currents and tidal streams offshore are weak, but inshore they are sometimes strong, notably in the Chenal du Four, Raz de Sein, Passage de la Teignouse and the Morbihan. As is to be expected, the streams tend to be faster off headlands.

The rates and even the directions of tidal streams may be affected by the wind, especially if it blows hard for a long time from one direction. In rivers and estuaries they may be affected by flood water from the land. They often run perpendicular to the coastline.

Tidal heights

The Admiralty *Tide Tables* give the most accurate predictions of tidal heights, but few yachtsmen carry them and the calculations are tedious.

Special tables (on the following page) have been prepared for this volume; these give adequate accuracy while being very much simpler to use. They are based on the principle that HW and LW heights can be found by taking the mean tide level (MTL) of the port and adding or subtracting the half-range of the tide for the day at that port.

The appropriate half-range is found by adding two index numbers: one for the day's tide (small near neaps, large near springs) and one for the port (small for a port with a small tidal range, and larger for one with a greater range). The index number for the day's tide is given in the tables in terms of the height of HW at Brest or Pointe de Grave, the standard ports used on this coast. The index number for each port is given, with the MTL, at the head of each chapter.

Detailed instructions, and an example of the calculations, follow.

Tide tables

From the *Nautical Almanac* take the time and height of HW Brest or Pointe de Grave. Note that in some nautical almanacs the times are as for Time Zone 1. From the chapter heading for the port take the time of local HW as compared with Brest or Pte de Grave, the port index and the mean tide level (MTL).

1. Calculate the time of local high water.
2. Calculate the interval between local HW and the time when the tidal height is required.
3. Along the top of the tide table, find the column with the nearest height of HW to Brest or Pte de Grave (in metres).

4. Note the corresponding tide index, add the port index, and locate the column headed by the total. Another way of putting this is that the port index tells you how many columns to move to the right.
5. Run down this column to the correct interval from local HW, calculated in 2 above, and read off the correction to the MTL. The answer will be in metres.

Example

Required: the height of tide at La Trinité on 19 August 1993 for 1630 French summer time (*heures locales*) = 1430 UT (Universal Time, GMT).

From an almanac: HW Brest (Time Zone 1) is at 1805 = 1705 UT, height 8·0m.

From chapter 32: La Trinité; HW -0015 Brest, index 1, MTL 3·2m.

Working Local HW is at 1705-0015 = 1650 UT.

Interval from HW = 1650-1430 = 2h 20min.

The table has a column for 7·9m, giving a tide index of 17; where there is no column for the particular tide height, use the nearest column. Adding the port index of 1 to 17 gives a total of 18. In the column headed 18 for interval 2h 20 the correction to MTL is 1·1.

Tide height will then be 3·2+1·1 or 4·3m.

There may well be differences of 0·1m or 0·2m from the more accurate tables, but this simplified system with no interpolation is good enough for practical purposes.

The first four lines of the table below suffice to find HW and LW heights.

Look up in the almanac the height of HW Brest or Pte de Grave. Line 3 gives the corresponding tidal index, to which add the port index, taken from the chapter heading or from below the plan.

Corresponding to this total index, the fifth line (interval for 0h 00) gives the half-range. Look up the MTL for the port, and add/subtract this half-range for HW/LW.

Coefficient

French tide tables quote the coefficient for the tide on a particular day and this number gives a useful indication of the range. A mean spring tide is given the coefficient 95 and a mean neap 45.

Equinoctial springs can reach 110 or even 120. A very feeble range might be given a coefficient of 20. As a rough guide, a spring tide can be thought of as having a coefficient of 100 and a neap tide as having one of 50.

...est HW	5·5	5·6	5·7	5·8	5·9	6·0	6·1	6·2	6·3	6·5	6·6	6·8	6·9	7·1	7·3	7·5	7·7	7·9	8·2
...e de Grave HW	4·0	4·1	4·1	4·2	4·3	4·3	4·4	4·5	4·6	4·7	4·8	4·9	5·0	5·1	5·3	5·4	5·5	5·7	5·9
...de index	0	1	2	3	4	5	6	7	8	9	10	11	12	13	14	15	16	17	18

Main correction table (left and right labels: *Interval from local HW*; upper half *Add to MTL (m)*, lower half *Subtract from MTL (m)*). The "add / port / index" labels span total-index columns 1–4, 6–9 and 11–14.

Interval	0	1	2	3	4	5	6	7	8	9	10	11	12	13	14	15	16	17	18	19	20	21	22	Interval
0h 00	0·8	0·9	0·9	1·0	1·1	1·1	1·2	1·3	1·4	1·5	1·6	1·7	1·8	1·9	2·1	2·2	2·3	2·5	2·7	2·9	3·1	3·3	3·5	0h 00
20	0·8	0·8	0·9	1·0	1·0	1·1	1·2	1·3	1·3	1·4	1·5	1·6	1·8	1·9	2·0	2·2	2·3	2·5	2·6	2·8	3·0	3·2	3·4	20
40	0·8	0·8	0·9	0·9	1·0	1·1	1·1	1·2	1·3	1·4	1·5	1·6	1·7	1·8	1·9	2·1	2·2	2·4	2·5	2·7	2·9	3·1	3·3	40
1h 00	0·7	0·8	0·8	0·9	0·9	1·0	1·1	1·1	1·2	1·3	1·4	1·5	1·6	1·7	1·8	1·9	2·1	2·2	2·3	2·5	2·7	2·9	3·1	1h 00
10	0·7	0·7	0·8	0·8	0·9	0·9	1·0	1·1	1·2	1·2	1·3	1·4	1·5	1·6	1·7	1·8	2·0	2·1	2·2	2·4	2·6	2·7	2·9	10
20	0·6	0·7	0·7	0·8	0·8	0·9	1·0	1·0	1·1	1·2	1·3	1·3	1·4	1·5	1·6	1·8	1·9	2·0	2·1	2·3	2·4	2·6	2·8	20
30	0·6	0·6	0·7	0·7	0·8	0·8	0·9	1·0	1·0	1·1	1·2	1·2	1·3	1·4	1·5	1·6	1·7	1·9	2·0	2·1	2·3	2·4	2·6	30
40	0·5	0·6	0·6	0·7	0·7	0·8	0·8	0·9	0·9	1·0	1·1	1·1	1·2	1·3	1·4	1·5	1·6	1·7	1·8	2·0	2·1	2·2	2·4	40
50	0·5	0·5	0·6	0·6	0·7	0·7	0·7	0·8	0·9	0·9	1·0	1·0	1·1	1·2	1·3	1·4	1·5	1·6	1·7	1·8	1·9	2·0	2·2	50
2h 00	0·4	0·5	0·5	0·5	0·6	0·6	0·7	0·7	0·8	0·8	0·9	0·9	1·0	1·1	1·1	1·2	1·3	1·4	1·5	1·6	1·7	1·8	1·9	2h 00
10	0·4	0·4	0·5	0·5	0·5	0·6	0·6	0·6	0·7	0·7	0·8	0·8	0·9	1·0	1·0	1·1	1·2	1·3	1·3	1·4	1·5	1·6	1·7	10
20	0·3	0·4	0·4	0·4	0·4	0·5	0·5	0·5	0·6	0·6	0·7	0·7	0·8	0·8	0·9	0·9	1·0	1·1	1·1	1·2	1·3	1·4	1·5	20
30	0·3	0·3	0·3	0·3	0·4	0·4	0·4	0·4	0·5	0·5	0·5	0·6	0·6	0·7	0·7	0·7	0·8	0·9	0·9	1·0	1·0	1·1	1·2	30
40	0·2	0·2	0·2	0·3	0·3	0·3	0·3	0·3	0·4	0·4	0·4	0·4	0·5	0·5	0·6	0·6	0·6	0·7	0·7	0·7	0·8	0·9	0·9	40
50	0·1	0·2	0·2	0·2	0·2	0·2	0·2	0·2	0·2	0·3	0·3	0·3	0·3	0·3	0·4	0·4	0·4	0·5	0·5	0·5	0·5	0·6	0·6	50
3h 00	0·1	0·1	0·1	0·1	0·1	0·1	0·1	0·1	0·1	0·1	0·1	0·1	0·1	0·2	0·2	0·2	0·2	0·2	0·2	0·2	0·2	0·3	0·3	3h 00
10																								10
20	0·1	0·1	0·1	0·1	0·1	0·1	0·1	0·1	0·1	0·1	0·1	0·1	0·2	0·2	0·2	0·2	0·2	0·2	0·2	0·2	0·2	0·3	0·3	20
30	0·1	0·1	0·1	0·2	0·2	0·2	0·2	0·2	0·2	0·2	0·3	0·3	0·3	0·3	0·3	0·4	0·4	0·4	0·5	0·4	0·5	0·5	0·6	30
40	0·2	0·2	0·2	0·2	0·3	0·3	0·3	0·3	0·3	0·4	0·4	0·4	0·4	0·5	0·5	0·5	0·6	0·6	0·6	0·7	0·7	0·8	0·8	40
50	0·3	0·3	0·3	0·3	0·3	0·4	0·4	0·4	0·4	0·5	0·5	0·5	0·6	0·6	0·7	0·7	0·7	0·8	0·9	0·9	1·0	1·0	1·1	50
4h 00	0·3	0·3	0·4	0·4	0·4	0·5	0·5	0·5	0·5	0·6	0·6	0·7	0·7	0·8	0·8	0·9	0·9	1·0	1·1	1·1	1·2	1·3	1·4	4h 00
10	0·4	0·4	0·4	0·5	0·5	0·5	0·6	0·6	0·6	0·7	0·7	0·8	0·8	0·9	0·9	1·0	1·1	1·2	1·2	1·3	1·4	1·5	1·6	10
20	0·4	0·5	0·5	0·5	0·6	0·6	0·6	0·7	0·7	0·8	0·8	0·9	0·9	1·0	1·1	1·1	1·2	1·3	1·4	1·5	1·6	1·7	1·8	20
30	0·5	0·5	0·5	0·6	0·6	0·7	0·7	0·7	0·8	0·8	0·9	1·0	1·0	1·1	1·2	1·3	1·4	1·5	1·6	1·7	1·8	1·9	2·0	30
40	0·5	0·6	0·6	0·6	0·7	0·7	0·8	0·8	0·9	0·9	1·0	1·1	1·2	1·2	1·3	1·4	1·5	1·6	1·7	1·8	2·0	2·1	2·2	40
50	0·6	0·6	0·7	0·7	0·8	0·8	0·9	0·9	1·0	1·0	1·1	1·2	1·3	1·4	1·5	1·6	1·7	1·8	1·9	2·1	2·2	2·3	2·5	50
5h 00	0·6	0·7	0·7	0·8	0·8	0·9	0·9	1·0	1·1	1·1	1·2	1·3	1·4	1·5	1·6	1·7	1·8	2·0	2·1	2·2	2·4	2·5	2·7	5h 00
20	0·7	0·7	0·8	0·8	0·9	1·0	1·0	1·1	1·2	1·3	1·4	1·4	1·5	1·6	1·8	1·9	2·0	2·2	2·3	2·5	2·6	2·8	3·0	20
40	0·8	0·8	0·9	0·9	1·0	1·1	1·2	1·2	1·3	1·4	1·5	1·6	1·7	1·8	2·0	2·1	2·2	2·4	2·6	2·8	2·9	3·1	3·3	40
6h 00	0·8	0·9	0·9	1·0	1·1	1·1	1·2	1·3	1·4	1·5	1·6	1·7	1·8	1·9	2·1	2·2	2·3	2·5	2·7	2·9	3·1	3·3	3·5	6h 00

Weather forecasts

Forecasts broadcast by the French coastal stations are more detailed than those broadcast by the BBC and the English coastal stations. The form of the forecast is: the general situation, followed by, for each area, firstly for the next 12 hours general weather type, wind direction and speed in knots, state of sea (*calme* to 0·1m, *belle* to 0·5m, *peu agitée* to 1·25m, *agitée* to 2·5m, *forte* to 4m, *très forte* to 6m = 20ft, *grosse* to 9m, *très grosse* to 14m, *énorme* the rest), swell (if necessary) and visibility in miles; secondly for the following 12 hours similar information in rather less detail; finally, the outlook. The forecasts are read slowly and repeated, so they are not hard to follow with even limited French. Some less familiar words: *brume* = mist, *coup de vent* = gale, *averses* = showers, *houle* = swell, *syroit* = southwest, *noroit* = northwest, *sudé* = southeast, *nordé* = northeast.

There are also forecasts broadcast by the national stations, including a special one for yachtsmen, during the summer only, on long wave.

The sea areas covered by this book are Ouest Bretagne (Brest to Quiberon), Nord Gascogne (Quiberon to Les Sables d'Olonne) and Sud Gascogne (south of Les Sables d'Olonne). The broadcasts are detailed below. The times are occasionally changed, but are given on a leaflet issued annually and obtainable from harbourmasters and marinas. A tape recorder is a useful aid to understanding a forecast.

Coastal stations

Times are French standard time, which is UT+1 (GMT+1); add one hour for French summer time.
Brest-Le Conquet 1673kHz, 179m; 0833, 1733, 2253. (Areas Ouest Bretagne, Nord Gascogne, repeated by Quimperlé 1876kHz, 159m; 0833, 1733.)
St Nazaire 1722kHz, 174m; 0903, 1903. (Areas Ouest Bretagne, Nord Gascogne, Sud Gascogne.)
Bordeaux-Arcachon 1820kHz, 165m; 0803, 1803. (Area Sud Gascogne.)

These bulletins are followed by notices about floating dangers, extinguished lights etc. Gale warnings are broadcast at H+03 and H+33 from Le Conquet, 1806kHz, OH+7 St Nazaire, 1687kHz, and EH+7 Bordeaux on 1862kHz, where EH/OH are even/odd hours of UT.

VHF stations

The following VHF stations transmit local forecasts at 0733 and 1233 *heures locales* (French time) (UT+2 during French summer time):

Ouessant	Ch 82	St Nazaire	Ch 23
Le Conquet	Ch 26	St Gilles,	
Pont l'Abbé	Ch 27	Croix de Vie	Ch 27
Nantes	Ch 28	La Rochelle	Ch 21
Belle Ile	Ch 25	Royan	Ch 23

Les Centres Régionaux Opérationnels de Surveillance et de Sauvetage (CROSS) Forecasts

CROSS CORSEN Ouessant. Announced on Ch 16 and transmitted on Ch 11 in French and English. Every 3 hours from 0150 to 2250 UT. Covering Manche Ouest, Ouest Bretagne and Nord Gascogne.
CROSS ETEL Announced on Ch 16 and transmitted on Ch 13, *heures locales*: 0400, 0830, 1410, 1910. Covering Penmarc'h to Sables d'Olonne.
S/CROSS SOULAC Ch 13 *heures locales*: 0800, 1100, 1430, 1800 (in winter), 1430 (in summer), 1900.

Yachtsmen's forecasts

France-Inter 164, 1829m. Forecasts are given at the end of bulletins, starting at the advertised time; now, 0645, 2005 *heures locales*.

Severe passages

With some trepidation a few passages marked as severe have been included for the benefit of those who may wish to use them in suitable conditions. They are strictly only for those with some local knowledge and reliable auxiliary power, in fine weather and good visibility, at the correct time of tide. They are generally narrow and beset by fierce tides which could quickly lead to disaster. It is hoped that they will not be a challenge to the foolhardy, who must keep clear of them. One is tempted to add that the French impose heavy fines upon foolhardy yachtsmen, but presumably anyone who is prepared to risk his yacht and the lives of himself and his crew is not going to be daunted by the prospect of tangling with the French police.

Port signals

The French authorities use two systems of signals to control the traffic into harbours. These are best explained by means of diagrams, which are based, by permission of the Service Hydrographique de la Marine, on those appearing in *Instructions Nautiques*.

By day and night three green lights one above the other signify that the port is open but that there are obstructions in the channel and vessels must navigate with caution.

Port signals diagrams

Figure (i) shows the international port signals used in large ports. Figure (ii) shows the simplified system used in smaller harbours. Supplementary signals are sometimes used; in particular, flag P of the International Code (Blue Peter) is often used to indicate open dock gates.

The traffic signals are not usually hoisted for yachts, and they should therefore be regarded more as a signal to keep out of the way of large vessels.

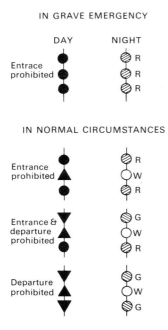

Fig. i. International port signals.

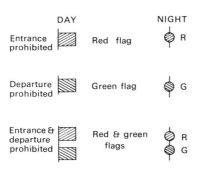

Fig. ii. Simplified system.

Charts

For the British yachtsman cruising in the Bay of Biscay the appropriate Admiralty charts are recommended. These cover the area well and are prepared with the conventions, abbreviations, soundings and compass roses with which he is familiar. General coverage is on a scale of approximately ½ inch to the mile, although from Brest to the Loire there is coverage on a scale of 1 inch or larger. They are particularly useful for passage-making, and in addition some areas, such as the Rade de Brest and the Morbihan, are covered on a scale suitable for detailed exploration in yachts. They are obtainable,

corrected to date of sale, from Admiralty chart agents, which means, in effect, that they must be obtained before leaving English waters. They can be kept corrected from *Admiralty Notices to Mariners*, published weekly and obtainable free (but not post free) from chart agents, or from the quarterly small craft summaries. Imray, Laurie, Norie & Wilson Ltd, Wych House, The Broadway, St Ives, Huntingdon, Cambridgeshire PE17 4BT ☎ 0480 462114 *Fax* 0480 496109 will supply Admiralty charts and publications. A list of charts is given on pages 12 to 15.

Imray, Laurie, Norie & Wilson Ltd publish seven coloured charts, Nos *C35* to *C42*, covering the coast from L'Aberwrac'h to the Pointe de Grave. They include large-scale insets of harbours. Quarterly bulletins of corrections may be obtained from the publishers, and more charts are in preparation.

The most complete coverage is naturally by the official French charts. The general coverage is on a scale of 1:50,000, with generous overlaps between adjacent charts, but there are also large-scale plans for many areas, such as the Glénan Iles, which are of great interest to the exploring yachtsman, but are not covered by large-scale British charts.

French official charts have no compass roses, so some form of protractor is needed. The Hurst Plotter, the Douglas Protractor, the Sestrel Course Setting and Compass Conversion Protractor and the Harries Direct Course Finder provide solutions with a variety of compromises between cost and convenience. Although modern French charts are very easy to read, the older ones are very finely engraved, and a chart magnifier is helpful in reading them.

Editions Grafocarte publish the Navicarte series of four-colour charts intended for yachtsmen. The standard scale is 1:50,000, with large-scale inserts. These charts show very clearly all features in which yachtsmen are interested and have legends which are also in English; bulletins of corrections are available. These charts are available from Librairie Maritime et d'Outremer, 17 rue Jacob Paris ☎ +1 46 33 47 48 *Fax* +1 43 29 96 77.

French official charts can be obtained from Librairie Maritime et d'Outremer (above); they should be ordered about two months in advance as delivery is sometimes very slow. They can also be ordered direct from Bureau des Cessions au Public, Service Hydrographique de la Marine, 29283 Brest Cedex. They may also be obtained, while cruising, from the authorised agents in the principal ports. These agents keep local charts in stock, but do not correct them after receipt. They usually require two or three days' notice to obtain ones of more distant parts. The French hydrographic office publishes weekly notices to mariners, but they are very expensive. However, it also publishes each April, primarily for yachtsmen, a summary of notices issued in the last 12 months affecting the French coast and adjacent waters. This summary, entitled *Recueil des Corrections de Cartes, 199-*, is not expensive, and enables one to make corrections.

Full lists of the abbreviations and conventional signs in use on French and British charts can be obtained, but a short list of the more useful ones, arranged in parallel columns to serve as a glossary, is given below.

Lights and beacons

British		*French*	
F.	Fixed	F.f	*Feu fixe*
Oc.	Occulting	F.o	*Feu à occultations*
Iso.	Isophase	F.i.	*Feu isophase*
Fl.	Flashing	F.é.	*Feu à éclats*
Q	Quick Flashing	F.sc.	*Feu scintillant*
VQ	Very Quick	F.sc.rap.	*Feu scintillant rapide*
IQ	Interrupted Quick Flashing	F.sc.d	*Feu scintillant discontinu*
Alt.	Alternating	F.alt.	*Feu alternatif*
Oc(2)	Group occulting (e.g. 2)	F.2o.	*Feu à occulta-tions groupées*
Fl(2+1)	Group flashing (e.g. 2 flashes, then 1)	F.2é.1é.	*Feu à éclats diversement groupés*
Dir	Directional light	F.d.	*Feu de direction*
obscd	Obscured		*Masqué*
occas	Occasional	occas.	*Occasionel*
	Sector	S. Sect	*Secteur*
destd	Destroyed	détr.	*Détruit*
vert	Vertical	V.	*Vertical*
hor	Horizontal	Hor	*Horizontal*
Bn.	Beacon	Bal	*Balise*
Tr	Tower	T	*Tour*
Bn Tr	Beacon tower	Tlle	*Tourelle*
Ro Bn,	Radiobeacon	R.C,	*Radiophare*
RC		R.D	*Circulaire, Directionnel*

Colours

(On French charts the colours of lights are in italics and those of the buoys/beacons themselves are in Roman.)

B.	Black	n.	*Noir*
Bu.	Blue (formerly Bl.)	bl.	*Bleu*
G.	Green	v.v.	*Vert*
Y.	Orange (formerly Or.)	org.	*Orangé*
R.	Red	r.r.	*Rouge*
W.	White	b.b.	*Blanc*
Y.	Yellow	j.	*Jaune*
W.	Whitewashed	bli.	*Blanchi*
Cheq.	Chequered		*à damier*
Vi.	Violet	vio.	*Violet*

Fog signals

Fog. Sig.	Fog Signal Station	Sal br.	*Station de sig-naux de brume*
Whis.	Whistle	Sif.	*Sifflet*
	Bell	Cl.	*Cloche*
	Siren	Sir.	*Sirène de brume*
Dia.	Diaphone		*Diaphone*
Reed.	Reedhorn		*Trompette*

Buildings and miscellaneous

Cas.	Castle	*Chau*	*Château*
Cemy	Cemetery	*Cimre*	*Cimetière*
Ch.	Chapel	*Chlle*	*Chapelle*
Chy	Chimney	*Chee*	*Cheminée*
Ch.	Church	*Egl, Cler*	*Eglise, Clocher*
Conspic.	Conspicuous	*Rem.*	*Remarquable*
CG	Coastguard	*Sem.*	*Sémaphore*
Fm.	Farm		*Ferme*
F.S.	Flagstaff (signals)	*Mt Sx*	*Mât de Signaux*
F.S.	Flagstaff	*Mt Pon*	*Mât de Pavillon*
	Gable		*Pignon*
Ho.	House	*Mon*	*Maison*
L.B.	Lifeboat	*Ston de sauv.*	*Station de sauvetage*
Mont	Monument	*Mont*	*Monument*
P.A.	Position Approximate	*P.A.*	*Position Approchée*
	Seamark		*Amer*
	Summit	*Set, Som.*	*Sommet*
Water Tr	Water Tower	*Chau d'eau*	*Château d'eau*
	Windmill	*Min*	*Moulin à vent*
Wk	Wreck	*Ep.*	*Epave*

British Admiralty charts

Chart	Title	Scale
20	Ile d'Ouessant to Pointe de la Coubre	500,000
304	Lorient Harbour	10,000
798	Goulet de Brest to Chaussée de Seine including Baie de Douarnenez	60,000
	Douarnenez: Morgat	15,000
1104	Bay of Biscay	1,000,000
2351	Anse de Bénodet to Chaussée de Sein	75,000
2352	Presqu'île de Quiberon to Anse de Bénodet	75,000
2353	Rade de Croisic to Presqu'île de Quiberon	75,000
	Le Croisic	20,000
2358	Morbihan including Rivière de Crac'h	25,000
2641	Pertuis Breton	50,000
2643	Ile d'Ouessant to Pointe de Penmarc'h	200,000
2645	Ile de Groix to Raz de Sein	140,000
2646	Pointe de Penmarc'h to Ile d'Yeu	200,000
2647	Les Sables d'Olonne to Bourgneuf	various
	St Gilles sur Vie; Port Joinville	29,200
2648	Pointe de la Coubre to Les Sables d'Olonne	various
	Port of Les Sables d'Olonne	25,000
2663	Ile d'Yeu to Pointe de la Coubre	200,000
2664	Pointe d'Arcachon to Pointe de la Coubre	200,000
2694	The Channels between Ouessant and the Mainland	50,000
2743	La Rochelle and La Pallice	15,000
2746	Pertuis d'Antioche	50,000
2748	La Charente – Ile de Aix to Tonnay-charente	20,000
2910	Approaches to La Gironde	50,000
	Le Verdon-sur-mer	25,000
2985	La Loire, St Nazaire to Nantes	30,000
	Port de Nantes	15,000
2989	Entrance to La Loire	15,000
3216	Approaches to La Loire	50,000
	Pornic; L'Herbaudière	15,000
3345	Chenal du Four	25,000
	Port du Conquet	10,000
3427	Rade de Brest	30,000

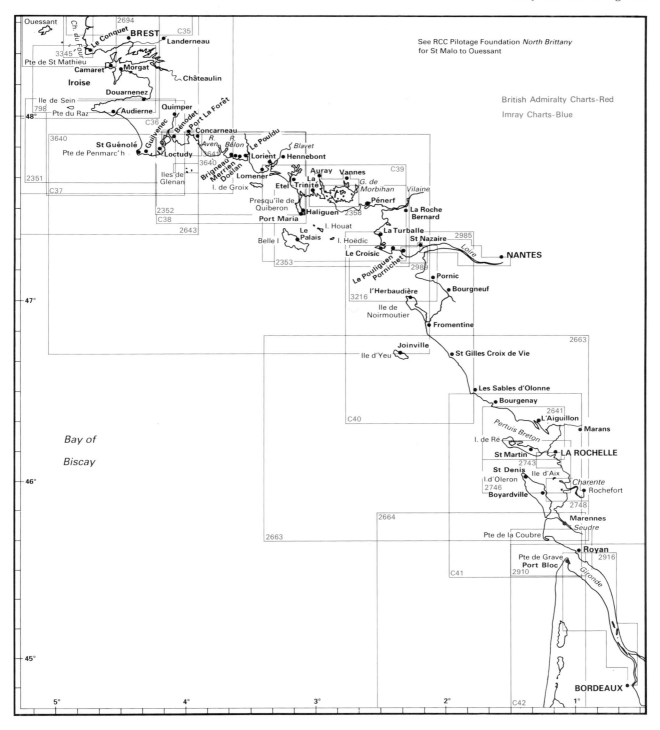

3428	Brest	15,000
	Port du Commerce	7,500
3640	Harbours and anchorages on the west coast of France	
	Point Joinville	10,000
	Le Guilvinec, Lesconil	15,000
	Saint-Gilles-Croix-de vie, Les Sables-d'Olonne	15,000
	Audierne	24,000
	Iles de Glenan	30,000
3641	Loctudy to Concarneau	20,000

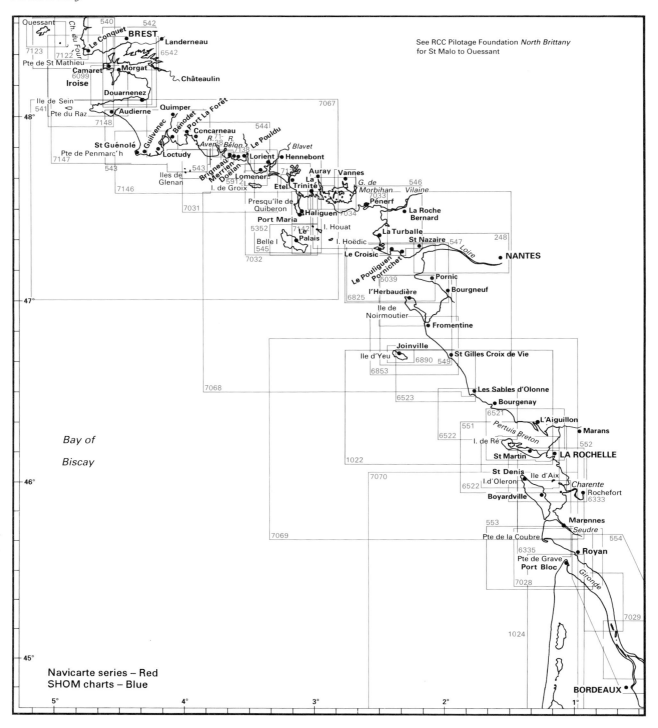

Ouessant
7123
7122
540
542
BREST
Landerneau
Le Conquet
Ch. du Four
6542
Pte de St Mathieu
Camaret
Morgat
6099
Iroise
Châteaulin
Douarnenez
Ile de Sein
541
Pte du Raz
7148
Audierne
Quimper
48°
Bénodet
Port La Forêt
7067
Concarneau
St Guénolé
Guilvenec
544
Le Pouldu
Blavet
R. 75
R.
Aven
Bélon
7138
Lorient
Hennebont
Pte de Penmarc'h
7147
Loctudy
543
Brigneau
Merrien
Doëlan
Auray
Vannes
Lomener
715
543
Iles de
Glenan
5912
Etel
La
Trinité
G. de
Morbihan
546
7146
I. de Groix
7033
Vilaine
7031
Presqu'île de
Quiberon
Pénerf
La Roche
Bernard
7034
Haliguen
Port Maria
La Turballe
5352
I. Houat
St Nazaire
547
248
Belle I
7142
Le
Palais
I. Hoëdic
St Nazaire
545
Le Croisic
Loire
NANTES
7032
Le Pouliguen
Pornichet
5039
Pornic
6825
l'Herbaudière
Bourgneuf
47°
Ile de
Noirmoutier
Fromentine
Joinville
St Gilles Croix de Vie
Ile d'Yeu
6890
549
6853
7068
Les Sables d'Olonne
6523
Bourgenay
6521
Bay of
L'Aiguillon
551
Pertuis Breton
Marans
6522
Biscay
I. de Ré
552
1022
St Martin
LA ROCHELLE
46°
St Denis
Ile d'Aix
7070
I.d'Oleron
6522
Charente
Rochefort
6333
Boyardville
Marennes
553
Seudre
7069
Pte de la Coubre
554
6335
Royan
Pte de Grave
Port Bloc
7028
7029
1024
45°
Navicarte series – Red
SHOM charts – Blue
BORDEAUX
5°   4°   3°   2°   1°

See RCC Pilotage Foundation *North Brittany*
for St Malo to Ouessant

SHOM (Service Hydrographique et Océanographique de la Marine) charts

As with the BA charts, these are listed in numerical order. Charts marked 'P' are available in the *Spéciale 'P' series*, folded on thin, water-resistant and tear-proof material. When a new French chart is issued, replacing a similar one of the same area, it is given a new number, unlike British charts where the old number is reused. The charts listed below are a selection from the official catalogue at the time of going to press.

Chart	Title	Scale
5039P	De la pointe de St Gildas au goulet de Fromentine, Baie de Bourgneuf	46,300
6099P	Baie de Douarnenez	45,800
6333P	De l'île de Ré à l'île d'Oléron, pertuis d'Antioche	47,500
6334P	De La Rochelle à Rocheforte, pertuis d'Antioche	47,600
6335P	De l'île d'Oléron à Corduan, pertuis de Maumusson	47,800
6470	Passes et rade de Lorient (may be superseded)	10,000
6521P	De la pointe du Grouin du Cou à La Rochelle, pertuis Breton, Ile de Ré	47,500
6522P	Des Sables d'Olonne à la pointe du Grouin du Cou	47,400
6523P	De Saint-Gilles-Croix-de-Vie aux Sables d'Olonne, Ile d'Yeu (partie Est)	47,200
6542P	Rade de Brest	30,000
6609P	De la pointe de Mathieu à Audierne, Goulet de Brest	45,800
6647P	Iles de Glénan partie Nord	20,000
6648P	Iles de Glénan partie Sud	20,000
6649P	Anse de Bénodet, ports de Bénodet et de Loctudy	15,000
6650P	Abords et port de Concarneau, baie de la Forêt	15,600
6679P	Cours de l'Odet - de Bénodet à Quimper	20,000
6825P	De Croisic à Noirmoutier. Estuaire de la Loire	46,700
6853P	Du goulet de Fromentine à St-Gilles-Croix-de-Vie. Ile d'Yeu	47,000
7028P	Embouchure de la Gironde - De la Pointe de la Coubre à la pointe de la Négade	45,000
7031P	De l'île de Penfret aux plateaux des Brivideaux – Abords de Lorient	50,000
7032P	De l'île de Groix à Belle Ile – Abords de Lorient	50,000
7033P	De Quiberon au Croisic	50,000
7034P	Golfe de Morbihan	25,000
7029P	La Gironde - De Mortagne-sur-Gironde au Bec d'Ambès, La Garonne et la Dordogne jusqu'à Bordeaux et Libourne (in 4 sections or 'cartouches')	45,000
	Port de Pauillac	20,000
	Port de Blaye)	20,000
7066P	D'île Vierge à la Pointe de Penmarc'h and Abords de Brest	150,000
7067P	De la Chausée de Sein à Belle Ile	150,000
7068P	De la Presqu'île de Quiberon aux Sables d'Olonne	150,000
7069P	De l'île d'Yeu à la pointe de la Coubre – Plateau de Rochbonne	150,000
7070P	De l'île d'Oléron au bassin d'Archachon	167,000
7138P	Ports et Mouillages en Bretagne Sud	
	Embouchures de l'Aven et du Belon	10,000
	Ports de Brigneau et de Merrien	7,500
	Port de Doëlan	7,500
	Embouchure de la Laïta	10,000
	Rivière d'Etel	10,000
7146P	Penmarc'h to Trévignon, with Iles de Glénan	50,000
7147P	De la chaussée de Sein á la Pointe de Penmarc'h – Baie d'Audierne	50,000

Navicarte charts by Editions Grafocarte

Chart	Title	Scale
243	Iles de Glénan	25,000
540	Argentan, Camaret	50,000
541	Morgat, Ile de Sein	50,000
542	Brest, Douarnenez	50,000
543	Audierne, Trévignon	50,000
544	Concarneau, Lorient, Ile de Groix	50,000
545	Lorient, La Trinité, Belle Ile	50,000
546	La Trinité, Le Croisic	50,000
547	Le Croisic, Pornic	50,000
549	Pornic, St Gilles, Ile d'Yeu	50,000
551	Ile de Ré, La Rochelle	50,000
552	La Rochelle, Ile d'Oléron	50,000
553	Royan, Gironde entrance	50,000
1022	St Gilles, La Rochelle	100,000

The Breton language

It is of interest, and sometimes actually of value to the navigator, to know the meanings of some of the commoner Breton words which appear in place names. Those who have cruised on the Celtic fringes of Britain will recognise some of them; the Irish *inish* corresponds to the Breton *inis*, and those who have cruised in West Highland waters will know the meanings of *glas* and *du*. I have no pretensions to a knowledge of Breton, but set down here the results of a few investigations.

The pronunciation is, or should be, more like English than French, with the final consonants sounded. The letters *c'h* represent the final sound of Scottish *loch* or Irish *lough* (but not English lock); there is indeed a word *loc'h*, meaning a lake or pool; *ch* is pronounced as in shall. The French books and charts do not always distinguish between these, and there may be some errors in this book in consequence. In France, as in England, mobility and the radio/TV are killing regional differences and *Raz* is now usually pronounced *Rah*; *Penmarc'h*, pronounced *Penmargh* a generation ago, is now often

Painmar, and *Bénodet* has gone from *Benodette* to *Bainoday* and collected an accent in the process. The most misleading example of this process is *porz*, which means an anchorage, possibly quite exposed and/or lacking in all shore facilities, not a port. This gets frenchified into *port*, and the French word *port* does mean a port, and not an anchorage, which is *anse* or *rade*.

A Breton glossary is hard to use because initial letters are often mutated into others, following complicated rules, depending on the preceding word. I have tried to meet this by suggesting, after the relevant letters, other(s) from which the initial might have come. Suppose that one wants to find the meaning of *I. er Gazek* (which is quite likely since *The Mare* seems to be the commonest name given to an islet). There is no word *gazek* in the glossary, but after G it says 'try K'; *kazek* means a mare; it mutates into *gazek* after *er*. Mutations of final letters also occur, but these do not usually cause difficulty in finding a word.

French	English
aber	estuary
anaon	the dead
al, an, ar	the
arvor	seaside
aven	river
B (try P)	
balan, banal	broom
bann, benn	hilltop
barr	summit, top
baz	shoal
beg	point, cape
beniget	cut, slit
benven,	
bosven	above-water rock
bian, bihan	small
bili, vili	shingle
bir, vir	needle, point
bran	crow
bras, braz	large
bre, brenn	small hill
breiz	Brittany
bri, brienn	cliff
C (try K)	
D (try T)	
daou	two
don, doun	deep
dour	water
du	black
ell	rock, shallow
enez	island
er a, an	the
fank	mud
froud, fred	strong current
freu	river
G (try K)	
garo, garv	rough

French	English
gavr	goat
glas	green
goban	shallow
gromell,	
gromilli	roaring
gwenn	white, pure
hir	long
hoc'h,	
houc'h	pig
iliz	church
izel	shallow
inis	island
kan(iou),	
kanal	channel
karn	cairn
kareg	rock
kastel	castle
kazek	mare
kein	shoal
kel(ou)	large rock
ker	house, hamlet
kern	summit, sharp peak
kleuz(iou)	hollow, deep
koad, goad	wood
kornog	shoal
koz	old
kreiz	middle
kriben	crest
lan, lann	monastery
marc'h	horse
melen	yellow
men	rock
mor,	
vor	sea, seawater
nevez	new
penn	head, point
plou, plo	parish
porz, porzig	anchorage

French	English
poul	pool, anchorage
raz	strait, tide race
roc'h	rock
ros	wooded knoll
ruz	red
ster	river, inlet
stiv, stiff	fountain, spring
teven,	
tevenneg	cliff, dune
toull	hole, deep place
trez, treaz	sand, beach
V (try B, M)	
W (try Gw)	
yoc'h	group of rocks

PORTS OF REGISTRATION

The ports of registration of fishing vessels may be identified by the letters on their bows, as follows:

AD	Audierne	MN	Marennes
AY	Auray	NA	Nantes
BR	Brest	NO	Noirmoutier
BX	Bordeaux	SN	Saint Nazaire
CC	Concarneau	VA	Vannes
CM	Camaret	YE	Ile d'Yeu
DZ	Douarnenez		
GV	Le Guilvinec		
IO	Ile d'Oléron		
LO	Lorient		
LS	Les Sables d'Olonne		

1. Chenal du Four

Charts

BA *3345, 2694, 2643*
Imray *C36*
SHOM *5287 P, 7066 P*
Navicarte *540*

Tidal data

Tidal heights (approx)
HW −0005 Brest
MTL 4·2m. Index 4
Heights of tide above chart datum
MHWS 7·1m, MLWS 1·3m, MHWN 5·5m, MLWN 2·9m

Tidal streams

The N stream begins about −0600 Brest, spring rates: 1 knot at 1 mile N of Les Plâtresses, 2¼ knots at St Pierre buoy (SW of Corsen), 5¼ knots at La Vinotière. The S stream begins about HW Brest, spring rates: 1 knot at 1 mile N of Les Plâtresses, 2½ knots at St Pierre buoy, 5 knots at La Vinotière. At Les Vieux Moines the stream is rotary clockwise, spring rates: at −0100 Brest, N 1¼ knots; at +0200 Brest, SSE 3½ knots; at +0500 Brest, SW ¾ knot; at −0600 Brest, WNW 1½ knots. The streams are considerably affected by the wind.

Depths

The main channel is deep.

Lights

1. **Le Four** 48°31'·4'N 4°48'·3W Fl(5)15s28m18M
   Horn(3+2)60s Grey tower
Chenal du Four leading lights 158·5°
2. **Kermorvan** 48°21'·7N 4°47'·3W
   Front Fl.5s20m22M Horn 60s Trompette(1)60s
   White square tower
3. **Saint Mathieu** 48°19'·8N 4°46'·3W
   Rear Fl.15s56m29M White tower, red top &
   DirF.54m28M 157·5°-intens-159·5° White tower
4. **Les Plâtresses** 48°26'·3N 4°50'·9W Fl.RG.4s17m
   6M 343°-R-153°-G-333° White octagonal tower
5. **Valbelle buoy (port)** 48°26'·.5N 4°50'·0W Fl(2)R.6s
   8m5M Whis
6. **Basse St Paul buoy (port)** 48°24'·9N 4°49'·1W
   Oc(2)R.6s7m4M
Chenal de la Helle leading lights 138°
2. **Kermorvan** 48°21'·7N 4°47'·3W
   Front Fl.5s20m22M Horn 60s White square tower
7. **Lochrist** 48°20'·6N 4°45'·7W
   Rear DirOc(3)12s49m22M 135°-intens-140°
   Octagonal white tower, red top
8. **Le Faix** 48°25'·8N 4°53'·9W VQ.16m8M Tower (N card)

9. **Le Stiff** 48°28'·5N 5°03'·4W Fl(2)R.20s85m24M
   Two white towers, side by side
10. **Pourceaux buoy (N card)** 48°24'·1N 4°51'·5W
    Q.7m8M
Both channels
11. **Corsen** 48°24'·9N 4°47'·7W DirQ.WRG.33m12-8M
    008°-R-012°-W-015°-G-021° White wall and hut
12. **La Grande Vinotière** 48°22'·0N 4°48'·5W Oc.R.6s
    15m5M Octagonal red tower
13. **Le Rouget buoy (starboard)** 48°22'·0N 4°48'·9W
    Iso.G.4s7m5M Whistle
14. **St Mathieu auxiliary** 54m at 291° from main tower
    Q.WRG.26m14-11M 085°-G-107°-W-116°-R-134°
    White tower
15. **Tournant et Lochrist buoy (port)** 48°20'·6N
    4°48'·3W Iso.R.4s7m5M
16. **Les Vieux Moines** 48°19'·4N 4°46'·5W Fl.R.4s16m
    5M 280°-vis-133° Octagonal red tower
Leading lights 007°
2. **Kermorvan** 48°21'·7N 4°47'·3W
   Front Fl.5s20m22M Horn 60s. White square tower
17. **Trézien** 48°25'·4N 4°46'·8W
    Rear DirOc(2)6s84m20M 003°-intens-011° Grey
    tower, white towards south

General

The Chenal du Four is the channel normally used by small vessels bound along the coast for Bay of Biscay ports; it saves distance and avoids the larger seas and heavy steamer traffic outside Ouessant. Those unfamiliar with the channel may think it presents special difficulties in navigation, but it is a wide, well marked route, and anyone who has piloted his boat along the north coast of France as far as Ouessant will find the Chenal du Four rather easier than some of the coastline that he has already passed. The difficulties lie rather in the facts that the strong tides and exposure to the Atlantic swell often result in steep seas, and the visibility is frequently poor. There are two other channels, the Chenal de la Helle, which is farther west and is also described here, and the Passage du Fromveur, SE of Ouessant, noted for the strength of its tidal streams, which attain 9 knots at extreme springs. In rough weather the Chenal de la Helle is to be preferred to the Chenal du Four.

The roughest seas do not occur in the Chenal du Four, but in the approaches. Eastward, between Ile Vierge and the Four lighthouse, northerly winds often bring a considerable swell, and a strong weather-going stream over an irregular bottom produces steep seas. With westerly winds, some shelter is found as the Chenal du Four is approached and the vessel first comes under the lee of Ouessant and then of the inner islands and shoals. The seas drop as soon as the tide turns fair.

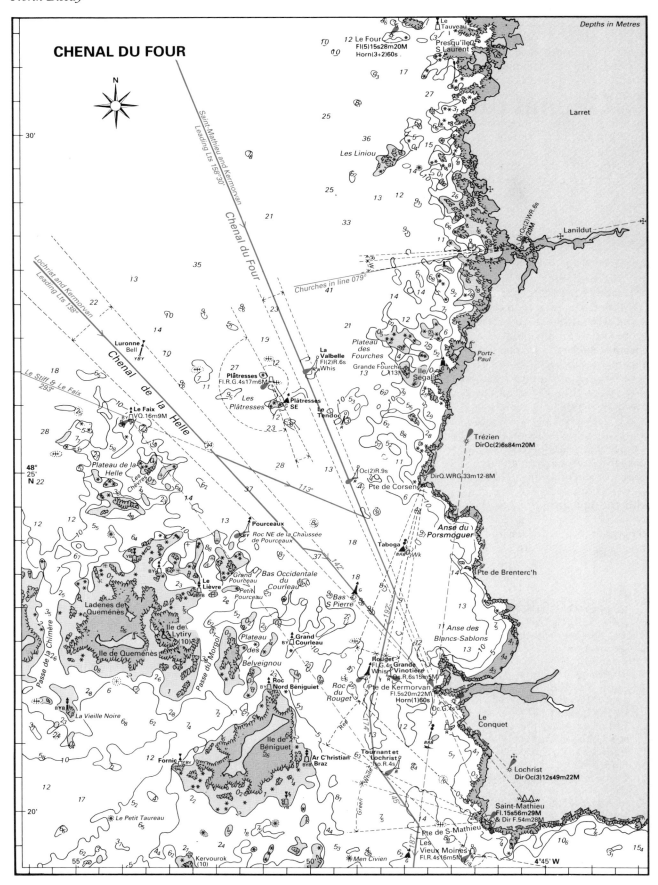

CHENAL DU FOUR

Depths in Metres

Larret

Le Four
Fl(5)15s28m20M
Horn(3+2)60s

Presqu'île
S Laurent

Les Liniou

DirOc(2)WR.6s
20M

Lanildut

Churches in line 079°

Plateau
des
Fourches

Portz-
Paul

Saint-Mathieu and Kermorvan
Leading Lts 158°30'

Chenal du Four

La
Valbelle
Fl(2)R.6s
Whis

Grande Fourche
13

Ile
Segal

Lochrist and Kermorvan
Leading Lts 158°

Luronne
Bell
Y BY

Plâtresses
Fl.R.G.4s17m6M

Les
Plâtresses

Plâtresses
SE

Le
Tendoc

Trézien
DirOc(2)6s84m20M

Le Stiff & Le Faix
293°

Chenal de la Helle

Le Faix
VQ.16m9M
BY

Plateau de la
Helle

Les
Chèvres

Oc(2)R.9s

Pte de Corsen

DirQ.WRG.33m12-8M

48°
25'
N 22

Pourceaux
Roc NE de la Chaussée
de Pourceaux

Anse du
Porsmoguer

Taboga
BRB Wk

Pte de Brenterc'h

Grand
Pourceau
Petit
Pourceau

Bas Occidentale
du
Courleau

Bas
S Pierre

Le Lièvre

Ladenes de
Quéménès

Passe du Morgol

Plateau
des
Belveignou

Grand
Courleau
BY

Anse des
Blancs-Sablons

Ile de
Lytiry
(10)

Ile de Quéménès

Passe de la Chimère

Roc
Nord Béniguet
BY

Roc
du
Rouget

Rouget
Fl.G.4s
Whis

Grande
Vinotière
Oc.R.6s15m5M

Pte de Kermorvan
Fl.5s20m22M
Horn(1)60s

Oc.G.4s

Le
Conquet

La Vieille Noire

Ile de
Béniguet

Ar C'hristian
Braz
BYB

Tournant et
Lochrist
Iso.R.4s

Fornic
BYBY

Lochrist
Dir Oc(3)12s49m22M

Le Petit Taureau

Saint-Mathieu
Fl.15s56m29M
& Dir F.54m28M

Pte de S-Mathieu

Kervourok
(10)

Men Civien

Les
Vieux Moines
Fl.R.4s16m5M

4°45' W

Plan 1

With a leading wind one will naturally arrange to pass the channel when the tide is favourable, but if the wind is ahead it is desirable to try to make the passage through the narrow part, where the tides run hard, at slack water. Coming from the north it is unfortunate that the tide turns in the Four channel before it does in the English Channel, so that starting from l'Aberwrac'h, say, on the first of the SW tide, most of the tide in the Four channel will have run to waste before one gets there. But one can cross the Iroise on the foul tide without difficulty, and reach the Raz de Sein as the tide turns fair again.

In fog or thick weather navigation is tricky in the Chenal du Four, and on entry the moment is opportune for Murphy to interfere with the electronic aids. He has also, on two occasions, extinguished the light on a buoy which then appeared out of the night, sporting a large bow wave, as the present editor rushed (fortunately) past on the tide.

If the outer marks have been sighted, and the visibility is sufficient to enable the towers and buoys to be seen at a reasonable distance, pilotage is possible even if the distant landmarks and lighthouses are hidden in the mist. With poor visibility, however, it is better to remain either in harbour or out at sea. A VHF-equipped yacht can be talked through even in nil visibility by the English-speaking radar station on Pointe St Mathieu, who listen on channel 16 and work on channel 12.

Coasting southward from Le Four lighthouse a fair offing should be given to Les Liniou and the Plateau des Fourches. The Chenal du Four may then be entered NE of Les Plâtresses tower (white), with the lighthouses of St Mathieu (white circular tower, red top) and Kermorvan (white square tower) in transit, bearing 158°. The remaining transits and marks are shown on the plan on page 18.

Except in certain parts, the area free from danger in normal weather is considerable; when it is rough the orthodox channel should be adhered to, as the overfalls are worse over an irregular bottom, such as the 3·7m patch SE of the Grande Vinotière.

If a vessel bound south is late on the tide she can avoid the worst of a foul tide by standing into the bay towards the Anse des Blancs Sablons, and again into the bay south of Le Conquet, but care must be taken to avoid the dangers.

Chenal de la Helle

Bring Kermorvan lighthouse to bear 138°, between the first and second houses from the right of five similar houses forming Le Conquet radio station. In good weather steer on this transit until Corsen lighthouse bears 012°, when steer 192° on this stern bearing. This transit leads across the Basse St Pierre (4·5m), marked by a buoy (starboard), which the transit leaves to port. In bad weather the shoal can be avoided, either by bringing the two white-painted gables, resembling pyramids, of Keravel (near St Mathieu lighthouse) in transit with Kermorvan, bearing 142°, or more simply by leaving the buoy to starboard.

By night

The transits are shown on the plan. Bound south, steer with Kermorvan[2] and St Mathieu[3] in transit, bearing 158°. Note that in a narrow sector each side of this transit St Mathieu shows a fixed white directional light as well as the flashing light that shows all round. For the Chenal de la Helle steer with Kermorvan[2] in transit with Lochrist[7], bearing 138°. To avoid the Basse St Pierre, if necessary, leave this alignment when Le Stiff light[9] on Ouessant comes in transit with Le Faix[8], bearing 293°, and steer 113° on this stern transit to join the Four channel alignment.

Chenal du Four, looking SE. Grande Vinotière centre, Kermorvan and Le Conquet far left, Pte de St-Mathieu far right.

Chenal du Four, steering south past Les Vieux Moines beacon tower and Pte de St Mathieu lighthouse.

In any case, when Corsen light[11] turns white steer in this sector, with the light astern, until the auxiliary light on St Mathieu[14] opens red. Then steer 174°, entering the red sector of Corsen until the Tournant et Lochrist buoy[15] is abeam, when the auxiliary light on St Mathieu will turn white and the light on Les Vieux Moines[16] will open. Then steer 145°, making sure that Kermorvan is brought in transit with Trézien[17], bearing 007° astern, before the green sector of St Mathieu auxiliary is left.

If proceeding south, steer nothing west of the 007° alignment; if going east or SE steer to leave Les Vieux Moines[16] to port.

Bound north

Put the reciprocal courses on the plan and this will enable the above directions to be followed in reverse.

Anchorages

The following temporary anchorages are available under suitable conditions:

Anse de Porsmoguer Good holding ground in sand in the pretty bay, with depths shoaling from 6m to zero. It is sheltered from N and E and popular for bathing. The village is about ½ mile to the north, but there are no shops there.

Anse des Blancs Sablons This wide sandy bay is free from dangers except off the headlands on each side. The anchorage is anywhere, in from 9m to 1m on a sandy shelving bottom which dries out nearly ¼ mile from the shore, except on the west side, where there is 3m close to the rocks off Kermorvan.

The peninsula protects the anchorage from the SW, and the land shelters it from the E and S. Yachts can work into this bay inshore against a foul tide, anchor there and slip round L'Ilette (off Kermorvan) when the stream becomes fair; note that there is a rock 200m east of this islet which is awash at chart datum. There is little stream in the bay, but often some swell. No facilities.

Le Conquet is a good anchorage in this inlet south of Pointe de Kermorvan. Leave the red La Louve tower to port and go in as far as draught and tide permit. For a full description see *North Brittany*, published by Imray.

Anse de Bertheaume (See plan page 22) This is a convenient bay, about 3 miles east of Pointe de St Mathieu, in which to wait before making the passage of Chenal du Four. It is sheltered from N and W, but exposed to the S and E. The Château de Bertheaume, on the SW corner of the bay, is itself fairly clean and can be passed at 100m, but 400m to the NE is Le Chat, an area of rocks nearly 200m across, with heads drying 6·6m and 7·2m. These are a particular hazard when they are covered near HW springs. Anchor in one of the two bays immediately north of Le Chat, going in as far as possible for shelter. Farther north and east the bottom of the bay is foul, with rocks. Village and simple shops one mile. If anchoring, keep well to the south of the local moorings, or alternatively borrow an available mooring.

2. Brest

Marina du Moulin Blanc
48°23'N 4°26'W

Charts

BA *2694, 3427*
Imray *C36*
SHOM *6609P, 6542P*
Navicarte *542*

Tidal data

Tidal heights
HW Standard Port
MTL 4·5m. Index 5

Heights of tide above chart datum
MHWS 7·5m, MLWS 1·5m, MHWN 5·9m, MLWN 3·1m

Tidal streams
Goulet de Brest. On the northern side the flood begins at −0535 Brest and runs E. On the southern side the flood begins at −0605 Brest, attaining 4 knots NE off Pointe des Espagnols, and continues in direction ENE towards the Elorn river. The ebb begins on the northern side at −0030 Brest, on the southern side at HW Brest. Within about 100m of the southern shore there are ENE and E eddies, which begin about +0100 Brest and continue until the flood begins. These eddies cause tide rips where they meet the main ebb from the Rade off Pointe des Espagnols.

Depths
Entrance channel dredged to 3 metres (1993). 2m at visitors' berths.

Lights
Only the buoys essential for Moulin Blanc are listed.
1. **Pointe du Petit Minou** 48°20'·2N 4°36'·9W
   Fl(2)WR.6s32m19/15M Shore-R-252°-W-260°-R-307°-W(unintens)-015°-W-065·5° 070·5°-W-shore
   Grey round tower W on SW side red top
   Ldg Lts 068° *Front* 420m NE DirQ Horn 60s Fog detector light F.G 036·5°-intens-039·5° same structure
2. **Pointe du Portzic** 48°21'·6N 4°32'·0W
   Oc(2)WR.12s56m19/15M 219°-R-259°-W-338°-R-000°-W-065·5° 070·5°-W-219° Grey 8-sided tower
   Directional light for Passe Nord 068°
   DirQ.54m22M same structure and for Passe Sud DirQ(6)+LFl.15s54m24M 045°-intens-050° same structure
3. **Basse du Charles Martel buoy (port)** 48°18'·9N 4°42'·2W Fl(4)R.15s Whis
4. **Fillettes W card buoy** VQ(9)10s Whis
5. **Roche Mengam** 48°20'·4N 4°34'·5W Fl(3)WR.12s 11/8M 034°-R-054°-W-034° RBR beacon tower
6. **Pénoupèle buoy (port)** Fl(3)R.12s
7. **No. 2 buoy (port)** Fl(2)R.6s
8. **No. 1 buoy (starboard)** Fl.G.4s
9. **No. 4 buoy (port)** long Fl.R.10s
10. **No. 6 buoy (port)** Fl.R.4s (well N of course)
11. **No. 3 buoy (S card)** Q(6)+L.Fl.15s (to be left to port)
12. **Beacon (port)** Oc(3)R.12s
13. **Moulin Blanc buoy (port)** Fl(3)R.12s
14. **Buoyed channel to Moulin Blanc**
    Starboard and port buoys *MB1* Fl.G.2s; *MB2* Fl.R.2s
    Marina entrance beacons Fl.G.2s, Fl.R.2s
    Buoy (E card) Fl(3)10s

General
Many yachts bound south stop the night at Camaret but avoid making the detour eastward to visit the Rade de Brest, which is in fact an excellent cruising ground in its own right, reminiscent of the Clyde.

Yachts are not very welcome in the commercial port, but the Marina du Moulin Blanc, offering all facilities, makes a good starting point for an exploratory cruise of the area.

Approach
The outer approach to Brest (Avant Goulet de Brest) is made with the twin lighthouses of Le Petit Minou (two adjacent white towers) in transit with the grey octagonal tower of Pointe du Portzic, bearing 068°. These lighthouses are on the north side of the Goulet de Brest. If the visibility is not good they may not be seen at first on rounding the Pointe de St Mathieu from Le Chenal du Four. However, if Les Vieux Moines tower and Le Coq port can buoy are left to port, the Charles Martel port-hand whistle buoy will be discovered close to the transit of 086°and the lighthouses should be in sight.

The outer approach from the SW, through the Chenal du Toulinguet, is described in chapter 5.

On approaching Le Petit Minou, bear to starboard and pass up the Goulet on the northern side of the midchannel shoals of Plateau des Fillettes. A W cardinal buoy marks the outer end and the BRB Roche Mengam beacon tower the inner end, with two port-hand buoys marking the northern limit of the southern channel.

When entering the Goulet from the SW, or on the ebb, the north coast of Presqu'île de Quélern is steep-to, with a useful eddy inshore. The central plateau is then left to port and La Cormoranderie (white beacon) on the northeast tip of the peninsula left well to starboard.

With the Pte du Portzic abeam, a line of port-hand channel buoys will be seen leading past the breakwaters of the naval base and the commercial port towards the bridge over the mouth of the Elorn river. The conspicuous white roof of the marine museum, on reclaimed land at the inner end of the harbour, makes a good landmark for the marina (see plan page 24).

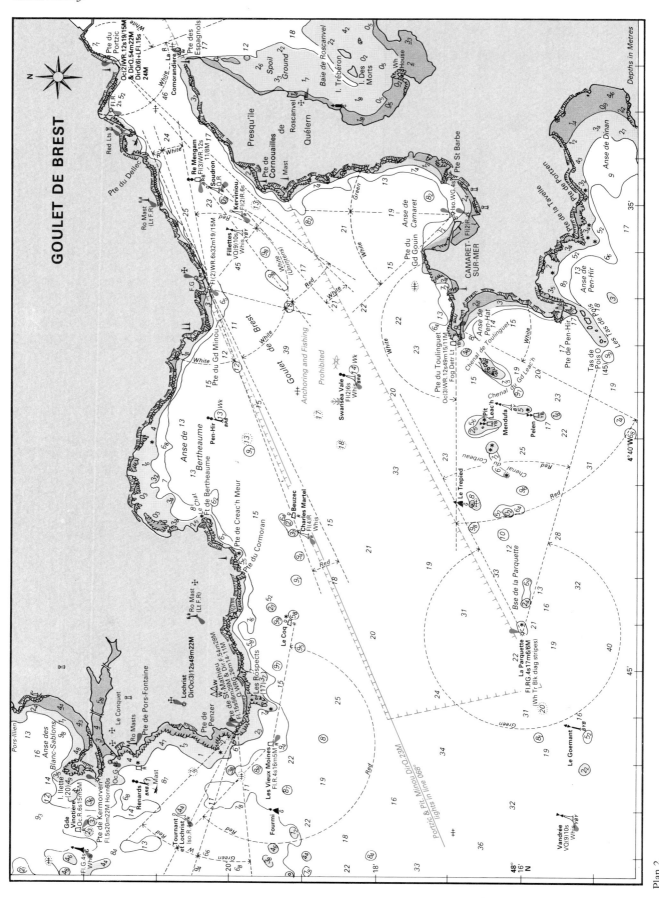

GOULET DE BREST

North

Depths in Metres

Plan 2

La Cormorandière and Pte des Espagnols, looking SE.

Pte du Portzic lighthouse, with Brest Jetée Sud behind it.

By night

From the Chenal du Four after rounding Pointe de St Mathieu, or from the west, identify the leading lights (068°) of Le Petit Minou[1] and Portzic[2] and steer on this transit until Charles Martel buoy[3] is close abeam to port. Then bear to starboard to pass between Pte du Petit Minou light[2] and Fillettes buoy[4].

Identify Roche Mengam tower light[5] and, leaving it to starboard, steer about 070° to acquire Penoupèle buoy[6]. Leaving Penoupèle close to port, steer 065° to follow the buoyed channel to Moulin Blanc buoy[13]. Leaving it to port, continue for about 200m before steering about 005° to locate the lights marking the narrow dredged channel. When MB1 and MB2[14] (see plan page 25) have been identified, steer between them on 007° to enter the marina.

Coming from Camaret, steer north to enter the intense white sector of Portzic[2] (Q(6)+LFl.6s). Alter to starboard and keep in this sector on about 047° until Roche Mengam tower[5] is abaft the beam to port, then turn onto 065° to acquire Penoupèle buoy[6] and continue as above.

Entrance

The Marina du Moulin Blanc is on the eastern side of the reclaimed land; on passing the port-hand buoy (Moulin Blanc) on the point, the small lateral buoys of the dredged channel into the marina will appear. Deep-draught vessels should leave the Moulin Blanc buoy 200m astern before turning in.

There is a central pier which divides the marina into two halves. The *capitainerie* is at the root of this pier and visitors' berths can be found in the northern half (see plan page 25).

Facilities

The staff in the *capitainerie* are most helpful and the marina is well equipped, with water and electricity on the pontoons, a fuel berth by the *capitainerie* (open 0900–1130 and 1400–1700), two wide slipways, a 14-tonne travel-lift, a 6-tonne crane and a large haul-out area.

There is a chandlery and there are engineers on site.

Showers are free, and there is a launderette in the marina, together with a bar/restaurant and a small food store.

Telecartes are necessary for all phones.

Outside the marina is a restaurant/food store. The bus service into Brest is frequent and passes a large supermarket. Get the bus ticket from the restaurant/food store.

Brest has all the usual facilities of a large town and there are chandlers, sailmakers and a shipyard with marine engineer close to the *port de commerce*.

With local bus services, good railway connections and a twice daily air service to Paris (not on Sundays), this commercial port, marina and major naval base is a pleasant place with all facilities and is convenient for changing crews.

3. Rade de Brest

Charts
BA *3427*
Imray *C36*
SHOM *6542P*
Navicarte *542*

Tidal data

Tidal heights (approx)
HW Standard Port
MTL 4·5m. Index 5
Heights of tide above chart datum
MHWS 7·5m, MLWS 1·5m, MHWN 5·9m, MLWN 3·1m

Tidal streams

For the Goulet de Brest, see chapter 2. The flood, beginning at −0605 Brest, in the south of the Goulet continues ENE to the Elorn and E towards Pointe Marloux. For the first half-hour the ebb is still running out of the estuary of the Aulne and there are tide rips where the two streams meet off Pointe des Espagnols. Half an hour later, at −0530 Brest, the flood stream divides off Pointe des Espagnols, one branch setting E and ENE as before, with an eddy setting towards Pointe Marloux. The other branch sets S into the Baie de Roscanvel and SE towards the Aulne at 2¾ knots springs. The ebb stream from the Elorn begins at HW Brest and from the Aulne about ten minutes earlier.

Depths
Given under the individual headings for the anchorages.

General

The Rade de Brest provides an excellent cruising ground, with many anchorages, beautiful creeks and two rivers that present no problems to bilge-keelers and can, with due care, be enjoyed by owners of deep-draught vessels. In bad weather it can be rough, especially with wind against tide, for there is often a fetch of five miles, but as it is sheltered on all sides it is free from the swell of the open sea. It makes an ideal place for a family cruise, or for filling in if caught by bad weather between the Four and the Raz.

Parts of the Rade are used for naval exercises, mining grounds etc. There are a few areas, marked on the charts, where anchorage or even passage is prohibited. The Rade is entered by the Goulet de Brest as described in the previous chapter.

L'Elorn river

This not unattractive river leads up to the pleasant old town of Landernau. It offers an interesting run, particularly for bilge-keelers. To find 3m in the channel, passage should be made near high water.

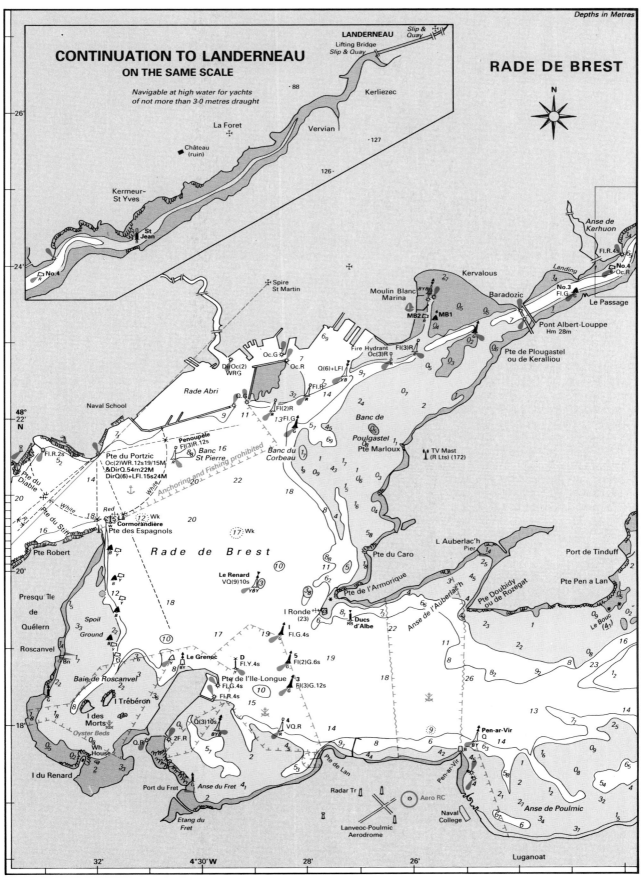

Depths in Metres

CONTINUATION TO LANDERNEAU
ON THE SAME SCALE

Navigable at high water for yachts of not more than 3·0 metres draught

RADE DE BREST

N

LANDERNEAU
Slip & Quay
Lifting Bridge
Slip & Quay

·88

La Foret

Château (ruin)

Kerliezec

Vervian

·127

126·

Kermeur-St Yves

St Jean

No.4

Spire St Martin

Anse de Kerhuon

Fl.R.4s

Landing

No.4 Oc.R

Kervalous

Moulin Blanc Marina

BYB

MB2 MB1

Baradozic

No.3 Fl.G.

Le Passage

Pont Albert-Louppe
Hm 28m

Pte de Plougastel ou de Keralliou

Fire Hydrant
Oc(3)R

Fl(3)R

Oc.G

DirOc(2) WRG

Oc.R

Q(6)+LFl

Fl.R.

Rade Abri

Q.G

Fl(2)R

13 Fl.G.

Banc de Poulgastel

Pte Marloux

TV Mast (R Lts) (172)

Naval School

Penoupèle
Fl(3)R.12s

Banc St Pierre

Banc du Corbeau

Anchoring and Fishing prohibited

Pte du Portzic
Oc(2)WR.12s19/15M
&DirQ.54m22M
DirQ(6)+LFl.15s24M

White

White

Red

Wk

Cormorandière
Pte des Espagnols

Pte du Diable

Pte du Stiff

Pte Robert

Rade de Brest

Pte du Caro

L Auberlac'h Pier

Port de Tinduff

Pte Pen a Lan

Pte Doubidy ou de Rozegat

Le Bouc

Presqu île de Quélern

Spoil Ground

Le Renard
VQ(9)10s

YBY

Wk

Pte de l'Armorique

Anse de l'Auberlac'h

Roscanvel

Bn

I Ronde
(23)

Ducs d'Albe
RB

Baie de Roscanvel

Le Grenoc

Fl.G.4s

D
Fl.Y.4s

5
Fl(2)G.6s

3
Fl(3)G.12s

I Tréberon

I des Morts

Oyster Beds

Q(3)10s

BYB

2F.R

Pte de l'Ile-Longue
Fl.G.4s

Fl.R.4s

VQ.R

Pen-ar-Vir
Q

BY

Pen-ar-Vir

Wh House

Q.R

I du Renard

Port du Fret

Anse du Fret

Etang du Fret

Pte de Lan

Radar Tr

Aero RC

Lanveoc-Poulmic
Aerodrome

Naval College

Anse de Poulmic

Luganoat

32'   4°30'W   28'   26'

Moulin Blanc marina, looking N. Moulin Blanc buoy right centre, conspicuous marine-museum roof left centre.

As the opening of the bridge must be arranged in advance, an overnight stay in Landerneau is to be expected and should not be regretted.

The Moulin Blanc port-hand buoy is one of the buoys marking the channel leading under the twin Ponts Albert-Louppe and into the river L'Elorn. From this buoy the river is navigable at all states of tide to deep-draught yachts for some four miles, up to the port-hand beacon St Jean.

Above this point the river shallows, but the channel, marked by rather small and widely spaced buoys, is navigable near high water to yachts drawing two metres for another four miles, up to Landerneau, where one can dry out against a wall. Half a mile below Landerneau is a swing bridge. This can be opened on request by telephoning in advance (☎ 98 85 16 16).

From the Moulin Blanc port-hand buoy a course of 070° leads to a starboard-hand buoy one mile distant. ¾ mile further on, construction of a second road bridge close upstream of the Pont Albert-Louppe (minimum clearance 28m) as part of the motorway extension was in progress in 1992. Anchoring was prohibited in the vicinity. The south bank of the river is thickly wooded, with interesting rocky outcrops on the ridge.

There are many houses and the town of Kerhuon on the north bank, with deep-water moorings inside the channel buoys. It should be possible to anchor in this stretch, or to pick up a vacant mooring on either side of the river up as far as St Jean. A dinghy landing can be made for supplies at Kerhuon on a slip, marked by a beacon with an orange top. At the eastern end of Kerhuon there is a wharf where the river curves north and then east again.

The yacht moorings in this stretch give a better indication of the channel than the small green buoys that mark it. Follow the curve round until the St Jean port-hand beacon is passed. After this there is a straight unmarked stretch of river. Keep in the middle and search with binoculars for the next of a succession of small green and red buoys marking the channel to Landerneau. From here on the channel winds in the river and it is important to follow the buoys closely in order to find a depth of 3m or more at HW neaps.

When the bridge opens, follow the straight channel into Landerneau. Passing the large sand-barge wharf to port, yachts may dry out against a short length of wall with a slipway on the port-hand side just below the road bridge marking the end of the channel. If there is space one may prefer to secure alongside one of the four ladders just below the bridge on the starboard side. Along the wall the bottom is hard and flat and there is 3m at HW neaps. Below the fourth ladder the bottom is foul.

Facilities

Landerneau has all the facilities of a fair-sized market town and is the junction where passengers on the Morlaix-Brest line can change for Quimper and the south coast of Brittany.

Lifting bridge for entry to Landerneau.

Landerneau, wall berths. Yachts on right have legs. *Capelan* (with bilge keels) on left, with deep-keel boat against wall behind her.

Rade de Brest, southern section

There is an area where navigation is restricted and anchoring prohibited around Ile Longue, the French naval base. Entry is also prohibited to an area east of the Naval College inside a line bearing 160° from the Pen-ar-Vir N cardinal buoy to the shore. Except for a visit to Roscanvel on the west side of Ile Longue or Le Fret on the east, it is best to keep out of this section of the Rade.

Roscanvel

An important feature of the Baie de Roscanvel is the tidal stream. The flood stream begins to run S into the bay at −0530 Brest, but one hour later the stream, running S down the E side of the bay, sweeps along the S shore and causes an eddy up the west side towards Pointe des Espagnols. By −0200 Brest the stream is weak in the inner part of the bay, but the north-going eddy on the west side attains 1 knot at springs. The ebb stream is simpler. It runs from Pointe de L'Ile Longue towards Roscanvel and Pointe des Espagnols, leaving only a weak stream in the south of the bay.

The east coast of Presqu'île de Quelern offers good protection from winds from the north through west to the southeast. From the Pte des Espagnols to the village of Roscanvel there are several small coves with yacht moorings, and there is a welcoming yacht club at Roscanvel which may loan a mooring on request.

Roscanvel has a double slipway, one running out east and the other south. It is a small holiday village, with village store, PO, café-bars, and an hotel with a good restaurant, grouped round the village green. The church spire is not visible from the northeast on approach, but there is water at all states of tide fairly close to the slips. Anchor off the slips clear of any moorings. The eastern slip dries at LW and

there are obstructions outside it. Towards LW approach the southern slip from the south and use the inside only. Further south anchorage is prohibited.

Rade de Brest SE section and L'Aulne river

The southeastern portion of the Rade has much to offer for the explorer. There are many bays and inlets along the north shore as the river L'Aulne is approached. Navigation is restricted along the south shore, but there is a regular ferry service from Brest to the Port du Fret SE of Ile Longue, with a bus connection to Camaret.

The number of yacht moorings along the north shore suggests that the area is generally sheltered in the summer, although a strong southwesterly could cause trouble.

To avoid shallows north of Pointe de l'Amorique make for Le Renard E cardinal buoy and then, if proceeding up L'Aulne, lay a course to leave the conspicuous islet Ile Ronde and two rectangular concrete 'Ducs d'Albe' three hundred metres to port. A course of 104° will then lead to the outer port-hand river-channel buoy (numbered 4), from which the buoys on the remaining channel can be located with binoculars. At present all the buoys are conical but are brightly painted in the correct lateral colours.

Anse de l'Auberlach

The hamlet of L'Auberlach lies at the head of a narrow bay running NE to the east of Ile Ronde. It has a short stone pier with a drying slip behind on which several fishing boats are hauled out. There are moorings, and it is possible to anchor outside the pier, with due attention to the vessel's draught, up to a line from the pier to the opposite shore. At LW neaps there was 4 metres depth 100m off the end of the pier on this line.

Keep clear of an experimental fish farm in the middle of the bay, marked by small, unlit yellow buoys.

Facility

A bar. Nearest shops 5km at Plougastel-Daoulas.

Le Fret

The Anse du Fret provides a pleasant, sheltered anchorage SE of Ile Longue. Close east of the ferry pier are a number of moorings, many of which were unoccupied in 1992. A course of 215° from Ile Ronde will lead through the prohibited anchorage area, well clear of the prohibited area close to the naval docks, and into the anchorage. Borrow a mooring or anchor in 2m, mud and gravel, in the bay east of the mooring area.

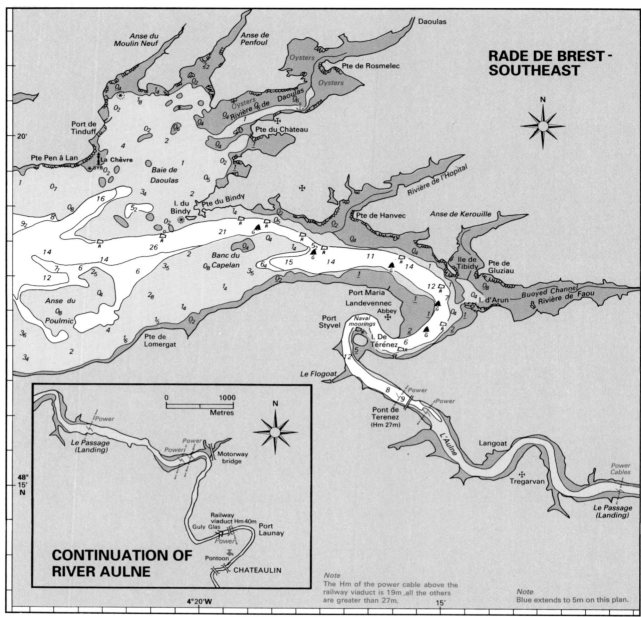

Plan 4

Facilities

A landing slip on the ferry pier (three ferries per day to and from Brest). Active sailing school, bars, good restaurant, *alimentation*, *charcuterie* and *depot de pain*. Bus service to Camaret.

Tinduff

This is in an inlet on the west side of the shallow Baie de Daoulas, half a mile to the north of Pointe Pen a Lan. In the approach this point must be given a berth of over a ¼ mile as there are shoals and La Chèvre rock (dries 3·1m, marked by an E cardinal beacon) off it with another rock (drying 4·1m) closer inshore.

The bay may be entered with sufficient rise of tide and there is 2m off the end of the pier, sheltered

from W and N with good holding. Keep clear of the experimental fish farm with *viviers* in the bay, marked by small, unlit yellow buoys.

Facilities

There are no facilities ashore save for two café-bars and a telephone kiosk. Nearest shops 6km at Plougastel-Daoulas.

Rivière de Daoulas

This runs into the NE corner of the Baie de Daoulas. The bay is shallow and can only be entered at sufficient rise of tide. There is a bar at the entrance to the river, but it is possible to anchor with complete shelter in 1·8m (mud) ¾ mile up-river, off the second slip.

Ile d'Arun, an island at HW, looking ENE into Rivière du Faou
(see page 30).

Landevennec Abbey, looking SW (see page 30).

There is a small village store at St Jean, 1km up the hill. It is possible, but difficult, to proceed upriver to Daoulas at springs, as the river dries 4·5m.

Rivière de l'Hôpital

The pretty entrance of this small river lies to the north of the entrance to L'Aulne. There is much local sailing activity here, but as the river dries it must be visited at HW.

Rivière du Faou

Upstream of the entrance to la Rivière de l'Hôpital, L'Aulne turns south into a large S bend. The mouth of la Rivière du Faou is on the east bank of the curve. The bar dries 0·6m and lies between the Ile de Tibidy and the charming little islet of Arun. North of this islet is a pool with 0·4m below datum, but further in the river dries. It is possible to go up to the substantial village of Le Faou at springs, but it is not very attractive and the river is said to be silting.

Rivière de L'Aulne

This is a beautiful river which winds between steeply wooded hills on either side and is quite comparable in charm with the Odet, though much less sophisticated. It is worth going out of the way to visit one of the quiet anchorages in this deeply sheltered river.

Keeping to the buoyed channel, described earlier, the river can be entered at all states of tide, with a minimum depth of 6m as far as the Pont de Térénez. At high water a yacht may cut across the Banc du Capelan (dries 0·4m).

On the south bank, inside starboard-hand buoy No. 7, at the start of the large S bend, are the drying jetty of Port Maria, off which one can anchor beside the moorings at neaps, and the attractive-looking village of Landévennec, with the abbey of Penform on the promontory behind. There are mud banks on both sides of the river and it is best to keep in the buoyed channel which curves S, W and NW behind the headland, avoiding the shallows round Ile de Térénez.

In the middle of the S bend there are some large mooring buoys, with a group of retired naval vessels attached, behind which it is possible to land at Port Styvel (not a port; see The Breton Language, page 16) and walk up a path through the woods to Landévennec, where there are shops, an hotel and the famous abbey, now restored.

From here on up the river winds between thickly wooded hills. The depth is ten metres or more as far as the Pont de Térénez (headroom 27m) and the bottom is rocky. However, there are several inlets where one can anchor out of the current, with soundings on mud. There are three on the starboard bank before the bridge, with a good restaurant on the opposite bank. Channel buoys cease at the naval

moorings, but there is enough water for deep-draught yachts to go up with the tide, keeping to the outside of bends, and to the middle where the river narrows, another twelve miles to the lock at Guily Glas.

At half tide, proceeding upriver above the bridge it is possible to find a depth of 4m or more to within a mile of the lock, after which the depth is reduced in some places to 2·4m at HW neaps up to the lock. Beyond the lock the depth is 3m. Six high-tension cables were seen to cross the river in March 1994 and measurements showed that all but one gave headroom of 27 metres or more. The sixth was just upstream of the Guily Glaz rail bridge (headroom 40m) and was half the height of the bridge arch, say 19 metres for safety. The cables are shown on plan 4, page 28.

Trégarvan, about two miles above the bridge on the south bank, is a reasonable anchorage; there are several local boats and a slip. There is also a landing at Le Passage, 2 miles further up. After that the banks become lower and reedy on one and then on both sides and there are no landings until the lock is reached.

The lock at Guily Glas operates from two hours before to one and a half hours after high water. On rounding the curve before the lock, it will be seen on the port-hand side of the river. In 1992 a direct approach led onto a mud bank. The channel led towards the weir to starboard of the lock and it was necessary to steer for the weir first and turn into the lock when about 150m off.

A popular transport restaurant by the lock was open in 1992. The depth in the river above the lock is 3m or more. One mile above the lock, on the port

The lock at Guily Glas

side, is Port Launay, a long curve of quays, backed by old houses under high tree-covered hills. Facilities are minimal, but there is a PO by the *hôtel de ville*, a *patisserie* and a small general store. The key of the shower on the river bank can be obtained from the *hôtel de ville*. A good hotel/restaurant, De Bon Accueil, with a pontoon for patrons, is a short walk upstream. A shallow patch opposite the restaurant is marked by two small green starboard buoys which are hard to see in the dusk.

A peaceful mooring at Port Launay.

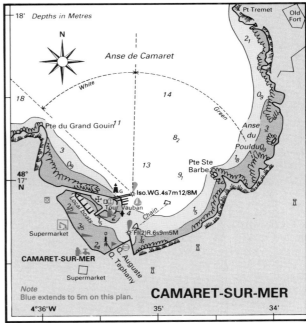

Plan 5

Most yachts passing through the lock carry on up to Châteaulin, which is a large town with banks, hotels, restaurants and all shops. Secure to the pontoon on the starboard bank or moor or raft alongside the quay. Along the canal from here to Nantes there are no facilities for masting and the bridges are low, but a substantial length has been reopened for pleasure traffic. In 1992 mooring charges were very reasonable, with free showers and toilets. A key for the showers is obtained from the tourist office, on the starboard bank above the rail bridge and weir. Launderette 300m upstream of tourist office.

Approaching the town, on the starboard side a large hypermarket will be seen. Run the bow into the bank, secure to a tree and store ship with ease and economy!

4. Camaret-sur-Mer

48°17'N 4°35'W

Charts

BA *2643, 798*
Imray *C36*
SHOM *6609P*
Navicarte *540, 542*

Tidal data

Tidal heights (approx)
HW −0015 Brest
MTL 4·2m. Index 4

Heights of tide above chart datum
MHWS 7·0m, MLWS 1·4m, MHWN 5·5m, MLWN 2·8m

Tidal streams
Tidal streams in the bay of Camaret are weak.

Depths

There are depths of 3m in the shelter of the outer breakwater, and the inner harbour is dredged to 2m or more in a channel leading to the pontoon berths.

Lights

1. **North mole head** 48°16'·9N 4°35'·2W Iso.WG.4s7m 12/8M 135°-W-182°-G-027° White pylon, green top
2. **South mole head** 48°16'·7N 4°35'·2W Fl(2)R.6s9m5M Red pylon

General

For yachts bound south, after passing through Le Four channel, Camaret is the most convenient port of call. It was once a considerable centre for shell-fishing vessels of all sizes, but the activity seems to be declining. The town is built along the edge of the harbour and has figured in many wars. The old fort on Le Sillon, on the north side of the harbour, and La Tour Dorée were designed by Vauban and date from 1689. Five years after their construction the defences repelled with heavy loss a combined Dutch and English attack, and in 1791 they won a victory against five English frigates.

Most of the inner harbour dries out, but there is a dredged area with pontoon berths. There are 60 to 70 places for visitors on the pontoons behind the outer breakwater, though it is a long way from the town.

Approach and entrance

The Anse de Camaret is entered between the Pointe de Grand Gouin on the west and Presqu'île de Quélern on the east; the bay is clear of dangers. To the west the high cliffy coast between Pointe de

Rounding Pte du Grand Gouin for Camaret. The breakwater head (arrowed) is left centre, with masts behind. Do not be misled into steering for the green tower off the western root of the breakwater.

Toulinguet and Pointe de Grand Gouin has no dangers more than 0·1M from the line of the shore and the above-water rocks. Southeast of Pointe de Grand Gouin there is shallow water in the rocky corner of the bay SW of a line from the point to the harbour entrance.

The long breakwater with a green beacon tower on its western end will be seen as soon as it is opened up to the SSE of Pointe de Grand Gouin. Leave the breakwater to starboard to enter the harbour or to find a berth on the outer pontoons.

By night

Approach in the white sector of the light on the northern breakwater[1] and round it at a reasonable distance.

Anchorage

There are many moorings, but anchoring is forbidden, in the bay southeast of the N mole in 3m or more.

The inner harbour, with pontoons for local boats.

It is convenient to berth alongside the pontoons connected to the south side of the N mole. However, they are exposed and damage may be suffered in strong winds.

Visitors' pontoons in the outer harbour. Lifeboat slip, with fuel berth, left of picture.

In 1988 an area in the inner harbour was dredged and the pontoons were extended, providing extra places for visitors. However, by 1992 all berths had been filled by local boats. There is a plan to dredge the inner harbour further and increase the number of pontoon berths.

Yachts which can take the ground could anchor in many parts of the harbour after consulting the harbourmaster. There is good hard standing off the quays in the middle of the SW side of the harbour, with a stern anchor and a bow line to the quay.

Facilities

Water and electricity on pontoons.

Showers and toilets.

Diesel from a long hose on the lifeboat slip. Refuel at HW or at other states of the tide after inspecting the bottom.

Ship chandler, shipbuilder and sailmaker.

All shops, two supermarkets, launderette, restaurants and bars.

There is a bus service to Le Fret, where one can take the ferry to Brest.

5. Chenal du Toulinguet

Passage notes

48°16'N 4°38'W

Charts

BA *798*
Imray *C3*
SHOM *6609P*
Navicarte *540*

Tidal data

Tidal streams

The S stream begins at +0015 Brest, the N at −0550 Brest, spring rates 3 knots. There is a cross tide at the northern end, the flood running to the E and the ebb to the W. To the S, between Les Tas de Pois and Cap de la Chèvre, the stream is weak, 1 knot springs, and runs almost continuously southwards.

Depths

As described here the channel has a least depth of 4·6m, though with care a greater depth can be carried.

Lights

1. **Pointe du Toulinguet** 48°16'·8N 4°37'·8W Oc(3) WR.12s49m15/11M 028°-R-090°-W-shore White square tower and house
2. **Pointe du Petit Minou** 48°20'·2N 4°36'·9W Fl(2) WR.6s32m19/15M Shore-R-252°-W-260°-R-307°-W(unintens)-015°-W-065·5° 070·5°-W-shore Grey round tower white on SW side, red top
3. **Pointe du Portzic** 48°21'·6N 4°32'·0W Oc(2)WR. 12s56m19/15M 219°-R-259°-W-338°-R-000°-W-065·5° 070·5°-W-219° Grey 8-sided tower

General

The Chenal de Toulinguet, which lies immediately west of the headland of that name, is a convenient passage for vessels bound south from Brest or Camaret, as it saves a long detour round the rocks and shoals outside.

On the east side of the channel is La Louve tower (W cardinal) on the rocks off the headland, and on

Chenal du Toulinguet, looking S towards Les Tas de Pois. Pte du Toulinguet lighthouse and *sémaphore* (signal station) on left, outermost Tas de Pois rock on right of picture, with La Louve W cardinal beacon tower (arrowed, to be left to port) close to the left.

the west side are the Roches du Toulinguet, with a rock named Le Pohen, which is steep-to and 11m high, nearest to the channel. The channel is over ¼ mile wide and carries a least depth of 4·6m. No directions are necessary other than to keep near the middle of the fairway between Le Pohen rock and La Louve tower. If proceeding SSE towards Cap de la Chèvre, note that the beacon on Le Chevreau was partially destroyed in 1987 and that a small W cardinal buoy is situated close west of the rock.

By night

The passage is possible by night if there is enough light to see the rocks and La Louve tower at 100m. There are no lights for the narrows itself and use must be made of two safe sectors. In the southern sector, Le Toulinguet light[1] shows white, bearing less than 028°, and the Pointe de Petit Minou light[2] shows open of Pointe du Toulinguet, bearing more than 010°.

In the northern sector Le Toulinguet light[1] shows white, bearing more than 090°, and the Pointe du Portzic light[3] shows open of the Presqu'île de Quélern, bearing more than 040°. This line passes very close to the rocks near La Louve tower, and it is desirable to keep Le Portzic light well open of Quélern.

From the south, enter in the southern safe sector and sail to its apex with Le Toulinguet light just turning red and Le Petit Minou light just shutting in behind Pointe du Toulinguet. From this point La Louve tower bears about 350° and Le Pohen about 270°. Steer to make about 310° to pass between them and into the northern safe sector.

From the north, enter in the northern safe sector, keeping Le Portzic light well open of Quélern as La Louve tower is approached. Once the tower has been seen, course can be shaped to pass through the channel, leaving the tower at least 200m to port, and out by the southern safe sector. From the apex of the northern safe sector, the course to steer is SW for 400m, thence SSE.

Chenal du Petit Leac'h

From the south at night this channel may be preferred, as Le Portzic light[3] can be held on a constant bearing of 043° to lead, with due allowance for tidal streams, between Pelen (S cardinal) and Basse Mendufa (N cardinal) (unlit) buoys to starboard and Petit Leac'h S cardinal beacon (unlit) to port. The channel is 600m wide with a depth of more than 10m.

Les Tas de Pois

48°15'N 4°38'W

There is no need to pass between these rocks, but as some may be interested in doing so (in good weather only) the following notes may be helpful. There are five rocks, which may conveniently be numbered from seaward as follows:

1. Tas de Pois Ouest, 51m high.
2. La Fourche, 16m high.
3. La Dentelé, 44m high.
4. Le Grand Tas de Pois, 65m high.
5. Le Tas de Pois de Terre, 58m high.

Les Tas de Pois, looking N. The yacht is sailing between La Dentelé and Le Grand Tas de Pois.

Between 1 and 2 is the widest channel. A midchannel course is clean. A rock dries 1·2m about 50m NE of 1 and there is a drying rock close to 2. Near LW it is therefore necessary to keep midchannel, if anything closer to 2.

Between 2 and 3 the channel is narrow but clean.

Between 3 and 4 keep closer to 3; there is a rock drying 0·6m close NW of 4.

Between 4 and 5 passage is only possible near HW; a rock dries 3·2m right in the middle of the narrow channel. Between 5 and the land there is no passage.

Anchorage

There is a snug anchorage in the Anse de Pen Hir, just inside Les Tas de Pois, in all winds but S or SE. There are no facilities ashore.

6. Morgat

48°13'N 4°32'W

Charts

BA *798, 2643*
Imray *C36*
SHOM *6099P*
Navicarte *542*

Tidal data

Tidal heights (approx)
HW −0010 Brest
MTL 4·1m. Index 4
Heights of tide above chart datum
MHWS 7·0m, MLWS 1·3m, MHWN 5·5m, MLWN 2·9m

Pte de Morgat lighthouse on hill, left. Marina breakwater extending to the right. The conspicuous white building is in the bay behind the marina.

Tidal streams

Inside the Baie de Douarnenez the streams are very weak.

Depths

The old harbour dries; depths in the marina are 1·8m to 4·0m.

Lights

1. **Basse Vieille buoy** (isolated danger) 48°08'·3N 4°35'·7W Fl(2)6s8m8M Whis
2. **Pointe du Millier** 48°05'·9N 4°27'·9W Oc(2)WRG.6s34m16-11M 080°-G-087°-W-113°-R-120°-W-129°-G-148°-W-251°-R-258° White house
3. **Pointe de Morgat** 48°13'·2N 4°29'·9W Oc(4)WRG. 12s77m15-10M 281°-G-301°-W-021°-R-043° White square tower, red top house
4. **Morgat buoy (port)** 48°13'·7N 4°29'·6W Fl.R.4s
5. **Morgat old breakwater head** 48°13'·6N 4°29'·9W Oc(2)WR.6s8m9/6M 007°-W-257°-R-007° White and red metal framework tower
6. **Entrance** between wave-breakers (pontoons *brise-lames*) port Fl.R.4s, starboard Fl.G.4s

General

Morgat is situated in the NW corner of the Baie de Douarnenez. It is a pretty, sandy bay, sheltered from the N and W by the land, and by the Pointe de Morgat on the SW, almost round to S. The village is a pleasant holiday resort with good beaches and the new marina makes it a popular port of call. It is more conveniently situated than Douarnenez as it is not so far east, and is nearer the Four channel and the Raz.

Approach

Cap de la Chèvre, 3½ miles to the south of Morgat, has fangs of rock extending seawards on all sides, especially to the SW, where the bottom is irregular

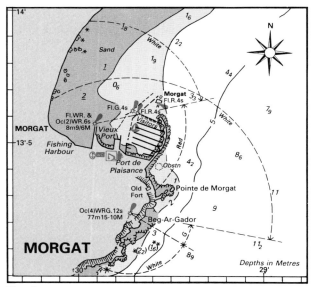

Plan 6

as far as the Basse Vieille whistle buoy. In westerly winds the approach from Cap de la Chèvre provides pleasant sailing, completely sheltered by the land. The cliffs are bold and their tops are covered with grass and heather; many sandy beaches lie at their feet.

Pointe de Morgat, a bold headland with a lighthouse on top (see photograph), hides the village and anchorage until it has been rounded. Two conspicuous above-water rocks at its foot can be passed closely, say within 50m. The breakwater of the new harbour lies just to the north of them, but there is a concrete obstruction in the intervening bay.

Approaching from the southeast, the only outlying dangers are the group of rocks, Les Verrès and La Pierre Profonde, which lie about 2 miles ESE of Pointe de Morgat. They are not marked, but they can be seen in daylight as they are respectively 12m and 7m high. There is a wreck 200m NE of Les Verrès, and Le Taureau (600m N of La Pierre Profonde and 1000m W of Les Verrès) dries. Approaching Morgat from this direction, leave La Pierre Profonde at least 200m to starboard.

By night

The dangers south of Cap de la Chèvre can be cleared by keeping in one of the two white sectors of Pointe du Millier light[2] until the Pointe de Morgat light[3] turns from red to white. Then steer in the white sector of the Pointe de Morgat light. On close approach keep clear of the coast with a course of not less than 035°, crossing the green sector of Pointe de Morgat light. Keep a lookout for unlit mooring buoys. The light on the old harbour breakwater[5] will open red, seen over the new breakwater; when it turns from red to white, alter course to leave to port the harbour entrance buoy[4]. There are green and red lights Fl.4s[6] marking the entrance between the wavebreakers (see plan).

Mooring

Yachts may anchor in 2m north and northeast of the wavebreakers. Anchoring is not permitted in the area enclosed by the breakwater and floating concrete wavebreakers. Entrance is in the gap between the wavebreakers, marked by red and green paint (red and green lights Fl.4s at night). Visitors secure to the S side of the long wavebreaker. There are 50 pontoon visitors' berths for yachts under 12m.

Facilities

Water and electricity on pontoons, fuel berth, showers, ice.

Drying slip, travel-lift, 6-tonne crane, large haul-out area. Engineers and sailmakers available from Camaret or Douarnenez.

¼ mile walk to the shops on the *plage*. Launderette in Crozon, the nearest large town (1·5 miles). Good bathing beaches nearby.

In calm weather a dinghy trip to the caves (Les Grandes Grottes de Morgat) is great fun. They lie along the cliff below the lighthouse.

Morgat marina.

7. Douarnenez

48°06'N 4°20'W

Charts

BA *798, 2643*
Imray *C36*
SHOM *6099*
Navicarte *542*

Tidal data

Tidal heights (approx)
HW −0010 Brest
MTL 4·2m. Index 4

Heights of tide above chart datum
MHWS 7·0m, MLWS 1·4m, MHWN 5·4m, MLWN 2·9m

Tidal streams

Tidal streams inside the Baie de Douarnenez are
very weak.

Depths

In Rosmeur the depths vary, but there is a considerable area with 3m to 5·5m. In the Rade du Guet the
depths shoal from 4m to 0·4m. In the marina at
Tréboul the dredged depth is 1·5m. In the wet basin
of Port Rhu the depth is 3m or more.

Lights

1. **Ile Tristan** 48°06'·2N 4°20'·3W Oc(3)WR.12s35m
   13/10M 138°-R-153°-W-shore Grey tower, white
   band, black top
2. **Tréboul breakwater head** 48°06'·1N 4°20'·4W
   Q.G.7m6M White column, green top
Fishing Harbour
3. **E-W mole, E head** 48°06'·0N 4°19'·3W Iso.G.4s9m
   4M White and green pylon
4. **N-S mole, N head** Oc(2)R.6s6m6M White and red
   pylon
5. **Elbow Rosmeur mole head** 48°05'·8N 4°19'·2W
   Oc.G.4s6m6M 170°-vis-097° White pylon, green top

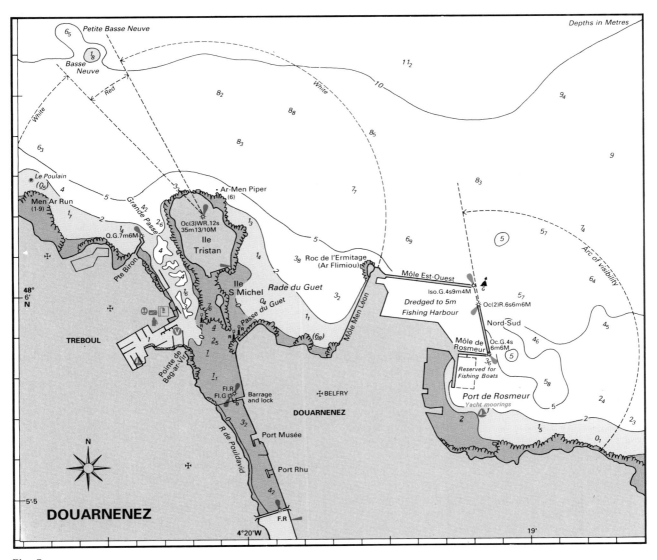

Plan 7

Douarnenez, looking SSW over Ile Tristan into the Rivière de Pouldavid. Tréboul fish and yacht harbour to the right.

General

Douarnenez is an important fishing harbour situated in the SE corner of the bay of the same name. It is off the beaten track of yachts bound south or north, as it lies 17 miles to the east of Pointe du Raz, but the detour is worth while. The town and harbour are interesting, with a superb museum of old craft. The town provides all facilities and the harbour protection in all weathers.

Approach

The only considerations in the approach are Basse Veur, with 4·7m over it, and Basse Neuve with 1·8m. Except near LW or when a sea is running these can be ignored. To clear them keep Pointe du Millier lighthouse (5 miles W of Douarnenez) open of Pointe de la Jument (3 miles W) until Ploaré church, at the back of the town, comes well open to the left of Douarnenez church and Ile Tristan lighthouse bearing 150°; the two churches and lighthouse are almost in one line. The town is easy to locate from seaward, with Ile Tristan in the foreground, the two churches, and the harbour mole to eastward.

By night

Navigate on Ile Tristan light[1] until the lights on the moles are picked up, then steer round them to the anchorage. Ile Tristan light has a red sector covering Basse Veur and Basse Neuve.

Anchorage and mooring

There are several anchorages or harbours at Douarnenez. As the vessel approaches, the first to be seen is the Rivière de Pouldavid, on the west side between the land and Ile Tristan. The river has been dredged to 3m and there is a yacht harbour, dredged to 1·5m, at Tréboul on the west side. In 1992 a barrage, with gate, was built across the river to provide a large wet basin for the museum at Port Rhu.

Next there is the Rade de Guet, an anchorage not much used, in the bay between the east side of Ile Tristan and the main fishing harbour. To the SE of the fishing harbour is the Port de Rosmeur. The following descriptions start with Port de Rosmeur and work back westwards.

Port de Rosmeur This lies to the east of the town; it is protected by land on the W and S and by the breakwater on the N. Though it is open to the E, the land there is only 1 or 2 miles distant. The northwestern half of the harbour is for fishing boats and there are many yacht moorings and *viviers* in the remainder of the bay. It may be possible to borrow a mooring. If not, anchor in around 5m outside the moorings. There is good holding in mud. Inshore the depths vary rather irregularly and once the 3m line is crossed they shoal quickly in places.

Fishing harbour Yachts may not use this harbour.

Rade du Guet This lies between Ile Tristan and the mole leading to Roche d'Ermitage (Ar Flimmou). It is sheltered except from winds from NW to NE, to which it is completely exposed. In offshore winds it is a good anchorage, with a convenient dinghy landing at the slip in Passe du

Douarnenez, looking SE into the Grande Passe for Tréboul. On close approach by day, the right-hand belfry bearing 145° clears Basse Veur and Basse Neuve.

The maritime-museum basin at Port Rhu, seen from the road bridge.

Guet. It is quieter than Port de Rosmeur. The depths decrease steadily towards the SW from 3m. Go in as far as draught and tide permit to get as much shelter as possible.

The Passe du Guet, leading from the anchorage into the river, dries 3·5m, the best water being on the southern side near the port beacons marking the slip. When the base of the first beacon is just covered there should be 1·5m in the Passe.

Rivière de Pouldavid This is entered through the Grande Passe, west of Ile Tristan. There are rocks close under the island shore, and the best water is nearer the breakwater head on the west side. The river is dredged to 2m and can also be entered through the Passe du Guet (dries 3·5m). There are two trots of mooring buoys on the starboard side in the channel. Visitors may moor, bow and stern, here if a place is vacant.

Tréboul A visitors' pontoon is in the channel before the turn to starboard into the Tréboul basin, dredged to 2m with finger pontoons on the outside. Space for two boats along the inside but not rafted, as there is a shelf along the wall. Passing this pontoon, turn to starboard to enter the basin. The visitors' pontoon is in the entrance on the starboard side. Visit the *bureau du port* on the quay or call on channel 9 to obtain a berth or a mooring in the channel.

Rivière de Pouldavid/Port Rhu This was once the commercial port. The wet basin was officially opened in 1993 together with a remarkable Maritime Museum, with some vessels in the museum building and others afloat in the basin. It is possible that visiting yachts of sufficient age and appropriate *gréement* may, by arrangement, be permitted to enter and moor. In front of the barrage the bottom dries 3m (mud and sand) for the most part.

Facilities

At Tréboul: water and electricity on the pontoons, fuel berth (the pumps are operated by card or on application to the harbourmaster), two cranes (6-tonne), showers, toilets, launderette, cafés, restaurants and shops. Market day Wednesday.

Shipyard in the fishing port. Marine engineers, repairs.

At Rosmeur: water tap near the dinghy slip and restaurants near the quays.

Douarnenez has all the usual facilities of a substantial town.

Nearest railway station and airport at Quimper.

8. Ile de Sein

Men Brial
48°02'·5N 4°51'W

Charts

BA *798, 2351, 2643, 2645*
Imray *C36, C37*
SHOM *6609P, 7067P, 5252*
Navicarte *541*

Tidal data

Tidal streams (approx)
HW −0005 Brest
MTL 3·8m. Index 3
Heights of tide above chart datum
MHWS 6·5m, MLWS 1·2m, MHWN 5·1m, MLWN 2·7m

Tidal streams

Between Ile de Sein and Tévennec the NW stream begins +0535 Brest, SE stream begins −0045 Brest, spring rates 3 knots. To the north of Nerroth the flood begins NNW at −0600 Brest, turning steadily to W by HW Brest. The ebb begins at +0200, running S.

Depths

The approach is deep until Nerroth is reached; thence the channel has 0·8m. In the anchorage there is 1·8m.

Lights

1. **Ile de Sein, main light** 48°02'·6N 4°51'·9W
   Fl(4)25s49m29M White tower, black top
   RC *SN* (···/−·) 289·5kHz 70M
2. **Men Brial** 48°02'·3N 4°50'·9W
   Oc(2)WRG.6s16m12-7M 149°-G-186°-W-192°-R-221°-W-227°-G-254° Green and white tower
3. **Kornog an Ar Braden buoy (starboard)** 48°03'·3N 4°50'·7W Iso.G.4s7m3M Whis
4. **Tévennec** 48°04'·3N 4°47'·6W Q.WR.28m9/6M 090°-W-345°-R-090° and DirIso.4s24m12M 324°-intens-332° same structure. White square tower and dwelling
5. **Le Chat** 48°01'·5N 4°48'·8W Fl(2)WRG.6s27m9-6M 096°-G-215°-W-230°-R-271°-G-286°-R-096° S card tower

General

On even the largest-scale British Admiralty chart, *798*, the Ile de Sein appears to be so surrounded by reefs and rocks that it looks unapproachable, especially when it is associated in one's mind with the fierce tides of the Raz. But, except in bad visibility or heavy weather, navigation in the area with a chart on a sufficiently large scale is not difficult because:

i. The plateau is compact on the NE and E sides and the fringes are indicated by the whistle buoy on the N, the above-water rock Ar Vas Du to the

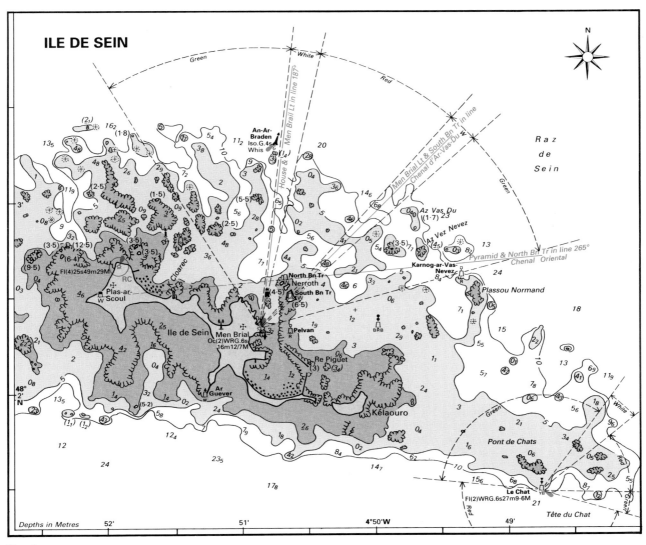

Plan 8

NNE, the Kornog ar Vas Nevez tower to the E and Le Chat tower to the ESE. There are no dangers if a vessel is over ½ mile seaward of these visible marks.

ii. The tidal streams on the Sein side of the Raz are not so strong as they are on the E side.

iii. The entrance channels are clearly marked. However, when visiting the island for the first time it is best to wait for settled weather, with clear visibility and neap tides.

The Ile de Sein is sufficiently detached from the busy world to remain largely unspoilt. Its inhabitants exist largely by catering for tourists, fishing, and farming small plots of soil won from hard rock, which is always so near the surface that it is difficult even to find sufficient depth for burying the dead. The entire male population left the island during the war to join the Free French forces in Britain. It is said that when Colonel de Gaulle, as he then was, reviewed the troops he said, 'Where is this Ile de Sein? It seems to be half France.'

The local fishing boats are mostly small, but the harbour is a base for larger vessels from Audierne and Douarnenez, which fish by day and anchor at Sein sufficiently early in the evening to patronise the numerous bars. When the fishing fleet is in the harbour is crowded, but there is still room for a few yachts.

Though there is considerable tripper traffic with the mainland, the island is a strange, out-of-the-way place. It is worth visiting, if only to see the curious rock formations, but it also has a practical use, as the harbour is convenient if you are late on the tide, especially when bound south. The facilities are quite good and the anchorage is secure in southerly and westerly winds. It is exposed to the N and NE; if there is a threat of winds from this quarter it is best to leave the Ile de Sein to visit another time, for if the winds are moderate there will be a swell in the harbour, and if they are strong it may be dangerous to remain.

Yachts that can take the ground can anchor in the bay south of the slips and can find 1·5m in places at LW neaps. The bottom is sand with some weed-covered stony patches. Inspect the bottom before taking the ground.

Men Brial. Entering from the N, the lighthouse and the black stripe on white wall to left of lighthouse form the leading line at 188°. On close approach Guernic G beacon tower is left to starboard.

Facilities

Several small shops, restaurants, PTT and bank (open 1630–1830 in 1992). Ship and engine repairs can be arranged, chandlery at the fishermen's cooperative shop. Water is scarce and yachts should bring enough with them.

The village has a considerable population; the houses are clustered together in a small area, providing shelter from the winds in narrow alleyways. Bread comes on first *vedette* from the mainland.

Approach

Nerroth is the key to pilotage in the Ile de Sein. Situated in the approach to the harbour, it looks like a small island. In fact it is composed of three very large rocks; only at low water does it form a continuous island, with a finger of rocks extending from its southern end to the eastern breakwater. There are two white masonry beacons, at its northern and southern ends, which are important leading marks.

North channel

This is the principal channel and the easiest for a stranger. The channel is deep until abreast of Nerroth, after which the depth is 1·4m to the jetties.

Having given a wide berth to all beacons and visible rocks (not less than ½ mile if approaching from the Raz), approach the Kornog an Ar Braden pillar whistle buoy (starboard) from the north. Bring Men Brial lighthouse into transit, at 188°, with the third house from the left by the quay; this house is painted white, with a black vertical stripe which should be kept just open to the left of the lighthouse if the latter tends to hide it.

This transit leaves both the buoy and the rock which it marks very close to starboard. It is advisable, therefore, to borrow say 50m to port until the rock is passed, as the tides set very strongly across the channel. Thence follow the alignment; there are drying rocks on either side, but no dangers for 50m on either side of the line. When Nerroth is abeam, if the tide is high, Pelvan concrete beacon (port, R) will come into transit with the E end of the eastern breakwater, bearing 155° (at LW the breakwater is obscured). Follow this transit (or steer 155° for Pelvan), leaving Guernic concrete beacon (starboard) to starboard.

When Guernic is well abaft the beam borrow a little to starboard of the transit, and when Men Brial lighthouse bears 220° the shoal is passed and course can be altered to SW for the anchorage.

By night

There must be enough light to make out Nerroth and Guernic concrete beacon on near approach. As it may not be easy to find the best water, it is desirable also that the tide should be high enough to allow some margin, preferably above half tide.

Enter in the white sector of Men Brial light[2], bearing from 187° to 190°, leaving Kornog an Ar Braden buoy[3] to starboard. When Nerroth northern beacon is abeam, alter course to 160° and enter the red sector of Men Brial, leaving Guernic tower 60m to starboard. When the other white sector of Men Brial is entered it is safe to steer for the anchorage.

Northeast channel

This channel carries 3·6m until it joins the north channel by Nerroth; thence depths are as for the north channel.

Make a position 300m NW of Ar Vas-du, a rock 1·5m (above MHWS). Here the white masonry beacon south of Nerroth will be in transit with Men Brial lighthouse bearing 224°; follow this transit. When the white masonry beacon at the north end of Nerroth bears 265° turn to starboard and, leaving the northern white beacon 100m to port, join the north channel.

By night

There is a white sector of Men Brial light[2] covering this channel, but sufficient light is needed for the deviation round Nerroth and into harbour.

East channel

This channel carries 2·3m until it joins the north channel by Nerroth; thence depths are as for the north channel.

The channel is entered 100m N of Kornog ar Vas Nevez tower (R). When coming up through the Raz be careful to avoid the shoals E and N of Le Chat tower (S cardinal), and Plassou Normand (drying 2·4m) to the SE of Kornog ar Vas Nevez tower. These shoals will be avoided if the tower is kept bearing less than 290°.

The leading marks for this channel are the white masonry beacon on the north end of Nerroth in transit at 264° with a pyramid, with fluorescent orange top, 300m S of the Ile de Sein main light-house. Also on the transit is Karek Cloarec, a rock which never covers, and behind it and just south of the transit is a monument (a cross of Lorraine) on Men Dai, a promontory rising to 18m above datum.

If the pyramid cannot be identified either of the above could be used instead, and they will in any case serve to confirm the identification. The marks must be held very closely, as Ar Vas Nevez, drying 5m, is close to the north of the transit, while shortly after there is a rock drying 1m close to the south.

On close approach to Nerroth, bear to starboard and round it to join the north channel, leaving the white masonry beacon 100m to port.

Near high water it is possible to make a short cut east of Nerroth by steering to leave Pelvan concrete beacon (port) close to port, then steering for 200m towards the southern quay to avoid rocks to starboard before rounding into the anchorage. This passage is a SEVERE one which cannot be recommended to strangers.

Anchorage

The anchorage is immediately off the lifeboat slip, near the Men Brial lighthouse and SE of it. Off the slip there is 1·8m, and there is 1m further to the SE. Near and south of the quays the whole harbour dries out. The fishing fleet enters the harbour in the evening, and is often there by day. Its position indicates the best water. The round red buoys belong to the fishermen and do not leave much room to anchor between them and the slip; it may be necessary to anchor to the east of them. Permission can sometimes be obtained to use one.

Men Brial. Drying anchorage in the southern bay. Inspect the bottom before taking the ground.

The anchorage is sheltered from S to NW, and from E below half tide. Swell enters if the wind goes into the north and the anchorage would be dangerous in strong winds from any northerly direction. It is also exposed to the east when the rocks are covered. Yachts should not remain in the anchorage if fresh northerly or easterly winds are expected. The bottom is a layer of mud over rock. The stream in the anchorage is weak.

9. Raz de Sein
Passage notes
48°03'N 4°46'W

Tidal streams

South-going, ebb stream

Position	Begins Brest	Direction	Spring rate, knots
Off Pte du Van	−0130	SW	1½
Between Sein and Tévennec	−0045	SE	2¾
Off La Vieille	−0045	SSE	5½
In centre of Raz	−0030	SW	5½
In southern part of Raz	−0045	SE	5½

There is a north-going eddy between La Vieille and a position near La Plate.

North-going, flood stream

Position	Begins Brest	Direction	Spring rate, knots
In southern part of Raz	+0535	NW	6½
In centre of Raz	+0550	NE	6½
Off La Vieille	+0535	NNW	6½
Between Sein and Tévennec	+0535	NW	2¾
Off Pte du Van	+0605	NE	2¾

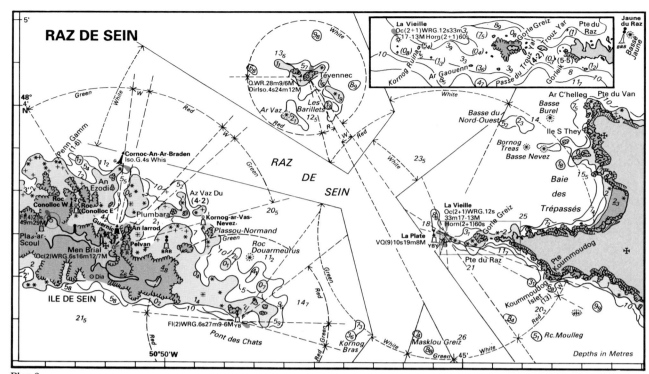

Plan 9

La Plate tower and La Vieille lighthouse, looking NE towards
Pointe du Van. Gorle Greiz is the large rock off the Pointe du
Raz, middle right.

Tévennec lighthouse, looking SW, with Ile de Sein main light-house to left of the rock.

Trouz Yar rock near LW, looking north. A fishing boat (arrowed) is coming through the Passe from the NW.

There is a south-going eddy for ½ mile north of La Vieille. In the inshore Passe du Trouz Yar the streams are much stronger and in the approaches to the pass they do not run true with the channel. They turn earlier, the S stream beginning about −0120 Brest; the time at which the N stream begins is not known, probably about +0445 Brest.

Lights

1. **Tévennec** 48°04'·3N 4°47'·6W Q.WR.28m9/6M 090°-W-345°-R-090° and DirIso.4s24m12M 324°-intens-332° same structure. White square tower and dwelling
2. **La Vieille** 48°02'·5N 4°45'·4W Oc(2+1)WRG.12s 33m17-13M 290°-W-298°-R-325°-W-355°-G-017°-W-035°-G-105°-W-123°-R-158°-W-205° Grey square tower, black top
3. **La Plate** 48°02'·4N 4°45'·5W VQ(9)10s19m8M W card tower
4. **Le Chat** 48°01'·5N 4°48'·8W Fl(2)WRG.6s27m9-6M 096°-G-215°-W-230°-R-271°-G-286°-R-096° S card tower
5. **Men Brial** 48°02'·3N 4°50'·9W Oc(2)WRG.6s16m 12-7M 149°-G-186°-W-192°-R-221°-W-227°-G-254° Green and white tower
6. **Ile de Sein main light** 48°02'·6N 4°51'·9W Fl(4)25s 49m29M White tower, black top RC *SN* (···/−·) 289·5kHz 70M

General

The Raz de Sein is the area between the Pointe du Raz on the mainland and the Ile de Sein. The scene viewed from the Pointe du Raz during gales, with the wind against a spring tide, is so impressive that it forms an inspiration to artists and photographers. Taken under reasonable conditions, however, the passage through the Raz presents no great difficulties and is a smoother passage than out at sea. It is largely a matter of timing. A yacht leaving the Four channel on the last of the fair tide can usually cross the Iroise, where the tides are less rapid and set nearly across the course, during the foul tide, so as to arrive at the Raz at the correct time, when the tide is just starting to turn fair.

The channel between La Plate tower and the rocks on the Ile de Sein is 2 miles wide. In the northern approach lies the island of Tévennec, surrounded by rocks; to the SW of Tévennec a rock, Basse Plate, narrows the western passage to 1½ miles.

Approach and passage

The Raz de Sein is rough, especially in the overfalls off La Vieille, even in moderate winds if they are contrary to the stream, as may occur with a fair tide if sailing south against a SW wind. When wind and tide are together the passage is smoother than outside. In light weather, at neap tides and in the absence of swell, the passage can be taken at any time by vessels having auxiliary power. The seas caused by the irregular bottom knock the way off a boat very quickly. Except when wind and tide are together, slack water for the passage is always to be preferred. The Raz is temperamental and the seas met there vary considerably, but in strong winds contrary to the tide the overfalls are dangerous.

From the north

Steer for La Vieille lighthouse, bearing 180°, about midway between Pointe du Van and Tévennec. When ½ mile off La Vieille, bear to starboard to pass west of La Plate tower (W cardinal), allowing for any tidal set. There are overfalls west of La Vieille and La Plate.

After passing La Plate the sea soon begins to moderate, but in rough weather the Masklou Greiz (9m) and Kornog Bras (3·6m) must be avoided as the seas break heavily over them. If proceeding seawards, the Pointe du Van in transit at 041° with Gorle Greiz, the large rock between Pointe du Raz and La Vieille, leads between the shoals. If bound for Penmarc'h, steer with Tévennec bearing 324° astern open to the left of La Plate.

By night

Steer for La Vieille light[2] at 180° in the white sector. When Le Chat[4] turns from green to white, steer in that white sector until the directional isophase light on Tévennec[1] opens; thence steer about 150° in that sector. Bound seaward, steer out in the first white sector of La Vieille, about 205°; bound for Penmarc'h, continue in the directional sector of Tévennec until clear. When Le Chat turns from green to red, bearing 108° the vessel is clear of the southern dangers.

From the northwest

The approach is between Tévennec and Ile de Sein. There is the Basse Plate ½ mile SW of Tévennec to be avoided; keep Koummoudog islet open to the right of Gorle Greiz, bearing 118°. The dangers off Ile de Sein are fairly well defined by the whistle buoy, Ar Vas Du rock (which never covers) and a R tower. Follow these dangers on the Ile de Sein side, leaving them ½ mile to starboard, and Le Chat tower (S cardinal) ¾ mile to starboard. Or steer for La Vieille in transit with the southern limit of the cliffs SE of the Pointe du Raz, bearing 112°. When ½ mile off La Vieille alter course to round La Plate as before.

The ebb stream SW of Tévennec is weaker than in the Raz, and the race itself appears weaker on the Ile de Sein side, though there is no official confirmation of this. In W or SW winds most of the passage is under the lee of the Ile de Sein plateau, and not so rough as east of Tévennec; care must be taken not to get onto Kornog Bras.

By night

Steer for Men Brial light[5] on Ile de Sein, in the white sector (186° to 192°). When La Vieille[2] turns from red to white, steer in this white sector until the directional isophase light on Tévennec[1] opens; thence proceed as described for the northern channel.

From the south

In good visibility keep Tévennec open to west of La Plate on a bearing of 327°. When ½ mile from La Plate, bear to port, avoiding overfalls.

If heading north, round the tower about ½ mile distant to steer 020° until, with due attention to tide, Jaune du Raz (BRB) isolated danger buoy is abeam to starboard.

At spring tides, counter the set of the flood stream towards the Tévennec dangers by holding La Vieille tower on a bearing of 180° when clear north of La Plate. If going west of Tévennec steer handsomely to port to make good a course of 295° from La Plate until the NE-going stream is entered.

The south coast of Pointe du Raz is steep-to, so that with visibility of ½ mile and otherwise favourable conditions it is possible to steer to sight the cliffs well to the east of the point and follow the coast west, keeping ½ mile off until La Plate tower has been identified.

By night

Passage at slack water is preferable. Keep in the directional isophase sector of Tévennec light[1] until, with Tévennec bearing 330°, La Plate[3] bears 110°. A course of 020° will then lead northwards clear of the Raz, while a course of 295° leads northwest between Tévennec and Ile de Sein.

Passe du Trouz Yar

This passage is SEVERE; see page 10. It can only be taken by those with experience of these waters, in calm weather, at slack water, with good visibility and with reliable auxiliary power.

Identify Gorle Greiz, which is the largest rock off the Pointe du Raz. At high water it appears as two large, slightly separated rocks with E Gorle Greiz, a smaller rock, close by to the ESE. Trouz Yar is the small rock midway between them and the shore. The passage lies between Gorle Greiz and Trouz Yar and is deep and clean, except for a 0·5m outlier to the north of the eastern end of Gorle Greiz.

Fishing boat passing south through Passe de Trouz Yar.

Approach on a N or SSW course, allowing for any cross set of the tide in the approach, and go through the centre of the channel, steering NNW (avoiding the outlier) if coming from the south or SSE when coming from the north.

Soon after slack water, even at neaps, the tide runs so hard that the yacht goes out of control, and any sea makes the passage highly dangerous. Note that the tide turns early in the pass; see page 45.

Anchorage

There is a good fair-weather anchorage in the Baie des Trépassés, sheltered between NE and SE, in which to wait for the tide. The bay is sandy and shelving, so anchor in the most suitable depth; the best position is in the centre, facing the valley.

10. Audierne

48°00'N 4°33'W

Charts

BA *2351, 2645*
Imray *C37*
SHOM *7147 P*
Navicarte *541, 543*

Tidal data

Tidal heights (approx)
HW −0030 Brest
MTL 3·1m. Index 1
Heights of tide above chart datum
MHWS 5·3m, MLWS 0·9m, MHWN 4·1m, MLWN 2·0m.

Tidal streams

In the approach the NW stream begins at −0515 Brest, the SE at +0025 Brest. Streams in the approach are weak, but strong in the harbour itself.

Depths

The approach is deep until ESE of Ste Evette mole, where there is a depth of 2·2m. The anchorage (with moorings) at Ste Evette has depths of from 1·0m to 3·0m. The entrance channel is dredged to 1m but is subject to silting. Yachts may lie afloat at the pontoons in 1·5m–2m at MLWS (1992).

Lights

1. **Pointe de Lervilly** 48°00'·1N 4°34'·0W Fl(2+1)WR. 12s20m14/11M 211°-W-269°-R-294°-W-087°-R-121° White round tower, red top
2. **Kergadec** 48°01'·0N 4°32'·8W DirF.R.44m9M 321°-intens-341° and DirQ.WRG.43m12-9M 000°-G-005·3°-W-006·7°-R-017° White tower, red lantern
3. **Jetée de Ste Evette head** 48°00'·3N 4°33'·1W Oc(2)R.6s2m7M Red lantern
4. **Jetée de Raoulic head Passe de l'Est Ldg Lts 331°** 48°00'·6N 4°32'·5W
   Front Oc (2+1)WG.12s11m14/9M White tower
   Kergadec Passe de l'Est *Rear* DirF.R
5. **Coz Fornic groyne** Oc.R.4s6m Grey mast
6. **Vieux môle groyne** Iso.R.4s7m Mast
7. **Pors Poulhan 3M ESE of entrance** 47°59'·1N 4°28'·0W Q.R.14m9M White square tower, red top

General

The port of Audierne, like all French fishing centres, is interesting and the harbour is picturesque. The outside anchorage at Ste Evette, while well protected except from the E and SE, is bleak and only suitable for a short stay when on passage. The entrance channel has been dredged and pontoons have been established in the inner harbour to cater for between 25 and 35 visitors.

Approach and entrance

At the mouth of the Goyen river, Audierne is situated in the NE corner of the bay of the same name. The white slate-roofed houses will be seen from a distance clustered on the hillsides, with another group above the village of Pors-Poulhan, 4 miles to the SE.

The entrance to the harbour can be dangerous in strong onshore winds and swell, but the Ste Evette anchorage is protected by the land and a breakwater, except from the E and SE.

Approach from the west and south

There are no dangers until the vessel approaches within one mile of Pte Raoulic, on which stands the harbour jetty. The channel, ½ mile wide, lies between Le Sillon and adjacent rocks on the west side and a group of rocks named La Gamelle, which only dry at springs, on the east side. If there is a swell the seas break on La Gamelle. There is a whistle buoy (W cardinal) ¼ mile SW and a bell buoy (S cardinal) ¼ mile SE of La Gamelle.

The approach may be made with the two lighthouses (white with red tops), one disused, to the west of Pte Raoulic in transit, bearing 006°. The rear lighthouse, Kergadec, is on the skyline, but the old front lighthouse, Trescadec, is on the foreshore in a gap between some houses and is not easy to locate. A good initial landmark is the microwave telephone-link mast a few degrees to the right of Kergadec.

This line leaves the whistle buoy (W cardinal) about 200m to starboard and passes over a 2·2m patch E of the Ste Evette mole. If bound for the anchorage, steer for the mole head when it bears NW and round it, but not very closely. If making for the inner harbour, leave the transit of the lighthouses and steer for the end of the Raoulic jetty when it bears 034° and is in transit with the rather small steeple of Poulgoazec church (St Julien), which may be detected situated on a grassy knoll on the eastern side of the river.

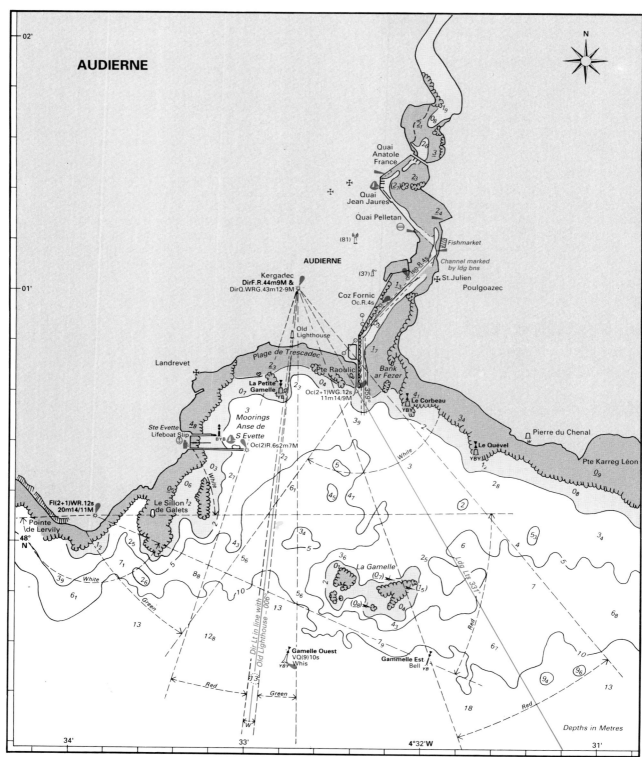

AUDIERNE

Audierne, looking north at half tide, showing the channel.

Audierne. 'Approach from the west and south' (see page 47). Kergadec lighthouse and the old lighthouse in transit (arrowed) on 006° left of picture. Conspicuous radio mast left centre and breakwater head (arrowed) far right.

By night

Enter the narrow white sector of Kergadec[2] quick flashing light (006°). When the light on the Ste Evette mole head[3] bears NW alter course for the Ste Evette anchorage. If proceeding to the inner harbour, alter course for the head of the Raoulic jetty when the light on it[4] turns from white to green, bearing 034°. Then keep just in the white sector to approach the jetty for entry. However, entry by night is not advised.

Southeastern approach

There is no difficulty in the southeastern approach as the channel between La Gamelle on the west and the land on the east is wide and carries a least depth of 2·5m on the leading line. However, Audierne is not easy to locate when approaching from the south, and it is best to follow the coast four miles or so offshore after rounding the Pointe de Penmarc'h.

Three conspicuous, equally spaced landmarks on the skyline indicate the harbour entrance from a distance of three or four miles. To the west is a church spire, in the centre over the Kergadec lighthouse a water tower and to the east a tall microwave telephone-link mast. Identify Kergadec light tower (white with a red lantern) and keep it on a bearing of 331° in transit with the Raoulic jetty head light tower, leaving La Gamelle well to port.

By night

Approach with Raoulic light[4] and Kergadec (F.R) light[2] in line on 331°. Pte de Lervilly light[1] has a red sector covering La Gamelle. When this light turns from red to white the way is open to steer for the Ste Evette anchorage.

The outer anchorage

The Ste Evette anchorage half a mile SW of the harbour is good. It is sheltered from W and N by the land and from the S by the mole, though some swell enters if there is S in the wind and this may be considerable if the wind is strong. The depths are 2·5 to 3·1m north of the end of the mole, decreasing steadily towards the shore. There are tightly packed moorings in the anchorage, with a charge collected for their use. There may be room to anchor east of them, with less shelter from the south. The holding ground is not very good and there are a few rocky patches. It is best to tuck in behind the mole as far as depths allow, so as to get out of the swell. The more northerly of the two slips, used by the ferries, extends a long way; the end is marked by an inconspicuous (E cardinal) beacon. A small tower (S cardinal) marks a rock, called La Petite Gamelle, in the northern part of the anchorage; west and north of this the bay is shallow.

Land at the ferry slip or, above half tide, at the little pier in the NW corner of the bay. There is a restaurant facing the bay at Trescadec and a small store at Kergadec, but most of the shops are in the town over a mile away. It is also possible to land at Raoulic jetty and leave the dinghy in a pond near its root, but this pond dries out towards low water.

Fuel is available close to the pier.

Audierne at LW. The pontoons had been cleared to receive a racing fleet.

The harbour

Much of the harbour or river mouth dries out at low water, and there is a bank which dries outside the entrance nearly one cable to the SE of Raoulic jetty head. The channel is dredged to 0·5m above LAT, but shifts and is subject to silting, so that it is best to enter within an hour and a half of high water. As a general rule, keep about 60m off the jetty as far as the bend in the wall some two cables from the entrance. The channel is indicated by a pair of panels with red and white chevrons, points uppermost, on the bank beyond the jetty. Thence the channel passes near the ends (marked by lit red beacons) of the two spurs, Coz Fornic and Vieux môle, projecting from the west side, after which it crosses over to run along the quay at Poulgoazec. Finally the channel swings back to the west bank along the Audierne quays and ends at the yacht pontoons.

Strangers are not advised to attempt this channel on a dark night.

Facilities

Audierne is a substantial town with a pleasant atmosphere which does attract tourists. The harbourmaster is most helpful and the mayor is keen for yachtsmen to enjoy their stay.

Water and electricity on the pontoons.

Depths at the visitors' berths vary from 1·5m to 2m. The banks of the dredged area are steep and care must be exercised when anchoring clear of the pontoons. Consult the harbourmaster.

There is a shipyard and repairs can be undertaken.

Municipal showers (open 1700–1900), garage and a Rallye Supermarché a short walk upstream past the bridge.

Audierne. Entrance channel at LW 1992. There was a yacht aground on La Gamelle.

Shops, banks, restaurants and hotels in the town close to the pontoons.

Bus service to Douarnenez and Quimper.

Fuel can be obtained from near the pier at Ste Evette, where there is also a *laverie automatique*.

11. Saint Guénolé

47°49'N 4°23'W

Charts

BA *2351, 2645*
Imray *C37*
SHOM *7147P, 6645P*
Navicarte *543*

Tidal data

Tidal heights (approx)

HW −0030 Brest
MTL 3·0m. Index 0
Heights of tide above chart datum
MHWS 5·2m, MLWS 0·9m, MHWN 4·1m, MLWN 2·0m

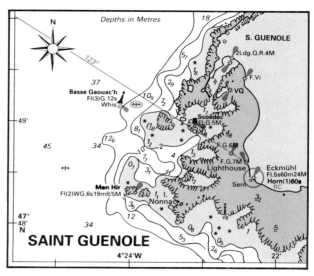

Plan 11

Tidal streams

For streams in the offing see under Penmarc'h (page 54). In the harbour the streams are weak, except in the final approach channel. 2m in the approach channel and anchorage.

Saint Guénolé. Looking SE over St Guénolé to Eckmühl lighthouse and *sémaphore*.

Lights

1. **Eckmühl** 47°47'·9N 4°22'·4W Fl.5s60m24M Grey 8-sided tower Horn 60s
RC *UH* (··–/····) 312kHz 50M
2. **Men Hir** 47°47'·8N 4°23'·9W Fl(2)WG.6s19m8/5M 135°-G-315°-W-135° White tower, black band.
3. **Basse Gaouac'h buoy (starboard)** 47°48'·7N 4°24'·2W Fl(3)G.12s Whis
4. **Passe de Grounilli Ldg Lts 123°** 47°48'·2N 4°22'·6W *Front* F.G.9m9M *Rear* F.G.13m9M Fluorescent orange-red spheres on white columns with black bands
5. **Scoëdec** 47°48'·5N 4°23'·1W Fl.G.2·5s6m3M Green tower
6. **Intermediate Ldg Lts 055·4°** 47°48'·7N 4°22'·7W *Front* VQ.5m2M *Rear* F.Vi.12m1M 040°-vis-070° Platforms on green and white metal columns
7. **Final Ldg Lts 026·5°** *Front* Q.R.8m4M Red mast *Rear* Q.R.12m4M Mast, red and white bands
8. **Entrance channel** two port buoys Fl.R, two starboard buoys Fl.G, followed by two red light columns Fl.R and two green light columns Fl.G

General

The small town of St Guénolé, situated about 1 mile north of Pointe de Penmarc'h, cannot be mistaken. It has a long and interesting history. Before the war the harbour, open to the westward, was untenable in bad weather sweeping in from the Atlantic. Then a sea wall was built, enclosing this entry, and a channel blasted through the rocks to the south; the quays were extended and the harbour was dredged. Although the entrance is exposed and dangerous in bad weather, the harbour now offers good shelter in all winds. A considerable fishing fleet is based here, but there is no local yachting activity. Yachts are not permitted to enter except in an emergency, but entry is described for interest.

No attempt should be made to enter the harbour except in settled weather, with no swell. A first entry should be made with the tide more than half up, in daylight; a night entry should not be attempted unless the channel is well known. There is very little room for error in following the channel.

St Guénolé, hazy approach on 123°. Arrowed from left: Scoëdec, port-hand buoy, rear leading mark, Eckmühl lighthouse, *sémaphore* (signal station).

St Guénolé entrance. Intermediate leading marks in transit (arrowed) on 055°.

Approach

From the north

Bring Eckmühl lighthouse on a bearing of 145° and make good this bearing until Men Hir black tower with white band, lying about 1 mile W of Penmarc'h, bears 175°. Alter course to make good this bearing, 175°, which leads clear of all the inshore dangers and about ¾ mile westward of St Guénolé sea wall. When Basse Gaouac'h whistle buoy (starboard) is 300m ahead the leading marks for the Passe de Groumilli will come in transit, bearing 123°. They are masonry columns with BW horizontal bands, with large fluorescent red • as topmarks. They will be seen to the left of Eckmühl lighthouse.

From the south

Give the Men Hir black tower with white band a berth of 800m to starboard. When it bears 090° steer 020° for the whistle buoy (starboard). Pass the buoy on either hand and hold the same course for 300m, when the marks for the Passe de Groumilli will come into transit (see above) bearing 123°.

Entrance

Enter with the BW columns with red • topmarks in transit, bearing 123°. This leaves the Pellenic rocks, which dry, close to starboard; Scoëdec tower (starboard G) will be seen on the port bow. After ½ mile, before Scoëdec tower is reached, a lateral port buoy will be left to port and the church of Notre Dame de la Joie, on the coast ½ mile north of Penmarc'h, comes into transit with Scoëdec tower, bearing 096°.

Passing the buoy, alter to port and steer 055·5° with the two intermediate leading marks (a pair of white columns with green tops) in transit. Identify

Steering S to round Pte de Penmarc'h. Men Hir beacon tower left centre, Eckmühl lighthouse with old tower and *sémaphore* right.

the four entrance-channel buoys (two port and two starboard), followed by the four metal light columns (two port and two starboard) marking the submerged breakwaters, and steer into the harbour.

By night

Only those who are already familiar with the harbour should attempt a night entry.

Anchorage and facilities

The pool is dredged to 2·5m. Anchor out of the way of the fishing boats, probably near the lifeboat house, although the bottom is foul and a tripping line should be used. The bottom is rock, covered with muddy sand.

All shops. Shipyard. Several hotels. Buses to Quimper. Museum of prehistoric megalithic culture about 1 mile distant. Water could probably be obtained from the fishmarket on the quay. No fuel nearby.

12. Pointe de Penmarc'h

Passage notes

47°48'N 4°22'·5W

Lights

1　**Eckmühl** 47°47'·9N 4°22'·4W Fl.5s60m24M Grey 8-sided tower Horn 60s
RC *UH* (··−/····) 312kHz 50M
2.　**Men Hir** 47°47'·8N 4°23'·9W Fl(2)WG.6s19m8/5M 135°-G-315°-W-135° White tower, black band.
3.　**Cap Caval buoy (W card)** 47°46'·5N 4°22'·6W Q(9)15s6m6M Whis

General

The Pointe de Penmarc'h is a low headland, in contrast with the very high octagonal lighthouse (Eckmühl) on it, which is 60m high. There are reefs of rocks extending in all directions from the headland, with numerous towers on them. In bad weather the whole scene is grim, but the point need not be closely approached except when on passage north of the Iles de Glénan. When rounding Pointe de Penmarc'h progress often seems slow, with Eckmühl lighthouse in sight for a long time, as the course follows an arc over 1 mile offshore.

Navigationally the principal consideration is the tidal stream. This does not compare in strength with that in the Four channel or the Raz de Sein, as the spring rates are only 1½ to 2 knots, except perhaps in the vicinity of the Men Hir tower.

Some 4 miles south of Penmarc'h the streams are rotary clockwise: N at −0325 Brest, E at −0020 Brest, S at +0240 Brest, WSW at +0600 Brest.

The tidal stream divides at the Pointe de Penmarc'h, the flood setting northerly towards Audierne and easterly towards the Iles de Glénan; the ebb sets in the opposite direction, the streams meeting off the Men Hir tower, where there are overfalls in rough weather. North of Penmarc'h the NNW stream begins at about −0540 Brest, the SSE at about +0025 Brest, spring rates 2 knots. South of Les Etocs the E and NE stream begins about −0600 Brest, the W and WSW at about HW Brest, spring rates 1½ knots. The streams on the coast eastward of Penmarc'h are much affected by wind.

13. Le Guilvinec

47°47'·5N 4°17'W

Charts

BA *2351, 2645*
Imray *C37*
SHOM *7146P, 6646P*
Navicarte *543*

Tidal data

Tidal heights (approx)
HW −0030 Brest
MTL 3·0m. Index 0

Heights of tide above chart datum
MHWS 5·1m, MLWS 0·9m, MHWN 4·0m, MLWN 2·0m

Tidal streams

Outside, the E stream begins about −0610 Brest, the W at HW Brest, spring rates 1·5 knots, but much affected by winds. There is negligible stream in the harbour.

Depths

On the main leading line the least depth is 2·8m, but more water can be found. The harbour is dredged to 3m to the inner ends of the fish quays and in the area of the visiting yacht mooring buoys.

Lights

1. **Basse Névez buoy (N card)** 47°46'·1N 4°19'·7W VQ.7m8M
2. **Spineg buoy (S card)** 47°45'·3N 4°18'·8W Q(6) +LFl.15s7m8M Whis
3. **Lost Moan** 47°47'·1N 4°16'·7W Fl(3)WRG.12s8m9-6M 327°-R-014°-G-065°-R-140°-W-160°-R-268°-W-273°-G-317°-W-327° White tower, red top
4. **Locarec** 47°47'·3N 4°20'·3W Iso.WRG.4s11m9-6M 063°-G-068°-R-271°-W-285°-R-298°-G-340°-R-063° White tank on rock
5. **Three Ldg Lts 053°** 47°47'·5N 4°17'·0W
   Front Q.7m8M 233°-vis-066° on starboard mole spur, white pylon
   Middle 210m from front Q.WG.12m14/11M 006°-W-293°-G-006° Red square on white pylon
   Rear 1100m from front DirQ.26m8M 051·5°-vis-054·5° Red square on white pylon in front of white gable end of building
6. **Capelan buoy (starboard)** 47°47'·2N 4°17'·5W Fl(2)G.6s
7. **N mole spur head** Fl.R.4s11m9M White tower, red top
8. **N breakwater head** Fl(2)R.6s4m5M Red structure
9. **S mole head** 47°47'·5N 4°17'·1W Fl.G.4s5m7M Round white hut, green top
10. **S mole spur** Fl(2)G.6s4m5M 078°-vis-258° Green structure

General

Situated some 4 miles east of Penmarc'h, Le Guilvinec (officially Guilvinec, but always called Le Guilvinec) is an important centre for fishing vessels of all kinds, and has processing factories. The town is not a tourist centre and derives its living entirely from the fishing industry. It has the attractions of a busy working town and there are a number of shops. Provided that care is taken to avoid the outlying rocks, the approach is straightforward and the harbour is sheltered. There is only limited room for yachts, which are tolerated rather than encouraged. Visitors are limited to a one-night stay and there is no local yachting activity.

Approach

The landscape east of Penmarc'h is dotted with white houses with grey slate roofs so that Le Guilvinec tends to be inconspicuous among them. It may be located by a somewhat thicker cluster of houses and the fishmarket, which is a long white building with a higher part at the west end, rather like a ship with the bridge aft. Also to be seen are the lighthouse, with a red top on the north mole, a conspicuous blue trawler travel-lift and the fluorescent orange-red ● topmarks of the leading line (these needed repainting 1992). (See photo page 56.)

Main western approach

From westward give Les Etocs, a prominent group of above-water and drying rocks, a good berth. Thence make a position 100m to the NW of Névez pillar buoy (N cardinal). This buoy lies 700m SE of Raguen tower (S cardinal), which is itself on the SE side of Les Etocs. In 1992 Raguen's topmark was missing and the pole was at an angle. From the position 100m NW of Névez buoy the leading marks should be in transit, bearing 053°. They are two enormous fluorescent orange-red spheres on orange-red columns.

The leading line crosses the Basse aux Herbes with a depth of 1·8m. Near low water, especially in rough weather, it may therefore be necessary to borrow 150m to starboard while the old Penmarc'h light tower is in line with Locarec tower, bearing 292°; at night, in the red sector of Locarec light[4].

After Basse aux Herbes is passed, return to the leading line, leaving Men Du concrete beacon (port) 200m to port, Capelan conical buoy (starboard) close to starboard, Rousse ar Men Du concrete beacon (port) 120m to port, and Groaïk tower (starboard) 200m to starboard.

From eastward make for the Basse Spineg whistle buoy (S cardinal), and either leave it close to starboard to make for the Névez buoy and enter on the leading line of 053°, or when the north mole lighthouse is identified, make for it, bearing not less than 020°, the lighthouse being seen just to the right of the fishmarket.

It is safe to steer in with the conspicuous lighthouse with a red top, on the north mole, bearing between 020° and 050°, until the buoys and beacons near the entrance are approached. On these bearings the north mole lighthouse will be approxi-

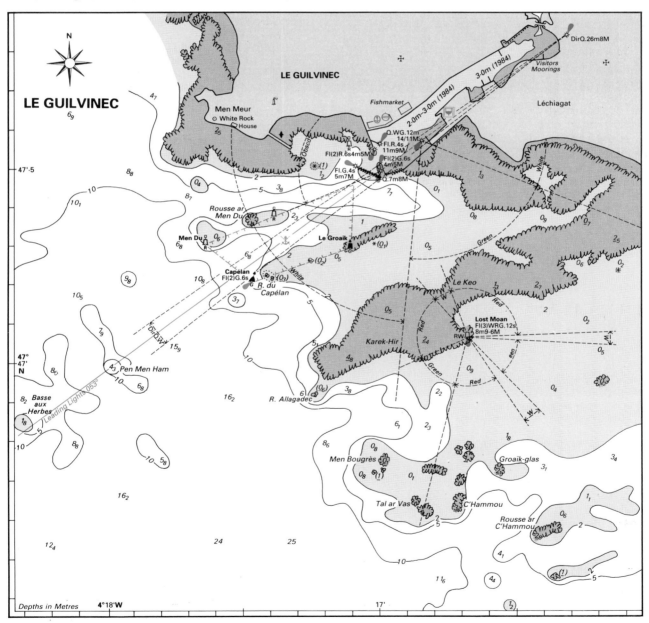

Plan 12

Le Guilvinec, looking NE along the leading line of 053° (markers arrowed).

Men-Meur, the white-painted rock (arrowed) for the southern approach. Capélan green buoy (arrowed), right centre.

Le Guilvinec entrance. Fishmarket left, white patch on break-water head to be left to starboard. Western approach leading marks arrowed.

mately in transit with the eastern edge of the fishmarket.

Southern approach

This is the easiest daylight route, with ample water, provided that the leading marks can be identified. Make a position midway between Les Putains (Ar Guisty) tower and Spineg buoy (S cardinal), 600m to the SW of Les Fourches rocks, which never cover, then identify the Men Meur white-painted rock, at the W end of the Guilvinec waterfront buildings, which transits a slender pyramid with large ♦ topmark a mile to rear on bearing 352°. Follow this transit for 1¾ miles to the Capelan buoy (starboard), which is left to starboard to continue as on the western approach.

By night

Entry by the main channel is straightforward.

Entrance and anchorage

Steer to leave the head of the outer southern mole (painted white) to starboard and then the northern mole head and spur to port. The northern mole head has a white rectangle with red border on the end. The ends of the spurs are marked by flashing red and green lights.

Le Guilvinec is an active fishing port and visitors must not get in the way. Yachts must not enter or leave between 1600 and 1830hrs and can only secure to a quay or a fishing boat in an emergency. On the starboard spur is a notice for visiting yachts. They must proceed to the upper end of the harbour and secure bow and stern to a pair of metal mooring buoys. There are three buoys; by rafting, six visiting yachts may be accommodated. Their stay may not exceed one night and a listening watch on channel 12 is required.

Visitors' moorings for one-night stay at head of harbour. (Most of the boats appear to be local!)

Facilities

The main part of town is on N side of harbour. Market day is Tuesday; excellent supermarkets. Showers at municipal baths near western pontoon on Thursdays, Fridays, Saturdays, and Sunday mornings.

14. Loctudy

47°50'N 4°10'W

Charts

BA *2645, 2351, 2352*
Imray *C37*
SHOM *7146P, 6649P*
Navicarte *543*

Tidal data

Tidal heights (approx)
HW −0030 Brest springs, −0010 Brest neaps
MTL 2·98m. Index 0
Heights of tide above chart datum
MHWS 5·05m, MLWS 0·85m, MHWN 4·0m, MLWN 1·95m

Tidal streams

In the offing the NE stream begins about −0610 Brest and the SW at HW Brest, spring rates 1·5 knots. In the harbour the spring rates are flood 3 knots, ebb 3·5 knots.

Depths

The least water in the approach is 0·9m. Off Loctudy there is 3m. Off Ile Tudy 1·0m or more may be found, and there is a deep pool with 5m on the opposite side of the channel just upstream of Ile Tudy jetty, with depths of 1m or more above and below it.

Lights

1. **Pointe de Langoz (Loctudy)** 47°49'·9N 4°09'·5W Fl(4)WRG.12s12m15-11M 115°-W-257°-G-284°-W-295°-R-318°-W-328°-R-025° White tower, red top
2. **Basse Bilien buoy (E card)** 47°49'·2N 4°08'·0W VQ(3)5s4m5M Whis
3. **Karek-Saoz** 47°50'·1N 4°09'·3W Q.R.3m1M Red truncated tower
4. **Les Perdrix** 47°50'·3N 4°10'·0W Fl.WRG.4s15m11-8M 090°-G-285°-W-295°-R-090° Black and white chequered tower
5. **Le Blas** 47°50'·3N 4°10'·1W Fl(3)G.12s5m1M Green pylon on pedestal

General

Geographically Loctudy and Ile Tudy (on the peninsula facing Loctudy across the river entrance) lie between Le Guilvinec and Bénodet. Likewise in character they stand midway between the wholly

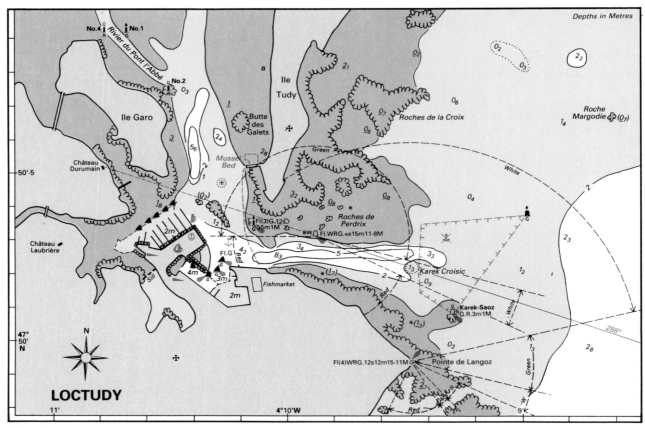

Plan 13

Looking west into Loctudy. Les Perdrix beacon tower is in transit
with Le Blas G beacon. Arrow over Château Durumain.

Entering Loctudy, with Château Durumain just open to right of Les Perdrix B/W chequered beacon tower on 288°.
Château Laubrière arrowed.

fishing port of Le Guilvinec and the holiday and yachting resort of Bénodet. At Loctudy and Ile Tudy fishing and sailing flourish together. The approach is sheltered in westerly winds and the harbour is secure. The estuary of the Rivière de Pont-l'Abbé is full of moorings, and the marina at Port Tudy, opened in 1991 but not fully developed by 1993, provides fuel and the basic facilities.

Approach

From the west the outside approach is the same as for Bénodet (see page 62), turning to port shortly after passing the Basse du Chenal buoy (E cardinal). Many will prefer to coast along the shore, which is considerably shorter.

Except near low water, it is sufficient after clearing Les Etocs near Pointe de Penmarc'h to leave not less than 500m to port Les Fourches (never cover), Ar Guisty tower (S cardinal), Reissant (S cardinal beacon on a small round rock which never covers), Les Bleds tower (S cardinal), Men Du tower (E cardinal), Karreg Hir tower (E cardinal), Men Bret tower (E cardinal) and Karreg Saoz tower (R). This course has a least depth of drying of 0·1m (Roche Glinec, between Karreg Hir and Men Bret).

Near low water it will be necessary to stand further offshore, using the chart and the outer buoys. Topmarks and paint were lost in the October gale of 1987 from Les Putains (or Ar Guisty) tower, Reissant beacon column and Les Bleds tower. The offshore marks on this coast are subject to damage which may not be repaired for some months.

From the E and SE the distant approach is the same as for Bénodet (see page 63) as far as Ile Aux Moutons. Thence steer more to the NW, leaving to port Les Poulains tower (N cardinal) and Men Dehou tower (E cardinal). Half a mile NW of Men Dehou is a rock with 2m over it. If necessary this can be left to the SW by keeping Ile Aux Moutons lighthouse midway between Les Poulains beacon and Men Dehou tower. Thence leave ½ mile to

port the buoys on Roche Malefic (W cardinal), Basse du Chenal (E cardinal) and Basse Bilien (E cardinal).

By night

Follow the direction for Bénodet (see pages 62 and 63) until the white sector of Les Perdrix[4] is entered. Then alter course to keep in this sector until within 400m of the lighthouse. There are no navigational lights in the river except for Le Blas[5] and it will be necessary to rely on the shore lights. A first entry should be made in adequate daylight.

Entrance

Enter with the Château Durumain (see photo page 58) open to the right of Les Perdrix black and white chequered tower on 288°. When Perdrix is about 500m distant alter course to port and steer 274° for the Château Laubrière, seen over the fishing harbour wall. When 100m from the wall turn upstream to starboard and follow the channel round into the marina.

When there is a heavy swell or in rough conditions, especially on the ebb, Karreg Saoz beacon (port) should be given a good berth; there are said to be isolated rocks near it as a result of blowing up a wreck.

If proceeding northward to the Ile Tudy anchorage, turn to starboard after passing the Banc Blas beacon (starboard), leaving the middle ground (which dries 1·8m) to port. Steer towards a position some 30m off the end of the jetty at Ile Tudy. 100m N of the jetty head is the Butte des Galets, a shingle patch, on which it is easy to ground when it is covered near high water.

Between 1800 and 1900hrs when the fishing fleet is returning entry is only permitted under power, sailing being prohibited.

Anchorage

The areas out of the fairways northwest of the fish quay and marina are now fully occupied by moorings. Only one or two corners are left for anchoring and if space is found further north it will entail a long dinghy journey against a fast tide.

Facilities

The marina was opened in the summer of 1991, when it had a fuel berth and temporary showers and toilets. Permanent buildings were to be constructed and chandlers and engineers were moving onto the site in 1992.

In Loctudy there are banks, *crêperies*, two restaurants, shops, a post office, a Rallye Supermarché just out of town, a launderette and a good vegetable market on Tuesdays (on road into town). Shipyard, marine engineer and chandler by the fishing port *criée* (market), where there is a top-class fishmarket at landing each evening.

The harbour is very animated when the fishing fleet is in, especially if dinghy racing is taking place as well.

Exceptionally interesting church.

Bus service to Pont l'Abbé and Quimper.

At Ile Tudy there are also shops and hotels, but it is rather less sophisticated. There is a water tap at the root of the jetty. Bus service to Quimper.

Rivière de Pont l'Abbé

As with other rivers, commercial traffic is no longer scouring the channel and it has silted. A visit to the town of Pont l'Abbé is still worth while, but the three-mile journey should perhaps be made in a dinghy with a reliable outboard.

15. Bénodet and Rivière Odet

47°53'N 4°07'W

Charts

BA *2645, 2352, 3641*
Imray *C38*
SHOM *7146P, 6679P, 6649P*
Navicarte *543*

Tidal data

Tidal heights (approx)

HW −0030 Brest springs, −0010 Brest neaps
MTL 2·72m. Index 0
Heights of tide above chart datum
MHWS 4·9m, MLWS 0·6m, MHWN 3·7m, MLWN 1·7m

Tidal streams

In the centre of the bay the streams are rotary clockwise, running N at +0600 Brest, NE at −0330 Brest, SE at +0015 Brest and SW at +0245 Brest, spring rate about 1 knot. In the river the flood begins at about −0540 Brest and the ebb at HW Brest, spring rate 2·5 knots.

Looking north into the Odet. Pte de Combrit lighthouse (white with red top) conspicuous lower centre. Bénodet main lighthouse (*pyramide*, tall white tower) conspicuous in Bénodet with Pte du Coq lighthouse (arrowed), on point, at 5 o'clock.

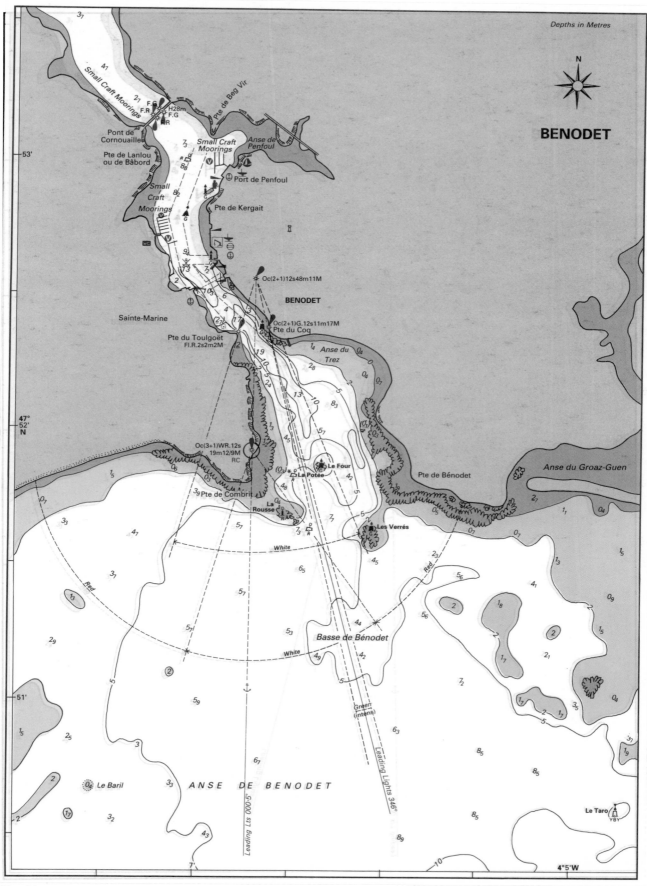

Depths in Metres

N

BENODET

Small Craft Moorings

4₁

3₇

2₇

F.G
F.R

H28m

F.G
R

Pte de Beg Vîr

Anse de
Penfoul

Pont de
Cornouailles

Small Craft
Moorings

7₃

R
8₈

Pte de Lanlou
ou de Bâbord

⊕ Port de Penfoul

8₂

Small
Craft
Moorings

G

Pte de Kergait

WC

V

9₄

0₅

Oc(2+1)12s48m11M

BENODET

Sainte-Marine

1₃

7

6

4

2

5

Oc(2+1)G.12s11m17M
Pte du Coq

Pte du Toulgoët
Fl.R.2s2m2M

1₇

1₉

1₄

Anse du
Trez

0₄

0₇

2₈

2

0₄

0₇

13

10

5

8₃

Oc(3+1)WR.12s
19m12/9M
RC

1₃

4₅

5₇

Le Four

La Potée

4₂

Pte de Bénodet

Anse du Groaz-Guen

3₉ Pte de Combrit

4₈

0₄

La
Rousse

7₇

5

Les Verrés

0₅

0₇

2₇

1₁

0₄

1₅

1₅

0₆

0₇

0₃

1₅

3₃

4₇

5₇

White

6₅

Red

2₃

5₆

1₃

1₇

4₁

0₉

3₁

5₇

1₃

Red

2

1₈

1₅

2₉

5₃

White

4₉

4₂

4₄

5₆

2

2₁

1₇

5

②

5₉

7₂

1₇

2₁

51'

1₅

2₅

0₄ Le Baril

3

3₃

A N S E   D E   B É N O D E T

Green
(intens)

6₃

8₅

8₅

3₅

0₄

3₇

1₉

2

1₇

3₂

4₃

Leading Lts 000·5°

6₇

Basse de Bénodet

Leading Lights 346°

8₉

8₅

Le Taro
YBY

7'

10

4°5'W

53'

47°
52'
N

Depths

The approach and entrance and the river for several miles upstream are deep. The upper reaches of the river dry.

Lights

Buoys to SW
1. **Cap Caval (W card)** 47°46'·5N 4°22'·6W VQ(9)15s Whis
2. **Karek Greis (E card)** 47°46'·1N 4°11'·4W Q(3)10s Whis.
3. **Basse Boulanger (S card)** 47°47'·4N 4°09'·2W VQ(6)+LFl.10s
4. **Bilien (E card)** 47°49'·2N 4°08'·0W VQ(3)5s Whis

Lighthouses
5. **Men Hir** 47°47'·8N 4°23'·9W Fl(2)WG.6s19m8/5M 135°-G-315°-W-135° White tower, black band.
6. **Pte de Langoz** 47°49'·9N 4°09'·5W Fl(4)WRG.12s 12m15-11M 115°-W-257°-G-284°-W-295°-R-318°-W-328°-R-025° White tower, red top
7. **Pte de Combrit** 47°51'·9N 4°06'·7W Oc(3+1)WR.12s19m12/9M 325°-W-017°-R-325° White square tower grey corners RC *CT* (–·–·/–) 288·5kHz 20M
8. **Pyramide (Bénodet main light)** 47°52'·5N 4°06'·8W Oc(2+1)12s48m11M White tower, green top
9. **Ile aux Moutons** Oc(2)WRG.6s18m15-11M White tower and building
10. **Pte du Coq Ldg Lts 346°** 47°52'·4N 4°06'·6W *Front* DirOc(2+1)G.12s11m17M 345°-intens-347° White tower, vertical green stripe *Rear* Pyramide Oc(2+1)12s48m11M 338°-vis-016° White tower, green top
11. **Trévignon** 47°47'·6N 3°51'·3W Oc(3+1)WRG.12s 11m14-11M 004°-W-051°-G-085°-W-092°-R-127° 322°-R-351° White square tower, green top

Buoys to SE
12. **La Voleuse (S cardinal)** 47°48'·8N 4°02'·5W Q(6)+LFl.15s Whis
13. **Grands Porceaux (N cardinal)** 47°46'·1N 4°01'·0W VQ.7m8M
14. **Jaune de Glénan (E cardinal)** 47°42'·6N 3°49'·9W Q(3)10s7m8M

Beacon
15. **Pte du Toulgoët** 47°52'·3N 4°06'·8W Fl.R.2s2m2M Red mast

General

The port of Bénodet, at the mouth of the river Odet, situated some 16 miles to the eastward of Penmarc'h, is one of the principal yachting centres in the north of the Bay of Biscay. With pontoons and numerous buoys on both sides of the river, it has good moorings and facilities and is a natural port of call for British yachts. The little town itself is a yachting and holiday resort where a yachtsman can get most of the things he needs. The only trouble is that it is terribly crowded in midsummer.

The Anse de Bénodet is a fine wide bay, some five miles across with sandy shores, sheltered from the N and W. The port of Loctudy lies on the west side and to the east lies the Baie de la Forêt, partially sheltered from the west, with marinas at Port de la Forêt and Concarneau. To the south there are the Glénan Islands, only twelve miles away.

The Odet river, which is completely sheltered, is navigable near HW nearly up to the cathedral city of Quimper; unless the yachtsman is in a hurry to sail south, he has plenty of local sailing to interest him. The whole bay is a centre of intense local sailing activity, with less popular waters to the west and to the southeast. Communications with England are good for crew changes.

Approach

From the west

After rounding Men Hir tower off Penmarc'h at a distance of ½ mile, make good 135° until Cap Caval W cardinal buoy is abeam to port. Then make good 120° to leave Spinec S cardinal buoy to port. If Ile aux Moutons light (white tower 18m and house) can be identified on a bearing of 083° hold it on this bearing, or make good a course of 083° for 8 miles, when Roustolou (E card) buoy should be seen ¾ mile abeam to port.

At this point Bénodet main lighthouse (white tower 48m with green lantern) will come into transit with Pte de Combrit light tower (white square tower, grey corners), bearing 000°. Alter course and steer on this transit, leaving Roustolou buoy to port and passing between Basse du Chenal E cardinal buoy (to port) and Basse Malvic W cardinal buoy (to starboard).

The passage between these last two buoys leads clear of dangers and into deep water, should identification of the transit marks at a distance prove difficult. Within a mile of Pte du Combrit alter course to starboard for the entrance.

In good weather a course can be followed closer to the shore, leaving Spinec buoy close to port, Les Putains (Ar Guisty) beacon well to port, and Karek Gris, Basse Boulanger and Billien buoys close to port.

By night

After rounding Men Hir tower[5] steer 135°, leaving Cap Caval buoy[1] to port and keeping in the white sector of Men Hir light[5]. When Ile aux Moutons light[9] turns from red to white on a bearing of 081°, follow this edge until Bénodet main light[8] comes into transit with Pte de Combrit[7] on a bearing of 000°. Follow this transit, watching the Pointe de Langoz light[6]; it will change from red to white to red to white to green to white. When it finally changes from green to white bearing 257°, the way is clear to turn to starboard to bring the Bénodet leading lights[10] in line on 346° and enter the river. Many lights other than those described will be seen.

It should be noted that yachts have been wrecked by following the Bénodet/Pte de Combrit transit of 000° onto the shore, under the impression that it led into the river.

Entering the Odet, with tall *pyramide* lighthouse left of centre and Pte du Coq lighthouse just below left. Les Verres G beacon tower far right and La Potée R buoy far left.

From the southeast

Leave Jaune de Glénan whistle buoy (E cardinal) to port and make good a course of NW, leaving Les Pourceaux about 1·5 miles to port. This rocky area is marked by a beacon tower (E cardinal) on its SE side and a buoy (N cardinal) on its NW side. Continuing the same course, leave Ile aux Moutons 1·5 miles to port, Les Poulains tower (N cardinal) to port, La Voleuse buoy (S cardinal) to starboard and Men Déhou tower (E cardinal) to port. The leading lighthouses of Bénodet should then be seen and course altered to bring them in transit on 346°, leaving Le Taro tower (W cardinal) to starboard.

By night

Before the Jaune de Glénan buoy[14] is abeam to port, get into the white sector of Ile aux Moutons light[9] and into or just south of the intense sector on a bearing of 285°. Continue in this sector until either the intense sector of the Concarneau rear leading light, Q, is entered, or Pte de Langoz light[6] is seen and Trévignon light[11] has turned from white to green bearing more than 051°.

When one or other of these occurs steer to starboard and enter the white sector of Pte de Langoz light, bearing 295°. Steer in the white sector of Pte de Langoz light until Pointe de Combrit light[7] opens white bearing 325°. Then steer for this light, crossing the green sector of Pte de Langoz light, and bring the Bénodet leading lights[10] in transit on 346°. Many lights other than those described will be seen.

Entrance

Bring the leading lighthouses in transit on 346°. The tower of the main light is conspicuous, but the front light, Le Coq, has been painted in green and white vertical stripes which tend to conceal it. It will be seen some way to the left of the conspicuous letters YCO on the grassy bank in front of the old yacht club building. This alignment leaves two buoys and one beacon (all port hand) to port and two starboard-hand beacon towers to starboard. When within 400m of Le Coq, bear to port and steer up the middle of the river between Pointe du Toulgoët port-hand beacon and a starboard-hand beacon tower.

By night

Entrance is straightforward, but the river will be found to be congested with moorings, and anchoring is prohibited in the channel until well beyond the bridge. The leading lights[10] lead clear of all unlit buoys and beacons. When within 400m of Le Coq[10], bear to port to pass halfway between Le Coq and Pte du Toulgoët light tower, Fl.R.2s[15]. Fixed red and green lights will be seen on the bridge and the shore lights may give some guidance. Those on the quays are left on all night.

Anchorage and mooring

There is good anchorage during offshore winds in the Anse du Trez on the starboard side of the entrance, especially if arriving in the dark. There is some hazard here from sailboard and Optimist schools, but it becomes peaceful at night. West of the Pointe de Combrit, the bay, with a long sandy beach, makes a pleasant lunchtime stop.

There are moorings, some of them marked *Visiteurs*, on both sides of the river up to and a short distance beyond the bridge. Anchoring is prohibited in this area. There are marina pontoons on the port side above Ste Marine and on the starboard side at the entrance to the Anse de Penfoul. Approach the visitors' berths in both marinas against the stream and with caution. A strong current sets across the pontoons during both flood and ebb. For west bank moorings apply to Ste Marine marina and for east bank moorings apply at the Port de Plaisance in the Anse de Penfoul.

It is possible at tide time to secure to the quay to do any business in the town and then go up the river where there is room to anchor.

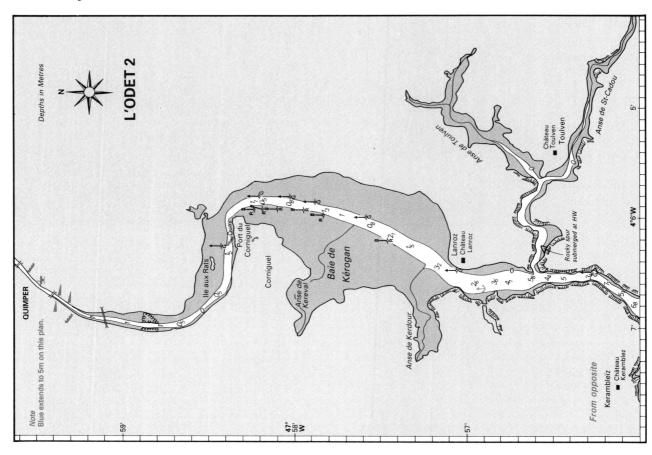

L'ODET 2

Depths in Metres

Note
Blue extends to 5m on this plan.

QUIMPER

Ile aux Rats

Port du
Corniguel

Corniguel

Anse de
Kereval

Baie de
Kérogan

Anse de Kerdour

Lanroz
Château
Lanroz

Anse de Toulven

Château
Toulven
Toulven

*Rocky spur
submerged at HW*

Anse de St-Cadou

From opposite
Kerambleiz
Château
Kerambleiz

Plan 16

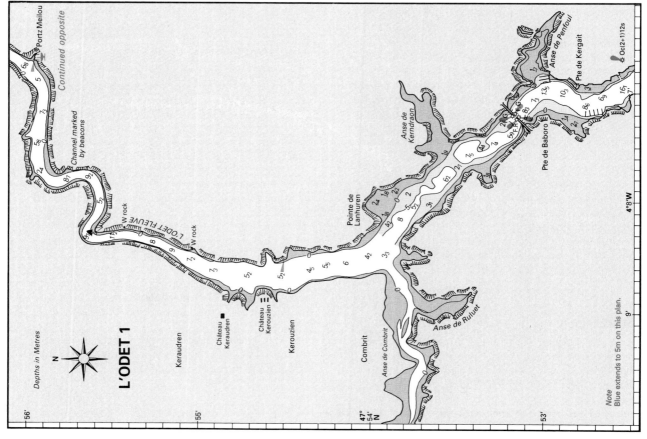

L'ODET 1

Depths in Metres

N

Portz Meilou

Continued opposite

*Channel marked
by beacons*

W rock
L'ODET FLEUVE
W rock

Keraudren

Château
Keraudren

Château
Kerouzien

Kerouzien

Combrit

Anse de Combrit

Pointe de
Lanhuren

Anse de
Kerndraon

Anse de Ruluet

Anse de Penfoul

Pte de Kergait

Oc(2+1)12s

Pte de Baboro

Pte de Penfoul

Note
Blue extends to 5m on this plan.

Plan 15

Facilities

All the facilities of a sophisticated yachting centre, with restaurants and hotels on both sides of the river. Food shops are of moderate standard.

Water and electricity on both marina pontoons, with a fuel pontoon at Anse de Penfoul. Showers and toilets in both marinas.

Groceries at café, *laverie automatique*, chandlery and engineers on Anse de Penfoul quay.

Yacht builders on both sides of the river.

Communications

Buses to Quimper from Bénodet and Sainte Marine.

Rivière Odet

The river Odet is a famous beauty spot, with steep, tree-covered banks, and ferries ply regularly from Bénodet to Quimper on the tide. There is no difficulty in sailing up the first five miles in depths of more than 2m. The deep water is in the middle and the only obstruction is a rock on the sharp turn to starboard, which is marked by a green conical buoy. There is 28m clearance under the bridge above Bénodet.

Above Lanroz the river is shallow, but well marked by beacons as far as the port of Corniguel; above that the river dries and the beacons are farther apart. A bridge prevents masted yachts from reaching Quimper, but yachts that can take the ground may anchor or borrow a mooring below the bridge and visit Quimper by dinghy, while motor yachts can carry a depth of drying 1·5m up to the first quays on the port hand in Quimper. The bottom here is hard and uneven for drying out.

There are no facilities on the way up the river, but everything can be got at Quimper, a large city, famous for its pottery, with an attractive cathedral with nave and chancel out of line.

A secret anchorage off the Odet.

In using the river, especially when anchoring, it is important to remember that occasionally large ships go up to Corniguel and need all the room there is. They must be given absolute right of way.

When looking for a place to anchor one wants to find a bight clear of the worst of the tide and where the mud has settled; in the river much of the bottom is rock. Among several such places the Anse de Combrit and the bay opposite Lanroz may be mentioned. There is a beautiful anchorage just below Lanroz in the Anse de Toulven inlet on the eastern side, but care must be taken to avoid a drying rocky plateau on the south side of the entrance where it opens out. Keep close to the north side of the channel. In this pool a large area has 1m depth and 2m can be found in which to swing on short scope. At the end of the first pool there is a rock with 1m or less, on the inside of the sharp turn to the N with mud on the S side.

Looking upriver from Ste Marine landing slip, with the road bridge behind the pontoons.

16. Iles de Glénan

Penfret lighthouse 47°43'·3N 3°57'·2W

Charts

BA *2645, 2352, 3640*
Imray *C38*
SHOM *7146P, 6647P, 6648P*
Navicarte *543, 243*

Tidal data

Tidal heights (approx)
HW −0025 Brest springs, HW Brest neaps
MTL 2·9m. Index 0
Heights of tide above chart datum
MHWS 5·0m, MLWS 0·8m, MHWN 4·0m, MLWN 1·9m

Tidal streams

Near the islands the streams are rotary clockwise, setting W 1 knot NW of the islands and S 0·25 knot to the NE at +0330 Brest, E 1 knot NW of the islands and NE 0·2 knot to the NE at −0230 Brest, SE 0·3 knot at HW Brest, and W 1 knot NW of the islands and S 0·2 knot to the NE at +0330 Brest; spring rates in each case. Amongst the islands the streams run in the direction of the channels, the flood setting N and E and the ebb S and W, spring rates up to 2 knots.

Depths

There is enough water in the anchorages for most yachts at all tides. Above half tide there is enough water to sail freely in the channels and in the large pool between Penfret and St Nicolas, but near low water the pilotage becomes intricate and a number of the channels cannot be used.

Lights

1. **Ile aux Moutons** 47°46'·5N 4°01'·7W Oc(2)WRG.6s 18m15-11M 035°-W-050°-G-063°-W-081°-R-141°-W-292°-R-035° White square tower and dwelling
   Auxiliary light DirOc(2)6s17m24M 278·5°-intens-283·5° Sync with main light
2. **Penfret** 47°43'·3N 3°57'·2W Fl.R.5s36m21M White square tower, red top
   Auxiliary light DirQ.34m12M on same structure
3. **Ile Cigogne** 47°43'·1N 3°59'·6W Q(2)RG.5s5m2M 106°-G-108°-R-262°-G-268° Red tripod shown 1st May to 1st October

Buoys
There are several lit buoys surrounding the islands, but these are not listed as it is inadvisable to enter the area at night.

Looking SSW over Ile de Bananec. Left centre, Fort Cigogne tower, with Ile du Loc'h behind. Far right, part of Ile St Nicolas, with the landing jetty.

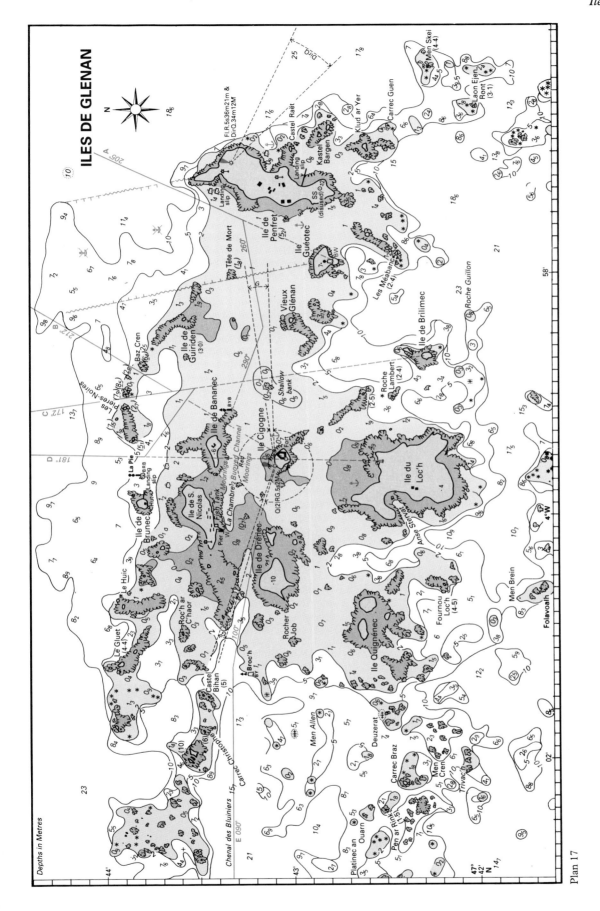

ILES DE GLENAN

N

Depths in Metres

Ile de Penfret (5.2)
Castel Raët
Kastel Bargen
Fl.R.5s36m21m & Dir.Q.34m12M
Landing slip
SS (disused)(0c2)
Ile Guéotec
BW
Klud ar Yer
Carrec Guen
Men Skei (14.4)
Laon Ejen Ront (3.1)
Les Méabanc (2.4)
Ile de Brilimec
Roche Guillon
Tête de Mort (1.8)
Vieux Glénan
Ile de Guiriden (3.0)
Baz Cren
Les Pierres-Noires
Shallow bank
Roche Lambert (2.4)
Ile de Bananec
Ile Cigogne
Fort
La Pie
Ile de Brunec
Landing slip
Le Huic
Ile de S. Nicolas
Fish Tank
Pier
La Chambre
Red Moorings
W. Moorings
Red Moorings
Ql(2)RG.5s3.M
Ile du Loc'h
Anse St. Yves
Le Gluet (14.4)
Roc'h ar C'haor
Ile de Drénec
Rocher Job
Broc'h
Castel Bihan (5)
Thistlestone
Chenal des Bluiniers
Carrec Cludu
Men Allen
Men Brein
Fournou Loc'h (4.5)
Ile Quignénec
Deuzerat
Men Du Cren
Trivach
Folavoalh
Carrec Braz
Platinec an Ouarn
Pen ar Rink (1.5)
4°W
47°42'N

Plan 17

67

General

Situated about 12 miles south of Bénodet and 10 miles from Concarneau, this archipelago is an intricate mixture of islands, rocks and shoals. It is the home of the Centre Nautique de Glénans (CNG), which is almost certainly the largest sailing school in Europe. Founded by Monsieur Philippe Viannay, it gives young people systematic training at all levels from basic seamanship to cruising and ocean racing. The main base of the CNG is on Ile Cigogne, with camps on the other Glénan islands, but there are centres in other parts of France and the rest of Europe, including one in Eire.

The fleets of CNG boats are in evidence everywhere among the islands. The CNG is very hospitable to visitors, but the latter should be careful not to impose on this hospitality as the *moniteurs* have a full programme.

The Ile de St Nicolas, where some of the more popular anchorages are, has a small café (which can on occasion supply bread), some holiday cottages, and the shellfish tanks of a famous restaurant.

The islands should be visited only in good weather as all the anchorages are somewhat exposed, at least at high water. They form a fascinating area to explore and practise one's pilotage, spending a week or more happily rock-dodging. It is hoped that the plans in this book will suffice for a quick visit, using the main channels, but for any exploration large-scale charts are essential.

From 1993 a speed limit of 8 knots has been imposed among the islands from 15th June to 15th September.

SHOM *6648* covers all the islands, despite being called *Iles de Glénan, partie Sud*, and shows many useful transits for alternative passages. SHOM *6647, Iles de Glénan partie Nord*, only covers Ile aux Moutons and Les Pourceaux. Navicarte *243* is comprehensive. British Admiralty *3640* plans, covering Audierne, Guilvinec, Lesconil and Glénan, may also be consulted. SHOM *7146 Penmarc'h to Trévignon* may be adequate for a brief visit. A vessel should be fully provisioned before going to the islands as there are no shops.

Approach

The main islands are easily distinguished by the conspicuous lighthouse on Ile de Penfret, the largest and most easterly of the group; a stone fort having a tall concrete tower, the top of which is painted black on the SE side, on Ile Cigogne; a disused factory chimney on Ile du Loc'h; some houses on the SE side of Ile de Drénec; the summer cottages on Ile de St Nicolas, and the shellfish tank (*vivier*) with adjacent house on the south side of the same island, which can provide a useful mark if they are not hidden behind the yachts in a crowded summer anchorage. A number of islets stretch out to the west of Ile de St Nicolas and the western edge of the archipelago is marked by Les Bruniers tower (W cardinal). The southern and southeastern sides are guarded by buoys (see British Admiralty *2352* or Imray *C38*).

Entrance

The entrances are described on the basis that one is aiming for La Chambre, the most popular and therefore the most crowded summer anchorage. Once inside the pool between Penfret and Bananec, the various alternative anchorages are easily reached.

The CNG people recommend the Chenal des Bluiniers western entrance and frequently use a northwest channel which leaves Castel Bihan rocks close to starboard (see SHOM *6648*). Yachts from Bénodet and Concarneau use the northern entrances and the feeling of all is that southern channels should not be used. For a stranger, the easiest entrance is that from the northeast. Once inside, the necessary landmarks can be more easily identified; exit can be made by another channel, which can then be used for a subsequent entry.

When manoeuvring in the pool, La Tête de Mort (dries 1·8m) is a well known hazard to be avoided; another is a shallow patch (drying 0·2m) 700m E of Cigogne.

Penfret lighthouse (left), with Ile de Guéotec beacon (right, arrowed) bearing 205°.

Northeastern entrance

• This channel carries a least depth of 1m, but passes close to shoals of 0·7m and should be treated as carrying that depth. Leave the northern end of Le Penfret 300m to port and steer 205° on the stone beacon on Ile de Guéotec. When Ile Cigogne concrete tower bears 260° alter course to make good the bearing, which also holds Penfret lighthouse dead astern. If the E cardinal beacon SE of Bananec can be located, alter course for it when it bears 290° and so avoid the shallow patch to the east of Cigogne. Alternatively alter onto 283°, steering for the wind generator on the western end of St Nicolas. Using either course, leave the east cardinal beacon SE of Bananec to starboard to enter the buoyed channel of La Chambre.

Northern entrances

All three entrances should be regarded as carrying 1m, although with careful pilotage through the pool, using a large-scale chart, more water can be found. In the approach care must be taken to avoid Les Pourceaux rocks, marked on their SE side by a tower (E cardinal).

The three entrances are taken in order from east to west; the easiest for a stranger is La Pie, the third. The vital clues to the first two entrances are four rocks which never cover: Baz Cren (dries 6·4m) in the E, then two adjacent rocks of Les Pierres Noires (drying 8·5m and 7·9m) and finally in the W a single Pierre Noire (dries 7·5m) with others to its SW which dry soon after HW. All these rocks stand on compact rocky bases and must be distinguished from Ile de Guiriden to the SE; this has a considerable sandy expanse, which covers near HW, leaving only the rocky head (dries 8·8m).

• The first entrance leaves Baz Cren (dries 6·4m) 50m to 100m to port steering on Fort Cigogne tower, bearing 212°. Once Baz Cren is fairly passed the vessel can bear to port as convenient. For this entrance the CNG use the chimney on Ile du Loc'h in transit with the E cardinal beacon southeast of Ile de Bananec on 200°. This is a positive transit to pick up but leaves an outlier of Les Pierres Noires, drying 2·8m and covered at HW, only 60m to starboard. When the islands were visited in 1992, the beacon was just being replaced, having recently been destroyed, and on close inspection the chimney was found to have two large holes in the base. It could fall in the near future.

• The second entrance leaves the two adjacent heads of Les Pierres Noires (drying 8·5m and 7·9m) 20m to 60m to port. Steer on Ile de Brilimec, bearing 172°, which leads fairly into the pool. As a check, Cigogne tower bears 200° in the entrance. This is a popular entrance for local yachts, but should not be used for a first visit, as Ile de Brilimec and Les Pierres Noires must be positively identified by close observation and there is a rocky plateau drying 2·6m, covered at HW, 100m to starboard.

• For the third entrance, La Pie, bring the chimney (if still in place) on Ile du Loc'h just open to the right-hand side of the Cigogne tower, bearing 181°. Steer so until inside Les Pierres Noires with La Pie beacon (BRB with 2 balls topmark, but do not leave it to port) abeam to starboard. Near low water the chimney dips behind the fort and one must then steer to leave La Pie beacon 100m to starboard. Except near high water there is no problem about knowing when Les Pierres Noires are passed, as a rock which dries 5·1m marks their SW extremity. However, this rock covers at HW springs. When La Pie beacon is in transit with the N side of Ile de Brunec, bearing about 280°, steer to port into the pool, unless heading for the anchorage north of Ile de Bananec, in which case steer straight on.

Western entrance

• The Chenal des Bluiniers carries a least depth of 0·5m drying, but it is safer to regard it as drying 0·8m. If this gives insufficient margin, it is better not to use this entrance, but to skirt the north edge of the rocks and enter by La Pie. Visibility of three miles is needed except towards high water.

Make a position 200m S of Les Bluiniers tower (W cardinal); if coming from the NW round this tower at not less than 200m distance. From this point steer E for Le Broc'h tower (N cardinal), keeping at least 100m S of a line joining all the dangers that show to the north and keeping Penfret lighthouse open to the north of Le Broc'h tower, bearing about 090°. Approaching Le Broc'h tower, leave it 100m to starboard and bring the semaphore, near the southern point of Ile de Penfret, open to the left of Fort Cigogne by the width of the fort (not the tower), bearing 100°. Steer so until the eastern part of Ile de Drénec is abeam to starboard; this island is in two clearly defined parts separated by a sandy strip which covers at HW. Thence steer 035° on the summer cottages to the east of the shellfish tank (*vivier*) to enter La Chambre. Near HW the detailed directions above can be disregarded; having passed Le Broc'h tower it is only necessary to sail 100m N of Ile de Drénec and then make straight for La Chambre or the pool as required.

For those already familiar with the islands: the transits shown on SHOM *6648* and British Admiralty *3640* may be used for entry, but it is necessary to identify the semaphore mast on Penfret at a distance of 5 miles as well as the farm buildings on Drénec.

Notes on entry by night and by the southeastern entrance are not included in this edition as it is felt that both operations should only be attempted after a thorough knowledge of the area has been acquired.

Anchorages

East of Ile de Penfret

This anchorage is in the sandy bay south of the hill on which the lighthouse stands. Approach with the middle of the bay bearing 270°. This leaves a rock

Second entrance for La Chambre (see page 69). Far left, the two adjacent heads of Les Pierres Noires. The ferry approaching will pass fairly close to the right-hand head to avoid the drying rock, just covered with breaking wave, centre of picture. Fort Cigogne tower bears 198°.

Beacons are frequently damaged or destroyed on this coast. A man is standing on Bananec E cardinal beacon plinth (below the left-hand edge of Fort Cigogne), ready to receive a new pole from the work boat. While the beacon is absent, a temporary buoy, to the left of the work boat, is placed close by.

drying 0·5m 200m to starboard and another, with 0·0m over it at LAT, 100m to port. This latter rock lies 150m N of an islet, Castel Raët, which dries 11m and is joined to Penfret by a ridge of rocks. There is a large metal mooring buoy on the N side of the bay, but it is preferable to anchor, on soundings, closer to the beach in sand, taking care to avoid patches of weed. The anchorage is well protected from the west but should not be used if there is any chance of a *vent solaire* during the night.

South of the islet is another bay with a slip and containing CNG moorings. This bay is unsuitable for anchoring.

Southwest of Ile de Penfret

There is a good anchorage in 2·5m outside the CNG moorings between the island and Ile de Guéotec. The tide runs fairly hard here, but the islands give a good deal of shelter even from the W and it is well sheltered from the E. This anchorage should normally be approached from the north; from the south the pilotage is intricate and requires the large-scale chart. At high water take care to avoid the rock (drying 5·2m) 150m off the shore opposite the CNG boatsheds.

East of Ile Cigogne

Anchor in 1m to 1·4m, north of the rocky ledge running SE from Cigogne.

La Chambre

This anchorage south of Ile de St Nicolas is the most popular one for visitors. The depths are up to 3m; although the best spots are occupied by moorings there is normally no difficulty in finding room to anchor. Do not anchor in the channel used by the *vedettes* and marked by small port and starboard buoys.

Avoid a rocky shoal which extends 350m SE from Ile de Bananec, the end marked by an E cardinal beacon. The bottom is also rocky for about 100m out along the south shores of St Nicolas and Bananec. Between the two islands, however, is sand. At low water they are joined by a sandy ridge, on either side of which bays are formed, drying 1m, which make excellent anchorages for yachts that can take the ground.

Coming from the pool, make for a position 100m S of the E cardinal beacon SE of Ile de Bananec. If La Chambre is full of yachts, follow the marked channel in until a suitable anchorage is found. If the shellfish tank is not obscured, keep it on 285° until Bananec is passed and then bear a little to port if wishing to proceed further into La Chambre. At low water depths of less than 1m may be encountered in La Chambre. The water is clear and it is necessary to look for a sandy patch on which to anchor as there is much weed.

Ile St Nicolas from the fort.

North of Ile de Bananec

There is a popular anchorage, with moorings, in the bay NW of Bananec and E of St Nicolas. The depth shoals from 2m; choose a spot according to tide and draught. There is a clean, sandy bottom. The anchorage is exposed to the N and E at high water and is not recommended except in calm conditions by the CNG.

17. Port La Forêt

47°54'N 3°58'·4W

Charts

BA *2645, 2352, 3641*
Imray *C38*
SHOM *7146P, 6650P*
Navicarte *543*

Tidal data

Tidal heights (approx)

HW −0025 Brest springs, −0005 Brest neaps
MTL 2·9m. Index 0
Heights of tide above chart datum
MHWS 5·0m, MLWS 0·8m, MHWN 3·95m, MLWN 1·95m

Tidal streams

Are weak in the bay.

Depths

The channel in Rivière de la Forêt is dredged to 1·2m or more.

Lights

1. **Cap-Coz shelter mole head** 47°53'·5N 3°58'·1W Fl(2)R.6s5m6M Red lantern on grey post, white hut
2. **Kerleven shelter mole head** Fl.G.4s8m6M Green lantern on grey mast, white hut
3. **Marina mole head** 47°54'·0N 3°58'·2W Iso.G.4s5m 5M Green lantern on grey mast
4. **Buoys marking entrance of channel** SE of Cap Coz mole head starboard; Fl(2)G.6s, port Fl.R.2·5s

General

Baie de la Forêt lies just to the NW of Concarneau. It is rectangular in shape, with shoals on each side of the entrance. It thus affords anchorage in most weather, even in SW winds. The shelter is sufficient for many local boats to lie on permanent moorings in the summer off Beg Meil. The E and NE sides of the bay are foul. The marina in the estuary at the head of the bay provides laying-up facilities for UK boats at a reasonable rate and is part of a planned holiday village complex which is slowly developing.

Approach and entrance

The entrance to the estuary lies to starboard of the wooded promontory of Cap Coz. Pass between the loose-boulder breakwaters of Cap Coz to port and Kerleven to starboard. The channel is well marked with lateral buoys and beacons. The moorings near the top of the estuary are reserved for fishermen, but there are a number of moorings for yachts up to 25m length on the port hand opposite the marina entrance in 2·5m. Turn sharply to starboard to round the marina breakwater head, marked by a named green and white column and pole.

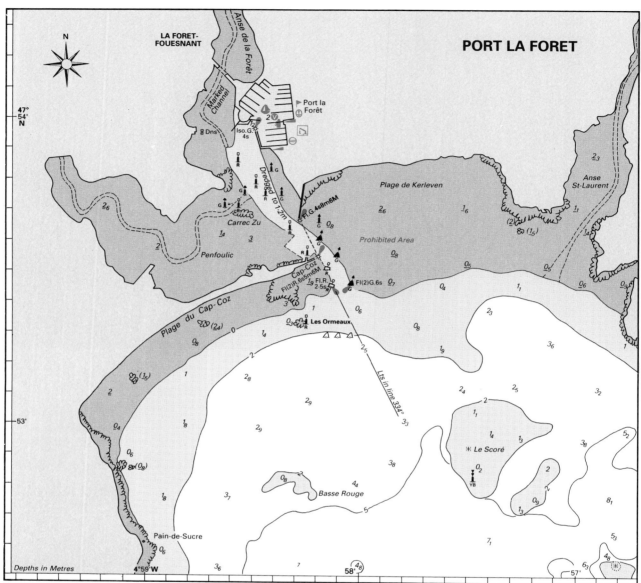

PORT LA FORET

Plan 18

La Forêt entrance. Cap Coz light on left, masts in the marina
seen over the Kerleven breakwater on the right.

Looking north into Port La Forêt.

By night

Cap Coz[1] and Kerleven[2] lights in line on 334° clears Le Scoré, a pair of lit buoys[4] mark the entrance to the channel and a night entry is possible if there is enough light to see any unlit channel buoys and beacons.

Mooring

There is room in the marina for several hundred yachts on pontoons with 2·5m to 3m below datum. Secure to the visitors' pontoon and obtain a berth from the *capitaine du port*.

Facilities

Water and electricity on the pontoons. Fuel berth, travel-lift, slipway and haul-out area. Engine yacht repairs undertaken.

Showers and toilets, groceries, café and chandlery in the marina.

One mile, crossing the tidal barrier and gate upstream of the marina entrance, to the town of La Forêt-Fouesnant (with a restaurant) on the west side of the bay. There are fairly frequent buses from the port to Quimper and Concarneau, so the marina provides a good stopping point for a crew change.

18. Concarneau

47°52'N 3°55'W

Charts

BA *2352, 2645, 3641*
Imray *C38*
SHOM *7146 P, 6560 P*
Navicarte *543*

Tidal data

Tidal heights (approx)
HW −0025 Brest springs, −0005 Brest neaps
MTL 2·9m. Index 0
Heights of tide above chart datum
MHWS 5·0m, MLWS 0·8m, MHWN 3·9m, MLWN 1·9m

Tidal streams

The streams in the harbour run at about 2 knots at springs.

Depths

The entrance is deep as far as La Médée tower, where there is a 2m shoal. The *avant-port* marina has 1m to 2m, but beware of rocks along the fuel-berth wall, which should only be approached near HW. The Anse de Kersos shoals steadily from 3m.

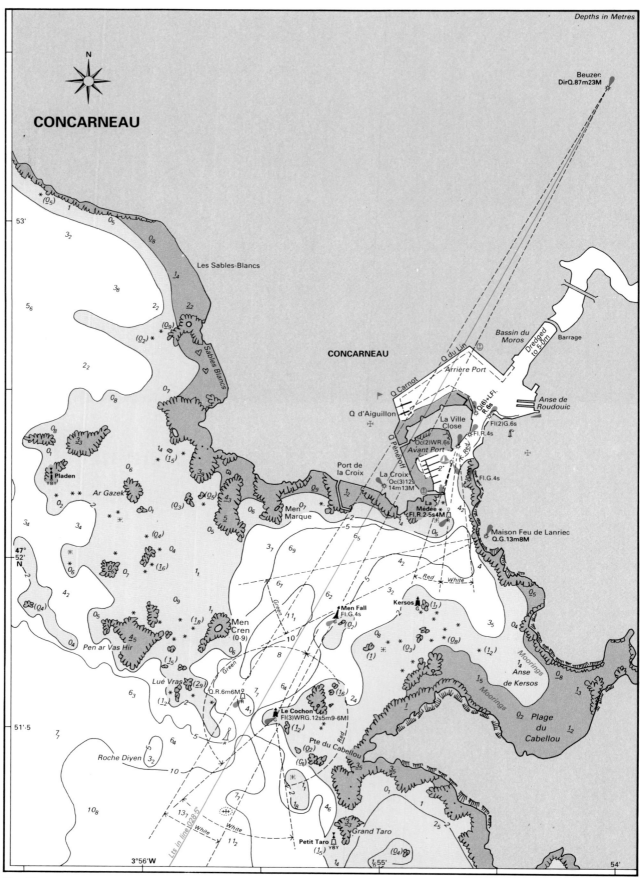

CONCARNEAU

Depths in Metres

N

CONCARNEAU

Beuzec
DirQ.87m23M

Les Sables-Blancs

Bassin du
Moros

Dredged
to 5.0m

Barrage

Arrière Port

Q du Lin

Anse de
Roudouic

Q Carnot

Q d'Aiguillon

Q(6)+LFl.
R.6s

La Ville
Close

Fl(2)G.6s

Sables Blancs

Q Pénéroff

Fl.R.4s

Oc(2)WR.6s

Avant Port

Pladen
YBY

Port de
la Croix

La Croix
Oc(3)12s
14m13M

Fl.G.4s

Ar Gazek

Men
Marque

La
Medee
Fl.R.2·5s4M

Maison Feu de Lanriec
Q.G.13m8M

47°
52'
N

Red   White

Pen ar Vas Hir

Men
Cren
(0.9)

Men Fall
Fl.G.4s

Kersos

Moorings

Anse
de Kersos

Green

Green

Lué Vras
Q.R.6m6M

Le Cochon
Fl(3)WRG.12s5m9-6Ml

Moorings

Plage
du
Cabellou

Roche Diyen

Red

Pte du Cabellou

3°56'W

Lts in line 028·5

White

White

Petit Taro
YBY

Grand Taro

1.55'

54'

Lights

1. **Le Cochon** 47°51'·5N 3°55'·5W Fl(3)WRG.12s5m9-6M 048°-G-205°-R-352°-W-048° Green beacon tower
2. **Basse du Chenal** 47°51'·6N3°55'·6W Q.R.6m5M Red beacon tower
3. **Men Fall buoy (starboard)** 47°51'·8N 3°55'·3W Fl.G.4s
4. **La Croix Ldg Lts 028·5°** 47°52'·2N 3°55'·1W *Front* Oc(3)12s14m13M Red and white tower **Beuzec** *Rear* Dir Q.87m23M Belfry
5. **Lanriec** 47°52'·1N 3°54'·6W Q.G13m8M Black window in white gable
6. **La Médée** 47°52'·1N 3°54'·9W Fl.R.2·5s4M Red beacon tower
7. **Passage de Lanriec** 47°52'·3N 3°54'·8W Oc(2)WR.6s4m9/6M 209°-R-354°-W-007°-R-018° Red tower below wall of La Ville Close
8. **Entrance to Port de Plaisance** on N end of wavebreaker Fl(3)R.12s red tube

General

Concarneau is an important fishing port with some commercial traffic and at present the inner harbour is wholly devoted to these activities. The *avant-port*, on the other hand, is wholly devoted to yachting, of which the port is a busy centre. During the storm of October 1987 pontoons and yachts were literally rolled up against the walls of the Ville Close.

The town is large and contains all resources. The Ville Close is picturesque, but so got up for the tourist that one can be put off. Though rather off the route to the south it is a place of character, at one time the main port for the sailing Thoniers whose graveyard is the Blavet river. Concarneau is worth a visit and is a good place for revictualling.

Approach and entrance

Whatever the direction of approach, the buildings on the hill rising up at the back of the town are unmistakable. Steer for a position about half a mile W of the tree-covered promontory, Pointe de Cabellou.

The official leading line is Beuzec belfry, on the ridge a mile inland, in transit with La Croix lighthouse, on the seafront, bearing 028·5°. The belfry is not conspicuous and La Croix is undetectable in front of an apartment block. Le Cochon green beacon tower is more easily identified and it is sufficient to leave it 150m to starboard and a red buoy and red tower to port.

Continue on this course for 600m to leave Men Fall (G) buoy to starboard. Round the buoy and steer 065° while attempting to identify the next mark, 'Maison Feu de Lanriec'. This is the end gable of a white house, among many white houses, with what appears to be a black window in the upper half. Binoculars may reveal the name in green under the window, and the mark can be identified for future reference on leaving Concarneau.

The channel is wide and, leaving Kersos G beacon tower 200m to starboard, it is sufficient to steer to leave La Médée R beacon tower to port to enter the *avant-port*. A floating wavebreaker is connected to the head of the harbour wall and visitors can secure along the inner side before visiting the harbour office to arrange for a berth.

By night

Approach in the white sector of Le Cochon[1] and bring Beuzec and La Croix lights[4] in transit on 028·5° or thereabouts. Hold this course past Le Cochon and Men Fall buoy[3]. As Men Fall buoy is passed, Lanriec Q.G light[5] will open. Steer about 070° in this sector until the Passage de Lanriec light[7] on the Ville Close opens red and then turns white. When it turns from red to white steer about 000° in the white sector, leaving La Médée[6] to port. There should be sufficient light to see to round the north end of the floating wavebreaker[8] and secure to the inside or raft to another yacht. The channel to the inner harbour, past the Ville Close, is marked by four lights, two fixed green to starboard and two fixed red to port.

Mooring

The charge for staying on the wavebreaker is the same as that for a pontoon berth. There is electricity but no water. It is claimed that there is less disturbance from the wash of passing vessels than there is at the visitors' pontoon berths. The outside of the wavebreaker is used by ferries.

If moving to a pontoon near the wall, beware at low water of the shallow rocky patch by the fuel berth.

On the north side of the Ville Close there are some rather crowded double-ended moorings for local boats. The inner harbour is fairly noisy and dirty and rather unattractive, and the quays are reserved for the fishing fleet.

There may be no places available in this popular harbour during the busy season. If so, the Anse de Kersos offers shelter from the N through E to SW, but is exposed to the W and NW. To anchor, go in clear of the moorings as far as draught and tide will permit. There are no facilities and it is a long and exposed journey in the dinghy back to Concarneau.

Should the wind be westerly, Beg Meil is not far off and will provide shelter, or a berth can be found at Port La Forêt.

Facilities

Showers, toilets and excellent *laverie* in the *capitainerie*. Water and electricity on the pontoons. Two good sailmakers and chandlers near the *avant-port*. Fuel berth, slipways. Workshops round inner harbour; all kinds of repair can be undertaken.

All the facilities of a large town. Shops of all kinds, banks, hotels and restaurants of every category. Large Rallye Supermarché behind the fishmarket N of the inner harbour. Ice from the fishmarket.

Concarneau, looking NE. The large block of flats in the middle distance left makes a fine landmark. La Croix (front leading mark) arrowed.

Approaching Men Fall G buoy (arrowed). Beuzec Spire (arrowed) is the rear leading mark for the approach. The front mark, La Croix white tower with red top, is directly under the head of the jib on the left-hand end of the grey-tiled A-frame building with white balconies (see also the air photo).

Men Fall G buoy is to be left to starboard before making the turn to steer 065° for Maison de Feu Lanriec (arrowed). The yacht under sail, on close approach, is turning to port to enter the harbour, leaving the red beacon, Médée, to port.

Sailing tunnymen leaving Concarneau in 1949.

19. Pointe de Trévignon

Passage notes

47°47'·5N 3°51'·3W

Lights

1. **Chausée Les Soldats - Roche Le Dragon**
   47°47'·9N 3°53'·3W VQ(9)10s11m7M W card beacon tower
2. **S breakwater light** 47°47'·6N 3°51'·3W Oc(3+1) WRG.12s11m14-11M Light obscured to S. Square white tower, green top

General

The early part of the flood stream divides at this headland, one branch turning NW towards Concarneau and the Baie de la Forêt, the other turning E, flowing past Ile Verte and along the land. The latter part of the flood flows S and E round the point. This pattern is reversed on the ebb. Between the Pointe de Trévignon and Ile de Groix the stream is weak.

There is a wide passage between Ile Verte and Ile de Raguenès, although rocks extend ¼ mile off each island. East of La Pointe de Raguenès is a sandy beach off which there are a number of summer yacht moorings. The island gives some protection from westerly winds and a pleasant overnight anchorage can be found in about 4m outside the moorings.

There is a delightful beach just over a mile NW of the port. The Musée de Pêche in the Ville Close is interesting. The annual *Fête de Pêche des Filets Bleus* is held on the second-to-last Sunday of August; a cheerful, noisy festival of Breton costume, dancing, music and wrestling, with an illuminated procession of boats.

Bus connection to railway at Quimper and Rosporden.

Looking SE over Pointe de Trévignon. Ile Verte is top right and Ile Raguénez top centre.

20. Aven and Bélon rivers

Port Manec'h

47°48'·1N 3°44'·3W

Charts

BA *2352, 2645*
Imray *C38*
SHOM *7031P, 7138*
Navicarte *544*

Tidal data

Tidal heights (approx)
HW −0025 Brest springs, HW Brest neaps
MTL 2·9m. Index 0
Heights of tide above chart datum
MHWS 5·0m, MLWS 0·8m, MHWN 3·9m, MLWN 1·9m

Tidal streams

The flood runs to the E and the ebb to the W at rates which are uncertain but not very great. The streams in the rivers are stronger.

Depths

The approach from the SSW and S is deep, but coming from the SE inside Les Verrès there is a shoal having 2·6m over it. The bars into both rivers vary and at times may dry, but channels over both bars are occasionally dredged by *sabliers* and depths of 5m were recorded near HW in 1992.

Lights

1. **Pointe de Beg-ar-Véchen** 47°48'·0N 3°44'·4W
   Oc(4)WRG.12s38m10-7M 050°-W(unintens)-140°-
   W-296°-G-303°-W-311-R-328°-W-050° White
   tower, red lantern

General

Both rivers are very pretty and offer good anchorage or mooring. Both offer good restaurants, but not much else in the way of shops except at Port Manec'h and Pont Aven; the Bélon is famous for its oysters. Both have shallow bars, but whereas that of the Bélon is impassable in bad weather, the Aven bar is sheltered and rarely breaks. It is perhaps for this reason that the Aven is much more visited than the Bélon. Given reasonable weather, the Bélon is more attractive than the Aven.

The large-scale plan on SHOM *7138* is most useful.

Approach and entrance

The entrance is easy to locate by the Beg-ar-Véchen lighthouse at Port Manec'h on the west side of the entrance. On the east side there is a large white masonry beacon with a black vertical stripe, on Pointe Kerhermen, with a beacon (starboard) off the tip of the point.

Approach can be made from any direction, having regard to the following dangers. To the W Les Cochons de Rousbicout lie ¼ mile off a small inlet, dry 0·3m and are unmarked. To the SE Les Verrès dry 2·6m and are marked by a BRB tower. An outlier, Le Cochon, lies half a mile NW of the tower and dries 0·6m. There is a clear passage between Les Verrès and the land, carrying a depth of 2·6m. Enter as convenient between Port Manec'h and the starboard beacon off Pte de Kerhermen, giving them a berth of 100m.

By night

The white sectors of Port Manec'h (Beg-ar-Véchen) light (Oc(4)WRG.12s) lead in. The red sector covers Les Verrès and the green sector the rocks along the coast to the SE. Having made the entrance, a stranger should anchor or pick up a mooring off Port Manec'h and wait for daylight.

Port Manec'h

On the point below the lighthouse is a white building with a grey roof. The short Port Manec'h breakwater, marked at its head by a red rectangle with a white border, runs upstream from the point. Behind it is a small quay and slipway. East of the breakwater are a number of white visitors' mooring buoys with 2·5m or more for deep-draught vessels. Upstream of them are a number of red mooring buoys. These provide double-ended moorings with heavy chain, but are in shallower water and are only convenient for boats of less than 10m length. There is a charge for using the moorings. A drying inlet runs west of Le Roc'h, the drying rocks marked by a red beacon at the Aven bar.

This inlet shoals towards a sandy bathing beach and provides a convenient anchorage, clear of the bathers, for shallow-draught vessels that can take the ground. There is a pleasant café/bar west of the beach.

Land at the quay or on the beach. There is water on the quay and there are shops, restaurants, an hotel and a Logie de France in the village. There is no post office or bank and the nearest garage is 5km.

Aven river

It should be noted that Le Roc'h, a group of drying rocks marked by a red beacon, is shown on SHOM *7138* as an islet when all except one are covered at MHWS. This is because the level for above-water heights on SHOM charts is taken as mean tide level instead of MHWS as on British Admiralty charts.

The river in general is shallow, and the position of the bar, which can dry 1m if it has silted, changes periodically; in 1992 there was a channel through it giving 5m near HW with a coefficient of 78. There

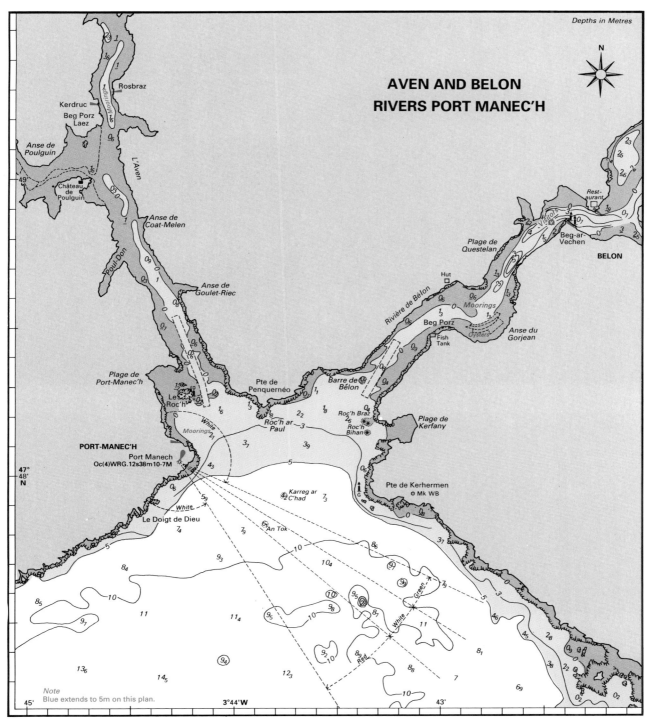

Plan 20

Looking W over Bélon river. Compare with plan.

Port Manec'h and entrance to Aven river.

Looking NE to entrance of Bélon river. Sailing yacht about to
enter. Conspicuous white mark with black vertical stripe on right
(see plan).

are pools up as far as Kerdruc and Rosbras, but these tend to be occupied by moorings for local boats. It is a pleasant river to explore near high water. A shallow-draught vessel may proceed beyond Rosbras, but must be prepared to take the ground.

For a first visit, in case silting has occurred, enter on a rising tide when the rocks marked by the red beacon are covered and one can expect at least 2m over the bar. Leave the beacon comfortably to port and proceed up the centre of the river. Half a mile up there is an inlet called Anse de Goulet-Riec on the eastern side. Here the river deepens for a little and 2m or more may be found. Moorings indicate the best places.

Farther up the river shoals to dry 0·6m and there is a large drying creek branching off to the west with a château at its mouth. Beyond the river narrows, with the quays and slips of Kerdruc on the west bank and Rosbras on the east. Between them is a long, deep pool with mooring trots on either side in up to 3m at LWS. It is possible to dry out alongside the quays in mud at Kerdruc and shingle and mud at Rosbras or to borrow a vacant mooring. The river runs at up to three knots and it is essential to moor bow and stern.

Rosbras can offer a water tap on the upper slip, toilets, and a bar/*crêperie* a short walk away. Kerdruc has a bar with food by the quay.

Above the quays the river widens and shoals. A channel marked sporadically by perches leads a further two miles to Pont Aven, and is navigable by shallow-draught vessels or a dinghy and outboard, although there is much weed. There is a quay drying 2 to 3m against which a yacht may berth. The picturesque town has shops and restaurants, is a famous haunt of artists and is well worth a visit.

Aven river. The slip at Kerdruc on left, Rosbras quay and slip on right.

If the curves of the channel have been memorised, it is possible to return downriver at night, armed with a good spotlight and making use of the reflecting bands which may be attached to some of the perches. Their continued existence must first be confirmed during the journey upriver.

Bélon river

Make a position about 100m W of the beacon (starboard) off Pte de Kerhermen; that is, about 200m W of the point itself. Thence steer about 005° for the rounded headland on the north side of the entrance. This course leaves a bay with a popular bathing beach, the Plage de Kerfany, to starboard and passes close to three small rocks awash at datum off Pte Kerfany, on the east side of the mouth.

With Pte Kerfany abeam to starboard, steer down the middle of the dredged channel on 035° for the little grey hut with a black window on the north

Bélon river entrance. Little grey hut (see text). Concrete fish tank on right of picture, with sun shining on the fish restaurant open to left of tank.

shore. After leaving a concrete fish-tank to star-board, the channel turns sharply to starboard and the best course is to keep close outside the line of moorings, backed by oyster beds in the large curving bay on the starboard side, leaving to port the inner bar which projects from the NW side of the river.

There are stakes marking oyster beds on the bar, and there are similar stakes planted in the bay and on both sides of the river so that it is not always easy to distinguish the channel. Coming out of the bay the channel leads straight upriver, keeping rather to the E side. Half a mile on, the river turns to star-board, and on the port-hand side of the curve in comparatively still, deep water (9m) are three large white metal mooring buoys for visitors, suitable for rafting.

Further on is a drying slip with a fish restaurant beside a quay. On the starboard bank is a long slip, with the lower end marked by a green beacon and the upper end leading onto the curving quay of Lanroit, where there is a restaurant but no shops. Here the river is wide, with many fishing-boat and yacht moorings, but it soon shoals. Above Lanroit, where it dries, there are extensive oyster beds, and yachts should not proceed much beyond the visitors' moorings.

Near high water it is possible to cross the outer bar rather than enter by the channel, but fresh winds from the S or SW quickly bring swell, making the bar impassable and entry by the channel inadvisable.

In July and August a shop for campers is open by the Plage de Kerfany.

21. Brigneau and Merrien

47°46'·9N 3°40'·2W & 47°46'·8N 3°38'·9W

Charts

BA *2352, 2645*
Imray *C38*
SHOM *7031P, 7138*
Navicarte *544*

Tidal data

Tidal heights (approx)
HW −0030 Brest springs, HW Brest neaps
MTL 2·9m. Index 0
Heights of tide above chart datum
MHWS 5·0m, MLWS 0·8m, MHWN 3·9m, MLWN 1·9m

Tidal streams
Outside the flood sets to the E, the ebb to the W; rates are weak. There is some stream in Merrien creek but little in Brigneau.

Depths
There is 1·7m just outside the entrance to Brigneau and 1m outside the entrance to Merrien. Brigneau dries 1m to 2m from the quay to the head of the harbour and Merrien dries 0·6m except in the dredged channel, which must be kept clear.

Brigneau. The ruined factory makes a good landmark. Green beacon pole (slightly bent) far right.

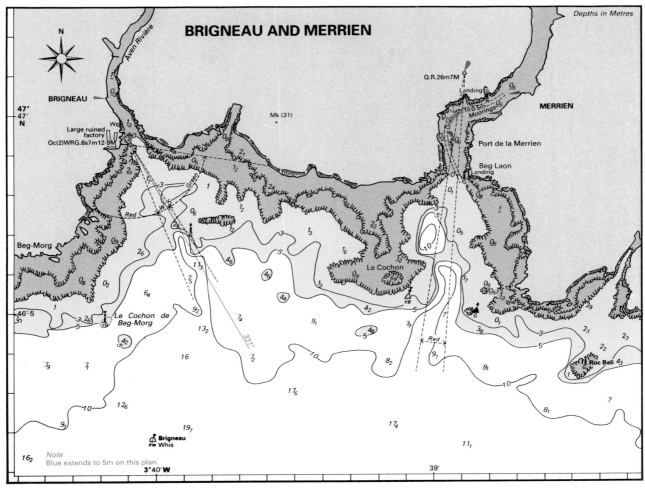

BRIGNEAU AND MERRIEN

Depths in Metres

Plan 21

Lights

1. **Brigneau mole head** 47°46'·9N 3°40'·2W Oc(2) WRG.6s7m12-9M 280°-G-329°-W-339°-R-034° White column, red top with name in white
2. **Merrien** 47°47'·1N 3°39'·0W Q.R.26m7M 004°-vis-009° White square tower, red top

Brigneau

The port of Brigneau lies in a small inlet about three miles SE of Port Manec'h. In onshore weather the swell gets right in and it is untenable, but in fine weather it is an interesting and pretty place for a visit. The quay dries out; in very fine weather one can stay afloat at the entrance, anchored or on a buoy.

At the beginning of the 20th century Brigneau was a busy sardine port. Now activity is divided between a sailing school and a small fishing fleet, with a Cooperative des Pêcheurs et de Plaisance.

Approach and entrance

The point to the west of Brigneau falls away to the low rocky spit of Beg Morg, with Le Cochon de Beg Morg (drying 0·3m) 400m off the point. ¾ mile due south of the entrance is an unlit RW landfall whistle buoy ('Brigneau'). From this point the port can be identified by the large ruined factory building on the west side, with the breakwater below. Steer due north for a point E of the breakwater, leaving to port a S cardinal beacon (badly bent 1992) on Le Cochon de Beg Morg, drying 0·6m. Leave 200m to starboard a green beacon on a rock awash at LWS and bear to port to enter the harbour, leaving the breakwater head, marked by a red rectangle with a white border, to port.

A leading line is provided on 331° using the Brigneau light structure as front marker and for rear marker (to the right of a white house with blue shutters) a white open tubular frame with a wire mesh rectangle at the top which is inconspicuous.

There are two trots of visitors' moorings on the E side of the harbour; the inner trot is very close to the rocky shore. At LAT there would be only 0·5m at the moorings, so they would not be suitable for deep-draught vessels. On entry one can either borrow a mooring or, if tide and draught permit, secure to the quay on the W side, without interfer-

Looking NE into Merrien (white light tower arrowed).

Merrien entrance. The white light tower (arrowed) has a house behind it. The two mooring buoys have recently been painted.

ing with the fishing boats. Shallow-draught vessels can continue up the harbc⸱ ⸱o the inner end of the quay and a wall, above which a wet basin is projected.

By night

Entrance can be effected without difficulty in calm weather by keeping in the white sector of the mole head light[1] on 335° until close to and then bearing to starboard to claim a mooring with the aid of a spotlight, or anchoring outside in 8m to starboard of the line, having passed the starboard beacon and with due attention to fishing buoys.

Facilities

There are water taps and electric points along the quay. Fuel in bulk is available (0700–1200 and 1300–2000) in the summer. (☎ 98 71 02 21). *Bartabac* with *épicerie* at the top of the square past the crane, and a café in the square.

Merrien

Particularly for bilge-keelers, or yachts equipped with legs, Merrien is a delightful place to visit. In calm conditions deep-draught vessels may anchor in 3m or more or secure to one of two large white metal buoys in the bay outside. Inside the entrance is a wide pool with flat sandy bottom which should be taken to dry 0·3m. Above the pool the river narrows and turns to starboard, leading to the village on the E bank and a trot of visitors' moorings where shallow-draught vessels can expect to lie afloat on most tides in complete shelter. As in the Aven and Bélon rivers, a channel is occasionally dredged (1987) from the entrance as far as the quay, but this will silt and should not be relied on.

Approach and entrance

The entrance is easy to identify from the west, ¾ mile E of Brigneau. From the east, the entrance will open after passing a headland topped by some holiday houses, white with grey roofs, 1¾ miles west of Doëlan.

Plan 21 on page 83 shows the dangers: to the W, a spit of rocks terminating in the ubiquitous Cochon, whose S cardinal beacon has been destroyed and replaced by a small conical buoy with ⚑ topmark. To the E rocks extend for 100m out along the side of the headland, marked by a green starboard beacon, destroyed in 1992 and replaced by a small green buoy somewhat inshore of their SW tip. 500m further E is an isolated rock, Roche Bali, marked in 1992 by a rusty pole, without its green ▲ topmark, lying 300m off a small creek.

From a position due south of the entrance to the river the white light tower will be seen at the head of the pool, backed by a large grey-roofed house with a gable on the E end. Keep the light tower on a bearing of 005° to enter the river or to anchor or moor outside.

At night

Entry to the pool is possible, though not advisable, keeping strictly in the narrow red sector of the light[2] on 005°. Should the light disappear it will be hard to make the correct course alteration to bring it back.

Anchorage

For a short visit, with enough water, the pool inside the mouth is inviting, with a sandy bottom except for a rocky patch (see plan 21). Keep out of the dredged channel and at least 50m offshore in the outer half as the sides are rocky. There are steps leading down on the starboard side of the entrance to a flat stone jetty, submerged at high water and marked by a green beacon. After the sharp turn to starboard there is another landing place on the port side, marked by a red beacon; the visitors' buoys and Merrien quay and slipways are on the starboard side of the channel. Do not proceed beyond the quay as the river is full of oyster beds.

Facilities

Water and electricity available on the quay. Fuel available 0700–1200 and 1300–2000 in the summer. Restaurant up the hill. Shops at some distance inland.

The harbourmaster is most helpful and also looks after Bélon and Brigneau.

22. Doëlan

47°46'·2N 3°36'·4W

Charts

BA *2352, 2645*
Imray *C38*
SHOM *7031P, 7138*
Navicarte *544*

Tidal data

Tidal heights (approx)
HW −0030 Brest springs, HW Brest neaps
MTL 2·9m. Index 0
Heights of tide above chart datum
MHWS 5·0m, MLWS 0·8m, MHWN 3·9m, MLWN 1·9m

Tidal streams

Outside the flood sets to the east, the ebb to the west; rates weak. There is little stream in the harbour.

Depths

There is 4m just inside the breakwater and the harbour was dredged to 2m in 1991 (see plan). The inner quays dry 0·7m to 1·5m.

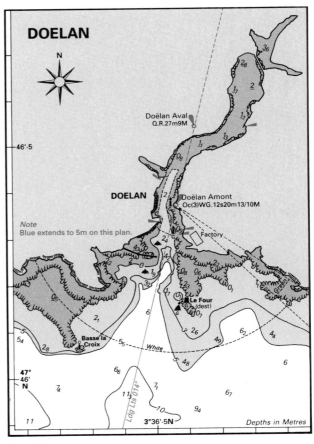

Plan 22

Lights

1. **Doëlan Ldg Lts 014° 47°46'·3N 3°36'·5W**
   Front Oc(3)WG.12s20m13/10M Shore-305°-G-314°-
   W-shore White tower, green band and lantern
   Rear Q.R.27m9M White tower, red band and lantern

General

The port of Doëlan, though larger than the other small ports on this coast, is still very small. It supports a small but active fishing fleet, and there are a number of yachts which take the ground at the back of the harbour, in shelter provided by a bend in the creek. The outer harbour is exposed to the S and entry should not be attempted except in settled offshore weather. It is a pretty little place and quite a resort for artists.

Approach and entrance

The port is easily recognised by the conspicuous factory buildings with slender chimney on the east side of the entrance and the two lighthouses that provide the leading line. Enter with the lighthouses in line bearing 014°. The transit leaves a red beacon to port and a green buoy, provisionally replacing a beacon tower recently destroyed, to starboard.

Looking NE into Doëlan.

By night

Approach and enter with the leading lights[1] in line on 014°. Coming from the direction of Lorient, a vessel can avoid the rocks SE of Le Pouldu (Les Grand et Petit Cochons) by keeping out of the green sector of the front light[1], which covers them.

Mooring

Visitors may raft with other yachts to a large white metal buoy or *Tonne à Flot* with a rail round its edge. There is one of these just outside and another inside the breakwater on the W side of the entrance, together with four orange visitors' buoys.

The fishermen are friendly to visitors, and it may be possible to borrow one of their moorings; for a yacht that can take the ground, it should be possible to borrow a mooring up-harbour.

Alternatively, one can dry out at one of the quays. Near the entrance to the harbour there is a landing slip and quay on the port side, a pair of slips forming a V on the starboard side. Other quays lie inshore of these slips. Local advice should be obtained before drying out. The inner quay on the port hand is not suitable as the bottom slopes outwards. The first two quays on the starboard hand should, however, be suitable, the bottom drying about 1·5m.

Doëlan entrance. The west breakwater head is between the two leading lighthouses.

Doëlan, looking up the harbour near LW.

Facilities

Water and electricity are available on the quays and there is a fishmarket on the outer port-side quay, Quay Neuf. There are bars and restaurants on both sides and it is possible that by 1994 provisions may be obtained and bread ordered from a bar on the W bank (turn right at the top of the square). There is a good chandlery S of the Hôtel Café du Port. The nearest shops are at Clohars Carnoet, 3km inland.

23. Le Pouldu

47°45'·8N 3°32'·2W

Chart

BA *2352, 2645*
Imray *C38*
SHOM *7031P, 7138*
Navicarte *544*

Tidal data

Tidal heights (approx)
HW −0030 Brest springs, −0005 Brest neaps
MTL 3·0m. Index 0
Heights of tide above chart datum
MHWS 5·0m, MLWS 0·8m, MHWN 4·0m, MLWN 2·0m

Tidal streams

Outside the flood sets to the E, the ebb to the west; the streams are weak. The streams in the river are fierce, up to 6 knots springs.

Depths

The bottom is sandy and both the position and the depth of the channel are liable to change. Without prior exploration it should be regarded as drying 2m, but there is more water when it can be found and there is a deep pool above Le Pouldu.

Lights

There are none. Keep well off at night.

General

Le Pouldu, at the mouth of the Laita or Rivière de Quimperlé, has a character quite different from its neighbouring ports. If we can liken the Aven to a miniature Salcombe and Doëlan to a miniature Dartmouth, here we have a miniature Teignmouth. It has a much more open valley, shifting sands and searing tides, and because of these it is much less frequented by cruising yachts.

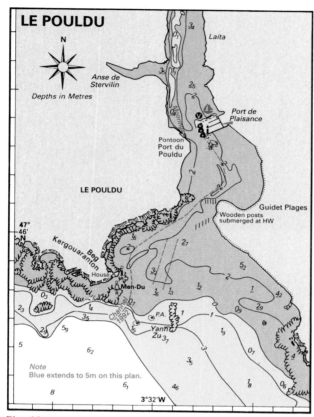

LE POULDU

N

Anse de
Stervilin

Depths in Metres

Laita

Port de
Plaisance

Pontoon
Port du
Pouldu

LE POULDU

47°
46'
N

Beg
Kergouaranton

House

Men-Du

Channel
1992

Yann
Zu

Guidet Plages

Wooden posts
submerged at HW

Note
Blue extends to 5m on this plan.

3°32'W

Plan 23

A visit is only practicable in fine settled weather, as the bar breaks heavily when the wind is onshore and, once inside, a change of wind can make departure impossible for several days. Exploration is an interesting exercise in a bilge-keeler, but can be disturbing in a deep-draught vessel, and should only be undertaken at mean tides, as there is scarcely enough water at neaps and the tides are uncomfortably strong at springs. At low water the anchorage outside is a deep peaty colour, justifying the name Le Pouldu (The black anchorage).

Approach

The entrance is not difficult to make out from a reasonable distance. A mile to the west is a group of grey-roofed holiday cottages behind a sandy beach. The land then rises, with low cliffs and a rocky cove, the eastern headland of which forms the western side of the entrance to the river. The town of Le Pouldu lies behind the cove. The eastern side of the entrance is low and sandy.

Approaching from the southeast, Le Grand Cochon S cardinal beacon tower was destroyed in 1992 and temporarily replaced by a small inconspicuous S cardinal buoy. Consequently, keep two miles offshore (until the tower has been rebuilt) and follow a long curving sandy beach, broken by rocky

Looking NE into Laita river and Le Pouldu.

Entrance to the Laita or Rivière de Quimperlé. Men Du red beacon tower centre left, with the former Fenoux pilot's station on the left and the first lateral port beacon pole (arrowed) on the right.

outcrops, to the cliffy headland, on the top of which is a white house with a round tower, the former Fenoux pilot's station.

The final approach is made with the headland bearing 010° to avoid rocks drying 0·6m and a shoal drying 1·3m 400m to the SSE.

Entrance

Without previous reconnaissance near LW or local advice, entry should only be attempted in calm conditions shortly before HW. Under these conditions the flood stream will not dictate the course followed, but there may be no indication of where the channel lies. It can only be misleading to give precise directions, as the channel shifts frequently and unpredictably. In general, a sandy spit runs out from the east side of the entrance, as shown in the plan on page 88.

The main channel follows the west bank and is marked by the red beacon tower at the entrance, followed by a port-hand beacon pole and, after curving to starboard, a second port-hand beacon pole near the end of a small rocky spit. In 1992 this was the channel which, except for the stream from the river, dried at LW. However, the strong tides tend to cut through the spit, so that the channel may follow the dotted lines shown on the plan, and a steep-sided sandy island may build up which can on occasion come close to blocking the under-cliff channel.

Leave the second beacon pole 40m to port and keep this distance off to avoid a rocky shelf. The river opens out, with a wide shallow bay to starboard, and the protecting breakwater of a marina, only suitable for small yachts, will be seen ahead on the east bank. In 1992 the channel was as shown by the dotted line on the plan. Normally the best water is more likely to be found by following the west bank until the next point is reached, with two hotels and a small jetty.

Thence one can cross to the marina, off which there are three red mooring buoys for visitors

(dredged but depth uncertain), or continue upriver to find deep water (2m or more) for anchoring along the west bank, at the entrance to a shallow creek, above a line of moorings. The holding appears to be good in spite of the stream and some weed. There is a drying sandbank in the middle of the river and there are many small-craft drying moorings on the eastern side and in the bay downstream.

The river is navigable at HW up to Quimperlé, but a bridge with 10m clearance two miles from the entrance prevents the passage of masted vessels.

Facilities

The pontoon on the west bank is for fishermen, but a dinghy landing is permitted, and there are two hotels close by, with Le Pouldu and its shops a mile down the road. On the east bank by the marina are restaurants catering for a camping site, and a large supermarket is situated a few minutes' walk round the bay towards the entrance.

Showers are available at hotel on west bank and water is probably available from the hotels and restaurants.

Looking upstream from Port du Pouldu, near LW.

24. Lomener

47°42'·1N 3°25'·8W

Charts

BA *2352, 2646*
Imray C38
SHOM *7031P, 5912*
Navicarte *544*

Tidal data

Tidal heights (approx)

HW −0030 Brest springs, −0005 Brest neaps
MTL 3·0m. Index 0

Heights of tide above chart datum
MHWS 5·1m, MLWS 0·9m, MHWN 4·0m, MLWN 2·1m

Tidal streams

Off the harbour the flood runs to the E and the ebb
to the W, spring rates 1 knot. There is no stream in
the harbour.

Depths

3m abreast the breakwater, shoaling steadily
towards the shore.

Looking SW over Lomener towards Ile de Groix, near LW.
Lomener lighthouse arrowed.

Light

1. **Anse de Stole** 47°42'·4N 3°25'·5W
   DirQ.WRG.18m10-8M 349·2°-G-355·2°-W-359·2°-
   R-005·2° White tower, orange top

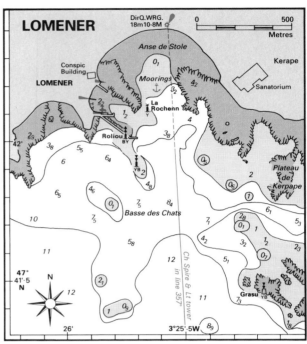

Plan 24

Approach to Lomener. Prominent block of flats (see text) far left, breakwater head (arrowed) left centre and Lomener light tower (arrowed) far right.

General

The port of Lomener, with the adjacent Anse de Stole, is a small harbour on the north side of the channel between Ile de Groix and the mainland. Exposed to the S, it would be uncomfortable in fresh southerly winds and dangerous in gales. However, a considerable fleet of fishing vessels and yachts lies on moorings, both in the harbour and in the Anse de Stole, so the shelter must be sufficient for normal summer conditions.

It is sheltered from the N and in fine settled weather, when the *vent solaire* is in evidence, it provides good shelter for a night's stop when on passage; better indeed than Port Tudy opposite, where the excitement in the outer harbour begins in the early hours of the morning when the wind freshens from the NE.

Approach and entrance

The harbour is not difficult to identify. It lies about halfway along the coast forming the northern side of the channel north of Ile de Groix, with a very prominent block of flats behind the breakwater (see the photo above). The approach is between the rocks round the Grasu S cardinal beacon tower and the shoal of Les Trois Pierres (0·9m) if the tide makes the latter relevant. Steer for the white tower with an orange top in the Anse de Stole in transit with the Ploemeur church spire (if visible behind the trees) on 357°. A S cardinal beacon marks a rock (drying 0·4m) 200m SSE of the breakwater head and an E cardinal beacon marks Roliou just S of the breakwater.

The plan on page 92 shows the drying, rocky spurs on both sides of the bay and the yellow beacon close to the tip of the western spur, sometimes surrounded by a circle of small yellow buoys where the fishermen store their *viviers*. Anchor where space and soundings permit, or borrow a mooring by arrangement in the Anse de Stole, making sure that there is room to swing. The beaches behind the breakwater and in the Anse de Stole are excellent for drying out. There is a landing slip on the spur inside the harbour. Avoid the breakwater wall as there are vicious rocks at its foot.

Facilities

Water and electricity on the quay. All the ordinary shops and restaurants of a small seaside resort. Shellfish can be bought from the fishermen on the quay. No post office or bank.

25. Lorient

with Kernével, Port Louis The Blavet river and Locmalo

Port Louis signal station
47°42'·7N 3°21'·8W

Charts

BA *2352, 2646, 304*
Imray *C38*
SHOM *7031P, 6470*
Navicarte *544*

Tidal data

Tidal heights (approx)
HW −0025 Brest springs, +0010 Brest neaps
MTL 3·0m. Index 0
Heights of tide above chart datum
MHWS 5·0m, MLWS 0·8m, MHWN 3·9m, MLWN 2·1m

Tidal streams

Outside, between the Ile de Groix and the shore, the flood sets E and SE, the ebb W and NW, spring rates ½ knot. The main flood and ebb into and out of the harbour run through the Passe du Sud, spring rate 1½ knots. In the Passe de l'Ouest there is a slack for two hours, starting at HW; the spring rates of the flood and ebb are 1 knot. The strongest streams occur in the narrows off the citadel of Port Louis, where the spring rate is 3½ knots; on extreme tides the ebb may reach 4½ knots if the rivers are in flood. The stream in the narrows sets to the W on to La Jument and Le Pot during the last of the flood and the whole of the ebb. Once through

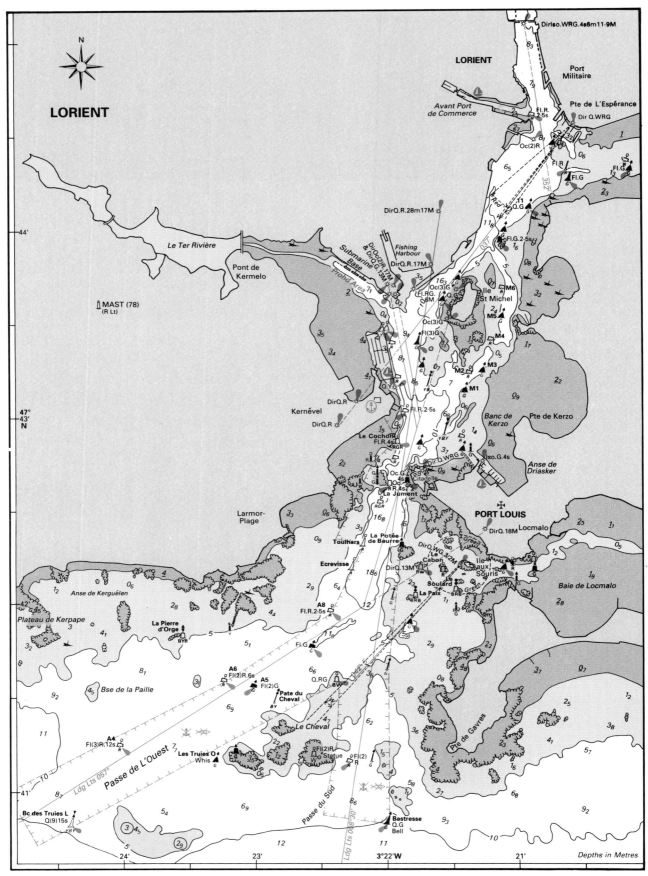

the narrows the streams are weaker; spring rates everywhere less than 2 knots. Generally the streams flow in the direction of the channels, but just to the north of the narrows the stream is rotary anticlockwise, the main strength being NE 1½ knots 4 to 3hrs before HW and SSW 1 knot 4 to 5hrs after HW.

Depths

The main channels are deep. Enough water can be found in all the usual anchorages, except Locmalo, for yachts of normal draught. In the Blavet, which has silted recently, 2·5m or more should still be found at half tide up to Hennebont. The Baie de Locmalo has 3m just inside the entrance, but as little as 0·6m off the pier at Locmalo.

Lights

Passe de l'Ouest

1. **Les Soeurs Ldg Lts 057°** *Front* 47°42'·2N 3°21'·7W DirQ.13M Tower, red and white horizontal bands
   Port Louis *Rear* 740m from front DirQ.18M Rectangle, red and white horizontal bands
2. **Les Trois Pierres** 47°41'·5N 3°22'·5W Q.RG.11m 6M 060°-G-196°-R-002° Tower, black and white horizontal bands
3. **4 buoys (port) and two buoys (starboard)** marking the channel are all lit, Fl.R or G
4. **Banc des Truies buoy (W card)** 47°40'·8N 3°24'·5W Q(9)15s

Passe de la Sud

5. **Bastresses Sud buoy (starboard)** 47°40'·8N 3°22'·0W Q.G Bell
6. **Les Errants buoy (port)** 47°41'·2N 3°22'·3W Fl(2)R.6s
7. **Halles du Port de Pêche Ldg Lts 008·5°** *Front* 47°43'·8N 3°21'·7W DirQ.R.16m17M White rectangle, fluorescent red vertical stripe
   La Perrière *Rear* DirQ.R.28m17M Fluorescent red rectangle, white vertical stripe

Port

8. **La Citadelle** 47°42'·6N 3°21'·9W Oc.G.4s6m6M 009°-vis-193° Green tower
9. **La Petite Jument** 47°42'·6N 3°21'·9W Oc.R.4s5m 6M 182°-vis-024° Red tower
10. **Ile Saint-Michel Ldg Lts 016·5°** *Front* DirOc(3)G.12s8m16M White tower, green top
    Rear DirOc(3)G.12s14m16M White tower, green top
11. **Kéroman Submarine Base Ldg Lts 350°** *Front* DirOc(2)R.6s25m17M Red and white horizontal bands
    Rear Dir Oc(2)R.6s31m17M Red and white horizontal bands
12. **Le Cochon** 47°42'·8N 3°22'·0W Fl.R.4s5m5M Red tower, green band
    Aero beacon Lann-Bihoué 47°46'N 03°26'W *LOR* (·−··/−−−/·−·) 359kHz, 80M

Locmalo

13. **W of Ile aux Souris** 47°42'·2N 3°21'·4W DirQ.WG. 6m3/2M 041·5°-W-043·5°-G-041·5° Green tripod

Lorient. Looking NE over Lorient. The conspicuous grain silo is at the centre of the picture, with the submarine pens to the left and Kernervel marina below. Ile St Michel is to the right of the silo, with the Blavet river in the distance (far right).

General

The city of Lorient is a combination of naval base, fishing harbour, commercial port and yachting centre. The naval base is in the north of the harbour, but to the south of the city the submarine pens remain as a reminder of World War II. Bombing devastated the city during the war, but it is now rebuilt and is a thriving place. It is the principal fishing port in Brittany; the fishing vessels, ranging in size up to the largest deep-sea stern trawlers, have the exclusive use of the Port de Pêche at the south end of the city, to the east of the submarine pens. Further to the north, at Kergroise, are the quays used by commercial vessels.

Port Louis, situated near the harbour entrance on the east side, also has a fishing fleet. It is named after Louis XIII, and the fortifications were created by Richelieu.

The principal yachting centres are the marina at Kernével, near the entrance on the west side, Port Louis opposite and the Port de Commerce in the centre of the city. Pontoons and moorings for local boats have been installed at several sites on the east side of the harbour, but at present visitors are encouraged to use berths in the principal centres.

The Port de Commerce in the centre of the city was the operational base of the French East India Company and it is from this that the city takes its name. There is still very limited commercial activity here – the ferries for Port Louis and the Ile de Groix start here and sand dredgers unload at the quays – but much of it is now devoted to yachting. Near the entrance there are pontoons and moorings for a considerable number of locally based boats, and the wet dock has been restored as a yacht harbour. It is reserved primarily for visiting yachts, for which it offers a convenient berth in the heart of the city.

Lorient is a good place for changing crew, as communications are good and there is plenty to explore if one has a day in hand.

It is possible to go up the river Blavet to Hennebont, whence with a draught not exceeding 0·8m one can enter the Brittany canal system. After going up the Blavet to Pontivy one climbs over the hills and down to Redon, whence one can reach St Malo, Nantes or the sea via the Vilaine.

Approach

The approaches to Lorient are partly sheltered by the Ile de Groix, some four miles to the SW. They are well marked and the huge white grain silo in the commercial port is conspicuous. There are two channels: the Passe du Sud and the Passe de l'Ouest. For a first visit, not all the leading marks are easy to identify and the front marker on the roof of the Port de Pêche wharf building can be obscured by a large trawler. The numerous buoys and beacons make navigation by day easy, though the plethora of lights can confuse at night.

A small-craft channel has been established W of the main channel past the citadel for access to the large marina at Kernével. At night use the main channel and beware of Le Pot unlit port-hand buoy. One night this was actually illuminated by searchlight by a kindly lookout on the citadel for a disorientated British yachtsman!

The larger ships using the port have little room to manoeuvre in the channels and all yachts should get out of their way in good time. Ships above a certain size carry a sphere by day (a red light at night) at the yardarm or masthead and these have absolute right of way over all other vessels. Sailing vessels must not hinder powered vessels of over 20m overall length.

Passe du Sud

The approach to this channel lies NE of the E end of Ile de Groix and ½ mile W of Pointe de Gâvres on the mainland. In good visibility, a group of some six tower blocks and a water tower are conspicuous to the W of the entrance and the tall white grain silo is conspicuous to the E.

Steer for the citadel on 010° until the leading marks are made out, or the yacht's position is confirmed by the channel buoys. The first buoy is Les Bastresses S (starboard, Q.G bell). To port will be seen Les Errants beacon tower (white with black ■ topmark), with a statue beside it, and further upchannel is the conspicuous beacon tower Les Trois Pierres, with BW horizontal bands. This is also left to port, after passing between Les Bastresses N (starboard buoy) and Les Errants (port buoy). The main channel, the Passe de l'Ouest, is then joined and is well marked to the citadel.

The day leading marks bearing 008·5° are on and behind the Fish Market Hall at the S end of Lorient; the front mark is a rectangular white board with a fluorescent red vertical stripe and the rear mark a fluorescent red board with a white vertical stripe. If these are not obscured by a trawler, they will lead up the channel and through the narrows.

Traffic signals, on the simplified system, are made for large ships only from the signal station on the citadel of Port Louis. No yacht should enter the narrows when one of these signals is shown.

By night

The leading lights[7] on 008·5° (Sync. DirQ.R) have an intensified sector extending out beyond both sides of the channel. Do not assume that if you are in the intensified sector you are in the channel, as some of the buoys are unlit. The transit should be maintained through the narrows, where La Citadelle[8] (Oc.G.4s) and La Jument[9] (Oc.R.4s) mark the port and starboard sides. The line passes close to Les Errants buoy[6] (port) (Fl(2)R.6s).

For movement by night in the harbour, see below.

Passe de l'Ouest. The rear leading mark (arrowed) is open to the right of the front mark, the red tower with a white band. On the right of the picture, the yacht with an orange and white sail is about to pass the BRB beacon tower La Paix, with the Baie de Locmalo behind.

Passe de l'Ouest

This channel, well buoyed, is entered ¾ mile S of the conspicuous Grasu tower (S card).

The outer leading mark is a tower on Les Soeurs rocks with red top, white centre and red base. The rear marker, seen to the right of the conspicuous spire of St Pierre church, is a panel above the walls of the citadel and has horizontal bands of fluorescent red (top), white, red and white (base). These are in transit on a bearing of 057°.

Hold this transit until Les Trois Pierres beacon tower (BW horizontal bands) is abaft the beam to starboard. The narrows will then open, and when the two white towers with green tops on the west side of Ile St Michel come into line bearing 016°, you may:

1. turn onto this transit to lead through the narrows,
2. carry on and enter by the 008° transit of the Passe du Sud, or
3. enter the Chenal Secondaire on the west side of the narrows.

By night

The intensified sector of the leading lights[1] (Sync DirQ) on 057° covers the channel and all the lateral buoys[3] are lit. While following up this transit, identify other relevant lights, particularly Les Trois Pierres[2] (Q.RG on this bearing) to starboard, as the turn to port is made when it is abaft the beam. Look for La Citadelle[8] (Oc.G.4s) and La Petite Jument[9] (Oc.R.4s), marking the narrows, and, ignoring the transit (016°) of the Ile St Michel leading lights[10] (Sync Oc(3)G.12s), when the leading lights over the Port de Pêche[7] (Sync DirQ.R) are in line bearing 008·5°, turn onto this transit to pass through.

Chenal Secondaire

This channel is unlit and passes over Le Cochon (dries 1m) but is convenient, given sufficient water, when making for Kernével marina, when the narrows are congested. Illuminated depth indicator panels have been situated on shore at each end of the channel as an experiment. One metre must be subtracted from the reading to allow for Le Cochon.

A spar buoy (RGR, preferred channel to starboard) marks the entrance to the channel. Leaving this buoy to starboard, the channel is seen to be marked by red and green beacons up to Le Cochon beacon tower (RGR), to be left to starboard, after which the main channel is re-entered.

Proceeding up the harbour

Passing through the narrows by the main channel, when Le Cochon beacon tower (RGR) is abeam the submarine pens will be seen, with two sets of leading lights on the roof. The green pair are for deep-draught vessels and the red pair are for general use. At night the green lights are switched on only at the pilot's request.

By day

Steer 350° with the RW marks in transit.

By night

Ignore the Oc(3)G.12s leading lights on Ile St Michel[10]; the Port de Pêche transit[7] leads over the Banc du Turc, SW of Ile St Michel. After passing La Citadelle, turn to port when the submarine base lights[11] (Sync DirOc(2)R.6s) are in transit on 350°.

The entrance to Kernével Marina is ½ mile NNE of the citadel on the W side of the harbour.

Continuing up harbour

By day

Follow the buoyed channel, leaving Ile St Michel to starboard and the fishing port quay and the grain silo to port, and turn to port to enter the Port de Commerce or to starboard to enter the Blavet river.

By night

The white sector of the DirQ.WRG light on Pte de l'Esperance leads past Ile St Michel on 037°, passing rather close to unlit channel buoys. For the Port de Commerce, when the Iso.WRG.4s light on the Port Militaire bridge turns from red to white, steer for it on 352°, leaving close to port the light Oc(2)R.6s on the end of the ro-ro jetty. Identify the

Entering the Rade de Port Louis. The citadel is on the right, with the conspicuous grain silo just to the left. The yacht is approaching the narrow gap between the citadel and La Jument red beacon tower.

Approaching the old Port de Commerce. The ro-ro jetty is on the extreme left. The port buoy marking the entrance is arrowed under the cranes.

Looking south into Port Louis. When approaching from the main channel, the red buoy is left to port!

light buoy (Fl.R.2·5s) on the S side of the Port de Commerce entrance and turn in, leaving it to port.

The entrance to the Blavet channel is marked by lateral buoys (Fl.G.4s and Fl.R.4s). Entry at night is not advisable without previous experience of the river in daylight.

Port de Plaisance Kernével

This marina was opened in June 1988 with 400 pontoon berths, half with 3m and the rest with 2m depth. Development of the marina is continuing and the facilities are increasing.

Entrance

A line of floating wavebreakers (*brise-lames*) secured to piles protects the marina. The southern entrance leads only to the fuel pontoon. In 1993 the northern entrance was used when looking for a berth. The future intention is to establish an entrance halfway along the wavebreakers.

Facilities

Fuel berth, slipway for hauling out. Showers and toilets in the *capitainerie*, which is a large late 19th-century mansion. There are a few shops and restaurants within walking distance in Kernével. Two large supermarkets are situated about a mile NW round the bay and there is a frequent bus service to Lorient, where chandlers, workshops and engineers can be found. The marina staff are most helpful, bicycles are available for shopping and free tickets are provided for the Bus de Mer running between Kernével, Port Louis and Lorient.

Port Louis

There are a large number of private moorings in the shoaling bay to the east of the citadel; these are only available on application to the yacht club. If anchoring, avoid the eastern side of the bay, where there are rocks and wrecks drying 3m and a ruined slipway.

East of the ruined slipway is a pier. A green beacon at its head marks the starboard side of a channel leading into some pontoons in the Anse Driasker, where, on application to the harbourmaster, it may be possible to find a vacant berth with 2m. Keep in the channel close to the pier as there are obstructions in the bay.

Further north, in bays on the east side of the Rade up to the mouth of the Blavet, are a number of pontoons for local boats, but the facilities ashore have not been investigated. Port Louis itself is a very interesting 18th-century walled town, with an excellent museum in the citadel, all ordinary facilities and a recommended Hôtel du Commerce.

Port de Commerce

The wet dock is a fully pontooned yacht harbour in pleasant surroundings, as the roads are well set back. Entry past the bridge and sill is only possible for one hour either side of HW springs and less at neaps. For a short stay it is more convenient to use one of the pontoon berths just outside the dock. Report to the *bureau du port* on arrival. For a long stay in the wet dock at a reduced charge, make arrangements with the harbourmaster.

The pontoons on the S side of the *avant-port* are for local boats; just past them is the Ile de Groix ferry berth. The *avant-port* is dredged to 3m, with 2·5m at the pontoons and 2·3m in the wet basin.

Facilities

Except for a fuel berth, everything is at hand for the wet dock and the outer pontoons. Fuel is obtainable at Kernével.

Water and electricity on the pontoons; showers and toilets (traditional French), shops, banks, main post office, chandlery; shipyards and sailmakers, slipway and crane or travel-lift in the *avant-port*.

Communications

The rail and bus services for Lorient are good and there are flights to Paris from Quimper.

Blavet river and Hennebont

Since 1988 the river has silted by about one metre and this process may continue. The tidal range is 4m at springs and 2m at neaps. At half tide it should be possible to find more than 2m all the way to Hennebont from the first road bridge, but there are two shallow patches where care must be taken:

1. After the first bridge (headroom 22m) the river curves to starboard and once past two lines of moorings, goes into a U-turn to port. At the start of this U-turn only 1·5m could be found at LWN.
2. Passing under the second road bridge (headroom 22m) the river again turns to starboard; on this bend the depth was 2·0m an hour before LWN.

The channel is buoyed or beaconed up to the first road bridge (headroom 28m), two and a half miles from the river mouth, with extensive mudbanks on the south side. The depth under the bridge at LW neaps was 5m. Above the bridge the river narrows and winds a further four miles to Hennebont.

A concrete obstruction with 1·5m over it at half tide is positioned under the second road bridge, approximately one third of the way out from the left supporting column. It would uncover at LWS, so when passing under the bridge keep to the centre, or to starboard if proceeding upriver.

Passing under the second road bridge and a rail bridge (headroom 21m), and arriving at Hennebont at HW −3 or half tide, the depth was found never to be less than 2·5m on a rising tide.

The river is a sad graveyard for sailing tunnymen, but is otherwise attractive, with plenty of bird-life. There are many possible anchorages on the way up to Hennebont, where there is a short-stay pontoon with 2m and visitors' moorings.

Facilities

Hennebont is a very pleasant market town (market in the square on Thursday mornings) with all shops, banks and restaurants. Fuel can be obtained from a garage close to the bridge on the port bank, and a good mile up the road, taking a right fork, is Centre Leclerc, a hypermarket with a launderette.

There is a water tap in the toilets close to the pontoon.

Good rail connections.

Graveyard of the sailing Tonniers in the Blavet river.

Moorings at Hennebont. *Capelan* is alongside the short-stay pontoon.

Locmalo

A pleasant anchorage, if sufficient depth can be found to stay afloat at low water, out of the tide, in the bay south of Port Louis.

Entry can only be made at sufficient rise of tide. There are two approaches, for both of which a large-scale chart, British Admiralty *304* or SHOM *6470*, is essential. The first is to approach north of La Potée de Buerre (8-sided green tower), with the north side of Ile aux Souris bearing 112°, in transit with the end of the ferry slip on the south side of the entrance to the Baie de Locmalo. This transit leads in between the rocks. On approaching Ile aux Souris, with a green light tripod on the detached above-water rock on its western side, alter course to

Locmalo. Looking SW over the Baie de Locmalo towards Ile de Groix. Locmalo entrance centre, the citadel and Rade de Port Louis far right.

leave Ile aux Souris to starboard and steer on the north side of the channel to pass between the red and green beacon towers. The channel curves NE towards the jetty at Pen er Run and an anchorage may be found in depths from 0·6m to 2·3m.

For the second approach, from the SW, pass between the two BRB towers, leaving La Paix to port and Le Soulard to starboard. Then steer midway between Le Cabon G tower (to port) and the green light tripod on the detached rock to the west of Ile aux Souris (to starboard) to join the channel already described.

The jetty, with slipways behind it, dries at LW, but affords a dinghy landing for a visit to Port Louis.

26. Ile de Groix

Port Tudy 47°38'·6N 3°28'·6W

Charts

BA *2352, 2646*
Imray *C38*
SHOM *7031P*
Navicarte 544

Tidal data

Tidal heights (approx)

HW −0030 Brest springs, +0005 Brest neaps
MTL 3·1m. Index 0
Heights of tide above chart datum
MHWS 5·1m, MLWS 0·9m, MHWN 4·0m, MLWN 2·1m

Tidal streams

Between the Ile de Groix and the mainland the flood runs to the E, the ebb to the W; spring rates ½ knot. Off Pointe de la Croix, at the eastern end, the flood runs to the S, the ebb to the N; spring rates ½ knot. To the SE of Les Chats, the southernmost point, the streams are rotary clockwise, the greatest rates being ESE ½ knot at −0130 Brest and SW 0·6 knot at +0230 Brest.

Depths

At Port Tudy 2m on the moorings, and the inner harbour dries; 2–3m in the wet basin. At Loc Maria 0·5m in the anchorage; the jetty dries.

Lights

1. **Pen Men** 47°38'·9N 3°30'·5W Fl(4)25s59m29M
   309°-vis-275° White square tower, black top
   RC *GX* (−−·/−··−) 298kHz 50M
2. **Pointe des Chats** 47°37'·3N 3°25'·3W Fl.R.5s16m
   19M White square tower and dwelling, red lantern
3. **Les Chats buoy (S card)** 47°35'·7N 3°23'·6W
   Q(6)+LFl.15s Whis
4. **Pointe de la Croix** 47°38'·1N 3°25'·0W Oc.WR.4s
   16m12/9M 169°-W-336°-R-345°-W-353° White
   pedestal, red lantern

Port Tudy

5. **East mole head** 47°38'·7N 3°26'·8W
   Fl(2)R.6s11m6M White round tower, red top
6. **North mole head** 47°38'·7N 3°26'·7W
   Iso.G.4s12m6M White round tower, green top

General

The Ile de Groix is a fairly high island, edged for the most part by cliffs, but falling away to the low Pointe des Chats in the southeast. It is about 4 miles long by 1½ miles wide. Although the coast is rocky, it is reasonably clear of outlying dangers for about 3 miles eastward from Pen Men, the westernmost extremity, on both north and south coasts. On the other hand, the eastern end of the island is foul; E of Port Tudy rocks extend 600m offshore, off Pointe de la Croix the sandy shoals extend 300m seaward and there are several dangerous wrecks further out, and S of Pointe des Chats the rocks extend 1 mile.

The main harbour, and the only secure one, is Port Tudy, halfway along the northern shore. It was formerly one of the principal tunny-fishing ports, since it was easy to make and leave under sail, but with the advent of the marine engine the tunnymen have gone to the more convenient mainland ports. Some inshore fishing activity remains, and the port is a very popular staging point for English and French yachts on passage along the coast.

Half a mile west of it is Port Lay, a small harbour protected by a breakwater. In addition to fishing boats a sailing school operates here, but the harbour dries out beyond the pierheads and the swell gets in when the wind is from the north. Although a suitable objective for a day sail, it is not a harbour in which to spend the night and is not treated in detail here. Yachts should not anchor off it, as it is in a prohibited anchorage zone, but there are a number of moorings, laid by the sailing school, which could be used for a short time by arrangement.

On the south side of the island is the pretty little harbour of Loc Maria, which is well worth a visit under the right conditions, but is dangerous if the wind comes in from the south.

Port Tudy

This is the only safe harbour in Ile de Groix. It is a very good one except in easterly and especially northeasterly winds, when the swell penetrates the outer basin between the pierheads. If the *vent solaire* is in evidence this happens in the early hours of the morning, and as yachts lie in tiers on the moorings in the outer harbour, and very few French yachts use springs when so doing, a noisy and enjoyable party is had by all.

Approach and entrance

The harbour is easily identified and the approach from the W and N is straightforward; there are some naval mooring buoys and a fish farm off Port Lay, but no other dangers. From the E and SE care must

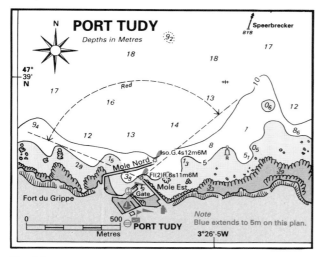

PORT TUDY

Depths in Metres

Plan 26

When close to the entrance bear to port and enter midway between the breakwater heads, steering in parallel to the northern breakwater; there are rocks at the base of the head of the eastern breakwater. If the ferry to the mainland is manoeuvring to enter or leave, stand off, as it needs all the room there is.

By night

The buoys in the approaches are unlit. The light (Fl(2)R.6s) on the eastern breakwater[5] is obscured over the dangers to the east of the harbour, so it is safe to steer in with this light showing and just open to the left of the light (Iso.G.4s) on the north breakwater[6]. It is obscured by the latter when in transit.

Looking north at the Pte de la Croix, the eastern point of Ile de Groix. Part of the long sand spit is exposed near half tide. The small light tower (white with red top) is arrowed.

Entrance to Port Tudy, from the northeast.

be taken to avoid the dangers off the coast, which extend in places outside the line of buoys and beacons. A safe course is with the harbour light-houses in transit bearing 217°. This leaves close to starboard a buoy (unlit, E cardinal) ½ mile off the entrance; the buoy marks a wreck with 9m over it. The transit then leaves 200m to port a rock with 0·6m over it, with other dangers marked by a red beacon closer inshore.

Anchorage and mooring

In the outer harbour yachts moor between the large white mooring buoys, ensuring that there is room for the ferry to manoeuvre. The harbour will be very crowded in the season, particularly at weekends. Use long warps and persuade your neighbours to use springs, making sure that spreaders will not foul when the swell gets up. There is a small charge for mooring. The landing slip is reserved for ferries, there is no room to anchor and the bottom is said to be foul.

The gate to the inner basin at Port Tudy is open. The yachts on the left of the picture are on drying moorings. Yachts waiting for the gate to open can secure to the slip, which is being used by the small ferry at HW. The Lorient car ferry is alongside (far right).

The inner harbour shoals inwards, but shallow-draught yachts can stay afloat at neaps moored bow and stern between rows of orange buoys where the bottom is about chart datum.

A wet dock has been formed from half of the inner harbour by installing a retaining wall and gates with a swing footbridge. Entry is possible between 0630 and 2200 some two hours either side of local HW. While waiting for the gates to open it is possible to secure to the inner landing slip if this is not being used by the sea taxi, but beware of a stone shelf protruding below the top end of the slip near the gates. This will probably be submerged when coming alongside.

Visitors will be directed to a berth in from 2m to 3m. Water and electricity on the pontoons; toilets and showers are available. Charges average in the wet dock.

Facilities

Showers and traditional French toilets behind the *bureau du port*. Fuel is available from the depot at the SE corner of the inner harbour. It will have to be carried. Marine engineer with hauling-out slip. Some chandlery. There are café/bars, and bread

may be obtained near the harbour. Launderette on quay. Up the hill in the town are all shops, a supermarket and an hotel.

Bicycles may be hired to explore this pleasant island. Frequent ferry to Lorient (Port de Commerce), whence good communications to all parts.

Loc Maria

This charming unspoilt little harbour is situated on the south of Ile de Groix, ¾ mile west of Pointe des Chats. The approach is open to the Atlantic, but the harbour itself is well sheltered from the W through N to E. A jetty provides some protection from the S, though with moderate southerly winds some swell penetrates round the end, and the harbour would be dangerous in strong winds or swell from this quarter. The harbour is shallow; the bottom dries as far as the head of the jetty, but depths of 1m may be found behind it, where most yachts will be able to lie afloat except at springs.

Approach and entrance

The distant approach must be made from the chart. If coming from the east or southeast it will be necessary to make a detour round Les Chats. The tidal streams are quite strong at springs, the ebb generally setting westerly and the flood easterly, but the directions vary from point to point.

Make a position 1 or 2 miles S of Loc Maria bay. On the eastern side will be seen the harbour and village, a green beacon tower offshore and a white masonry beacon on the shore. On the western side is another smaller village. Between the two villages is a small group of houses on the NW side of the bay, with a small masonry beacon in front of them (see photograph).

Approach with the green beacon tower (starboard) bearing 005° until the houses and beacon to the NW of the harbour have been identified. The lead for the channel, which carries about 0·2m, is the masonry beacon in transit with the centre window of the white cottage bearing

Entrance to Loc Maria at half tide. The house and small beacon (leading marks for entry) are arrowed, with a starboard beacon pole below. The two yachts are in the anchorage and should be afloat at LW.

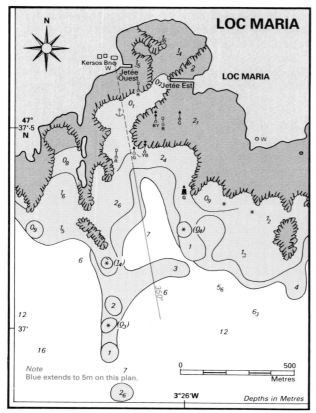

Plan 27

about 350°. This cottage is the right-hand one of three, and has a lean-to shed on its right-hand side (see photograph); the windows have blue shutters.

Follow this transit, passing between a port and a starboard beacon, until the vessel is about halfway between the two cardinal beacons to starboard, marking the middle ground; near low water, deeper water may be found by borrowing to the west when the outer port-hand beacon comes abeam. Then bear to starboard for the pierhead, keeping rather closer to the inner port-hand beacon. There is a shallow channel for local boats, to the east of the middle ground marked by a port and a starboard beacon, but it should not be used.

There are no lights and a night entry should not be attempted.

Anchorage

The harbour is choked with small-boat moorings and there is no room to anchor and remain afloat. Vessels that can take the ground may anchor with a kedge astern after inspecting the bottom for rocky patches. Others may anchor outside the harbour with good holding just west of the leading line, with the outer middle-ground beacon (S card) in transit with the green beacon tower, and the head of the jetty bearing about 060°. Soundings should be taken when coming to anchor, when swinging and when leaving. The middle-ground shoal extends westward beyond the beacons. Lying alongside the jetty is impossible owing to the lines on small-boat moorings, but it may be used for landing.

Facilities

Shops, a bar and a *crêperie* in the village. A pleasant mile and a half walk to Port Tudy. Good bathing beaches.

27. Etel

Entrance 47°38'·6N 3°12'·9W

Charts

BA *2352, 2646*
Imray *C38*
SHOM *7032P, 7138*
Navicarte *545*

Tidal data

Tidal heights (approx)
HW −0015 Brest springs, +0015 Brest neaps
MTL 3·2m. Index 0
Heights of tide above chart datum
MHWS 5·1m, MLWS 1·4m, MHWN 4·1m, MLWN 2·3m

Tidal streams

The tidal streams offshore do not exceed 1 knot and are much affected by wind. Streams in the river attain 4 to 5 knots at springs, but are somewhat weaker for 1½ hours after high and low water. The streams continue to run the same way for about one hour after high and low water. That is to say, a vessel arriving on the bar at high water will find that the tide is still flowing strongly into the river. On spring tides there is hardly any slack.

Depths

The bar varies greatly; it usually has about 0·5m, but has been known to dry 4·5m. Once over the bar the channel is deep but narrow for a short section 400m inside the entrance (see plan page 103). Above the Fish Quay 8m can be expected in the channel as far as the bridge.

Lights

1. **Plateau des Brivideaux** 47°29'·2N 3°17'·4W
   Fl(2)6s24m9M BRB masonry tower, name on side
2. **West side of entrance** 47°38'·7N 3°12'·8W
   Oc(2)WRG.6s13m9-6M 022°-W-064°-R-123°-W-330°-G-022° Red metal framework tower
3. **Epic de Plouhinec head** Fl.R.2·5s7m2M Red metal beacon

General

The Etel river should not be approached by night, or in bad visibility, or on the ebb. First visits are not recommended in strong onshore winds. Otherwise, Etel is fun. It is a delightful place, with its clean blue water and extensive sands.

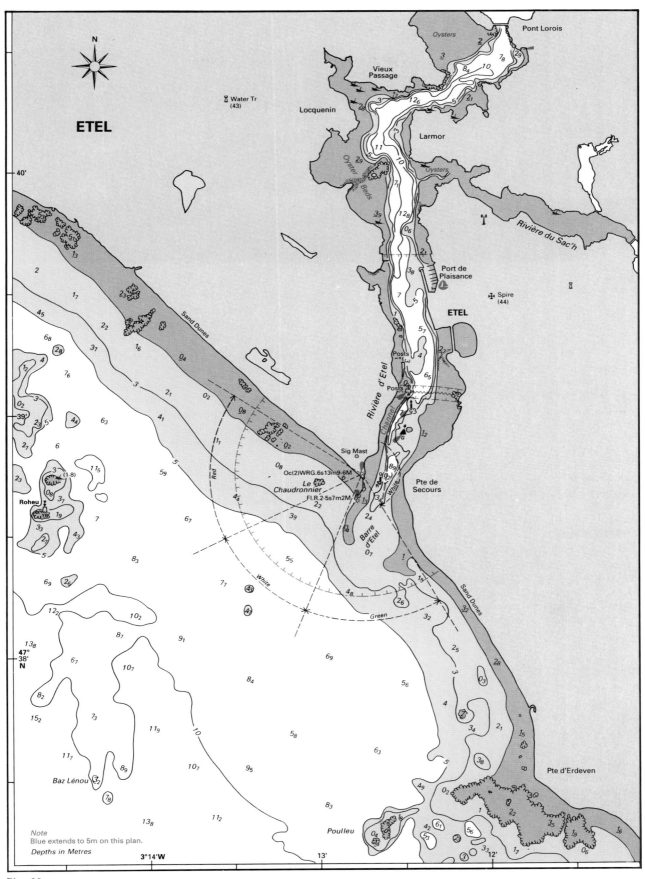

ETEL

Pont Lorois

Oysters

Vieux
Passage

Locquenin

Larmor

Water Tr
(43)

Rivière du Sac'h

Oyster Beds

Oysters

Port de
Plaisance

ETEL

Spire
(44)

Rivière d'Etel

Sand Dunes

Posts

Posts

Sig Mast
Oc(2)WRG.6s13m9-6M

*Le
Chaudronnier*
Fl.R.2-5s7m2M

Pte de
Secours

*Barre
d'Etel*

Roheu

(1·8)

Sand Dunes

Pte d'Erdeven

Baz Lénou

Poulleu

Note
Blue extends to 5m on this plan.
Depths in Metres

3°14'W

13'

12'

Plan 28

Looking NE towards Etel, near HW. Fenoux (signal station) and conspicuous water tower arrowed.

The entrance lies on the mainland halfway between Lorient and Quiberon, 8 miles due east of Groix. The aspect of the coast is low and sandy, but Etel can be recognised by its church tower with, to the east, a water tower dominating the dunes. Three miles to the NW the church steeple of Poulhinec and two tall radio masts will be readily identified. To the S, the rounded hummock of Rohellan island will appear. A mile W of the actual entrance, the beacon tower (S cardinal) on Roheu rocks, which are covered at HW, will be left to port. A mile S of the entrance, in the direction of Rohellan, will be seen the Poulleu (Poul-haut) rocks.

Entrance

A convenient approach is with the water tower bearing 042°. While making the approach it is essential to contact the Fenoux (semaphore) station and to keep at least ½ mile off until contact has been established. In the past this was achieved by hoisting an ensign to the masthead, and directions for entry were signalled with the semaphore arm.

For a vessel not equipped with VHF it is still possible to use the semaphore, by telephoning 97 55 35 59 in advance and giving the operator an ETA. With VHF, call 'Sémaphore d'Etel' on channel 16 or directly on 13.

The following signals are displayed from the semaphore mast:
1. Arrow horizontal: sea too rough, no entry for any vessels.
2. Black ball: no entry for undecked vessels under 8m length.
3. Red flag: Not enough water or pilot not on duty.

For entry
1. Arrow vertical: continue on course.
2. Arrow inclined left: steer to port.
3. Arrow inclined right: steer to starboard.

The pilot, Madame Josiane, is famous in France as the only woman pilot. Once contact has been established, she may give the instructions in clear, simple French or, for the sake of tradition, use the semaphore arm. It is as well to have a felicitous phrase ready for when the pilot signs off as one enters the river proper.

Entrance to the Rivière d'Etel at HW. Pilot's signal mast arrowed. Etel church spire right centre, water tower (far right).

On leaving, after consulting the harbourmaster, keep a listening watch on the pilot's channel and she will call you as you approach the bar.

In 1988 the river was entered along a line from Roheu beacon tower to the red pole framework beacon on the end of a training wall off the spit (Epic de Plouhinec) in front of the light-tower (see photograph). In 1992 a long sand spit had grown out from the training wall and more water was available in the centre of the entrance. The stream is weak outside the bar, but may reach six knots as the port-hand beacon is passed. Shortly after entering the river continue up along the west side, where the best water may be found (see plan page 000). Approaching the Fish Quay soundings will increase.

It is possible that from 1994 the entrance will be buoyed in season.

By night

The entrance bar should not be attempted at night.

Anchorage and mooring

There is a small marina behind the fishing jetty with 12 places for visitors of less than 15m overall, with a least depth of 2·5m. Do not secure to the main jetty, which is reserved for the fishing fleet, and keep clear of the ferry berth on the innermost pontoon.

It is now hard to find an anchorage in the river that is not full of moorings, and when anchoring it is necessary to get far enough in (by sounding) to be out of the main stream, especially at springs. A kedge is essential to stop swinging into the shallows. Keep clear of oyster beds and look out for mooring buoys, which can run under in the current and only show at slack water.

A possible anchorage is just south of the conspicuous lifeboat house at the SW corner of the quays. One can anchor or borrow a mooring off Magouër, on the W bank. To obtain a mooring anywhere along the W bank, apply at Magouër, not Etel.

Just above Etel the holding is good on both sides of the river, but springs run at 6 knots and there are oyster beds in the shallows. There is a good anchorage just above Vieux Passage, but do not go far into the bay as the bottom is foul. Finally, an anchorage recommended by some is just into the northern side of the bay on the E bank below Pont Lorois. The southern part of this bay is foul.

Facilities

Water and electricity on the pontoons. Hose on the quay. Ice from the fish hall and fuel from the quay. Gas bottles can be filled at the camping store on the NE corner of the swimming and boating pool. Showers (free) and toilets (traditional French style) in the *capitainerie*. Helpful staff. Shops, bars and good restaurants, excellent supermarket. Oysters and fish sold in front of supermarket. No launderette, but dry cleaners will do laundry. The town caters well for holidaymakers; market day Tuesday. There is a large camping site on the dunes south of the town.

La Mer d'Etel

The description below has been retained in the present edition even though a visit involves passing under the bridge at the entrance to La Mer d'Etel, which should only be attempted after first consulting the harbourmaster, and then only with a robust inflatable, fitted with a powerful motor.

Above the bridge, Pont Lorois, said to have a clearance in the region of 9m, there is a wide expanse of water, the arms of which extend 5 miles inland. No official charts are available for the Mer d'Etel, which, except for the currents (up to 10 knots under the bridge) and a larger tidal range, might be compared with Poole Harbour. There is 2m in the main channel for the three miles up to La Pointe du Verdon. While this is no place for a seagoing yacht, it is an interesting place to explore in a dinghy with sufficient power to cope with the currents. There is an ancient oratory at St Cado, which is a good place for a picnic, as are the many islands in this inland sea.

After passing under the bridge keep to port to round a green (starboard) beacon. Then cross over to leave the red beacon to port. The river up to this point is strewn with islets and submerged rocks over which strong eddies swirl. From there on up the stream should be weaker and exploration may commence.

Pontoons for yachts at Etel, looking upriver.

28. Belle Ile

Le Palais 47°21'N 3°09'W

Charts

BA *2346, 2353*
Imray *C39*
SHOM *7032P*
Navicarte *545*

Tidal data

Tidal heights (approx)
HW −0030 Brest springs, −0005 Brest neaps
MTL 3·0m. Index 1
Heights of tide above chart datum
MHWS 5·2m, MLWS 0·8m, MHWN 4·0m, MLWN 1·9m

Tidal streams

In the channel to the NE of Belle Ile the streams are rotary clockwise, except close to the shore. They set NW at low water, SE at high water; spring rates up to 1½ knots at the north end and in the middle and about 1 knot at the south end. The streams probably run harder close to the north and south points of the island. The streams in the harbours are weak.

Depths

The approaches to the harbours are deep. Le Palais has 3m at the usual moorings. Sauzon inner harbour dries; 1m or more should be found in the outer harbour. Port du Vieux Château (Ster Wenn) has about 1·5m.

Lights

1. **Goulphar** 47°18'·7N 3°13'·6W Fl(2)10s87m26M Grey tower, red lamp
2. **Pointe des Poulains** 47°23'·3N 3°15'·1W Fl.5s34m 23M White square tower and dwelling, red lamp
3. **Pointe de Kerdonis** 47°18'·6N 3°03'·6W Fl(3)R.15s 35m15M White square tower and dwelling, red lamp
Le Palais
4. **South jetty** 47°20'·8N 3°09'·1W Oc(2)R.6s11m11M White round tower, red lantern
5. **North jetty** 47°20'·9N 3°09'·1W Fl(2+1)G.12s11m7M White tower, green top
Sauzon
6. **West jetty** 47°22'·4N 3°13'·1W Q.G.9m6M White tower, green top
7. **NW jetty head** 47°22'·5N 3°13'·0W Fl.G.4s8m8M White tower, green top
8. **SE jetty head** 47°22'·5N 3°13'·0W Fl.R.4s8m8M White tower, red top

General

Belle Ile is the largest island off the south coast of Brittany, being about 10 miles long and up to 5 miles wide. The NE coast is fairly free of outlying dangers except at its ends, off Pointe des Poulains and Pointe de Kerdonis. This side of the island is sheltered from the prevailing winds and has two harbours, Le Palais, which when not overcrowded is one of the best in Brittany, and Sauzon, with its drying inner harbour, excellent for vessels which can take the ground. Sauzon also has an outer harbour with moorings and an anchorage outside, both comfortable except during the *vent solaire*, when they can be unpleasant.

The Atlantic side of the island is rugged and deeply indented, and has a profusion of rocks. It is picturesque and the island attracts many tourists. The only inlet on this side that provides some kind of harbour is the Port du Vieux Château (Ster Wenn), 1 mile south of Pointe des Poulains. This has no quay, roads or facilities, but has become a popular objective for yachts since attention was drawn to it in the first edition of this book. The danger is that here the Atlantic swell can rise and bar the entrance.

Le Palais

Le Palais is a very good harbour, and there is a good anchorage outside in offshore winds. It can, however, become crowded and uncomfortable in July and August. The harbour itself has a narrow entrance facing SE, but some swell can enter. Winds from the NE are worst; strong NE winds cause seas to break over the breakwater. Even strong NW winds can cause some swell in the harbour, but it is well sheltered from the S and W. If the outer harbour becomes too uncomfortable it is possible to dry out in the inner harbour or go into the wet dock, which has a marina. Once a principal sardine-fishing port, Le Palais is now mainly a holiday resort, though some fishing continues. It is very popular not only with yachts on passage but also with the large fleet of yachts in the Baie de Quiberon, so that in the afternoon the harbour fills rapidly, especially at weekends. The town is the capital of Belle Isle, so there are shops of all kinds.

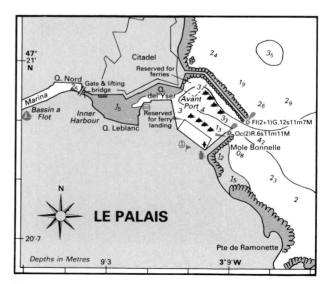

Plan 29

Le Palais, looking SW.

Le Palais entrance. Look out for the ferries!

Approach and entrance

The citadel makes identification easy and there are no dangers in the approach. Steer for the lighthouse on the end of the northern jetty. Keep a sharp lookout for the frequent ferries from Quiberon, which enter and leave at speed, taking up most of the channel. If the way is clear, enter giving a wide berth to the southern pierhead, which has a rock at its base, and to the northern one, where the bottom is foul for some distance in along the wall.

By night

As by day, keeping a sharp lookout for the unlit buoys which are sometimes moored near the entrance.

Anchorage and mooring

Outside the harbour, anchor to the east of the north jetty in 3m, keeping well clear of the fairway. This is a safe anchorage, with good holding ground, in offshore winds. Anchoring is prohibited between the citadel at Le Palais and the approaches to Sauzon, because of cables, but the anchorage noted above is just clear of the prohibited area, and two large mooring buoys have been placed here for visitors' use.

Inside the harbour, yachts secure fore and aft between three rows of mooring buoys and to the wall of the north jetty. The buoys are rather close together for yachts of 10m or more. Make sure that your neighbours are secured bow and stern. Use fenders and springs, and check that spreaders will not foul, as yachts are subject to movement from incoming swell. Yachts also secure between two rows of buoys to port inside the entrance.

Part of the inner harbour has been dredged, but most of the berths are occupied by fishing boats. It is possible to dry out bow to the north wall on either side of the grid, with a stern mooring if one is available. However, the bottom is foul along the north wall leading into the inner harbour (see plan). White stripes on the walls reserve spaces for fishing boats.

The wet-dock gates are open from about 1½ hours before to 1 hour after high water between 0600 and 2200. Beyond the wet dock and a lifting bridge opening daily at 0700hrs lies La Saline marina, completely secure, with water and electricity on the pontoons. Consult the harbourmaster before attempting to enter the wet dock and marina.

Facilities

Water, showers and toilets by the *capitainerie*. Also showers at the caravan park, up the hill beyond the marina. Fuel by long hose from the root of the southern breakwater. Haul-out facilities, marine and electrical engineers, chandlery. Banks, hotel, restaurants, café/bars and a good selection of shops.

Communications

Frequent ferry service to Quiberon. Rail, bus and air links at Quiberon. It is possible to hire bicycles and cars to explore the island.

Sauzon

Situated less than two miles SE of Pointe des Poulains, this once peaceful little harbour is now full of yachts in season, but is still a very pleasant place to visit, and is a secure haven for vessels which can take the ground. The moorings in the outer harbour and the anchorage outside provide shelter from the S and W but no comfort when the *vent solaire* blows. There is some local fishing and active sailing.

Approach and entrance

The harbour is not hard to identify except when the sun is behind it. The Gareau beacon tower (starboard) off the Pointe du Cardinal north of the entrance will be seen if approaching along the coast in either direction. The ends of the two outer breakwaters are marked by low white lighthouses with red and green tops, while behind them can be seen the old taller lighthouse, also white with a green top.

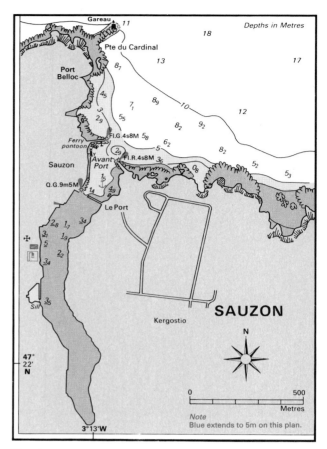

Plan 30

By night

The main light[6] (Q.G.9m6M) and the two jetty head lights[7, 8] (Fl.G.4s and Fl.R.4s) are obscured by the Pointe du Cardinal when approaching from the NW, but one can navigate by the Pointe des Poulains light[2] (Fl.5s34m23M) until they open Pick up a buoy on the west side of the entrance, or enter (with a good spotlight, as the harbour is very crowded and ill-lit).

Anchorage and mooring

There are moorings outside the outer north mole, with room to anchor outside them clear of the fairway.

Between the outer and inner moles on the east side there are some mooring buoys for single mooring with better shelter; the old port tower still stands there and the bottom round it is foul. Between the moles on the west side, the situation may not be immediately obvious: inside the ferry berth a yellow pole beacon, × topmark, marks the N end of a flat ledge about 5 metres wide, covered at half tide, and extending in about halfway towards the main lighthouse. Parallel to the ledge are two rows of mooring buoys. Depending on the number in the harbour, yachts can moor bow and stern along the two lines of buoys or raft to another yacht. When the harbour is crowded during the summer, up to eight yachts may be rafted between two buoys.

The inner harbour dries out, having a firm sandy bottom. Single-keel yachts may find a space to lie

Calm-weather anchorage and moorings outside Sauzon.

Looking up the inner harbour at Sauzon at LW.

against a wall after consulting the fishermen. Many French yachts are now fitted with legs or *béquilles*, and the new verb *béquiller* means to take the ground and dry out (*échouer*) with legs. English yachts similarly equipped or with bilge-keels may join them, either moored bow and stern in the lines of buoys (red to port and green to starboard of the channel) inside the entrance, or, further up the harbour, by laying out bower and kedge anchors and adjusting the lie at low water if warps or chains are over those of nearby boats. It may also be necessary to dig the anchor in or it will not hold, as the bottom is hard sand and shingle.

The creek is over 500m long and if there is a crowd near the entrance there is plenty of room higher up for those prepared to dry out for longer each tide.

Facilities

Water tap at the root of the inner W jetty. Water tap, municipal showers and toilets on the E wall of the inner harbour. Hotels and some good restaurants. There are some shops, but many have been converted to cater for a growing flood of tourists. Bicycles may be hired.

Port du Vieux Château (Ster Wenn)

This anchorage is in a fjord on the west coast of Belle Ile, a little over a mile south of Pointe des Poulains. It was described in the first edition of this work as one of the most beautiful in France; in consequence it has become also one of the most overcrowded by day visitors. It has also been likened to a lobster pot: easy to get into and hard to get out of. The onset of bad weather, or heavy swell, which can be caused by bad weather elsewhere, would make the entrance a deathtrap.

The sailing directions and plan should be regarded with caution, as the largest-scale chart published is on too small a scale to show much detail. The names Pointe Dangereuse and Pointe Verticale are fictitious, though appropriate; the name Pointe du Vieux Château (Beg en Nuet) on the plan is attached to what is believed to be the correct point – official charts differ.

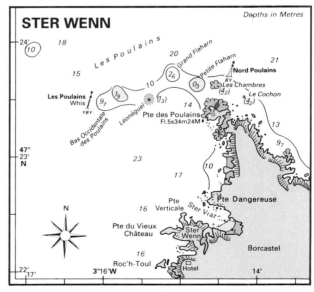

Plan 31

Looking south into an uncrowded Ster Wenn.

Approach and entrance

In the approach from northward the dangers off the Pointe des Poulains must be avoided and the tidal charts must be consulted, as the streams are strong near the point and set across the rocks. A detour may be made round Poulains Basse Occidentale buoy (W); a yacht without auxiliary power should not risk being becalmed between this buoy and Port du Vieux Château with a northerly running stream. Alternatively, if the rocks of Les Chambres and Le Cochon are showing, as they generally will be, the Pointe des Poulains may safely be rounded close inside them.

The Port du Vieux Château is divided into two parts: the main inlet, called Ster Vraz, which is seen from seaward, and a smaller inlet called Ster Wenn, which opens out on the south side of Ster Vraz. Ster Vraz is 400m wide and 900m long. Ster Wenn is only 50m wide and 500m long.

The entrance to Ster Vraz is harder to locate than it appears on the chart, as there are several inlets looking similar from seaward, but on nearer approach it is easy to identify. The north side of Ster Vraz is encumbered with rocks as much as 300m off Pointe Dangereuse, but the southern side is steep-to, there being 15m almost alongside. Pointe Verticale forms a vertical cliff on the south side of the entrance and it is this cliff which makes identification easy.

Ster Wenn, with Les Poulains lighthouse in the cleft.

Some ¾ mile south of Pointe Verticale the Hôtel de l'Apothicairerie is conspicuous on the skyline.

Pointe Verticale, then, lies one mile SE from the Poulains Basse Occidentale buoy, but it is better not to approach the last half mile on this bearing for two reasons: one, because due allowance must be made for the stream which may be setting across the entrance to Ster Vraz; two, because approaching from a more westerly direction ensures that a good berth is given to the sunken rocks off Pointe Dangereuse and the northern arm of Ster Vraz. The stream weakens as Ster Vraz is entered, and so does the swell, especially in southerly winds.

The cliffs along the southern shore of Ster Vraz may be skirted in safety. No sign or hint of the existence of Ster Wenn will be seen until, quite dramatically, the entrance opens up to starboard. Open Ster Wenn fully, when course may be altered sharply to starboard to enter. If Ster Wenn is overcrowded, there is a possible day anchorage further up Ster Vraz; use only in calm weather. Keep to starboard and look out for many rocks as the beach is approached. Most of the rocks occupy the northern half of the inlet; they provide some shelter for local fishing boats.

Anchorage

Ster Wenn is deep near the entrance and shoals gradually up to a sandy beach after a small fork. A cable is slung across the inlet at the fork to provide moorings for small fishing boats. On both sides iron rings are set into the rock above the high-water line. Drop anchor in the middle of the inlet (1·5m or more) and take a stern line ashore to one of the rings. The holding is good, but make sure that the anchor is well dug in before going ashore. On returning you may find several yachts rafted to you with slack cables and shore lines, and their owners may require some gentle encouragement if you are to survive a *vent solaire* during the night.

The water is smooth in all winds except NW. It seems inconceivable that any sea can make the double turn to enter this snug retreat, even in a severe gale. It is stated, however, that surge enters when there is a heavy onshore wind, and that the anchorage is therefore dangerous. Accordingly, the anchorage must be regarded only as a fair-weather one.

Facilities

There is a dinghy landing on the beach and a path leading up the valley to the road. Turn left and Sauzon can be reached after a walk of some 3 miles. Turn right and visit the Grotte de l'Apothicairerie (¾ mile), a cave that is worth seeing, so named after the rows of cormorants that sometimes line the ledges, looking like the jars of coloured liquid in an old chemist's shop. There is a tourist shop and café above the cave. The hotel was rebuilt in 1991.

Belle Ile has a long and interesting history. Owned at one time by the Counts of Cornouaille, it was presented in the 9th century to the Abbey of St Croix at Quimperlé. An English fleet was driven off in 1548, but a raid was successful in 1573 after the monks had sold the island to the Retz family. Van Tromp attacked the island in 1673 and it was finally taken in 1761 by the British under Admiral Keppel. Two years later Belle Ile was restored to France by the same treaty that gave Nova Scotia to England. A number of Nova Scotian families returning to Europe settled in the island and introduced the potato some years before the vegetable became popular on the mainland.

During the Second World War a contingent of German soldiers occupied the barracks in the citadel at Le Palais.

29. Presqu'île de Quiberon

Charts

BA *2353, 2646*
Imray *C38, C39*
SHOM *7032P, 7033P*
Navicarte *545*

Tidal data

For tidal information and lights, see under the individual ports.

General

The name of Quiberon is familiar because it was the scene of the great sea-battle in 1759, when, in a November gale and gathering darkness, Hawke led his fleet into the bay to victory among the rocks and shoals and strong tides which will be described.

The peninsula itself is about 5 miles long and is joined to the mainland by a sandy neck which is little over 100m wide. North of this a narrow arm of sand dunes continues for some three miles before widening to merge with the broader mainland. The total length of the projection seawards is therefore about 8 miles. The geological formation continues for nearly 15 miles to the SE, in the shape of an archipelago of rocks, islets and shoals, between which are navigable passages, to be described in the next chapter. Houat and Hoëdic are the only inhabited islands in this archipelago.

Presqu'île de Quiberon itself looks somewhat sinister from seaward; it is sandy in the north but rocky towards the south, and was formerly strongly fortified. Ashore, however, the whole peninsula is dotted with seaside resorts, for it has a long coast-line and the sandy beaches are ideal for bathing. The town of Quiberon is the capital and there are two harbours a little over half a mile apart, Port Maria on the SW side and Port Haliguen on the NE. Quiberon has a population of about 4,000, a railway station, an airport and many shops, for it serves the whole district. Accommodation varies from the luxury hotel to the camping site.

Port Maria is closed to yachts except in an emergency. The harbour is very crowded with fishing boats and the ferries to Belle Ile. Port Haliguen, the yacht harbour for Quiberon, has all the facilities of a marina. The NE side of the peninsula is sheltered from the prevailing winds and there are several anchorages available in winds from NW to S. At Port d'Orange, 2½ miles farther north, there is merely a jetty and a somewhat indifferent anchorage. There are oyster beds in parts of the NW corner of the Baie de Quiberon, marked by orange buoys.

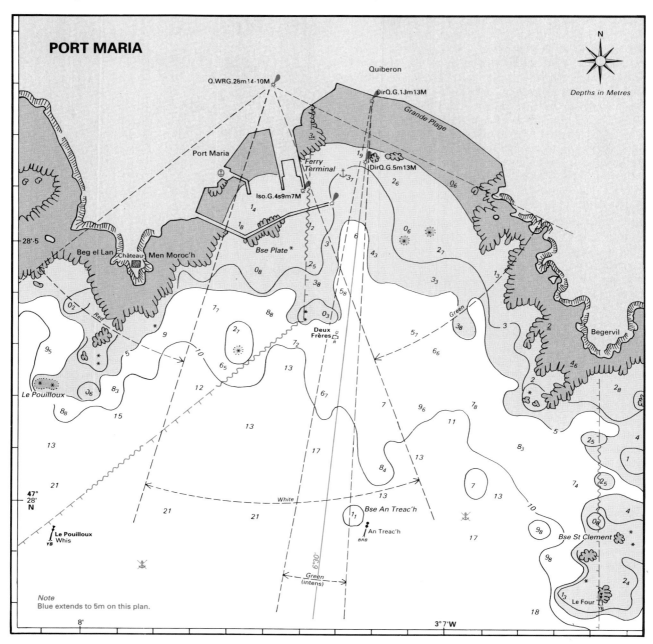

Plan 32

Yet further north on the NE side of Quiberon peninsula is an almost landlocked bay, but it is very shallow in both the bay and the approaches, except for a winding unmarked channel. Here is the Anse du Po, which is only one mile from Carnac, where the alignments of standing stones form one of the greatest sites of the megalithic culture.

The only other harbour on the Quiberon peninsula is Portivi, on the west side. This is exposed to the west, and when there is a heavy swell the sea is said to break nearly one mile to seaward. The anchorage is, however, a pleasant one in fine weather.

Port Maria

47°28'·5N 3°07'·3W

Tidal heights (approx)

HW −0030 Brest springs, HW Brest neaps
MTL 3m. Index 1

Heights of tide above chart datum
MHWS 5·3m, MLWS 0·9m, MHWN 4·1m, MLWN 2·1m

Tidal streams

Some 3 miles SW of Port Maria the streams are rotary clockwise, the main strength being SE (1½ knots at −0300 Brest) and NW (1½ knots at +0400 Brest). There is no stream in the harbour.

Looking SE over Port Maria into Quiberon bay. The
conspicuous château on Beg el Lan is arrowed.

Depths

Maximum about 2m; much of the harbour dries.

Lights

1. **Main light** 47°28'·8N 3°07'·5W Q.WRG.28m14-
   10M 246°-W-252° 291°-W-297°-G-340°-W-017°-R-
   051°-W-081°-G-098°-W-143° White tower, green
   lantern
2. **Ldg Lts 006·5°** 47°28'·6N 3°07'·2W
   Front DirQ.G.5m13M White tower, black band and
   black top
   Rear DirQ.G.13m13M White tower, black band and
   black top
3. **East mole head**; 47°28'·6N 3°07'·4W
   Iso.G.4s9m7M White tower, green lantern
4. **S breakwater head** 47°28'·5N 3°07'·2W
   Oc(2)R.6s9m7M White tower, red lantern

General

This is an artificial harbour, sheltered from all
winds, situated just E of Beg el Lan on the SW
extremity of the Quiberon peninsula. There is a
conspicuous château with towers on this point. The
harbour is used by many fishing vessels and is the
terminal for the ferries to Belle Ile. Yachts are only
permitted to enter in an emergency; a notice on the
port-hand wall in the entrance, stating that any stay
is limited to 72 hours, gives the restrictions.

Approach and entrance

The approach is well marked. Coming from the W
or NW a whistle buoy (Le Pouilloux, S cardinal) is
left to port over ½ mile from the entrance. Then
steer 070° until the leading marks, two white
masonry beacons with black bands and black tops,
E of the breakwater, come into transit, bearing
006°. Leave Les Deux Frères can buoy (R) about
150m to port and follow the transit carefully, as a
drying rock has been reported close to it, about
200m N of the buoy. When the harbour entrance
opens up behind the breakwater steer in.

By night

The main light[1] has 5 white sectors. Approach in
the white sector where the light bears N or between
340° and 017° (an arc of 37°). In good time bring
the leading lights in transit and steer so until the
entrance between the S breakwater and E mole
opens up.

Anchorage

The deep water (1·4 to 2·2m) lies on the SE side of
the harbour parallel with the southern mole, and
rocks and rocky bottom lie on the landward side.
There are rocks at the base of the mole, which
should not be approached too closely. The berth at
the E mole is used by the ferries to Belle Ile and
anchoring in the harbour is not permitted. Much of
that which remains is taken up by fishing-boat
moorings.

   In settled northerly winds it is possible to anchor
clear of the fairway and W of the seaward leading
light, subject to fishing-boat and ferry wash. Yellow
buoys define the swimming and pedal-boat area. Do
not anchor inside these. Should it be necessary to
find a berth in the harbour, apply to the harbour
authorities.

Facilities

Water tap at ferry terminal. Several hotels, restaurants and shops of all kinds. Ferries to Belle Ile and Houat. Bus service to Carnac and Auray. Railway and airfield at Quiberon (1km). Good chandlery.

Port Haliguen

47°29'·4N 3°05'·9W

Tidal heights (approx)

HW −0020 Brest springs, +0005 Brest neaps
MTL 3·1m. Index 1

Heights of tide above chart datum
MHWS 5·4m, MLWS 0·8m, MHWN 4·1m, MLWN 2·0m

Tidal streams

Off the harbour the N stream begins at −0600 Brest and the S stream at +0100 Brest; spring rates 1 knot.

Depths

The approach is deep. In the harbour there is up to 3m.

Lights

1. **Port Maria main light** 47°28'·8N 3°07'·5W
   Q.WRG.28m14-10M 246°-W-252° 291°-W-297°-G-340°-W-017°-R-051°-W-081°-G-098°-W-143° White tower, green lantern
2. **Marina, new breakwater head** 47°29'·4N 3°06'·0W
   Oc(2)WR.6s10m12/9M 233°-W-240·5°-R-299°-W-306°-R-233° White tower, red top
3. **Old breakwater head** 47°29'·3N 3°06'·0W
   Fl.R.4s10m5M 322°-vis-206° White tower, red top

4. **NW mole head** 47°29'·4N 3°06'·1W Fl.G.2·5s6m6M White column, green top
5. **Pier head** 49°29'·3N 3°06'·0W Fl.Vi.2s5m Purple column

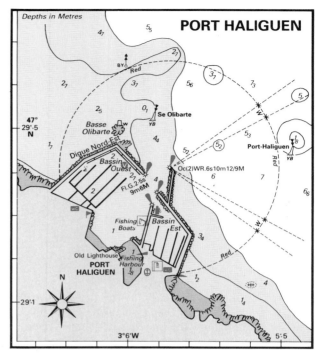

Plan 33

Looking north over Port Haliguen.

Port Haliguen entrance, with the old harbour lighthouse (unlit) right ahead. Turn to starboard round the right-hand breakwater head for the visitors' pontoon.

General

Port Haliguen is an expanding yacht harbour. A simple village encircles the old drying harbour. Every yachting facility is provided by the marina, there are excellent beaches handy and the resources of Quiberon are only ½ mile away. This is a pleasant harbour, but the facilities are some distance from the visitors' pontoon.

Approach and entrance

The approach to the Baie de Quiberon through the Teignouse is described in the next chapter. Port Haliguen is situated less than 2 miles NW of the SE extremity of the Quiberon peninsula. The immediate approach is easy, passing midway between La Teignouse lighthouse and the S cardinal buoy Sud Banc de Quiberon on a course of 305°, leaving to starboard the S cardinal buoy Port Haliguen.

Enter between the breakwaters and turn to starboard for the visitors' pontoon, which runs along the inside of the breakwater. Report to the harbour office, which will allocate a permanent berth if the authorities wish you to move.

By night

Approach in the white sector of Port Maria light[1] 246°-252°, or in one of the white sectors of Port Haliguen Marina light[2] 233°-240·5° or 299°-306°. Keep a lookout for unlit buoys and avoid the protective spur off the E breakwater head on entering.

Mooring

Anchoring is not permitted in the yacht harbour. Visitors secure to the pontoon along the wall of the northwestern basin. Mooring buoys for very large yachts may be available in the northwestern basin. Should the visitors' berths be full, the *accueil* pontoon is beside the fuel pontoon in the southeastern basin (see plan), not far from the main harbour office.

Facilities

The facilities of a major marina. Water and electricity on the pontoons, showers and toilets. Fuel pontoon, slip, crane, travel-lift, engineers, club.

Bread available at café at the port. A 15-minute walk on road towards Quiberon is a large supermarket with fish and oysters on sale outside. Hotels, restaurants, banks and all shops in Quiberon, 1 mile away, where there are connections by bus, train and plane to all parts. This is a good place for a change of crew.

30. La Teignouse, Le Beniguet, Ile aux Chevaux, Les Soeurs

Passage notes

Charts

BA *2353, 2646*
Imray *C39*
SHOM *7033P*
Navicarte *545, 546*

Tidal streams

La Teignouse NE begins −0600 Brest, SW begins HW Brest, spring rates 2·5 knots.
Le Béniguet NE begins −0540 Brest, SW begins +0040 Brest, spring rates 2 knots.
Ile aux Chevaux (rounding the SE point of Houat) and **Les Soeurs** NNE begins +0540 Brest, SSW begins −0030 Brest, spring rates 2 knots.

Depths

All four channels are deep.

General

For a distance of some 15 miles SE of Quiberon there are reefs of rocks, shoals and the two islands of Houat and Hoëdic. Between the reefs and rocks there are several navigable passages, but only the four that are suitable for the stranger will be described. The Passage de la Teignouse is the big-ship route, well lit at night; it is about 3 miles from Quiberon. The Passage du Beniguet, which lies

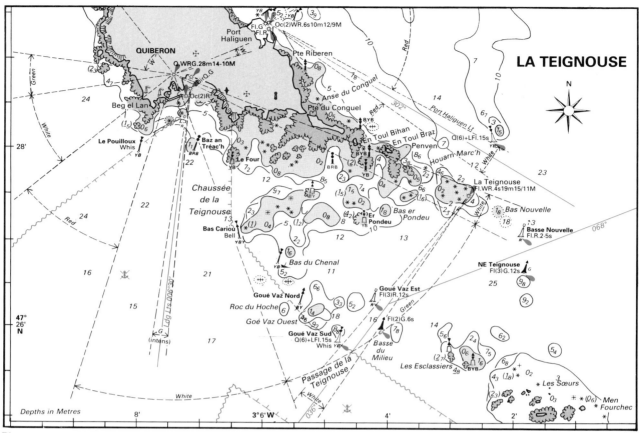

Plan 34

La Teignouse lighthouse, from the south.

close NW of Houat, is narrow but quite straight-forward by day; there are no lights at night. The Passage des Soeurs lies between Houat and Hoëdic; it is wider than Le Beniguet, but also unlit. The Passage de l'Ile aux Chevaux is the short route between Le Palais and Hoëdic.

Passage de la Teignouse

Lights

1. **Port Maria main light** 47°28'·8N 3°07'·5W Q.WRG.28m14-10M 246°-W-252° 291°-W-297°-G-340°-W-017°-R-051°-W-081°-G-098°-W-143° White tower, green lantern

2. **La Teignouse** 47°27'·5N 3°02'·8W Fl.WR.4s19m 15/11M 033°-W-039°-R-033° White round tower, red top

3. **Goué Vas Sud buoy (S card)** 47°25'·8N 3°04'·9W Q(6)+LFl.15s Whis

4. **Basse du Milieu buoy (starboard)** 47°25'·9N 3°04'·2W Fl(2)G.6s9m5M

5. **Goué Vas E buoy (port)** 47°26'·3N 3°04'·2W Fl(3)R.12s

6. **NE Teignouse buoy (starboard)** 47°26'·6N 3°01'·9W Fl(3)G.12s

7. **Basse Nouvelle buoy (port)** 47°27'·0N 3°02'·0W Fl.R.2·5s

8. **Port Haliguen** 47°29'·4N 3°06'·0W Oc(2)WR.6s 10m12/9M 233°-W-240·5°-R-299°-W-306°-R-233° White tower, red top

9. **Sud Banc de Quiberon buoy (S card)** 47°28'·0N 3°02'·4W Q(6)+LFl.15s

General

This is a well marked channel, ¼ mile wide, and small vessels have plenty of margin, as there is deep water on either side of the marked channel. There are no difficulties other than those caused by bad visibility or bad weather. The strong tides cause a steep sea when wind and tide are opposed, so that with a contrary wind the passage should be taken as near slack water as possible.

From the southwest

Bring the white lighthouse on La Teignouse to bear 036°. This line leads S of Goué Vas Sud buoy (S card), which must not be confused with Goué Vas NW buoy (N card), situated ½ mile to the NW of it. Steer on this course, 036°, leaving:

Goué Vas Sud buoy (S card) 200m to port,
Basse du Milieu (starboard) 200m to starboard,
Goué Vas Est buoy (port) 200m to port.

When this last buoy is abeam alter course to 068°. The official lead for this is the church at St Gildas, 10 miles away, bearing 068°, but all that is necessary is to steer out between Basse Nouvelle buoy to port and La Teignouse NE buoy to starboard.

From the east

Plot the above courses on the chart (British Admiralty *2353* is good for this) and reverse.

By night

Enter the white sector (033° to 039°) of La Teignouse light[2] before Port Maria main light[1] turns from white to green. Steer in this sector between the buoys. When the vessel is approximately between Basse du Milieu[4] and Goué Vas Est buoys[5] alter course to 068° to pass between the two eastern buoys[6, 7].

From the east or north

Avoid the dangers off La Teignouse by keeping in the white sector of Port Haliguen light[8] 299°-306°. Enter between the two eastern buoys[6, 7] and steer 248° to pass between Basse du Milieu and Goué Vas buoys[4, 5]. Steer out 216° between the buoys in the white sector of La Teignouse light[2]. When Port Maria main light[1] turns from green to white all dangers are passed.

There are several short cuts that can be taken by day, making allowance for conditions of wind and tide. While these have not been included in the present edition, they can still be explored with the assistance of a large-scale chart such as British Admiralty *2353* or SHOM *7033*.

Passage de Béniguet

For the plan of this passage see under Houat in the next chapter, page 119.

General

This is an easy daylight passage lying immediately to the NW of the island of Houat, and is often used by yachts going between Belle Ile and Houat.

Coming from the SW, leave Le Rouleau tower (W cardinal) about 600m to starboard and steer about 030° to pass between Le Grand Coin tower (E cardinal) and Bonnenn Braz tower (W cardinal). Keep closer to Le Grand Coin tower and well clear of Bonnenn Braz and the shoals with a least depth of 1·5m which extend 600m to the NNE of it. Le Grand Coin tower bearing 240° (and in transit with Le Palais citadel, if the visibility is good) clears these shoals.

Use this transit when leaving Baie de Quiberon and alter to 210° when Le Grand Coin is 400m distant.

Passage de l'Ile aux Chevaux

For this passage see plan page 119, or chart BA *2353* or SHOM *7033*.

General

This is the direct fine-weather route from Le Palais to Hoëdic, and is an attractive alternative to Le Beniguet for reaching Houat.

Steer E from Le Palais for the Ile aux Chevaux. The Pot de Fer, 1 mile NNW of Ile aux Chevaux, may be passed on either side. It is marked by a BRB spar buoy and can be cleared safely by keeping the northern tangent of Ile aux Chevaux clear to the N or clear to the S of Hoëdic. Keep 400m N of Ile aux Chevaux; the outlying danger dries 5·7m and hardly ever covers.

Bound for Houat, steer to leave Beg Pell (13m high) 200m to port; there is a rock with 1·3m over it about ½ mile to the SE. Beg Pell and the rocks north of it are steep-to and can be passed at 200m. Thence, leave the Men er Houteliguet (or Houtelligued) BRB tower 100m to starboard. To port will be seen the dramatic sweep of Tréac'h-er-Goured, one of the sights of Brittany.

Entering the Passage du Béniguet from the SW near LW.
Arrowed from the left: (A) Le Grande Coin BYB beacon tower, (B) Bronnenn Braz YBY beacon tower, (C) Men er Brog rock, (D) Le Rouleau YBY beacon tower.

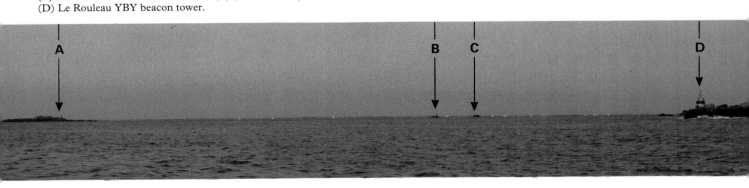

It is a magnificent beach for bathing. British Admiralty *2353* and SHOM *7033* mark it as being within a prohibited anchorage area, but Navicarte *546* shows an anchorage, and in July 1988 *Capelan* joined over one hundred yachts in the bay. The evening was delightful, but 0130 saw navigating lights come on and riding lights extinguished as the fleet weighed and stood out to clear the lee shore in a violent *vent solaire*.

SHOM confirmed in 1992 that both Tréac'h-er-Goured and the other bay, Tréac'h-Salus, are in areas in which anchoring is prohibited because of submarine cables, and that yachts found to be at anchor are liable to prosecution. However, both bays were full of yachts during summer 1992.

Cross the bay if proceeding to Port de St Gildas, leave the rock Er Yoc'h (18m high) 100m to port and the beach on the point En Tal well to port, and round Er Jenetëu (16m high), leaving it 100m to port, to enter Port de St Gildas.

Bound for Hoëdic, leave Men er Vag shoal, marked by a BRB spar buoy, to starboard. The clearing mark is Le Palais breakwater open N of Ile aux Chevaux astern. Thence, leave Les Soeurs tower (W cardinal) to starboard and follow the directions for the Passage des Soeurs given below.

Passage des Soeurs

For this passage see plan page 119, or chart BA *2353* or SHOM *7033*.

Bound northeast

Note that Er Rouzès tower beacon (E cardinal), shown on uncorrected charts, was destroyed in 1993. A temporary buoy marked its position; this should be replaced in 1994 by a metal beacon.

Make a point 400m W of Er Palaire tower (W cardinal), which is itself 1 mile W of Hoëdic. If the visibility is good this will bring the church of St Gildas in transit with Er Rouzès beacon (E cardinal) bearing 019°. If St Gildas church, which is on the mainland 10 miles away, cannot be seen, bring Er Rouzès beacon (or buoy) to the left of Les Soeurs tower (W cardinal) by three to four times the height of the latter. Leave Les Soeurs tower 100m to starboard. The channel is quite wide and it is not necessary to follow the alignments closely. Having passed Les Soeurs tower, steer out as requisite.

Bound for Hoëdic, do not bring Les Soeurs tower to bear more than 255° until the west side of Hoëdic is shut in behind the Pointe du Vieux Château, bearing 175°. This point is the NW headland of Hoëdic, and shoals extend northwards of a line between the point and Les Soeurs.

Bound north, leave Er Rouzès beacon (or buoy) (E cardinal) at least 200m to port.

31. Houat and Hoëdic

Charts

BA *2353, 2646*
Imray *C39*
SHOM *7033P*
Navicarte *546*

Tidal data

Tidal heights (approx)
HW −0030 Brest springs, HW Brest neaps
MTL 3·0m. Index 1
Heights of tide above chart datum
MHWS 5·2m, MLWS 0·7m, MHWN 4·1m, MLWN 1·9m

Tidal streams

The tidal streams in Passages du Beniguet and des Soeurs are given on page 115. North of Hoëdic the NE stream begins at −0600 Brest, the SW stream at HW Brest; spring rates 1½ knots. Half a mile E of Les Grands Cardinaux the flood runs NNE, the ebb SW; spring rates 1½ knots.

Depths

In the harbour at Houat there is 2 to 2·5m near the breakwater; the southern side of the harbour dries. Half Argol harbour (on Hoëdic) dries; there is 2m in the entrance.

Lights

1. **Houat Port de St Gildas N mole** 47°23'·5N 2°57'·4W Fl(2)WG.6s8m9/6M 168°-W-198°-G-210°-W-240°-G-168° White tower, green top
2. **Buoy (N card)** 47°25'·1N 2°56'·5W VQ marking N corner of shellfish-culture zone (*zone conchylicole*)
3. **Buoy (E card)** 47°24'·9N 2°56'·1W Q(3)5s marking NE corner of shellfish-culture zone
4. **Hoëdic Port de l'Argol breakwater head** 47°20'·7N 2°52'·5W Fl.WG.4s10m9/6M 143°-W-163°-G-183°-W-203°-G-143° White tower, green top
5. **Grouguéguez (Les Grands Cardinaux)** 47°19'·3N 2°50'·1W Fl(4)15s28m13M Red round masonry tower, white band

English yacht encounters French yacht with island looming out of the mist. Englishman, "What is that?" Frenchman, "That is WHAT!" (Told by a French yachtsman who pronounced the 'a' as in 'hat'.)

Houat

Houat is a strangely shaped island about 2 miles long, lying 7 miles east of Le Palais and 10 miles south of La Trinité. At its eastern end there are long promontories. En Tal, on the NE, is low; the southern one is higher, with offlying rocks. Between these headlands lie the remarkable sands of Tréac'h-er-Goured, and the old Port er Beg, destroyed by a violent tempest in 1951. The new harbour, Port de St Gildas, lies to the west of En

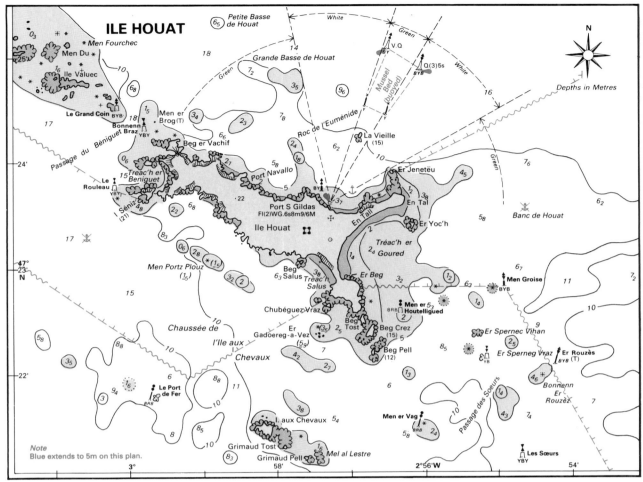

Plan 35

Tal. This harbour is very snug and well protected from the swell, but it is small and the local fishing boats nearly fill it. As it is a popular objective for a weekend sail from the mainland, it becomes very overcrowded and should only be visited midweek during the season.

Approach

The easiest approach is from the north and east. From the north one will try to come down with the ebb stream, but it is better to avoid arriving near low water, so as to have room to manoeuvre inside the harbour.

From the north steer towards the eastern end of the island. Nearly one mile N of it is the conspicuous rock La Vieille (14m high) and NNE of it a shellfish-culture zone marked by a N cardinal and an E cardinal buoy to the north and two yellow buoys to the south. Once La Vieille is identified it is easy to locate the harbour, which bears 200°, ¾ mile from it. Pass either side of the shellfish zone and La Vieille, which is clean to the N and E but less so to the SW; shoals extend about 200m to the S. A convenient lead passing W of the rock is to keep the church in transit with the breakwater lighthouse.

From the east the outer NE rock, Er Jenetëu (16m high), can be passed at a distance of 100m. There are rocks near the direct line from it to the harbour, and a yacht should stand well out into the bay before shaping up for the harbour.

By night

Green sectors of the breakwater light[1] cover La Vieille and also the dangers to the east and west of the harbour. Approach in either white sector and anchor off the harbour, or enter if there is enough light to berth. The shellfish zone lies in the green sector of the breakwater light, and the N cardinal buoy[2] marking the N corner and the E cardinal buoy[3] marking the NE corner are both lit.

Entrance and mooring

There are two rows of moorings for yachts running parallel to the breakwater, which is reserved for fishing boats. The bottom shoals behind the second row of moorings and a rock must be avoided if they are to be approached. Enter between the breakwater and the first row of moorings if there is room to pick one up or raft to another yacht. If the harbour is full, anchor in the bay to the east in 2m. The holding here is not good and in fine weather it is exposed to the *vent solaire*. Port Navallo (see plan), a small bay one mile to the west, offers better holding, as does the next bay west, which has a sandy beach.

Many yachts anchor off Tréac'h-er-Goured and Tréac'h-Salus, despite the fact that these are shown on charts as prohibited because of underwater high-tension cables. Treac'h-Salus offers good protection from the *vent solaire* in fine weather. The anchorage in Tréac'h-er-Beniguet is also attractive, sheltered from N through E to S.

Facilities

Water from the public tap in the village centre, toilets on the pier. The shops can supply simple needs and tourist fodder, but they are limited. 3 hotels, cafés. Good shrimping and cockling off Tréac'h-er-Goured. The island is noted for its succession of wild flowers: roses in May, carnations in June, yellow immortelles in July and sand lilies in August. There are wonderful beaches on the north side of En Tal, at Tréac'h-er-Goured in the east, Tréac'h-Salus in the SE and Tréac'h-er-Beniguet in the west.

St Gildas de Rhuys

(With acknowledgements to the late Sabine Baring-Gould)

Gildas was one of the many Britons who emigrated to Armorica as a result of the Saxon invasion. Armorica became known as Lesser Britain and the current language became British, identical with that spoken in Wales and at one time in Cornwall.

Together with Irish followers of St Patrick, Gildas and other Britons founded missionary colleges to evangelise the land. As in Cornwall, many place names are derived from these missionaries, who are all classed as saints.

Gildas was the son of Cau, prince of Alcluyd or Dumbarton. Cau and all his family were driven south by the Picts and Saxons and took refuge in North Wales, where Maelgwn Gwynedd gave them

lands. All his sons entered religion except for the eldest, Hywel, who lost his life in a quarrel with King Arthur.

Gildas was a married man and had several sons, amongst whom the most notable was Kenneth, hermit of Gower, who came to Brittany with his father and became a founder there.

When aged thirty, Gildas settled at Rhuys, near the Gulf of Morbihan. Here he wrote a scurrilous letter against the princes and clergy and people of Britain, reviling in it Maelgwn, who had treated his family so well. He later turned against Conmore, Regent of Domnonia, who had richly endowed his lands, and caused his death.

When St Brendan visited him, although the Irish travellers arrived in cold and wintry weather he refused them hospitality, but the Irishmen broke down the gates and forced themselves upon the sour British abbot.

St Gildas died in 570 when visiting Houat, and in accordance with his wishes his body was placed in a boat and pushed out to sea. Two months later, on 11 March, the boat was washed ashore at what is now the entrance to Crouesty Marina. A chapel was built at the spot, and according to Baring-Gould, writing in 1920, a procession leaves St Gildas annually to visit the site. The chapel can be seen on the south side of the marina entrance. It has been rebuilt several times, having suffered damage in storms. Its history is recorded on a plaque by the porch.

Hoëdic

This island, rather over 1 mile long and ½ mile wide, lies about 4 miles SE of Houat. There are many detached rocks off its west, south and east coasts. There are two harbours. Argol harbour, on the N side, is very small; most yachts will prefer to lie outside. Port de la Croix, the southern, drying, harbour, and its approaches are dangerous in winds from the S and E, but in settled fine weather offer the best anchorage.

Hoëdic, looking south over Port de l'Argol. The drying Port de Croix (arrowed) can be seen on the south side of the island.

Port St Gildas from the north. The breakwater head light is at 7 o'clock in relation to the church spire.

Tréac'h-er-Goured bay, looking south. The ruined breakwater of Port er Beg is arrowed.

Approach

From the north make for the centre of the island, taking care to avoid La Chèvre in the close approach (see below). From Houat, leave Men Groise E cardinal beacon (see plan page 119 and Er Rouzès E cardinal buoy or metal beacon (replacing a tower destroyed in 1993) to starboard. Thence steer for the north side of the island, keeping Houat church open to the S of Er Rouzès beacon or buoy; this line passes SW of La Chèvre. From the east, making for the north side of the island, leave Beg Legad, the NE point of the island, about 400m to port to clear a drying rock (marked by a N cardinal beacon) NW of the point and continue into the bay.

La Chèvre, a small group of rocks drying 1m, marked by a BRB beacon, is the principal danger on this approach.

For the approaches from the south and west, see chapter 30.

By night

Approach in one of the white sectors of the harbour light[4]. Green sectors cover La Chèvre and dangers to the east and west of the approach.

Anchorages

L'Argol harbour has room for 20 to 30 visiting yachts in settled weather. To avoid sunken rocks in the approach and outside anchorage, do not bring the head of the eastern jetty to bear more than 180°. The bottom shoals steadily; anchor in 2m, 60m from the beach, just inside the entrance to port or raft in less water with other yachts, using three tonne mooring buoys. A road leads to the village.

The southern harbour is best approached using a French chart (SHOM *7033*). The harbour itself dries 2·8m and is often crowded; most yachts will prefer to anchor outside, where there is good shelter from the *vent solaire* in fine weather. If the French chart is not on board, approach with the S cardinal tower Madavoar (see plan page 122) in transit with the right-hand edge of the fort, bearing 320°. On close approach, leave the tower to starboard and make for a point to the S of Men Cren starboard beacon tower, fetching a slight curve northwards to avoid rocks which must be left to port SE of Men Cren. Anchor S of Men Cren tower. Yachts which can take the ground, and others at neaps, can pass between Men Cren tower and the port-hand beacon tower and anchor beside other vessels. Thence the way to the harbour is open.

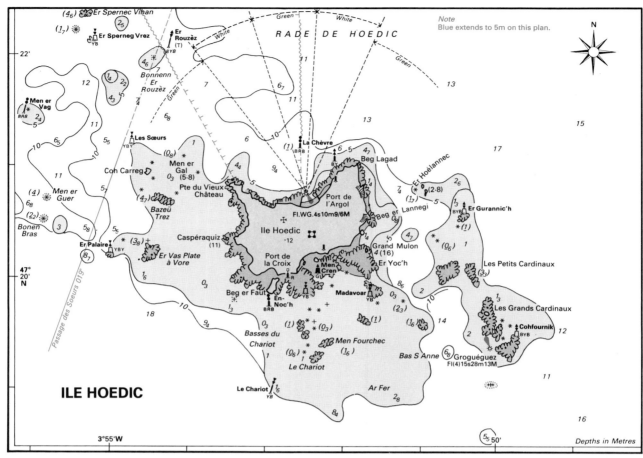

Plan 36

There is an anchorage suitable for a visit by day off a sandy beach north of Grand Moulon, a rock 14m high rising out of rocky flats which cover (see plan). This is approached from Beg Lagad, the NE point of the island, keeping 300m offshore and avoiding a rocky spur extending SE from Beg-er-Lannegi, the northern headland of the bay. Anchor with soundings on sand, avoiding any patches of weed. This and other anchorages round the island are frequented by French yachts from the mainland, but room to anchor can usually be found.

Facilities

It is best for a yacht to be fully provisioned and watered before visiting Hoëdic. The island boasts one small hotel, one *alimentation*, a baker, two *crêperies*, two cafés and a couple of 'chicken take-away' establishments (not McDonald's). There is a shower and toilet block with fresh-water tap on the right on the way up from the harbour.

Port de l'Argol, looking west.

32. La Trinité

47°35'N 3°01'W

Charts

BA *2353, 2646*
Imray *C39*
SHOM *7033P*
Navicarte *546* (if updated)

Tidal data

Tidal heights (approx)

HW −0015 Brest springs, +0015 Brest neaps
MTL 3·2m. Index 1

Heights of tide above chart datum
MHWS 5·4m, MLWS 0·8m, MHWN 4·3m, MLWN 2·0m

Tidal streams

The currents outside vary from point to point. 4 miles south of La Trinité the flood sets NNE, the ebb SW; spring rates 2 knots.

Depths

The river is deep in the channel until the last reach, approaching the quay, where there are patches with only 2m.

La Trinité, looking north, with homecoming yachts funnelling into the channel.

Lights

1. **La Trinité Ldg Lts 347°** 47°34'·1N 3°00'·4W *Front* Q.WRG.11m10-7M 321°-G-345°-W-013·5°-R-080° White tower, green top
2. *Rear* DirQ.21m15M White tower, green top
3. **Le Petit Trého buoy (port)** 47°33'·5N 3°00'·7W Fl(4)R.15s
4. **La Trinité-sur-mer Dir Lt 347°** 47°35'·0N 3°01'·0W DirOc.WRG.4s9m13-11M 345°-G-346°-W-348°-R-349° White tower
5. **S pier head** 47°35'·1N 3°01'·5W Oc(2)WR.6s6m10/7M 090°-R-293·5°-W-300·5°-R-329° White tower, red top
6. **No. 12 (port buoy)** Fl.R.2·5s
7. **No. 5 (starboard buoy)** Fl.G.2·5s
8. **No. 7 (starboard buoy)** Fl(3)G.12s
9. **No. 9 (starboard buoy)** Fl.G.2·5s
10. **Marina pierhead** Iso.R.4s8m5M White framework tower, red top

General

La Trinité, situated 1½ miles up the river Crac'h on the west side, is one of the most popular yachting centres in the Bay of Biscay. It is not in itself exceptionally pretty, but it has good facilities and good communications, and is the centre for a remarkably interesting cruising area which also affords good courses for racing. It is, in consequence, more of a place to yacht from than to visit, though visitors are made welcome and all reasonable needs can be met.

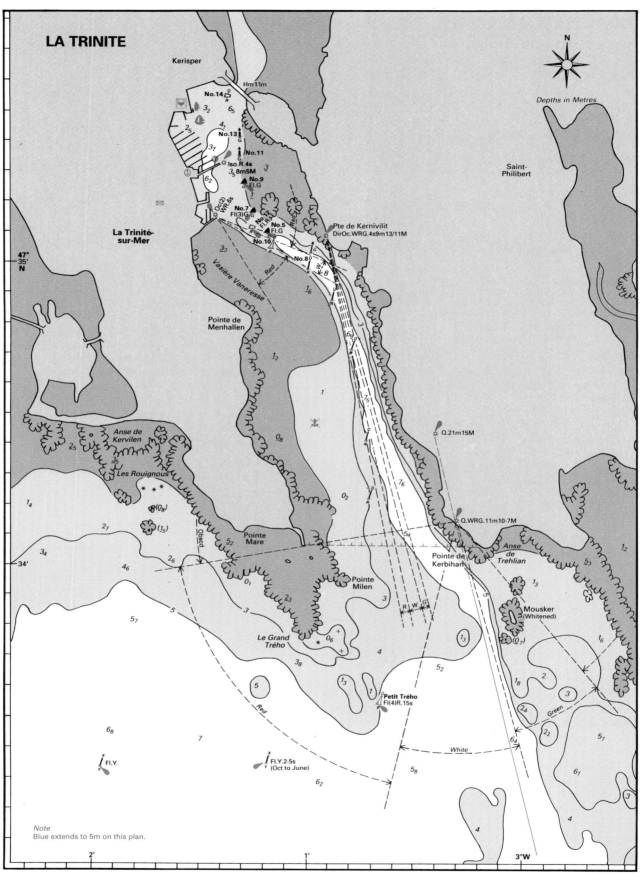

LA TRINITE

Kerisper

Hm 11m

No.14

No.13

No.11

Iso.R.4s
8m5M

No.9
Fl.G

No.7
Fl(3)G

No.12
Fl.R.

No.5
Fl.G

No.10

No.8

Pte de Kernivilit
DirOc.WRG.4s9m13/11M

La Trinité-
sur-Mer

Saint-
Philibert

Oc(2)
WR.6s

Vasière Vaneresse

Pointe de
Menhallen

47°
35'
N

Depths in Metres

N

Q.21m15M

Anse de
Kervilen

Les Rouignous

Q.WRG.11m10-7M

Obscd

Anse
de
Trehlian

Pointe
Mare

34'

Pointe de
Kerbihan

Mousker
(Whitened)

Pointe
Milen

R | W | G

Le Grand
Trého

Green

Petit Trého
Fl(4)R.15s

White

Red

Fl.Y.

Fl.Y.2·5s
(Oct to June)

2'

1'

3°W

Plan 37

Leading light towers for the approach to La Trinité are not easy to identify. The front tower appears in the centre of the white house's end. The top of the rear tower shows light green in the trees just to the right of the front tower.

In the marina the shelter is excellent from all except strong S and SE winds, which send in a sea near high water when La Vaneresse, the sandbank protecting the harbour, is covered. In addition to its yachting activity, La Trinité is a great centre for oyster culture. Anchoring is prohibited in the main channel between the entrance to the river and the town. Speed limit 5 knots. Power vessels over 20m overall, barges and oyster-culture vessels under tow have priority over all other vessels.

Approach

The entrance to the river is not conspicuous. It is most easily identified by the rear leading lighthouse, although this is masked on some bearings.

By day

Approaching from La Teignouse, a wooded hill about 30m high will be seen to the west of the entrance. La Trinité nestles behind it, but there are some villas on it. To the east the lighthouse will be seen. Some two miles S by W of the entrance lies Le Souris BRB spar buoy; this must not be confused with Le Rat BRB spar buoy, situated about one mile to the NNW of Le Souris. From a position 500m E of Le Souris buoy, Le Petit Trého buoy (port), 1½ miles due N, will be easy to find; this buoy marks the outer dangers on the port side of the entrance to the river.

From the S or SE leave the conspicuous island of Méaban 1½ miles to starboard, leave the Buissons de Méaban buoy (S cardinal) to starboard and make for the leading line, the two lighthouses in transit bearing 347°. Many of the dangers on the east side of the leading line are marked by beacons, but Roche Révision, with 0·2m over it, is unmarked.

Entrance

The river is entered between Mousker rock (3m high), painted white on top, to starboard and Le Petit Trého buoy to port. Follow up the channel, which is well marked by buoys, as shown on the plan. Near No. 3 buoy (starboard) there is a shoal with about 2m over it; yachts of deep draught should consequently keep close to No. 10 buoy (port) near low water.

By night

Approach with the leading lights[1, 2] in transit, bearing 347°, or in the white sector of the directional light[4]. When the pierhead light[5] turns from red to white continue in the white sector of that light, with due regard to buoys lit and unlit.

Mooring

Anchoring is forbidden below the bridge (clearance 10m at HWS). Visitors' berths at the marina on the first or second pontoon above the breakwater. A marina launch will normally meet a visiting yacht and direct her to a berth.

Facilities

Water and electricity on the pontoons. Showers and toilets at the *bureau du port*. Launderette, ice, fuel and all the facilities of a busy yachting centre; crane, 25-tonne travel-lift, chandlers, shipyard, repairs of all kinds, but charges are high. Good but very busy Volvo agent. Scrubbing berth, with a level concrete bottom, by the yacht club.

In the town: banks, hotel, restaurants and all shops. Good fishmarket at the head of the marina. Bus to Auray and other localities.

The Carnac Alignments

The Quiberon district is famous for the large number of megaliths, stone circles, tombs and stone rows in the area. A visit to the Carnac Alignments is highly recommended and La Trinité is an ideal base from which to start. There is a bus service to Carnac, from which the Alignments can be reached on foot; the ancient tomb, built in a huge artificial mound now surmounted by a Chapel of St Michael, can be visited en route. An alternative is to hire a bicycle for the visit. On a hot summer's day it is a long walk to the Alignments and back, as the editor discovered.

There has been much debate as to the purpose of the Alignments and the surrounding megaliths. The late Professor A. Thom made a detailed study of the area and concluded that it was a vast astronomical observatory for predicting solar and lunar events.

33. Morbihan

Entrance 47°32'·8N 2°55'·3W

Charts

BA *2358*
Imray *C39*
SHOM *7034P*
Navicarte *546*

Tidal data

Tidal heights (approx)
HW Port Navalo HW Brest springs, +0025 Brest neaps
Note that HW Vannes is HW Navalo +0204 springs and +0123 neaps
MTL 2·8m. Index 0
Heights of tide above chart datum
MHWS 5·0m, MLWS 0·7m, MHWN 3·9m, MLWN 1·9m

Tidal streams

Outside, in the middle of the bay, the streams are rotary; SSW at +0200 Brest and on to NNE at −0400 Brest, they then swing anticlockwise to N at −0200 Brest and back to SSW at +0200 Brest, spring rates 1 knot. Nearer the entrance the streams strengthen. Off Port Navalo the flood begins −0400 Brest, the ebb at +0100 Brest, spring rates 5 knots.

Depths

The approach and entrance are deep.

Note Tidal information for the interior of the Morbihan is given below under the headings Auray river, Vannes channel and southern and eastern Morbihan.

Lights

1. **Port Navalo** 47°32'·9N 2°55'·1W Oc(3)WRG.12s 32m15-11M White tower and house
2. **Port de Crouesty Ldg Lts 058°** 47°32'·6N 2°53'·9W
   Front DirQ. Red panel with vert white stripe
   Rear DirQ. White tower
3. **Crouesty N jetty head** Oc(2)R.6s9m7M White square tower, red top
4. **Crouesty S jetty head** Fl.G.4s9m7M White and green square tower
5. **Le Grand Mouton beacon (starboard)** 47°33'·8N 2°54'·8W Q.G
6. **Grégan** 47°33'·9N 2°55'·1W Q(6)+LFl.15s3m8M S card tower

General

This inland sea, which receives the waters of three rivers, though it is fed mostly by the tide, has an area of about 50 square miles. Since the megalithic era the land has sunk, or the sea level has risen, according to S. Baring-Gould, by some 10 metres, and a partly submerged stone circle can be seen on the islet Er Lannig to the south of Gravinis island. Just south of this circle is another, fully submerged, which could present a hazard. Today the islands of the Morbihan are said to be equal in number to the days of the year, but in fact there are no more than 60 and this figure includes the isolated rocks. Many are wooded and all, with the exception of Ile aux Moines and Ile d'Arz, are privately owned. Most are uninhabited, and in these cases landing is not objected to. Ile Berder is a convalescent home, and it is usual for visitors wishing to penetrate inland to ask permission. Ile aux Moines, with its pine woods, restaurants, good shops and *plage*, is the island most visited.

Ile d'Arz has picturesque walled farms, such as Ker Noel. The Séné peninsula (known as L'Angle and lying east of Boëdig) was the home of the Sinagots, a separate community of fishermen. On Gravinis, a guide will conduct visitors coming by launch from Larmor Baden round the celebrated carved tumulus. Sadly, landing from yachts is no longer permitted.

As a cruising ground the Morbihan is exceptionally interesting, and it offers innumerable anchorages in sheltered water. Only near the narrow entrance off Port Navalo is it open to the sea. Within the entrance, off Grand Mouton rock and south of Ile Longue, Gravinis and Ile Berder, the streams attain 8½ knots at extreme spring tides. They are fierce in the narrows between the islands, but farther from the entrance they moderate and in the upper reaches are not strong.

Navigation in the Morbihan is not as difficult as it appears on the chart, as the islands are easy to identify. There is deep water in the main channels and dangers are marked by beacons and buoys. Charts BA *2358* and SHOM *7034* are recommended if it is intended to explore the more out-of-the-way channels. The best time for cruising is at neaps, but even then the navigator will have to be quick in his pilotage, as with a fair stream the speed across the ground will be greater than he expects.

It is a help to plot courses on the chart and to tick off the landmarks as they pass.

The tidal streams are often fast enough for their direction to be seen from their surface appearance. In 1951 *Isabel*, an 80-tonne ketch, under sail, was spun through 360° south of Gravinis, and it is

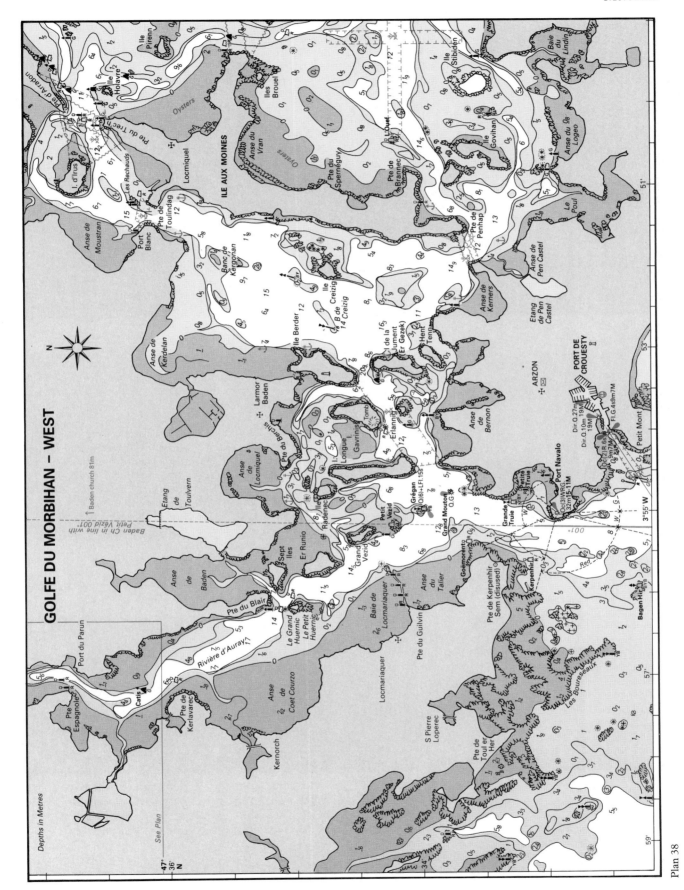

Morbihan

Plan 38

127

Looking NE across the entrance to the Morbihan. Port Navalo is far right.

On approaching the Morbihan entrance for the first time, binoculars are useful for identifying the leading marks (arrowed), Baden church spire in transit with Petit Vézid white beacon on 001° (see next photo).

The transit for the entrance to the Morbihan, Petit Vézid beacon and Baden spire on 001°. The tide is running hard!

reported that some years later the Brixham trawler *Provident* went up the channel like a carousel. However, except in the vicinity of Le Grand Mouton, the streams tend to follow the directions of the channels. Sometimes they run on one side of the channel and there is a slack or reverse eddy on the other, with a clear dividing line between them. Using the eddies, those with local knowledge can make surprising progress against a foul tide. If you leave the main channel, begin to turn in good time, or you will be swept past your destination.

Approach and entrance

The outer approach to the Morbihan presents no difficulty. Peering above the trees is Port Navalo lighthouse, on the east side of the entrance, with a second tower like a lighthouse close to it; more conspicuous from the southwest are the Petit Mont, a hill 42m high, on the peninsula 1 mile to the SE of it, and the white lighthouse within Crouesty marina.

Make Basses de Méaban S cardinal buoy and, leaving it to port, approach the entrance and identify the leading marks. These are the white pyramid on Petit Vézid in transit with Baden church spire 3 miles behind it, bearing 001° (see photographs). Follow this transit through the narrows, leaving Petit Mont ¾ mile to starboard, Bagen Hir E cardinal tower ½ mile to port and Port Navalo lighthouse 200m to starboard. This transit leads close to the Pointe de Port Navalo. On the ebb there can be a strong eddy, running along the shore from the entrance to Crouesty marina and round the point, which facilitates passage into Port Navalo bay to await the flood.

The flood sweeps past the Pointe de Port Navalo and swings across towards the Pointe de Kerpenhir, then back towards Le Grégan tower. The approach is rough on the ebb if there is an onshore wind. The entrance channel is marked on its western side by two towers, Kerpenhir (port) and Goëmorent (port), and on its eastern side by the Grande Truie tower (W cardinal), on the northern side of Port Navalo bay.

For further directions for the Auray river see below, and for the Vannes channel page 132.

A gale warning light is shown by day from Port Navalo lighthouse. IntQ for force 6 to 7 and Q for force 8 and above, between 1 July and 15 September.

By night

There are no lights in the Morbihan. If it is not quite dark it is possible to use the Port Navalo lighthouse to get into Port Navalo and wait for daylight, but it is easier to enter Crouesty marina, which has leading lights.

For Port Navalo, enter the white sector of Port Navalo light[1] on about 010° and keep on the west side of the sector. Petit Mont (42m) will be left to starboard; when the Crouesty leading lights are in transit, bear a little to port, just into the red sector. Round the lighthouse at a distance of 150m and, passing through the white sector of the light, pick up a vacant mooring clear of the pier in 1m or less. The bay is full of moorings and it is not advisable to anchor without light.

For Le Crouesty: enter the white sector of Port Navalo light[1] as before on about 005°. When the Crouesty leading lights[2] come into transit on 058°, turn to starboard onto this transit and steer into the marina, securing to the pontoons along the starboard wall or to a waiting pontoon under the *capitainerie*.

Le Crouesty

This marina has been built in the bay south of Port Navalo and is useful if one arrives at the entrance to the Morbihan at the wrong tide. It also has a large supermarket, at the head of the north basin with a fishmarket outside. This is excellent for storing ship before entering to explore the Morbihan.

The entrance opens on passing Petit Mont, and it is only necessary to follow the buoyed channel, carrying 1·5m, to pass between the outer piers. Leading marks are the lighthouse and a red panel with a vertical white stripe.

Facilities

Water and electricity on the pontoons, fuel pontoon, showers, toilets, good launderette. Bank open Tuesday, Friday and Saturday. Cafés and food shops round the marina, excellent supermarket. Chandlers, engineers, crane, 45-tonne travel-lift. PO at Arzon (½M).

Port Navalo

There is a tolerable anchorage in depths of 1·5m off the end of the pier, but it is exposed to the S and W and disturbed by the wash from ferries. The shoaling bay is full of moorings and it may be possible to arrange to borrow one further in near neaps.

Facilities

Land at all tides at the outer jetty, but dinghies must not be left blocking the way for passengers on the ferries. At tide time land at the eastern jetty by the village. Simple shops and restaurants. Ferries to Auray and Vannes.

Departure

When leaving on the flood to enter the Morbihan, steer boldly out into the stream to avoid being set on to the Grand Mouton; see page 132.

Auray river

Tidal data

Tidal heights (approx)
HW Auray: +0005 Navalo (average, varying springs and neaps)
MTL 1·9m

Heights of tide above chart datum
MHWS 3·4m, MLWS 0·4m, MHWN 2·75m, MLWN 1·0m

Tidal streams
Flood begins −0510 Navalo, ebb begins +0025 Navalo, spring rates 3 to 3½ knots.

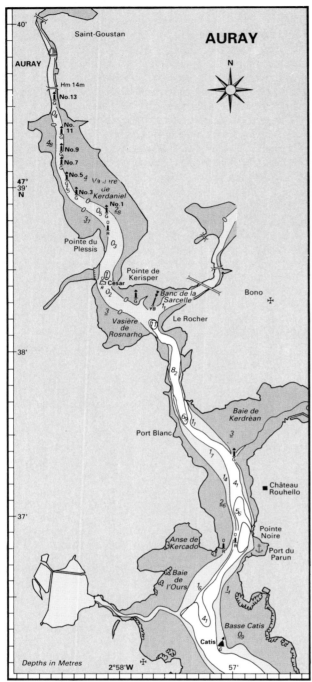

Plan 39

St Goustan. Auray is up the hill on the right.

Depths

The river is deep as far as Le Rocher, though the last mile of the deep channel is narrow, so that it may be better to regard it as carrying 1m. Above Le Rocher it shoals rapidly and the bottom is only just below datum. The mooring area at Auray in midstream has been dredged to 3m, and more in places, but the quays dry (mud!).

General

This fine river on the west side of the Morbihan provides eight miles of varying scenery. The town of Auray, at the head of the navigable river, stands on a steep hill on the west side of the river, with the old port of St Goustan on the east side. Auray is quite a large town; much of it is fifteenth century, with the steeples of the church and chapel standing on the hill.

The old port of St Goustan is now small, but at one time had a substantial trade. Benjamin Franklin landed here from America to negotiate a treaty with France during the War of Independence. The river runs southwards between wooded shores, through a narrow cleft at Le Rocher, then gradually widens out between mud banks and oyster beds until near the entrance it merges into the Morbihan scene of islands and fast tidal streams.

The river is often visited by English yachts, but is relatively less popular with the local people, so that one can easily find quiet spots away from the crowds. Auray has good communications, so that it is quite a good place for changing crew.

The river

In passing the Morbihan entrance (see page 128), keep nothing E of the 001° transit of Le Petit Vézid pyramid and Baden church. When the tide is up a bit one can pass fairly close to Goëmorent tower (port), but there is only 1·4m some 300m E of it and near LW the leading line must be held strictly.

The tidal set over Le Grand Mouton at the entrance to the Vannes channel presents a real hazard at this point, whether a vessel intends to proceed up to Auray or to Vannes.

If bound for Auray, when Goëmorent is on the port quarter it is desirable to leave the leading line, alter to port and steer 345° for the centre of Er Runio (Ile Renaud). When Petit Vézid beacon is abeam, steer 333° for E Harnic (port) buoy to the right of Le Grand Huernic (Harnic) islet, easily recognised by two conspicuous clumps of trees. Beyond El Grégan the tides set fairly up and down the channel, except for local sets between the islands on the east side, particularly north of Grand Vézid.

Steer to leave Le Grégan tower (S cardinal) 400m to starboard. Petit Vézid, Grand Vézid and Er Runio will also be left to starboard; when E Harnic buoy (port) has been identified, leave it close to port and pass between N Harnic buoy (port) and a green (starboard) beacon off Pte du Blair.

North of this the channel is wide, though there is a big shallow bay, the Anse de Coët-Courzo, to port. A course of 325° will take the yacht to the port-hand buoy off the Pointe de Kerlavarec and on to the Catis buoy (starboard). Here the channel is narrower and there are extensive mud flats on either hand. The yacht should be steered in a gradual sweep round the mud on the starboard hand until she heads for the middle of the narrows off Pointe Espagnole with the Château Rouhello (conspicuous with lawn in front and trees on either side) well open. Steer for the château when it bears 025°, leaving the two red (port) beacons on the end of Pointe Espagnole (the first marking the end of a long slipway) to port.

The withies on the oyster beds help to identify the channel. Above Pointe Espagnole the deep water lies on the east side of the river off the château. Then, as the Baie de Kerdréan opens, the channel bears to port towards the narrows seen ahead. The shallow *anse* is left to starboard, together with the green beacon marking the edge of the mud. The deep channel now crosses to the other side. This is the narrowest part of the river, which becomes much prettier, passing between steep, rocky shores and thick woods to Le Rocher.

Since the river's deep part ends above Le Rocher, it can only be navigated up to Auray with sufficient rise of tide. The channel almost dries, but there is plenty of water in the pool at Auray. The channel is clearly marked, the trickiest part being where it crosses the remains of a Roman bridge ½ mile above Le Rocher. There is a drying shoal in midstream marked by César, a red buoy, which should be left well to port. The only visible remnant of the bridge is a flat square of turf over stones on the bank to port.

Anchorages

One of the beauties of the Morbihan is that it is possible to find an endless variety of anchorages according to weather and individual preference for solitude or company, steep banks or saltings. Some well known anchorages are given, but many others can be found.

Locmariaker This village is on the west side of the river near the entrance, opposite the Vézid islands. There is a channel to it, with about 0·6m, marked by port-hand beacons, but it is narrow and used by the ferries. The quay dries 1·5m. Yachts can take the ground between the village quay and the *vedette* jetty. It is possible to anchor off the entrance and go in by dinghy, but this anchorage is rather exposed and subject to strong tides.

Larmor Baden This village lies 1 mile to the east of the Auray river, between it and the Vannes channel. It is approached from the Auray river by passing between Grand Vézid and Er Runio (Ile Renaud), leaving Ile Radenec to starboard and keeping in the northern half of the channel to avoid a rock and a drying patch 200m N and 200m NE of Radenec. It can also be approached from the Vannes channel by passing close east of Ile Longue, or more simply between Gravinis and Ile Berder. It is possible to anchor near Pointe de Berchis or farther to the east and closer to the pier, but there are many moorings here and it might be more convenient to arrange to borrow one. The tides run hard through the channel (flood E, ebb W), and it is best to work into one of the bays as far as draught and depths allow.

Le Rocher Once an excellent and popular anchorage, but now full of permanent moorings. If one is available, land at the small inlet downstream on the east side.

Port du Bono An inlet to starboard just north of Le Rocher. There is 1m as far as the jetty and 0·5m at the quay, but the holding is bad. The new bridge, but not the old, has ample clearance. A dinghy excursion can be made to the hamlet and chapel of St Avoye; land on the port side ½ mile above the old bridge at Le Bono.

St Goustan The clearance of the road bridge just below the port is 14m at HWS. It has been reported that a yacht with a mast height of 15m made contact at half tide; since the range is only about 3m and the level would be affected by heavy rainfall, yachts with a mast height of over 13m should proceed with caution.

There are moorings in the middle of the river opposite the quays and visitors' fore and aft moorings below the bridge. There is enough water at most tides over a considerable length. The water shoals rapidly on the turn to the old bridge; especially at springs, the ebb pours violently through the bridge and eddies make the upper end of the deep water an uneasy berth. The quay should be used only as a temporary berth at high water, and the large floating restaurant-cum-sightseeing vessel must be given plenty of room to manoeuvre and berth. There is a dinghy pontoon near the old bridge which is useful at LW to avoid the mud!

Facilities

All shops and restaurants at Locmariaker, Larmor Baden and Le Bono, but nothing at Le Rocher. At St Goustan, a *bureau du port* and showers; there are simple shops and restaurants on the quay, a good fish market in the square, and all the facilities of a substantial town up the hill at Auray, including a marine engineer. Market day Monday. Good train service, though the station is some way from the town and further from St Goustan. Buses to all parts, including La Baule for the airport and Carnac for the megaliths.

Vannes channel

Tidal data

Tidal heights (approx)
HW Vannes +0204 springs, +0123 neaps on Navalo
MTL 1·9m

Heights of tide above chart datum
MHWS 3·4m, MLWS 0·4m, MHWN 2·7m, MLWN 1·0m

Tidal streams

Inside the Morbihan entrance the stream divides, a weaker portion running up the Auray river. Part of this sweeps past Larmour Baden and rejoins the main Vannes channel at the south end of Ile Berder, where it causes turbulence and a back eddy close to the shore. The main torrent follows the main channel; the spring rate is about 8 knots. The irregularities of the channel produce whirlpools, and the yacht's head is thrown from side to side, but not so as to make it difficult to keep in the channel. The way the water climbs up the Grand Mouton is remarkable.

Once through the narrows south of Ile Berder the rate decreases a little, but the stream continues in a narrow jet towards Ile Crëizig, and thence passes near the Ile aux Moines to the narrows NW of that island. Here the stream is fierce, sweeping across from the Pointe des Réchauds in a wide curve along the mainland side and south of Ile d'Irus. This sets up an eddy, so that NW of Ile aux Moines the current runs SW almost continuously.

After passing the narrows north of Ile aux Moines the stream fans out and becomes weaker, nowhere exceeding 4 knots. The ebb stream roughly reverses the flood, but it is important to keep towards the south side of the narrows between Ile Berder and Ile er Gazek (Ile de la Jument) if one does not want to be swept up the channel west of Ile Berder to Larmor Baden. It is important to realise not only that high water is progressively later as one goes up the channel (1½ to 2hrs between Port Navalo and Vannes), but also that the streams do not turn until about 1½ hours after local high water or low water.

Depths

The channel is deep to Ile aux Moines; thence deep water can be carried to Ile de Boëdig, but the deep channel is very narrow in places and it is easier to regard it as carrying 2m. Thence to just downstream of Conleau it carries 3·2m, after which it shoals progressively, but there should be adequate depth for vessels approaching or leaving Vannes near high water.

The channel

Before entering the Morbihan it is advisable to plot the succession of compass courses up to Vannes on the chart. This will make it easier to identify the islands and the relevant gaps between them as the vessel speeds up the channel. Tick the islands off on the chart as they flash past. Note that some of the names on British Admiralty *2358* may not match those on the French charts. The latter are used in this pilot.

After passing the entrance (see page 128), immediate steps must be taken to avoid being swept by the tide onto the Grand Mouton rock, which lies to starboard and is marked by a green beacon with a green ▲ topmark. Hold the Baden/Petit Vézid transit and turn sharply to starboard only when the Grand Mouton is safely abaft the beam. The channel is now clear before you. Leave Ile Longue to port, a beacon (starboard) and the islet of Erlannig with its partly submerged stone circle to starboard, Gravinis to port (there is a landing place here, marked by beacons), a buoy (starboard) and Er Gazek (Ile de la Jument) to starboard, and Ile Berder to port.

A wide expanse of water, some of it shallow, now opens, but it is best to keep in the jet of the tide setting towards the small Ile Creïzig. Leave to port the two cardinal buoys marking middle grounds, steering midway between the second and the N end of Ile Creïzig. After passing this, turn towards the north, keeping fairly close to (but not less than 200m off) the Ile aux Moines shore. This avoids the Kergonan shoal, which dries in places.

The stream sets strongly through the narrows between Ile aux Moines and the mainland, and Les Réchauds rocks, marked by two beacons (starboard), are left to starboard. Thence the channel is straightforward, the critical points being well marked.

Leave Ile d'Irus to port, two beacons (starboard) on Pointe du Trec'h to starboard, a tower (port) and a beacon (port) on Truie d'Arradon to port, a buoy (starboard) off Pointe d'Arradon to starboard, and the yachting centre of Arradon, with three port and two starboard buoys, to port. Steer to leave the green (starboard) beacon W of Ile de Logoden 100m to starboard and round Le Petit Logoden, leaving it 100m to starboard and Drenec buoy (starboard) to starboard.

An alternative and rather shorter channel carries 1·8m. After passing Pointe du Trec'h, leave Holavre tower (starboard) to starboard and pass south of Ile de Logoden, rejoining the other channel to leave the next buoy, Drenec (starboard), to starboard.

The channel continues in a curve to the northeast, leaving a W cardinal buoy (Boëdig) and Roguedas tower (starboard) to starboard. North of Ile de Boëdig the continuation of the channel is not obvious from a distance. As one passes north of Boëdig the narrow gap opens up dramatically. When it is fully open turn sharply to port and steer through it. Coming out of this narrow passage, the yachting centre of Conleau is to port and a wide expanse of shallow water lies ahead. The channel through this is marked by beacons; at the far end it takes a very sharp turn to port and its bottom is only just above datum. Thence the channel is very narrow, though well marked by beacons, and there is only just room to pass oncoming traffic. The channel gets progressively shallower and is about

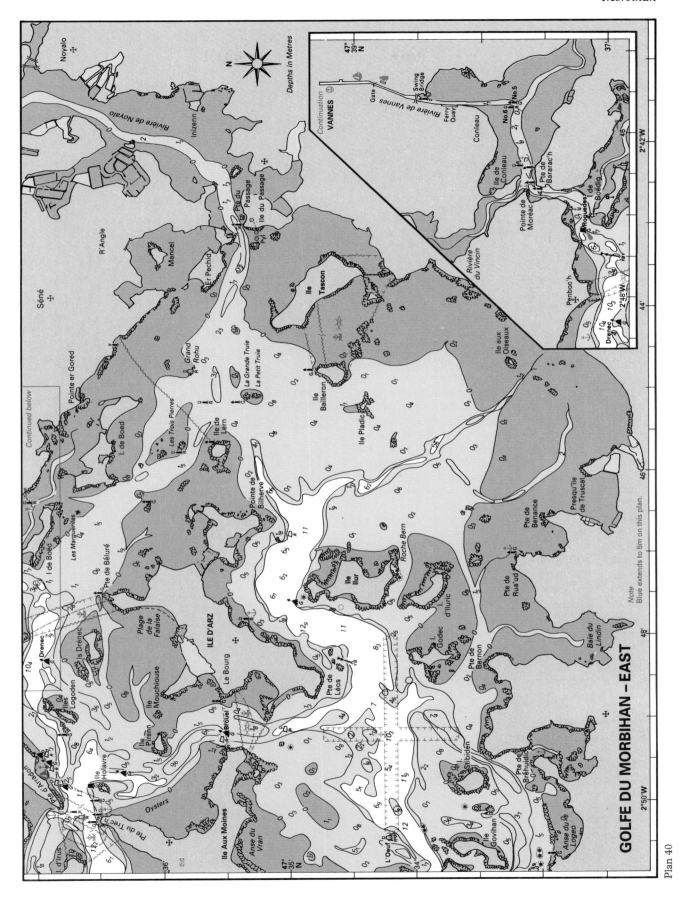

GOLFE DU MORBIHAN – EAST

Plan 40

Depths in Metres

Note
Blue extends to 5m on this plan.

Continuation
VANNES

The concealed entrance to Vannes. Boëdig chapel (arrowed) has sunlit roof. To enter the narrows, the green beacon tower Roguédas must be left to starboard.

1·2m above datum when it reaches the vedette quay on the port bank.

A short distance past the vedette quay is a swing bridge. This is operated from the *capitainerie* at the Vannes wet basin. Closed-circuit television cameras show the situation on the road and in the channel. If the bridge is not open, secure to the waiting pontoon on the starboard side.

The gate for the wet basin at Vannes is open between 0800 and 2200 in season for a maximum of 5 hours, depending on the requirement to maintain a depth of 2·4m at the pontoons. As a rough guide, according to the harbourmaster, it will open at HW Navalo. Regulations state that the bridge will open for ten minutes every half-hour while the gate is open. In fact the harbourmaster may operate the bridge at his discretion, depending on road traffic, should there be vessels waiting to pass. Harbour office listens Ch 9.

Lights: Red – Stop. Yellow – boats that can, proceed under bridge. Flashing green – get ready. Green – Go.

The visitors' pontoon in the wet basin is on the starboard side, but a launch may direct you to a vacant berth on arrival.

Anchorages

With the large-scale chart many anchorages can be found; some of the better known ones are:

Ile Longue There is a NE-facing bay on the SE end of this island where the water is slack when the tide is running hard in the channel. The bottom shelves rapidly, but there is room to anchor on soundings. Some use the 4·9m (rocky) patch (see British Admiralty 2358), where the water is still. The island is private and landing is not allowed.

Larmor Baden see page 131.

Ile er Gazek (Ile de la Jument on British Admiralty 2358) On the east of the island out of the tide. A good place to wait for a fair tide.

Ile Berder To the E of the island, NW of the S cardinal buoy, or farther north in the Mouillage de Kerdelan. A good anchorage with little stream. Yachts on moorings indicate the best areas.

Ile aux Moines There is a small marina on the NW corner with a few pontoon berths for visitors and

Anchorage out of the stream SE of Ile Longue. The yacht in the stream is making a good 10 knots over the ground.

some visitors' moorings. It is also possible to anchor to the NE of the moorings. It is worth working out the depths carefully because the bottom slopes very gently for a long way before suddenly dropping into deep water. To have more than just enough water one has to go a long way out with a deep-draught vessel and so will tend to be more in the tide, though the tides are not too strong if one gets well into the bay. There is no official information about tidal constants for this point; take high water as +0100 Brest, MTL 2·9m; these constants are only estimates and some margin should be allowed. A fine-weather anchorage exposed to the W and SW is south of Pte de Toulindag, the NW tip of the island.

Anse de Moustran This is the bay just north of Port Blanc on the opposite side of the narrows to Ile aux Moines. The best spots are occupied by moorings, so that one is pushed out into deeper water where the tide is strong. If the wind comes up against the tide the yacht sheers about. As the bottom is sharp sand, some years ago Professor Black's yacht *Black Jack* lost all the galvanising on 10 fathoms of chain in one night in this anchorage.

Arradon A popular yachting centre. Moorings for visitors, or anchor outside the moorings. Rather exposed in southerly weather near high water.

Ile de Boëdig There is a pleasant, secluded, sheltered anchorage in the bight at the NW end of the island. The island is private and there is no landing.

Conleau The inlet to the SW of the peninsula is full of moorings. The best available anchorage is in the bight on the port side just before the far end of the narrows. There are usually some fishing boats here. The restaurant on the Ile de Conleau is recommended.

Vannes Entry has already been described above. Port signals: green light, departure prohibited; red light, entry prohibited; red above green, entry and departure prohibited.

A timetable for the gate's operation is available at the *capitainerie* on the W bank. ☎ 97 54 16 08 or 97 54 00 47. VHF Ch 9.

The wet dock, 600m long, has a pontoon bridge for pedestrians halfway up which is broken when the gate is open. The quieter pontoons are on the W bank below the pontoon bridge.

Facilities

There are no facilities at all at Iles er Gazek, Berder and Boëdic. Facilities are very limited at Arradon. At Port Blanc (Anse de Moustran) fuel and water are available, with a *capitainerie* and tourist bureau. On Ile de Conleau there is a good restaurant. At Ile aux Moines there are all the usual village shops and hotels and restaurants near the quay.

Vannes is an attractive cathedral city of historic interest with banks, hotels, restaurants and all the facilities of a large town. Market day Tuesday. Water and electricity on the pontoons, showers and toilets by the *capitainerie*, which provides a good regional *Météo*. Yacht yard with fuel berth outside the gates and chandlers in the town. Vannes is a main rail centre and communications by rail and bus are good, making it a good place for a change of crew. Buses from Conleau and Vannes marina pass the railway station. There is an airfield north of the city and a regular ferry service from below the swing bridge to Conleau, Ile aux Moines, Port Navalo, Auray and other points in the Morbihan.

Ile du Passage, at the eastern end of the Morbihan. Depths are continually changing in this area, but with a reliable echosounder it is an interesting and uncrowded place to visit.

Southern and eastern Morbihan

Tidal heights (approx)

HW Le Passage +0204 springs, +0128 neaps on Navalo
MTL 2·0m

Heights of tide above chart datum
MHWS 3·5m, MLWS 0·6m, MHWN 2·9m, MLWN 1·1m

General

An interesting alternative after passing between Iles Berder and Er Gazek is to proceed south of Ile aux Moines. Beyond the narrows the channels, though well marked, wind between mudflats and are probably best taken by a stranger on a rising tide. The tidal streams are not so fierce as in other parts of the Morbihan. Between Ile aux Moines and Ile d'Artz the flood runs to the S.

Anchorages

Anse de Kerners Anchor outside the local boats. Water, showers and provisions in season.

Anse de Pencastel Anchor outside the moorings.

Anse de Penhap This is a peaceful anchorage in the south of the Ile aux Moines. Get in as far as draught and soundings will allow and you will be right out of the streams.

Between Ile aux Moines and Ile d'Arz Those requiring solitude may find it southwest of the anchorage shown on British Admiralty *2358* south of Ile Pirren. Shallow-draught vessels must keep clear of the oyster beds. Landing at the Pointe de Brouel and at the slip W of Pointe de Brouel. All shops on Ile aux Moines in the Bourg, 1 mile walk. Ile d'Arz is more primitive but has shops.

Ile du Passage This is the last anchorage where one can lie afloat. However, the depths in the channel appear to alter from year to year, and a vessel drawing 2m should proceed with caution.

Anchor midstream in the narrows to the north of the island; the tide is strong. Quiet and rural, it has no supplies. This used to be the base for the Sinagots, fishermen living at Séné, who sailed an individual type of brown-sailed lug-rigged schooner with conspicuous skill. A few of these survive, sailed as yachts.

34. Pénerf

Rade de Pénerf 47°30'N 2°39°W

Charts

BA *2353, 2646*
Imray *C39*
SHOM *7033P*
Navicarte *546*

Tidal data

Tidal heights (approx)

HW −0020 Brest springs, HW Brest neaps
MTL 3·2m. Index 2

Heights of tide above chart datum
MHWS 5·5m, MLWS 0·8m, MHWN 4·3m, MLWN 2·1m

Tidal streams

Between Pointe du Grand Mont and the rivermouth the flood has a spring rate of 1 knot, the ebb 1½ knots. In the passes the streams run three knots springs when the rocks are uncovered, but only 2 knots ENE and WSW when the rocks are covered.

Depths

In the central pass 0·5m, in the east pass 4·5m. Inside, the river is deep as far as Cadenic.

Light

1. **Le Pignon** 47°30'·1N 2°38'·9W Fl(3)WR.12s6m 9/6M 028·5°-R-167°-W-175°-R-349·5°-W-028·5° Red tower

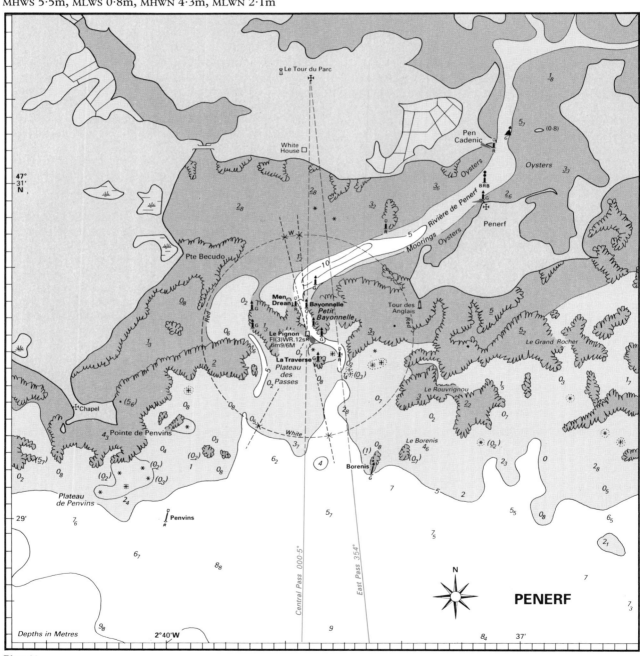

Plan 41

Pénerf, looking east over Le Pignon red beacon tower (foreground).

Leading marks for entry to Pénerf. Le Pignon red beacon tower in transit with the steeple of Tour de Parc church on 000·5°.

General

This quiet and unspoilt river, 6 miles west of the entrance to La Vilaine, is sheltered from the Atlantic swell by groups of rocks and the peninsula on which Pénerf is situated. The village is small, combining oyster culture with being a minor holiday centre. A fair number of yachts and fishing boats are moored off the village of Pénerf, with others off Cadenic, on the other side of the river ½ mile further up. There is still plenty of room for visitors. There are many rocky ledges near the entrance. They are well marked with beacons, but the channels are very narrow in a wide expanse of water; it is not safe for the stranger in bad weather or poor visibility, as an error could have serious consequences.

Loss of trees during the storm of October 1987 has made the main leading mark, the spire of Le Tour du Parc, visible once more. It was for some years obscured from view, and this may well recur at some future date.

Approach

Pointe de Penvins, 1½ miles SW of the entrance, is easy to identify. It is low, with a conspicuous octagonal mosque-like chapel on it. Half a mile SSE of Penvins chapel is the Penvins buoy (port), which is left to port. To the ENE of Penvins chapel are Le Pignon tower (red) and the Tour de Pénerf, also called Le Tour des Anglais, looking like a chess castle and painted white.

Enter the bay with the Tour des Anglais roughly in transit with Pénerf church bell-tower, bearing about 030°.

Approaching on this transit, identify:
1. Le Pignon red beacon tower,
2. a conspicuous water tower to the north,
3. a prominent white house with a single gable, on the shore to the right of the water tower,
4. the steeple of Le Tour du Parc church, above the trees to the right of the white house.

Beware of heavy fishing netting in the approach.

Entrance

There are three passes into Pénerf. The west pass can be disposed of by saying that although it is preferred by the local fishermen in strong westerly winds, it is not well enough marked for strangers, who anyway have no business to be entering this port in strong westerly winds. The central pass is the easiest, but is not deep enough to be used at low water. The east pass is less easy to follow but is deep.

Central pass

This pass carries a least depth of 0·5m.

If the steeple is clearly visible, bring it in line with Le Pignon tower bearing 000°. Should the spire become obscured, Le Pignon in transit with the white house bearing 359° will serve.

These transits will leave Borenis spar buoy (starboard) 800m to starboard and La Traverse beacon 150m to starboard, with a port-hand beacon for the east pass beyond it.

On close approach to Le Pignon tower, bear to starboard and leave the tower 40m to port. Thence steer to leave the Bayonelle beacon, replacing the Grand Bayonelle (starboard) tower (destroyed), 20m to starboard; this course leaves to starboard two beacons (starboard) on the S end of Le Petit Bayonelle rocks, and to port Men Drean beacon.

After passing between the Bayonelle beacon and Men Drean beacon, hold the same course for nearly 200m, until another starboard-hand beacon has come into transit with Pénerf village. Then alter course to steer ENE for the boats on moorings off the village over one mile away. Leave the beacon (starboard) 100m to starboard, and a beacon (port) halfway to the village about 200m to port, as it is well up on the mud.

East pass

This pass carries 4·5m if the directions are followed, but the pass is narrow and there are rocky shoals to the east of it which it is essential to avoid. Before finally committing the yacht to the pass, that is to say before passing the outer port-hand beacon, the following marks should be positively identified:

1. The port-hand beacon on the east side of La Traverse.
2. The Men Drean beacon (port) beyond Le Pignon tower.
3. The starboard beacon, Bayonelle, east of Men Drean.
4. The two starboard beacons opposite Le Pignon.

Approach on 030° with Pénerf church tower just open to the left of the Tour des Anglais. When the Tour du Parc steeple and the port-hand beacon on La Traverse have been identified, they will come into transit on 354°. Turn onto this transit to enter the pass. If La Traverse port-hand beacon has not been identified by the time Borenis spar buoy (starboard) is abeam, about 600m distant, go back.

The transit leaves very close to starboard a rock with 1·3m over it. When within 100m of La Traverse beacon, alter course to leave it 20m to port. After passing it, continue to steer about 355° for another 100m until a course of 300° will lead between Le Pignon tower (port) and the southernmost of the two green beacons (starboard) on Le Petit Bayonelle, to the east of Le Pignon. Steer this course and alter as necessary to leave the two green beacons 30m to starboard and Le Pignon to port. Thence, passing between Bayonelle beacon (starboard) and Men Drean beacon (port), follow the directions given above for the central pass.

When leaving by the east pass, it is important to bring La Traverse beacon (port) in transit with Le Tour du Parc steeple quickly in order to avoid contact with the eastern rocks.

By night

Le Pignon[1] is lit (Fl(3)WR.12s6m9/6M), with white sectors covering the central channel. However, a fair amount of light would be needed to go up the river, and strangers are not recommended to attempt a night entry.

Anchorage

The most convenient anchorage is off Pénerf slip, the end of which is marked by a green beacon (starboard), but moorings now extend downriver for several hundred metres below the slip as well as above it. There were no moorings marked *visiteurs* in 1992. Should a mooring be borrowed, the outer ones are in the tide and one must aim off accordingly when going to and from the shore in a dinghy. About 200m upstream is an isolated danger beacon (BRB), which should be left to port by visitors. North of this the channel tends to the west bank, where there is a slip, the end marked by a red beacon (port), with moorings in 3·5m, mostly occupied by the fishing boats of Cadenic. A green buoy (starboard) on the other side of the channel marks the edge of the extensive mud flats and oyster beds on the east side of the river. A quiet overnight anchorage may be found upstream of the Cadenic moorings, but some report that the tide runs hard and the holding is not good.

Facilities

All shops, café and restaurant at Pénerf. Café but no shops at Cadenic, but a travelling shop calls daily; orders for it could, no doubt, be left at the café.

35. La Vilaine

The Breton Canals

Entrance channel buoys
47°30'·5N 2°28'·5W

Charts

BA *2353, 2646*
Imray *C39*
SHOM *7033P*
Navicarte *546*
Grafocarte *Carte Guide: Navigation Fluviale de Voies
Navigables de Bretagne*

Tidal data

Tidal heights (approx)

HW −0025 Brest springs, HW Brest neaps
MTL 3·2m. Index 2
Heights of tide above chart datum
MHWS 5·5m, MLWS 0·8m, MHWN 4·3m, MLWN 2·1m

Tidal streams

Normal for an estuary of this size. Above La Roche
Bernard and up as far as Rennes the river can be
closed to navigation for a time after heavy rain.

Depths

The closure of the Arzal Dam has caused silting in
the estuary and the line of the buoyed channel is
subject to alteration. Depths in the channel have
decreased since 1988.

In 1992, 0·8m could be found over the bar south
of Pointe de Penlan and there was a least depth of
1m in the channel to Arzal. Above Arzal, vessels
drawing 1·3m can proceed up to Rennes with an
occasional drive through soft mud. A vessel drawing
1·2m can usually navigate from Rennes to Dinan,
except in a dry summer. In 1992, due to a water

shortage, the locks were only operated during
weekends and depths were less than 1m in places,
but in 1993 there was sufficient water for passage
throughout the summer.

General

On a summer's day few places are prettier than La
Vilaine, running between meadows where cows
ruminate, or between rush-covered banks or rocky
cliffs.

Above the Arzal dam there is a tideless lake. This
is not a tidal-power scheme like that on the Rance
in north Brittany, with its rapid changes of level.
The intention is to improve the river for drainage
and navigation and to reactivate the port of Redon.
So far little commercial traffic to Redon, which
would scour the channel and so maintain the depth,
has developed.

At Redon the river connects with the Breton canal
system, by which shallow-draught vessels can travel
between the Bay of Biscay and St Malo.

Lights

1. **Basse de Kervoyal** 47°30'·4N 2°32'·6W DirQ.WR.
   8/5M 269°-W-271°-R-269° Bn tower S card
2. **Basse Bertrand** 47°31'·1N 2°30'·7W Iso.WG.4s6m
   9/6M 040°-W-054°-G-227°-W-234°-G-040° Green
   tower
3. **Penlan** 47°31'·0N 2°30'·2W Oc(2)WRG.6s26m15-
   11M 292·5°-R-025°-G-052°-W-060°-R-138°-G-180°
   White tower, red bands
4. **Pointe du Scal** 47°29'·7N 2°26'·8W Q.G.8m4M
   White square tower, green top
5. **Channel buoys** No. 1 Fl.G.2·5s, No. 2 Fl.R.2·5s,
   No. 4 Fl(2)R.5s, No. 5 Fl(3)G.6s, No. 6 Fl(3)R.6s,
   No. 8 Fl(4)R.7s

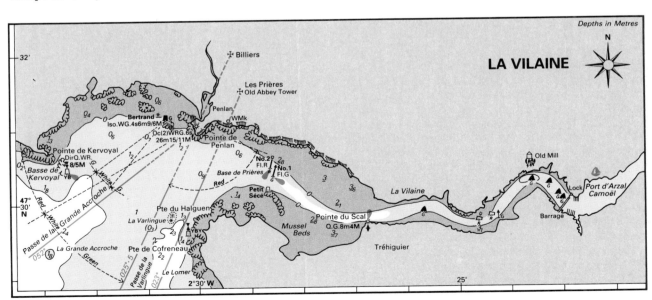

Plan 42

Looking east up the Vilaine. Tréhiguier and Pointe du Scal low right. The Arzal dam arrowed.

Pointe de Penlan lighthouse bearing 027°, with Billiers church tower to the left.

Approach and entrance

In the approach to La Vilaine the depths on the outer bar are not less than 0·8m, except for La Varlingue, a rock drying 0·3m, situated only ½ mile off Pointe du Halguen, which marks the SE side of the entrance. In good weather, with a sufficient rise of tide, it is only necessary to steer a midchannel course.

With any sea or swell, conditions are rough on the bar, especially on the ebb, and it is better to enter or leave on the last of the flood. Directions for the three recommended passes across the bar are given below, for use when the conditions call for them.

The western pass, Passe de la Grande Accroche, carries 1·2m least water to the bar and is lit, but the sea breaks heavily in it in strong onshore winds. Passe de la Varlingue, the eastern one, carries 1·3m and is not lit, but is preferable in heavy W or SW weather, as the shallow part is inshore and gets some protection from the Grande Arroche bank to seaward. The landmarks shown on the charts and described in earlier editions of the pilot are virtually impossible to see from a yacht due to the growth of trees. For the Passe de la Grande Accroche and for the SW approach one must employ the Pointe de Penlan lighthouse. The Passe de la Varlingue should only be attempted if the leading marks can be positively identified.

Passe de la Grande Accroche

Make the Plateau des Mâts (S cardinal) buoy and, leaving it 300m to port, steer on 058° for Pointe de Penlan lighthouse. Leave Pte de Kervoyal tower (S cardinal) about 600m to port and La Grande Accroche (1·9m) shoal about 300m to starboard. When the Pte de Kervoyal tower bears 270°, with the Tour des Anglais at Pénerf (white tower with castellated top), if it can be seen, just open to the left, make good 090° into the estuary to pick up the port and starboard buoys that mark the channel.

From the SW

Pass Ile Dumet on either hand and steer for Pointe de Penlan lighthouse, bearing more than 025° (with Billiers church tower open to the left of the lighthouse) to leave La Varlingue (dries 0·3m), off Pointes du Halguen and Cofreneau, to starboard and less than 040° to leave La Grande Accroche (1·8m) shoal to port. When Pointe de Kervoyal tower (S cardinal) bears 270° proceed as in the western approach.

This leads in 0·8m to the outer pair of small port and starboard channel buoys north of the Petit Secé tower (white). Follow the narrow channel defined by Nos 2, 4, 6 and 8 port buoys, with starboard buoys Nos 1 and 5 opposite Nos 2 and 6. Note that the Tréhiguier lighthouses in transit define a line which now dries. East of Tréhiguier there is one starboard buoy (lit) which should be left 100m to starboard, after which steer to leave a port buoy (lit), numbered 2 in a new sequence, close to port. The deep water tends to be nearer the north bank, with drying mud banks along the south bank. Mussel beds occupy the mud flats on either side of the channel.

After the port buoy a green beacon is seen on the bank ahead. Make a turn to port and identify a disused windmill tower with a black conical roof over the trees on the north bank. Grounding was avoided in 1992 by steering on a course between the beacon and windmill until a turn to starboard could be made to enter the buoyed channel into the lock.

In 1993 a second port buoy, No. 4 (lit), was installed on the turn to port, closely following No. 2, and a starboard buoy, No. 1 (lit), was placed on the turn to starboard. This is followed by starboard buoys 3 and 5 (lit) and a fourth unlit starboard buoy leading into the lock. If these buoys are maintained in future the danger of grounding will be considerably reduced.

By night

Approach in the white sector of Penlan light[3], between 052° and 060°. The sectors of Basse Bertrand light[2] can be disregarded. When the DirQ.WR light of Basse de Kervoyal light[1] turns from red to white, steer 090° in this narrow sector to pass between the first pair of red/green channel buoys[5] and follow the channel buoys to Tréhiguier, beyond which the channel is not well lit. Due to channel changes a night entry should only be attempted when weather and tide conditions are very favourable.

Passe de la Varlingue

This pass carries 1·3m to the bar and leads through a narrow channel between a W cardinal tower off Pointe de Cofrenau and La Varlingue (dries 0·3m); the transit must be closely held. The leading marks are the tower of Abbaye de Prières in transit with a white wall beacon (in front) and Avalec Mill (1½ miles behind), bearing 023°; the wall beacon is not easy to locate. Follow this transit until the Petit Secé tower (white) bears 105°, then steer to make good 090° until Nos 1 and 2 starboard/port buoys N of Petit Secé are picked up.

Should there be doubt about the identification of the Abbaye square tower, an alternative is to pass outside La Varlingue by keeping Billiers church clock tower in transit with Penlan lighthouse bearing 025°. Make the alteration in good time and use the SW approach if Billiers church tower is not seen, with Pointe de Penlan lighthouse bearing more than 025°.

The river

The lock is on the north side of the river, adjacent to the conspicuous control tower. The approach channels from above and below are buoyed and the danger area above the dam spillway is marked off by yellow buoys with a × topmark. The lock is worked in daylight hours between 0700 and 2000, except on public holidays, e.g. 14 July and 15 August. The sill level is 2m below datum, but there is only 1m just outside, preventing use close to LW; the level above the lock is maintained at 4·5m above datum (3·5m during floods). At HWS there may therefore be a small drop on passing through the lock into the river. The road bridge above the lock is raised as necessary to allow masted vessels to pass.

Securing in the lock is awkward as there can be substantial turbulence. If alongside the wall, rather than rafted to a boat that is so secured, pass bow and stern warps round the chains hanging down the walls and tend them and your fenders as the level rises or falls. Do not be in a hurry to unmoor as there will be further turbulence when the gates open and salt and fresh water mix.

The river is very beautiful for some distance above La Roche Bernard; further up, the hills draw away and the scenery is less interesting. Masted vessels can go all the way up to Redon, which is a town of some character. There is a swing bridge at Cran. Sound three blasts on your horn on approach or telephone in advance (99 90 21 93).

A power cable with 23m headroom crosses the river downstream of the Cran bridge, halfway between the bridge and Foleux.

Above the dam a midchannel course should be followed. Be careful not to cut corners; rather tend to keep to the outside. A few special dangers are marked on the lateral system.

Anchorages and facilities

Tréhiguier A convenient anchorage near the entrance; it is exposed to W and NW winds. Anchor outside the moorings of local craft in soft mud. Land at the slip; restaurant.

Arzal A marina (Camoël) on the south bank with a substantial extension (Arzal) on the north bank.

All the facilities of a large marina, with water and electricity on the pontoons, showers and toilets on both sides, *capitainerie* at present on the south bank, fuel berth on north side at entrance to lock. Haul-out facilities, repairs and laying up under cover on the north side. The villages of Arzal and Camoël are both about 2 miles by road, but food supplies may shortly be available in the marina, which has a good restaurant.

La Roche Bernard Excellent anchorage and several moorings in the river. There is a marina in the small inlet on the starboard side, but the berths are often all reserved. There is another marina in the river below the bridge, with a visitors' pontoon running along the bank downstream of the finger pontoons, and many mooring buoys.

Water and fuel on the quay. Hot showers can be had; *laverie* at 'Le Camping'. Chandlery and marine engineer. All shops in the town, ¼-mile walk up the hill, with a number of excellent restaurants.

Foleux Some 4 miles above Roche Bernard, in peaceful surroundings by the old ferry slips, there are moorings and some pontoons on both sides of the river, with a restaurant on the north bank.

Redon A small marina has been built in the old dock, surrounded by picturesque old warehouses. At present there is no commercial traffic. Rather basic showers and toilets by the *capitainerie* on the port-hand side of the entrance. Fuel berth nearby; crane for masting on the other side. A good chandlery at the top of the basin on the port-hand side. There are all shops, banks, hotels and restaurants in the town, which is a major rail centre offering good communications.

The marina and bridge from Roche Bernard.

The Breton canals

The canals offer a convenient route for shallow-draught yachts which do not relish the long haul round the western end of France, where the seas can be rough. Any yacht which can safely reach the Channel Islands can easily get from there to St Malo and thence have a most pleasant rural passage to the interesting and relatively sheltered waters of the Baie de Quiberon.

The passage is especially attractive to motor yachts, but there are cranes at each end which the crew can use to lay the mast of a sailing yacht on deck; the crew should be sufficiently experienced to do this without calling on outside help. Limits on size dictate that width must not exceed 4·5m and headroom above the waterline 2·7m. Permissible draught varies, but will never be more than 1·3m, and 1·2m or 1·1m are more usual official limits. If rainfall has been low, 1·0m draught may be difficult.

The normal, and quickest, route is from St Malo to Rennes by the Canal d'Ile et Rance, from Rennes to Redon by La Vilaine Canalisé and thence to the sea via the lower reaches of the Vilaine, about 130 nautical miles with 62 locks. The locks are worked from 0630 to 1930, with a short lunch break. There are speed limits of 6km/h (3·2 knots) in the canal north of Rennes, and 10km/h (5·4 knots) in the river between Rennes and Redon. By keeping going reasonably hard the passage can be made in five days. It is also possible to turn aside at Redon and go up to Josselin, carrying on from there over the hill to Lorient. The draught limit is 0·8m. For Nantes, leave the Vilaine at Bellions lock, below Redon; the canal direct from Redon is now closed.

At present no permit is required, nor is any charge made for a single return journey, but the French Government Tourist Office (FGTO), 178 Piccadilly, London, W1V 0AL, ☎ 0891 244123, should be applied to for a list of dates of *chomages*, when sections of the canals are closed for maintenance. It is also desirable before setting out to obtain an up-to-date copy of the *Carte Guide: Navigation Fluviale de Voies Navigables de Bretagne*, produced by Grafocarte. This has strip maps of the canals with directions in French, English and German, and can be obtained from Imray, Laurie, Norie & Wilson Ltd if it is not available in a local chandlery or bookshop.

Building sand appears now to be transported by road, and there is little sign of the sand-barges that once provided uneasy companionship in the locks of the Vilaine.

The lock-keepers are careful when letting in the water, and with ordinary care no damage is to be expected. A plank slung across fenders, with an apron to protect the ship's side, should suffice during the passage. Small motor tyres are no longer allowed in French canals, as they have a tendency to break off, sink and jam the lock gates.

There are strong currents as a lock fills, and the yacht must be securely moored and the lines tended as the water rises; moor near the lower gates if possible, but somebody has to be in front if two or three yachts share a lock.

It may help to fit blocks at bow and stern so that the mooring lines can be led to the cockpit and tended by one person, who could use the sheet winches in a sailing yacht. Officially the lock-keepers are not required to help with mooring lines, and north of Rennes a crew member should be put ashore before entering the lock to handle the lines; help with the gates is appreciated (especially since the keeper is normally a woman) and will speed the passage. South of Rennes the locks are larger and it is less easy to get ashore; here the lock-keepers will usually help willingly with the shore lines.

There are cranes to help with masting at Dinan and Redon, the limits which can be reached by masted vessels; there are cranes at St Malo and La Roche Bernard, but these deprive one of some pleasant sailing. There are also cranes at Nantes and Lorient for those using these variants.

The route

St Malo-Dinan Accessible to masted vessels. The lock at Le Chatelier is only available for about 4 hours during the high-water period in the Rance. Information on the times of operation of the Barrage and Le Chatelier locks may be obtained in St Malo (☎ 99 46 21 87). The upper reaches are shallow out of the channel, but this is clearly marked.

Dinan-Rennes Ile et Rance canal. A straightforward canal section, with 47 locks, of which 11 in quick succession (L'Escalier) climb to the top. Yachts of draught near the maximum will have trouble with soft mud in places. This mud is carried in by water courses joining the canal. If you begin to drag, try to see which side the flow has come in; the best water will be near the opposite bank. Having found it, open up the engine and force a way through; the bad patches are not very long. The engine water-cooling intake should be inspected regularly, as it may become blocked with weed or grass cuttings from the towpath.

Ecluse de Boël, on the Vilaine river below Rennes.

Fuel at Dinan and refuel at Rennes. It may be possible to fuel at Betton, but the fuel berth at Tinténiac has closed.

Rennes-Redon Canalised portion of the river Vilaine. There are 12 locks. The river is wider here; the best water is usually about one third of the way from the towpath bank (left bank to Pont Réan, right bank thereafter). There is a channel of the requisite depth all the way, but it is easy to get out of it and go aground. In some places the distance of the channel from the bank is indicated by notices on the towpath, with an arrowhead and a figure indicating the distance in nietres.

However, there are other shallows, and if an echo sounder is available it is as well to use it regularly between Boel and Malon. Do not trust the advice of fishermen; they have seen shallow-draught vessels travelling in parts of the river outside the proper channel and imagine that all boats can take the same course. Beware of the fisherman, who can sometimes leave four rods and lines poking out through the reeds while he lunches elsewhere, expecting yachtsmen to avoid them. It is a courtesy to slow down when passing fishermen in full view; to quote the English translation in an old guide: 'Anglers would otherwise have their feet watered, and you would hear everything but congratulations...!'

The river is closed to navigation in times of flood.

Entering Redon, you will come to a stop-gate for flood control. Check the signs to see that it is open before passing through. The locks on either side directly below the stop-gate are no longer in use. After passing the stop-gate, turn sharp right at the junction if you want to enter the dock, or go straight on and turn left for the sea.

Facilities

Nearly all the villages on the route have a café-restaurant which can supply a very adequate meal at a reasonable price; one is off the tourist route and does not have to pay tourist prices. They also have food shops. Beware, however, as some shops will close for a month in the summer and a whole village has been found to be closed for August. A number of the lock-keepers are pleased to sell farm and garden produce. Water can be had at the 'campings' at Tinténiac (where it sometimes tastes of chlorine) and Pont Réan, at the quays at Guipry, Port Roche, Rennes and Redon and by hose at Beslé. There are hot showers at Pont Réan, cold at Tinténiac. Some hotel/restaurants will provide a shower while your meal is prepared (at Guipry, for instance). There is a launderette near the yacht berths at Rennes and there are washing facilities at Tinténiac and Pont Réan.

The main road runs alongside the canal in Rennes and there is traffic noise all night, but it is well worth making a stop for supplies and fuel by day. Excellent hypermarket and banks in a shopping precinct on the right bank close to the yacht berths, and a garage from which fuel may be obtained on the left bank after passing through the lock into the Vilaine.

36. La Turballe

47°21'N 2°31'W

Charts

BA *2353, 3126, 2646*
Imray *C39, C40*
SHOM *7033P, 6826*
Navicarte *546, 547*

Tidal data

Tidal heights (approx)

HW −0025 Brest springs, +0030 Brest neaps
MTL 3·0m. Index 1

Heights of tide above chart datum
MHWS 5·3m, MLWS 0·6m, MHWN 4·1m, MLWN 2·0m

Tidal streams

In the middle of the Rade du Croisic the streams are rotary clockwise and weak. At HW Brest the direction turns southerly and at LW Brest it turns northerly, spring rates ½ knot. Between the Pointe du Croisic and the Plateau du Four the pattern is similar, but the rates may be greater; SW at +0250 Brest.

Lights

1. **Jetée de Garlahy (west breakwater head)**
   47°20'·7N 2°31'·0W Fl(4)WR.12s13m10/7M 060°-R-315°-W-060° White metal frame, red top
2. **Ldg Lts 006·5°** DirF.Vi.11m3M 004°-intens-009° White masts, orange tops
3. **Digue Tourlandroux (northern end)** Fl.G.4s7m 6M White tank, green top.

   Siren 1 long every 10 minutes

La Turballe entrance bearing 005°. Dredger operating to right of entrance.

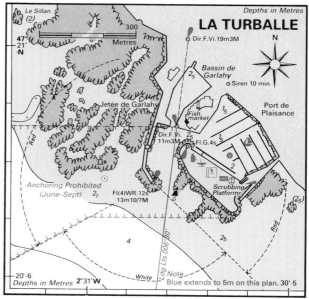

Plan 43

General

La Turballe is a busy fishing port two miles north of Le Croisic, with a fishing fleet of some 60 trawlers. The inner harbour has been dredged and developed so that half of it is a small fishing-boat harbour and the other half a yacht harbour, with pontoon berths for some 280 yachts. 20 pontoon berths are available to visitors.

Entry is possible in winds of force 5 or 6 from the east through south to southwest and the land provides good shelter from stronger winds from the west through north to northeast.

Approach and entry

Rocky shoals extend offshore to the north of the harbour, which should be approached from the SW. Seen from the west, the long white-walled fish market, with a water tower some distance behind, makes a good landmark, and a red beacon tower is situated just west of the entrance. South of the entrance there is 2m to within 300m of the long sandy beach.

Entry is made on a course of about 005° (the leading lights being on 006·5°), as the deep water appears to be nearer the west breakwater. Once past the breakwater head, turn sharply to starboard to enter the yacht harbour.

By night

Approach in the white sector of the W jetty head light[1] Fl(4)WR.12s, steering to leave it to port, and enter in the intense sector of the violet leading lights (in line on 006·5°)[2]. After passing the W breakwater head, make a sharp turn to starboard round the light flashing green every 4s, marking the starboard side of the entrance to the yacht harbour[3].

Facilities

Water and electricity on the pontoons, fuel berth (takes card), or fuel from nearby garage, showers and toilets, 16-tonne crane, 140-tonne travel-lift and slipway. Boatyard can take yachts of up to 16m; wood or fibreglass and engine repairs undertaken. Chandlers, banks, baker, restaurants and bars close to the marina in the old town.

La Turballe is developing as a holiday resort with quite a large summer population and provides all facilities. Good sandy beaches to the southeast of the harbour. Although it is crowded in summer, access to the marina in La Turballe is easier than entry to Le Croisic, making it a useful stopping place on this part of the coast.

37. Le Croisic

47°18'·5N 2°31'W

Charts

BA *2353, 3126, 2646*
Imray *C39, C40*
SHOM *7033P*
Navicarte *546, 547*

Tidal data

Tidal heights (approx)

High water −0025 Brest springs, +0030 Brest neaps
MTL 3·0m. Index 1
Heights of tide above chart datum
MHWS 5·2m, MLWS 0·6m, MHWN 4·0m, MLWN 2·0m

Tidal streams

In the middle of the Rade du Croisic the streams are rotary clockwise and weak. At HW Brest the direction turns southerly and at LW Brest it turns northerly, spring rates ½ knot. Between the Pointe du Croisic and the Plateau du Four the pattern is similar, but the rates may be greater; SW at +0250 Brest.

The streams in the entrance to the harbour are very strong; west of the Mabon rocks they exceed 4 knots at springs 3 hours before and 2½ hours after HW Brest.

Depths

On the leading line the channel is dredged to 2·3m as far as the Fish Quay, and to 1·5m as far as the second entrance. From there a narrow channel *dérocté à* 0·5m runs some 30m out from the wall to the upper end of the entrance into the Port de Plaisance, which dries 1·7m.

Lights

1. **Jetée du Tréhic head** 47°18'·5N 2°31'·4W Iso.WG.4s12m13/10M 042°-G-093°-W-137°-G-345° Grey tower, green lantern
2. **Basse Hergo tower** 47°18'·7N 2°31'·6W Fl.G.2·5s5m3M Green beacon tower
3. **First Ldg Lts on 156°** DirOc(2+1)12s10m18M Fluorescent orange rectangles on white pylons
4. **Intermediate leading lights on 174°** Q.G.5m11M Fluorescent white rectangles with vertical green stripe on white and green pylons
5. **Final leading lights on 134·5°** DirQ.R.6m11M Red and white chequered rectangle, front on white pylon, red top, rear on fish-market roof
6. **Les Rouzins port buoy** 47°18'·2N 2°31'·1W Q.R
7. **Le Grand Mabon tower** Fl.R.2·5s6m5M Red beacon tower

General

The harbour of Le Croisic is situated in the SE corner of the Rade du Croisic. The town is a popular holiday resort with a busy fishing harbour, and is associated with Batz and La Baule to the eastward to form a district noted for its bathing sands and holiday amenities. A large yard for building GRP fishing trawlers was completed in 1989 and a substantial new fish-market building was already in use. There is a yacht builder, and much yachting activity takes place.

Yachts that can take the ground may use the basin of the Port de Plaisance and there is a good sheltered anchorage outside, though the best spots are occupied by permanent moorings. The entrance channel is shallow and exposed to the W and NW, and in fresh onshore winds it is rough, owing to the shallow and irregular bottom. If approached on the flood with sufficient rise of tide it presents no difficulty.

Approach

The streams are strong and for this reason the best time for entry at springs is within the last hour of the flood, when they are weakening. It is difficult to enter against the ebb. At neaps there is more latitude and by following all the transits a yacht can use the channel at any state of tide.

Approaching from the west or northwest, steer into the bay until the leading marks are identified.

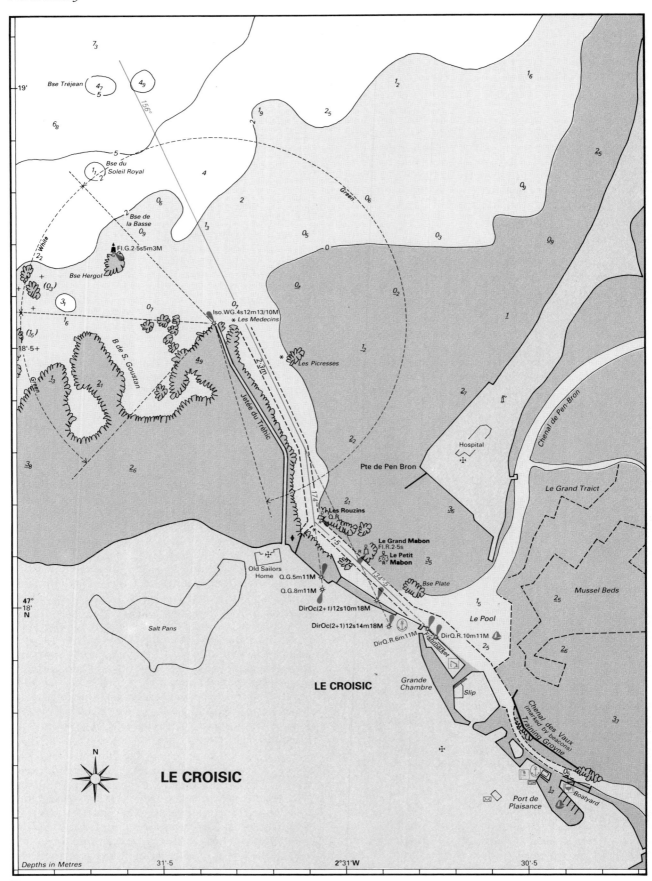

Bse Tréjean

156°

Bse du
Soleil Royal

Green

White

Bse de
la Basse

Fl.G.2·5s5m3M

Bse Hergol

Green

B de S. Goustan

Iso.WG.4s12m13/10M
* Les Medecins

* Les Picresses

Jetée du Tréhic

219m

Les Rouzins
Q.R.

174°

1·5

Le Grand Mabon
Fl.R.2·5s

Le Petit
R Mabon

Bse Plate

Pte de Pen Bron

Hospital

Chenal de Pen-Bron

Le Grand Traict

Mussel Beds

Old Sailors
Home

Q.G.5m**11M**

Q.G.8m**11M**

DirOc(2+1)12s10m18M

DirOc(2+1)12s14m18M

DirQ.R.6m11M

132°·5

Fishmarket

DirQ.R.10m11M

Le Pool

**47°
18'
N**

Salt Pans

LE CROISIC

Grande
Chambre

Slip

Chenal des Vaux
(marked by beacons)

Training Groyne

Boatyard

N

LE CROISIC

Port de
Plaisance

WC

Le Croisic, looking SSW. Compare with plan.

Entering Le Croisic. The first set of leading marks in transit (arrowed) on 156°.

The church tower, with an unusual near-Byzantine belfry, is conspicuous behind the primary leading marks. Also conspicuous are the broad white three-storeyed building with grey roof and central spire to the west of the root of the Jetée du Tréhic (a hostel for the disabled) and the long white building with central belfry of the isolation hospital on the Pen Bron peninsula, to the east of the entrance.

Approaching from the south, the extensive Plateau du Four with its conspicuous lighthouse lies on the west side and the Pointe du Croisic with its offlying rocks to the east. Near the eastern side of this passage is the Basse Castouillet, with a least depth of 0·3m. This shoal is marked on its western side by a buoy (W cardinal). After leaving this buoy to starboard steer about 045° towards La Turballe, which lies ahead conspicuously, until the leading marks for Le Croisic (a pair of fluorescent orange rectangles bearing 156° with the church tower behind) are in line.

Entrance

Steer in with the church belfry bearing 157° until the orange leading marks have been identified and then bring them into transit bearing 156°. On close approach the Hergo green tower (starboard) will be left 300m to starboard and the transit leads in about 100m E of the end of Jetée du Tréhic. To port the sands dry. Proceed up the channel inside the breakwater on the transit of the leading marks. On passing the bend in the breakwater, steer 174° on the transit of the intermediate leading marks, a pair of fluorescent white rectangles with a green vertical stripe, 100m to the left of the lifeboat station.

Approaching the lifeboat slip, if the intermediate line is being followed, the final leading marks (a pair of red and white chequered rectangles) will be seen beyond Le Grand Mabon tower (port). The rear mark is on the fish-market roof, with the front mark on the quay. Turn onto their transit of 134·5°.

Hold this transit until close to the fishing quay to avoid a rocky patch (drying 2·5m) to port, then steer to leave the quays about 50m to starboard if bound for the yacht basin. A training wall of stakes on the port side of the narrow channel to the yacht basin is marked by red beacon poles. If looking for a mooring, turn to port when the fish market is abeam to starboard and search 'Le Pool'.

If one is late on the tide one meets an ebb which runs like a torrent off the Grand Mabon at springs.

By night

Follow the transits as by day (leading lights 3, 4, and 5). Notice particularly that the white sector of Le Trehic light[1], which leads clear of the distant dangers, such as Le Four and Ile Dumet, leads right onto the nearby rocks; the close approach must be made in the green sector. The street lighting on the quays is good and there is no difficulty once they are reached.

Moorings and anchorage

'Le Pool' is a fair size, and provides good anchorage, though much of it is occupied by yachts on moorings. Mussel beds cover the drying banks of Le Grand Traict, but the narrow and steep-sided Chenal de Pen Bron runs up the east side of the peninsula, containing more moorings and a possible anchorage. There are no visitors' moorings, but it might be possible to borrow a mooring in Le Pool or Chenal de Pen Bron, or to anchor, after taking soundings, clear of the moorings and with a trip-line, as the bottom is foul with old chain. The ebb runs very hard in the Chenal and even in the anchorage the streams are strong.

The harbour has a curious pattern of islands called *jonchères*, with drying basins (*chambres*) behind them in which vessels lie. The original character has been changed by the building of bridges to the islands so that only one remains in its original isolated state.

The first entrance gives onto the first, La Grande Chambre. To port there is a patent slip and scrubbing hard. At one time a good place to try for a drying berth was just inside on the right, where one could set up a line to hold the yacht against Le Quai des Yachts. Fishing boats occupy most of the town side of this *chambre*, and the new fish-market hall (*Halle de Criée*) has been built on the Jonchère de

Le Croisic. Looking downstream from the boatyard at LW.

The yacht basin entrance seen from the boatyard. Note the deep-keel yacht outside against the wall.

Lenigo, making it a busy quay to moor alongside.

It is probably advisable to avoid the first four entrances and make for the Port de Plaisance in the Chambre des Vases. Deep-keel yachts can dry out against the wall outside on a hard, level bottom and those that can take the ground can enter and secure bow to a pontoon with a stern mooring. The *capitainerie*, with a shower and toilet cabin, is on the wall at the entrance.

Facilities

The facilities are those of a holiday resort and a fishing and yachting port. Banks, hotels, restaurants and all shops. Water and electricity on the pontoons. Water from the quays. At present there is no fuel berth for yachts, but fuel may be obtained from a garage in the town. Yacht yard with haul-out facilities, marine engineer and good chandlery. Ice from the *criée*.

Communications

Railway station and buses to La Baule, where there is an airport.

38. La Baule – Le Pouliguen

47°16'·4N 2°25'·4W

39. La Baule – Pornichet

47°15'·5N 2°21'·0W

Charts
BA *3216, 2646*
Imray *C39, C40*
SHOM *6825P*
Navicarte *547*

Tidal data
Tidal heights (approx)
HW – 0035 Brest springs, +0020 Brest neaps
MTL 3·0m. Index 1
Heights of tide above chart datum
MHWS 5·3m, MLWS 0·5m, MHWN 4·1m, MLWN 1·8m

Tidal streams
Approaching the Baie du Pouliguen from the west, the stream 1 mile south of the Pointe de Penchâteau runs east from –0530 Brest, maximum rate 1 knot, turning westerly at +0030 Brest.

The tidal streams in the Baie du Pouliguen are irregular in direction, the flood running generally north round the Pointe de Penchâteau and northeast towards Pornichet, while the ebb runs south or southwest, rates up to about 1 knot. In the north of the bay itself the tide tends to run always westerly. In the Pouliguen river the tidal streams can attain 4 knots at springs and care must be exercised when approaching or leaving a pontoon.

Depths
The Le Pouliguen channel dries and the rocky sill should be assumed to dry 1·2m. In the pool there is water to float vessels drawing up to 2m. The marina at Pornichet has up to 2·5m in the main berths.

Lights
1. **Les Guérandaises buoy (starboard)** 47°15'·0N 2°24'·3W Fl.G.2·5s
2. **Penchâteau buoy (port)** 47°15'·3N 2°24'·5W Fl.R.2·5s
3. **Les Petits Impairs** 47°16'·0N 2°24'·6W Fl(2)G.6s 6m6M Green metal structure
4. **Le Pouliguen, S jetty** Q.R.13m9M 171°-vis-081° White column, red top
5. **Pornichet, W breakwater head** 47°15'·5N 2°21'·1W Iso.WG.4s11m11/8M 084°-G-081°-W-084° White tower, green top
6. **Pornichet entrance west** Fl.G.2s3m2M
7. **Pornichet entrance east** Fl.R.2s3m2M

General
La Baule is a sophisticated international beach resort with a casino and innumerable hotels and restaurants of all grades. It may be reached by train, or by air to St Nazaire or its own smaller airport. There are two harbours, Le Pouliguen and Pornichet. The approach to the former dries out and it is essential for strangers to enter around high water. Pornichet is a modern marina providing 1,150 berths for yachts of all sizes. It is available at all states of the tide. The bay is sheltered from northerly and westerly winds and is often smooth in summer. Both harbours are very crowded in high season and vessels of over 10m are often turned away from Le Pouliguen.

Approach to Le Pouliguen
Le Pouliguen is situated in the NW corner of the bay of the same name, and is some 6 miles E of Le Croisic. The best approach from any direction is the western passage between the Pointe de Penchâteau red pillar buoy on the west side of the bay and the ledges and rocks to the SE, which extend nearly 4 miles to the Grand Charpentier lighthouse. Even from the east it is better to approach south of the Grand Charpentier along the Chenal du Nord in the entry to the Loire. There is an inshore passage which can be followed using British Admiralty *3216* or a French chart; this channel joins the western channel south of La Vieille beacon (starboard).

The approach is sheltered from the N through W to SW, but southerly swell breaks in the shallow water, and it is fully exposed to the SE. The sands shift, and if the available margin of depth is very small it is worth seeking the advice of local yachtsmen or the club boatman.

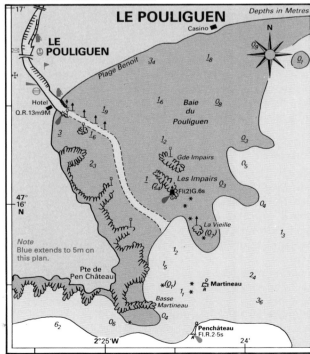

Plan 45

Looking NW into Le Pouliguen at half tide.

Entering at half tide in 1992 with the church spire visible over the hotel (see text). The slender white light tower on the west pier-head arrowed.

Leave the Penchâteau red pillar buoy 100m to port. Thence steer 020° to leave the Basse Martineau buoy (port) also to port. There is an anchorage about 400m NNW of this buoy where a yacht may await the tide in good weather.

Entrance

Shortly before high water proceed towards the entrance, leaving La Vieille beacon (starboard) and Les Petits Impairs tower (starboard) well to starboard, and two red beacons 150m to port. Close to the harbour entrance are five green starboard beacons, the third and fourth a triangular arrangement of three parallel poles. The fifth, a slender wooden pole, marks the tip of a spur of the training wall, covered at HW. To port there are two red beacons, the outer being unpainted and lacking a topmark in 1992, the inner one marking the edge of the entrance channel. The channel usually lies closer to the red beacons than to the starboard ones and the entrance should be approached with the top

of the church spire visible to the left of the tall right-hand section of the hotel (see photograph).

Enter with the church spire open between the pier heads. The lighthouse on the west pier head is a very slender white structure with a red top. This is left to port and the vessel then proceeds between stone embankments. Special care must be taken on near approach to the entrance as the channel is narrow, between high sands on either side. The slender wooden beacon on the starboard side lies well inside the line of rather thicker iron beacons marking the approach and must not be overlooked.

By night

The lights are few in number and some local knowledge is desirable for a night entry.

Mooring

The west side of the river is mainly reserved for fishing boats.

There are yacht pontoons along the east bank all the way up to the road bridge, with visitors' berths near the entrance. Berths are allocated by the yacht club boatman.

Facilities

Water and electricity on the pontoons. The fuel berth on the starboard side on entering had been removed in 1992 but should be reinstalled in 1994. The fuel berth upstream of the bridge by the yacht club cannot be reached by masted vessels.

Pontoons on the east side of the river. Harbour staff may direct you to a berth. Beware of the strong stream when entering or leaving a berth.

All the facilities of a sophisticated yachting centre. The yacht club, with showers and toilets, is a large and clearly labelled building on the La Baule side above the first road bridge. It is hospitable to visitors and its boatman acts as harbourmaster. There are all shops handy in Le Pouliguen, and yacht yards, chandlers and marine engineers are all close at hand. There are many hotels and restaurants in this holiday town.

Approach to Pornichet

From the Penchâteau and Guérandaises light buoys, the white lighthouse at the end of the outer mole can be made out amongst the buildings at the eastern end of La Baule, bearing 083°, and course should be altered towards it. An unlit green conical buoy marking the northernmost extremity of the Guérandaises shoal is left to starboard.

Entrance

The entrance faces north, and it is not until close approach that the red and green beacons marking the underwater projections from the pierheads will become clear; course must be altered to pass between them.

Looking east over Pornichet. The Loire estuary is visible in the distance.

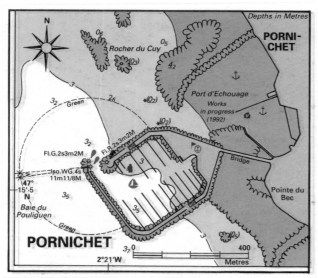

Plan 46

By night

The approach is covered by the white sector of Pornichet pierhead light (Iso.WG.4s), which can be seen from 081° to 084°. This sector just excludes the Penchâteau light buoy and the Guérandaises unlit buoy (starboard); the Guerandaises light buoy lies 400m S of this white sector. The beacons in the entrance show flashing red and green lights.

Mooring

There are 10 pontoons (A-J) on the southern side of the harbour and 4 (K-N) on the northern. The heads of all these are allocated to visitors, together with the whole of pontoon J and the west side of pontoon I, although these are only suitable for boats of under 6m length. All the main berths carry a depth of 2·8m. As the bottom is soft mud, vessels of deeper draught will sink their keels into it and remain upright.

Facilities

One of the best equipped marinas on the coast.

VHF Ch 9 0800–2000. Fuel pontoon immediately to port on entry. Water and electricity on the pontoons; showers, toilets, ice, restaurant and chandlery shop (chart agent) in marina, with limited groceries, a wine merchant and a laundry. Yacht yard with 2-tonne travel-lift; large slipway and grid.

Across the causeway to the mainland there are many shops, hotels and restaurants.

40. Pornic

47°06'·5N 2°07'·0W

Charts

BA *3126, 2646*
Imray *C40*
SHOM *5039P*
Navicarte *547*

Tidal data

Tidal heights (approx)

HW −0035 Brest springs, +0020 Brest neaps
MTL 3·1m. Index 2
Heights of tide above chart datum
MHWS 5·6m, MLWS 0·6m, MHWN 4·3m, MLWN 2·0m

Tidal streams

Outside the flood runs E and the ebb W, 2 knots springs. The streams in the harbour are weak.

Depths

There is 1·5m to the fairway buoy. The marina entrance is dredged to 2m but can silt between dredgings. Inside the marina 2·0m at pontoons A to D but 1·5m at the visitors' pontoons. The depths shoal rapidly at the entrance to the old harbour and the channel to the inner basin dries 1m, the basin itself drying from 1·3m at the north quays to 1·8m at the south quays.

Lights

1. **Saint Gildas** 47°08'·0N 2°14'·8W Q.WRG.23m11-6M 264°-R-308°-G-078°-W-088°-R-174°-W-180°-G-264° Metal framework structure on white house RC *NZ* (−·/−−·) 308·5kHz 40M
2. **Pointe de Noëveillard** 47°06'.6N 2°06'·9W Oc(3+1) WRG.12s22m13-9M Shore-G-051°-W-079°-R-shore White square tower, green top, white dwelling
3. **Marina elbow** Fl(2+1)7s4m3M Grey pole
4. **Off marina SW breakwater head** Fl(2)R.6s4m4M Black column, red top
5. **Off marina E breakwater head** Fl.G.2·5s4m2M Black column, green top
6. **Gourmalon breakwater head** Fl(2)G.6s4m8M White mast, green top
7. **Fairway buoy (RW)** 47°06'·5N 2°06'·6W LFl.10s
8. **Inner basin entrance** Q.R to port, Q.G to starboard

General

The Baie de Bourgneuf is a big wide bay east of the Loire, formed between the mainland to the north and east and the Ile de Noirmoutier on the south. The bay is exposed to the west and shallows progressively. There is plenty of water for yachts and although there are many shoals and rocks they are, with the exception of the Kerouars bank in the northern part, well marked, so that there are few navigational difficulties except in thick weather. There is no exit from the bay to the south between

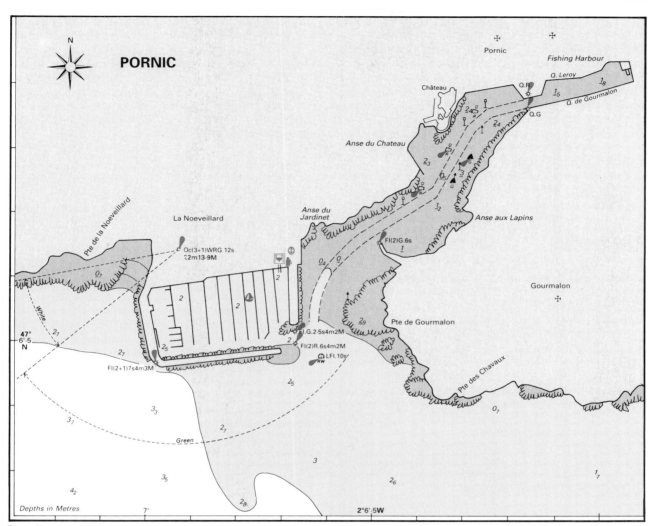

PORNIC

N

Pornic

Fishing Harbour

Q. Leroy

Q.R

Château

1_8

1_5

Q. de Gourmalon

2_4

2_4

Q.G

Anse du Chateau

2_3

0_5

1_2

Anse du Jardinet

Anse aux Lapins

Pte de la Noeveillard

La Noeveillard

Fl(2)G.6s
1

0_7

Oc(3+1)WRG.12s
22m13-9M

0_4

0_2

Gourmalon

White

2

2

2

Pte de Gourmalon

47°
6'·5
N

2_7

2_9

2_5

2

Fl.G.2·5s4m2M

2

Fl(2)R.6s4m2M

2_7

2_5

LFl.10s
RW

3_3

Fl(2+1)7s4m3M

2_5

3_7

Green

3

0_7

Pte des Chavaux

2_7

3_5

1_7

4_2

2_8

2_6

Depths in Metres

7'

2°6'·5W

Plan 47

Pornic, looking NE. The small right-hand yacht is approaching
the fairway buoy on the curve of the muddy water.

Ile de Noirmoutier and the mainland except for shallow-draught vessels at high water, as there is a causeway, drying at low water, across which there is insufficient depth at any state of the tide.

The harbours, however, are poor, except for Pornic and L'Herbaudière. Those on Noirmoutier are described in the next chapter. Pornic harbour, situated halfway along the northern shore of the Baie de Bourgneuf, is rather off the route for foreign yachts. The harbour is easy of access in reasonable weather and supports considerable local yachting activity. It is a pretty little place which is well worth a visit. Bluebeard's castle overlooks the harbour just seaward of the quays.

Approach

In the outer approach from the SW the outlying dangers to the north of Ile de Noirmoutier are well marked by a series of buoys and towers. From the NW care must be taken to avoid the Banc de Kerouars, which is unmarked except for a buoy, La Couronnée (starboard), one of the channel buoys for the Loire entrance, one mile off its western end and Nord Couronnée buoy (N cardinal), marking a rock which dries 1·9m. The least depth near the eastern end is 1m and is unmarked. To the north of the bank there is a passage over ½ mile wide and ½ mile off the land, or entry can be made south of the bank if it is not safely covered.

Leave the tower of Notre Dame (BRB topmark two spheres) about ½ mile to starboard and steer for the RW fairway buoy at the entrance to Pornic, leaving it to starboard on arrival.

Entrance

Marina

Do not attempt entry within 1½ hours either side of low water at springs. Enter the marina between the two red (port) and the green (starboard) steel columns. These columns and their associated lights are placed in the entrance and not on the break-

Leave the RW fairway buoy to starboard and enter the marina between the right-hand red metal beacon and the green metal beacon.

water heads. Once inside keep clear of the south wall, which is lined with submerged rocks. The east breakwater head is also foul, with a partly submerged knuckle extending diagonally into the marina. Manoeuvring among the pontoons is not easy in an onshore wind. There are 165 berths for visitors. Yachts of up to 10m length can secure to pontoons P2 and P3 and those over 10m to P1 and the ends of the other pontoons.

Facilities

VHF Ch 9. Water and electricity on the pontoons, showers and toilets, ice. Fuel berth, 20-tonne travel-lift. Café/restaurant and food shops in the marina. Engineers and sailmaker in the town.

Old port

The inner harbour dries about 1·3m, and it is assumed that no attempt will be made to go up the harbour unless the tide has risen sufficiently to float the yacht there. On this basis there is sufficient water in the outer part of the harbour provided that course is set roughly near the centre. Just beyond the marina a beacon (starboard) marks a rock to starboard. The breakwater, which extends from the E side of the entrance (Pointe de Gourmalon), is marked at its end by a green beacon.

Above the breakwater the channel is marked by red and green beacons and buoys. The beacon posts should not be confused with various other posts, mostly white, erected for swimmers to dive from. There is a silting problem in the harbour east of the marina entrance. The RW fairway buoy must be left to starboard and entry should not be attempted near LW.

By night

The white sector of the main light[2] clears the Banc de Kerouars and Notre Dame rock. The marina and Gourmalon yacht harbour can be reached, but strangers should not attempt to go up the harbour.

Pornic, looking down the inner fish harbour, which dries, towards Bluebeard's castle.

Anchorage and mooring

Berth in the marina. Yachts which can take the ground can use the Gourmalon yacht harbour.

Yachts can also berth alongside the quays in the inner harbour. The quay on the north side of the entrance to the inner harbour is prohibited, and immediately inside the entrance to port is the berth reserved for the Noirmoutier ferry. The north side is the best, though it is principally used by fishing vessels. Not only is the water deeper here (dries 1·3m), but the quay is stone faced, with many recessed ladders. On the south side, where the local yachts mostly berth, the mud dries about 1·8m; the quay is faced with vertical wooden rubbing piles, though there are again plenty of ladders.

Facilities

The facilities of a small holiday town. All shops, several restaurants and hotels. Marine engineer. Diesel at the south quay; petrol close by. Club house and showers at Gourmalon yacht harbour.

Communications

Bus and branch railway line.

41. Ile de Noirmoutier

L'Herbaudière 47°02'N 2°18'W

Charts

BA *2646, 3216* (as SHOM *6825P*, northern part of island only)
Imray *C40*
SHOM *5039P*
Navicarte *549*

Tidal data

Tidal heights (approx)

Tidal information is given below for the NE side of the island; for Fromentine see page 159.
HW −0040 Brest springs, +0015 Brest neaps
MTL 3·0m. Index 2
Heights of tide above chart datum
MHWS 5·3m, MLWS 0·6m, MHWN 4·1m, MLWN 1·9m

Tidal streams

In the middle of the entrance to the Baie de Bourgneuf the tide is rotary clockwise: at +0425 Brest, NW 1·5 knots springs; at −0325 Brest, 1·7 knots SE; at −0025 Brest, turning to SW; at +0225 Brest, NW 1·0 knot springs.

In Chenal de la Grise, at the NW end of the island, NE begins at −0625 Brest, 1·5 knots springs; SW begins −0100 Brest, 2 knots springs. Off Bois de la Chaise SE begins −0600 Brest, NW begins −0040 Brest, spring rates 1·5 knots.

Depths

L'Herbaudière has 1·5m to 2·2m at the pontoons; the entrance channel is dredged to 1·5m. Bois de la Chaise has about 1·5m. Noirmoutier dries about 2·5m.

Lights

1. **Ile du Pilier** 47°02'·6N 2°21'·6W Fl(3)20s33m29M Grey stone tower
   Auxiliary light Q.R.10m11M On same structure, covering Les Boers
2. **Pointe de Saint Gildas** 47°08'·0N 2°14'·8W Q.WRG.23m11·6M 264°-R-308°-G-078°-W-088°-R-174°-W-180°-G-264° Metal framework structure on white house. RC *NZ* (−·/−−··) 308·5kHz 40M
3. **Basse du Martroger** 47°02'·6N 2°17'·1W Q.WRG. 11m9·6M 033°-G-055°-W-060°-R-095°-G-124°-W-153°-R-201°-W-240°-R-033° N card beacon tower
4. **Passe de la Grise S card buoy** 47°01'·7N 2°19'·9W Q(6)+LFl.15s
5. **La Pierre Moine** 47°03'·4N 2°12'·4W Fl(2)6s14m9M Isolated danger tower
6. **L'Herbaudière west jetty head** 47°01'·6N 2°17'·9W Oc(2+1)WG.12s9m10/7M 187·5°-W-190°-G-187·5° White column and shelter, green top. Horn 30s

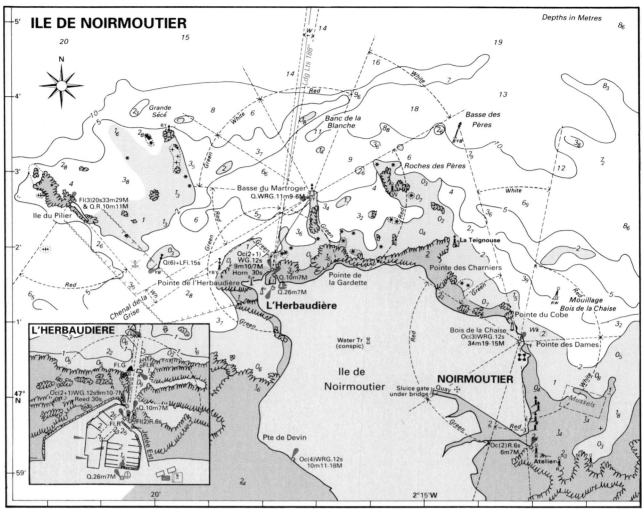

Plan 48

7. **Ldg Lts 188°** *Front* Q.10m7M 098°-vis-278° Grey post
   Rear Q.26m7M 098°-vis-278° Grey post
8. **East jetty head** Q(2)R.6s8m4M Red tripod
9. **Lifeboat slip** Fl.R.2s Red casing
10. **Entrance channel** buoys two starboard Fl.G.2s, one port Fl(2)R.5s
11. **Pointe des Dames** 47°00'·7N 2°13'·3W Oc(3)WRG. 12s34m19-15M 016·5°-G-057°-R-124°-G-165°-W-191°-R-267°-W-357°-R-016·5° White square tower
12. **Port de Noirmoutier jetty head** 46°59'·3N 2°13'·1W Oc(2)R.6s6m7M White column, red top

General

The Ile de Noirmoutier is a long, narrow, sandy island measuring about 9 miles from NW to SE. It is separated from the mainland by the narrow Goulet de Fromentine. North of the Fromentine bridge is a causeway carrying the old road from the mainland to the island. This is so high that although it covers at high water it is not safe for a deep-keel boat to attempt to cross over.

The island, which was invaded by the English in 1388, by the Spanish in 1524 and by the Dutch in 1674, is now invaded only by crowds of summer holidaymakers. L'Herbaudière, in the north, has a

marina in a rather bleak spot. It is, however, a convenient passage anchorage. Bois de la Chaise is an open anchorage, though with enough shelter to be the summer base for yachts. Noirmoutier town dries and can only be reached near high water (high water springs for deep-draught yachts), and Fromentine, on the mainland by the bridge, is approached over a shallow bar exposed to westerly winds and swell, though it is easily accessible at high water in offshore winds. There are shoals and rocks extending a long way off the island; they are adequately marked, but call for care in the approach.

South of Lorient, and more especially south of the Loire, one must keep a lookout for the *nombreux orins de casiers* which appear round the N and W coasts of Noirmoutier. To the north, a line of lobster pots is usually marked by a dan buoy at each end. From Noirmoutier to the south a line of very small floats will be seen to stretch between the two dan buoys and one should avoid crossing the line.

Approach and entrance

The island is well placed in the middle of the French charts, SHOM *5039* and Navicarte *549.*

There is at present no British Admiralty equivalent, but British Admiralty *3216*, showing the northern part of Noirmoutier, is adequate for entry to L'Herbaudière from the north.

Approaching from the N, the landmarks to look for are the tall twin lighthouses on Ile du Pilier, the conspicuous red and white radio mast on the NW tip of the island and an easily identified water tower, with a wide tank and a flat conical top, painted red, to the SE of L'Herbaudière. Although there are a number of shoals – Le Four, La Blanche, La Lambarde, Kerouars – to avoid, they lie in the approaches to St Nazaire and the Loire and are consequently very well marked.

L'Herbaudière

If making for L'Herbaudière, the entrance lies 500m E of the radio mast. Steer for Basse du Martroger tower, leaving Grand Sécé N cardinal tower ¾ mile to starboard. ½ mile NW of Martroger tower, when the radio mast bears 195°, the harbour can be identified by a slender chimney close to the west and the large red-roofed lifeboat house to the east of the entrance. From here the entrance channel should bear 190°, marked by one lateral port and two starboard buoys and by two port-hand beacons.

In conditions of poor visibility it is not easy to identify the marks and in 1993 the leading lights[7] were established. These are automatically switched on in daylight if visibility is reduced.

Bois de la Chaise

Bound for Bois de la Chaise, it is best to pass at least 1½ miles N of Martroger tower to avoid the Banc de la Blanche, with a least depth of 1·8m. Passing close to the south of Banc de la Blanche buoy (N cardinal), steer for Pierre Moine BRB tower and alter to leave Basse des Pères buoy (E cardinal) close to starboard, with Pierre Moine tower 1·3 miles to port. From this point Noirmoutier spire is conspicuous bearing 182° and a course of 153° should lead to the small RW buoy marking the Bois de la Chaise anchorage, ½ mile NW of the Pointe des Dames. A wooden pier projects from this headland, which is steep and tree-covered, with only the top of the lighthouse showing above the trees.

Anchorage

There are a few moorings for visitors inshore of the RW buoy and there is plenty of room to anchor in from 1·5m to 3m NE or SE of the pier but clear of a wreck (2m) 400m ENE of the pier.

From the S or SE

Unless going to Fromentine, it will be necessary to clear Les Boers, after which one can pass through the Chenal de la Grise. This channel carries 3·3m. It is marked on its NW side by a buoy (S cardinal) and on its SE side by a beacon (W cardinal) marking Rocher Patou, off Pointe de l'Herbaudière. This beacon should be given a berth of at least 200m. Basse du Martroger tower (N cardinal) in transit with the Rocher Patou beacon, bearing 050°, clears all the dangers of Les Boers. A midchannel lead is the tower of Ste Marie church, on the mainland, in transit with Martroger tower, bearing 058°. In the channel, pass rather closer to the buoy than to the beacon and continue until the entrance of L'Herbaudière harbour has been identified by the large red-roofed lifeboat building on the east side and the slender chimney behind the west jetty. Steer for the entrance when it bears 190°.

If proceeding to Bois de la Chaise, steer to leave the Basse du Martroger tower 200m to starboard. There are shoals to the E and ENE of Basse du Martroger; although there is a thin pole beacon on these shoals, it is ½ mile inside the northern edge. A safe course is to keep the Rocher Patou beacon off Pointe de l'Herbaudière in transit with Martroger tower, bearing 230° astern, until the Basse des Pères buoy (E cardinal) bears 090°, then alter course to pass 200m south of it. Thence steer to give the Pointe des Dames a reasonable berth. The anchorage is described above.

By night

The following directions lead to L'Herbaudière.

From the northwest Approach in the white sector of Basse du Martroger light[3] bearing 124° to 153° and then in the white sector of L'Herbaudière light[6] bearing 187·5° to 190°. Identify the leading lights[7] Q on 188° and follow this transit towards the entrance. Finally, leave the Fl.G light buoys[10] close to starboard.

From the south Go through the Chenal de la Grise in the white sector of Basse du Martroger light[3], bearing between 055° and 060°. When L'Herbaudière light turns white, steer in this sector on 187·5° to 190° and pick up the transit of the leading lights[7] Q on 188° leading towards the entrance, leaving the Fl.G light buoys[10] close to starboard.

L'Herbaudière

There are two starboard-hand buoys and one port in the near approach, together with two port-hand beacons. The channel is no wider than the entrance, so do not stray. Alter to starboard on passing the west breakwater and then round the slipway and lifeboat station to port to enter the marina. The visitors' pontoon (F) is on the west side in the entrance of the marina with 2·3m depth.

Facilities

Water and electricity on the pontoons. Fuel berth, 25-tonne crane, slipway and grid. Showers, toilets and launderette; telephones, ice, café/restaurant, *superette* with provisions, fruit and wine. Engineers and chandlers. In the village there are shops, but a bank was not sighted. Large camping site on the west point.

Looking SW over L'Herbaudière near LW. Radio mast arrowed.

Entering L'Herbaudière at half tide. The radio mast, slender chimney and lifeboat station make good landmarks.

Bois de la Chaise

This open anchorage is sheltered from the W and S. It is exposed to the N and E, but the fetch is not more than 5 miles and, in summer, yachts lie on moorings here. It is an attractive situation, though the facilities are limited. There are some moorings for visitors and space to anchor outside, keeping clear of the wreck some 400m ENE of the pier. Land at the steps halfway along the pier; the end must be kept clear for the ferries.

Facilities

Two restaurants, a paper shop and a *patisserie* (which does not sell bread). Good shops in Noirmoutier, 1½ miles' walk. There is a big camp site behind the beach to the south. In the summer a general shop opens to serve the camp, with a butcher in July and August. To reach them, it is easier to land on the beach to the south of the anchorage than to walk round from the pier.

Noirmoutier

This port is reached by a long, straight, narrow channel. It should be regarded as drying 2·5m and is therefore not accessible to deep-draught yachts at neaps.

Should a visit by sea be intended it is strongly recommended that an inspection at low water be made beforehand. Bicycles can be hired at L'Herbaudière and the ride is pleasant over this flat island.

Noirmoutier is a busy port and the quays are occupied by fishing boats and the flat barges used for oyster culture. The bottom is hard rock with a mud overlay and on occasion the channel is scoured by opening the sluices to the inland water. This takes away a foot or so of mud on the first sluice and leaves the sloping mud banks along the quays in an unstable condition.

Enter with the tide; not all the outside berths will have mud, and it is best to pick a berth using a sounding pole to test for mud, and then to tend warps until safely grounded. It will probably be necessary to raft to another yacht, and on occasion rafted boats may tip and cross masts, or even fall outwards into the scoured channel.

Looking up towards Noirmoutier during a bicycle recce.

Approach and entrance

South of the channel training wall a rocky shelf, covered with oyster beds, stretches out some four miles to the ENE, with several passages marked by beacons. The old approach runs north of a curving line of 5 red (port) beacons on the northern edge of the shelf. This approach does not dry as far in as Atelier, the second beacon out from the training wall, but since there is a drying 2·5m patch at the entrance it is more convenient to wait until there is sufficient water in the channel and use the line of green beacons to approach along the shore.

Coming south from the Bois de la Chaise anchorage, when there is considered to be enough water, keep about 400m offshore, passing over a sandy bottom (drying 1·6m) inshore of a mussel bed. A line of green (starboard) beacons marking the ends of stone groynes will be seen along the shore,

Noirmoutier. The channel has just been scoured and the outermost yacht is resting on gravel.

curving to starboard into the entrance of the channel. While taking soundings, follow the line of beacons round to the entrance and thence continue up the marked channel to the town. The best water at the entrance is on the south side near the training wall.

Moor to the first quay on the starboard hand, before the crane is reached. Farther up the quays are shallower. The mud is very soft, so the keel will probably sink in, with any luck leaving the yacht upright.

Facilities

All shops; restaurants and hotels. Shipyard and marine engineer. A pleasant town.

Fromentine

46°54'N 2°10'W

Tidal data

Tidal heights (approx)

HW −0045 Brest springs, +0015 Brest neaps
MTL 3·2m. Index 1
Heights of tide above chart datum
MHWS 5·3m, MLWS 1·1m, MHWN 4·2m, MLWN 2·0m

Tidal streams

Ingoing stream begins −0530 Brest, 5 knots springs; outgoing begins −0130 Brest, 8 knots springs.

Depths

The bar varies in position and depth; it dries about 1·5m.

Lights

No lights are included here. It is not advisable to attempt entry at night.

General

The Goulet de Fromentine, between the south of Ile de Noirmoutier and the mainland, has not a very good reputation among yachtsmen, as the entrance is on a lee shore if the wind is in any westerly direction and the bar of sand dries and shifts in position. The streams are very strong in the narrows and run seaward for 8½ hours, from about 1½hrs before high water to 1½hrs after low water. The channel is, however, well buoyed, and as it is used all the year round by the Ile d'Yeu ferry it may be regarded as fit for navigation in reasonable weather conditions.

The editor's visit in 1992 was most unpleasant. The substantial moorings between the bridge and the Fromentine pier had been removed and yellow buoys marked the bathing area off the beach. The moorings above the pier were not heavy enough to hold in the strong outgoing tide and a force 6 NE wind. Large clumps of Japanese seaweed were float-

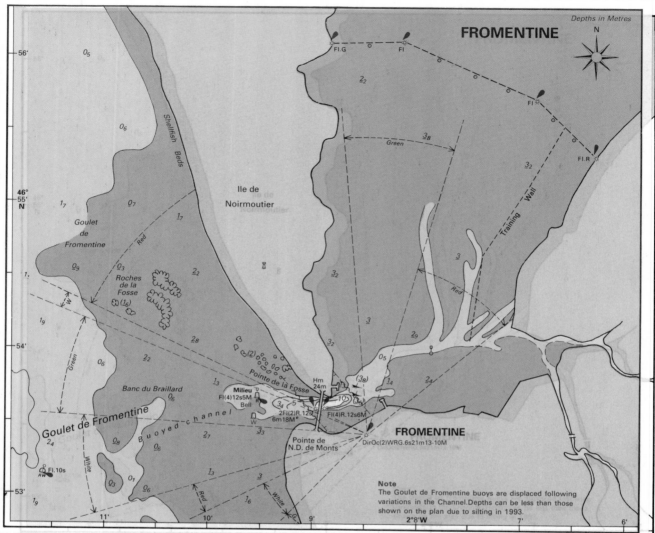

Plan 49

ing down on the tide and winding round mooring chains and propellers. An uncomfortable night was spent at anchor on the Noirmoutier side. Conditions were the same the following day and it was not possible to attempt the crossing of the causeway to confirm Mr Paul Dane's directions (below).

Approach and entrance from the NW

Deep-draught vessels must on no account approach from the Baie de Bourgneuf, as there is a causeway which dries 3m with guide posts and raised refuges between the island and the mainland. In 1987 Mr Paul Dane surveyed the passage in a bilge-keel ketch drawing 1·1m. He has kindly supplied the directions included in this edition.

The coast of Noirmoutier and the mainland south of it merge together into a line of sand dunes when viewed from seaward. There are several windmills painted white with black tops on the Noirmoutier side, and a very conspicuous water tower. Notre Dame des Monts lighthouse, with a water tower in the background, is at Fromentine. Half a mile seaward of the bridge are two beacon towers, the northern one red and the southern one white.

Fromentine, moorings and ferry jetty on the Noirmoutier side. Wind force 6, tide 4 knots. Note the weed on the mooring buoy and on the chains to the boats!

The sea shoals some 6 miles west of the entrance, before the landmarks can be located if the weather is at all thick. Accordingly, it is best to fix the vessel's position precisely on the buoys SW of Les Boers, Réaumur (W cardinal) and Le Bavard (S cardinal), if approaching from the NW.

Although the Ile d'Yeu ferry uses the port near HW, strangers would be unwise to attempt it in a strong onshore wind, or if there is a swell high enough to break on the shoals. If it is not rough and the approach is made during the last two hours of the flood, there will be plenty of water over the outer shoals, the shallowest being Basse de l'Aigle, with 2·9m over it. The landfall buoy Fromentine (RW, bell) is situated 1·95 miles at 264° from Fromentine lighthouse.

From this buoy pairs of red and green buoys mark the channel across the bar to the beacon towers, one red and one white. Passing between them the channel deepens, and a starboard-hand buoy indicates the channel to the main navigation arch of the bridge, which is clearly marked (clearance 27m). A red buoy (port) marks the lead of the channel to the Fromentine pier. To the north of this buoy are two wrecks, exposed at LW.

Approach from the SW

This really starts from the Basse de l'Aigle buoy, from which you set course for the landfall buoy, Oc.4s (spherical RW with radar reflector) 46°53'·1N 02°11'·6W. On the flood tide there is a set to the south. Before reaching the landfall buoy you will see a large water tower on the S end of Noirmoutier and the very large bridge joining the mainland and the island. The channel is well buoyed and most of the buoys have radar reflectors. Buoys are changed when necessary by the ferry operators. The centre span of the bridge is lit.

Anchorage

Depending on draught, either off the jetty on the E side of Pte de la Fosse (Noirmoutier), with less tidal stream, or off the shore just west of the ferry jetty off Fromentine and just east of the cable area. The buoys to the E of the Fromentine ferry jetty are not too suitable, as the ground tackle is light and there is a lack of water at LWS. The streams in the fairway are very strong, about 5 knots, but they moderate towards the shore. Anchor as far in as draught and tide will allow.

Owing to the strength of the tide it is said to be unwise to leave a yacht unattended while at anchor, and this would certainly be true at the top of springs. If going in to the Pte de la Fosse side, beware of the E-boat wrecks just N of the channel; they lie between the first and second red buoys after you pass under the bridge, so turn in either before the first red buoy or after the second. It is not practical to row across the stream to Fromentine in the dinghy and the bridge is a long way round.

Facilities

Water at both ferry jetties; ask the ferry operators. Fromentine is a small holiday resort with hotels, restaurants and small shops. Ferry to Ile d'Yeu. At Pte de la Fosse, on Noirmoutier, there is a small hotel, which combines a bar/restaurant, tobacconist and small shop for bread etc., about 3 minutes' walk

from the ferry office. Alternatively, take a walk or taxi over the bridge to Fromentine.

Passage north from Fromentine over causeway

French directions state that there should be more than 1·5m over the causeway 2hrs before HWS but not more than 1m at HWN.

The directions below are compiled from Mr Paul Dane's survey in *Pampa Mia*, a bilge-keel ketch drawing 1·1m, in July 1987. The chart used was French, SHOM *5039P*, but Navicarte *549* might be preferred. The editor was unable to confirm the directions in 1992 as conditions were unsuitable.

The causeway is about 2 miles long and 30m wide, constructed of stones and small rocks. The roadway is *pavée* and about 10m wide. It is the highest object in the immediate area, and calculations put the height as being 2·64m above St Nazaire datum. (Note: SHOM *5039* shows sand drying 3m S of Bal à Hune and drying 2·7m N of the refuge.)

There are three refuges or *bals à hune* on the causeway. On either side of the eastern refuge are beacons to indicate the best place to cross. The starboard beacon is west and the port beacon (to be left to starboard going north) is east of the refuge, which is a wooden structure mounted on a stone and concrete plinth, the top of which is 2·1m above the level of the causeway. From this it follows that when the plinth is just covered the causeway may be crossed between the refuge and the port-hand beacon with a minimum depth of 2·1m.

The tide makes from the south, comes in quickly and runs over the causeway across the sands to meet the tide rising on the north side. From a position 100m off the end of the Fromentine ferry jetty, make good a course of 030° up the channel to pass 15m to the east of a spar which is located approximately 400m from the eastern *bal à hune* on a bearing of 199°. Do not borrow east, as there is a training wall further E, covered at HW. After passing the *bal à hune*, set course to make good 355° to clear the oyster beds.

Fine on the port bow you will see a prominent water tower bearing 351° from the *bal à hune*, and on the starboard bow, north of Pornic, another water tower with a RW radio mast close west bearing 002° from the *bals à hune*. This course crosses La Préoire rocky plateau, drying 2·9m. To avoid it, turn onto 040° 2½ miles from the *bals à hune*, when the water tower on the southern end of Noirmoutier bears 205°. This course will lead to Le Fain channel, where there is sufficient water to leave Goeland lateral starboard buoy to starboard (although it is a starboard-hand channel buoy when going south) and a green (starboard) beacon to port.

The way is then clear to Pornic. As an alternative, those equipped with Navicarte *549* can find their way across the extensive rocky shelf south of the port of Noirmoutier to an anchorage off Bois de la Chaise.

42. Ile d'Yeu

Port Joinville 46°44'N 2°21'W

Charts
BA *2663*
Imray *C40*
SHOM *6853P, 6890*
Navicarte *549*

Tidal data

Tidal heights (approx)
HW −0020 Brest springs, +0010 Brest neaps
MTL 3·1m. Index 0
Heights of tide above chart datum
MHWS 5·3m, MLWS 0·8m, MHWN 4·2m, MLWN 2·1m

Tidal streams
There is considerable variation in the directions and rates of the streams round the island and tidal charts should be consulted. Generally the streams are weak, but there are local variations close inshore and there can be 2 knots at springs off the NW tip of the island, running NE at −0400 Brest and SW at +0200 Brest.

Depths
The principal harbour, Port Joinville, is dredged to 1·5m, with a wet basin (3·7m) and a marina (2·5m). Port de la Meule dries, but there is an anchorage outside that can be used in offshore winds, as can that further east in Anse de Vieilles.

Lights

1. **Petite Foule-Feu Principal** 46°43'·1N 2°22'·9W
   Fl.5s56m24M Square white tower green lantern
   Trumpet (1) 60s RC *YE* (− ·−−/·) 303kHz 100M
2. **Les Chiens Perrins** 46°43'·6N 2°24'·6W
   Q(9)WG.15s16m8/4M 330°-G-350°-W-200° Beacon tower, W card
3. **Pointe des Corbeaux** 46°41'·4N 2°17'·1W
   Fl(2+1)R.15s25m20M White square tower, red top
4. **La Sablaire** buoy (S card) 46°43'·7N 2°19'·4W
   Q(6)+LFl.15s
5. **Port Joinville NW jetty head** 46°43'·8N 2°20'·7W
   Oc(3)WG.12s6m11/9M 150°-W-232°-G-279°-W-285°-G-shore White metal frame, green top
   Horn(3)30s
6. **Quai du Canada Ldg Lts 219°** *Front* Q.R.11m6M
   Pylon
   Rear 85m from front Q.R.16m5M Mast
7. **Passerelle de la Galiotte inner end** Fl(2)R.5s1M
   Gare Maritime pier head Iso.G.4s7m6M
8. **Port de la Meule** 46°41'·7N 2°20'·6W
   Oc(3)WG.12s9m11/9M 150°-W-232°-G-279°-W-041·5° Grey square tower, red top

General

The Ile d'Yeu, situated about halfway between Belle Ile and La Rochelle, is the furthest from the mainland of the outlying islands off the coast of the Bay of Biscay. It measures about 5 miles long and 2 miles across. The only deep harbour, Port Joinville, is an important fishing port, especially for tunny, with good berths at the quays and an anchorage outside sheltered from the prevailing winds. The town is a pleasant one, with excellent facilities, as the island is a popular one for visitors.

The south coast of the island is very rocky and deeply indented by the action of the Atlantic seas. There are two bays that can be used as temporary anchorages in offshore winds. In one of these is the narrow winding inlet which forms Port de la Meule, which, although Lilliputian, is the only other harbour in the island. The other is Anse des Vieilles, near the SE corner of the island. The bay west of the ruined château looks inviting, but from the land it is seen to be full of rocks.

Despite its lack of good harbours Ile d'Yeu appears very prosperous, perhaps because the fishing industry is so active. The houses are whitewashed, with brightly painted doors and shutters. The whole island seems trim and well cared for; it is high, windswept and bracing.

The coastline is magnificent, especially on the southern side, where, overlooking a rock-studded bay, there are the ruins of an eleventh-century castle, much damaged by the English, complete with dungeons and moats. In recent history Marshal Pétain was imprisoned near Port Joinville and his simple tomb is to be seen in the cemetery there. The island is well worth a visit and, although the marina is very crowded in the summer, it provides a convenient port of call when bound for La Rochelle.

Port Joinville

This harbour, on the north side of the Ile d'Yeu, is exposed to N and E winds, though the extension to the NW mole has improved the shelter. Swell enters in strong winds from these directions and there is sometimes a surge during gales from other directions. None of this, however, affects the berths in the yacht marina or in the wet basin, which are completely sheltered. It is the only safe harbour in the island.

Approach and entrance
The high water tower will be seen just behind the town; in the distance this is more conspicuous than the island's main lighthouse. The town and the breakwaters at the harbour entrance are easy to locate from seaward; an approach with the water tower bearing 224° will lead in.

On the east side of the entrance is the Passerelle de la Galiotte, a walkway on concrete columns with an elbow giving the outer half a lead of ENE, outside which are a 0·2m drying patch and a red can buoy 100m NE of the head. The NW breakwater arm has been extended and the light has been moved to a metal frame tower. The old light tower is still in position, but no longer lit.

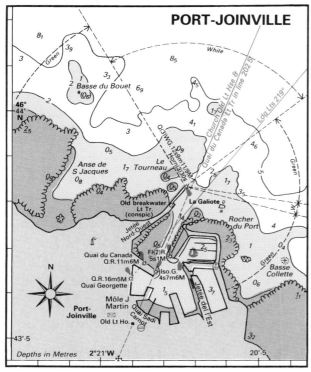

Plan 50

Anchorage and mooring

There is an anchorage in 3 to 4m (sand and mud) ½M east of the port in Anse de Ker Châlon, a bay with rocky outcrops on either side, Rocher Ronde to the W (drying 2·3m) and some rocks in the sand close inshore. It is advisable to keep at least 600m offshore. In the port beware of the grid, whose position is marked by red lines on the wall of the west side of the Jetée de l'Est, with its large ice-factory building.

There are only three pontoons in the marina, which can easily become crowded. The harbour-master likes visitors to telephone (51 58 38 11) to arrange a berth before arrival, or to call on VHF Ch 9. Entry to the wet basin is possible two hours either side of high water. It is intended for the fishing fleet, but yachts may moor by arrangement with the harbourmaster. Keep clear of the west side of the harbour and the ferry terminal.

Facilities

Water and electricity on the pontoons, fuel berth at entrance to marina. Toilets, showers and telephones in the marina. Ice from the factory. 5-tonne crane, slip, grid, shipyard, marine engineer, chandlery at fishermen's cooperative, sailmaker (who is, how-ever, more used to trawlers' riding sails than to yacht work). In the town are banks, hotels, restau-rants, all the usual shops, a good supermarket and, all-importantly, several bicycle-hire firms.

There is a regular ferry service to Fromentine, on the mainland; also, in summer, to St Gilles Croix de Vie, and less frequently to Les Sables d'Olonne.

Enter the harbour leaving the NW breakwater head 50m to starboard; on reaching the Passerelle elbow, bear to port (as the western side of the outer harbour dries 0·5m) and round the inner end of the Passerelle to enter the marina.

By night

Approach in the white sector of the NW breakwater light[5] and enter the harbour with the leading lights in line[6] bearing 219°.

Looking NW over Joinville. Water tower far left, with lighthouse (arrowed) behind.

Entering Joinville with the leading lighthouses and church in transit.

Port de la Meule

46°41'·7N 2°20'·7W

A picturesque but tiny fishing harbour on the south side of Ile d'Yeu, which is rewarding to visit if one is lucky enough to get the right conditions of offshore wind, but is to be avoided in unsettled weather. The harbour is crowded with small fishing boats, with the occasional trawler at anchor in the entrance. The fishermen much prefer yachts to anchor outside; they report that in the summer there can be ten or more yachts at anchor during *le weekend*.

Approach and entrance

The entrance is not conspicuous, but lies between two fairly prominent headlands, Pointe du Châtelet (La Panrée), with a white stone cross, 1½ miles to the west, and Pointe de la Tranche, ¾ mile to the SE, behind which there are, on high ground, a conspicuous white semaphore tower and a red and white radio mast. Another landmark is the ruined castle 1 mile to the W. The ruins are of similar rock to the cliffs behind them, but can be made out on a clear day.

From seaward the entrance has little to distinguish it from the other inlets on this coast until it is opened up, when the white panel on the side of the lighthouse and the white chapel at the NE end of the inlet can be seen. The bay in which Port de la Meule is situated is clear of offlying rocks, except for those off the headlands and in the immediate vicinity of the cliffs. Steer for the lighthouse, bearing 022°, allowing for any set of the tide.

On near approach a headland on the west side of the entrance will lie to port. This has rocks off the south end, which are well off the line of approach, but there is also a reef projecting eastward almost facing the headland on the opposite side. These rocks can usually be seen as the swell breaks on them, but an incoming vessel should borrow to starboard to give them an offing.

The headland on the east side, which is an island (Tête Jaune) at high water, does not project seawards as far as the west headland does. There are rocks off its southern extremity, which it is convenient to regard as a short, underwater continuation of the headland.

In the near approach, first give reasonable clearance to the reef of rocks to port, then keep the inlet between the lighthouse and the cliff on the east side open, steering parallel with the eastern side of the inlet. When within the entrance, where there is 4m, lobster-pot buoys will be seen on the west side; these are an aid to navigation, as the outer ones are

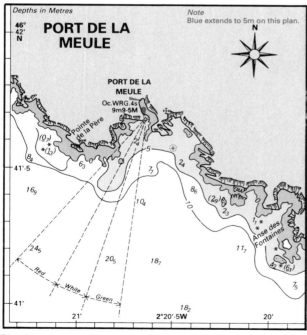

Plan 51

La Meule. Entrance.

La Meule, near HW.

usually laid where they may be treated as port-hand marks, to be left close to port. On the opposite, east, side there are a few rocks at the foot of the cliffs, and one of them lies close to the channel. Hence, if proceeding to the quay, a vessel should now keep rather W of the centre and turn sharply to port round the point on which the lighthouse stands.

There is shelter at the quay in normal conditions with the wind from W through N to E, but if the wind goes into a southerly quarter the swell will surge right in and the harbour will be untenable. In southerly gales even the local boats move round to Port Joinville.

By night

Night entry cannot be recommended to a stranger.

Anchorage and mooring

In settled offshore winds it is practicable to anchor in the entrance, though some swell comes in even in NE winds. The bottom is rocky and there is little swinging room, so two anchors are necessary.

The harbour dries; the fishermen are helpful, but say that there is really no room for a yacht. It would be wise to seek their advice before entering. There are three slips; the best walls to lie against are between the first and second (although there are said to be some stones on the bottom here), or between the second and third, where it will be necessary to keep clear of the chain moorings for fishermen's dinghies. The bottom is rocky off the first slip and above the third.

Facilities

There are two restaurants, but almost no other facilities. There are paths over the hills and the cliffs to east and west. The ruined castle one mile to the west is interesting.

Anse des Vieilles

46°41'·7N 2°18'·5W

This attractive bay with a sandy beach on the SE coast, 1¼M from Pointe des Corbeaux, can be entered from the SE. Avoid the line of rocks, the Ours des Vieilles (the outermost drying 3·5m), which runs out for 600m in a southeasterly direction from the Pointe des Vieilles, on the west side of the bay. It is advisable not to attempt entry unless equipped with SHOM *6890*, or at least Navicarte *549*.

There is a small drying harbour on the west arm of the bay. The anchorage in 3m in the centre of the bay is sheltered from northerly winds.

43. Saint Gilles Croix-de-Vie

46°41'N 1°56'W

Charts

BA *2647*
Imray *C40*
SHOM *6853P, 6523P*
Navicarte *549, 1022*

Tidal data

Tidal heights (approx)
HW −0020 Brest springs, +0010 Brest neaps
MTL 3·1m. Index 1
Heights of tide above chart datum
MHWS 5·3m, MLWS 0·8m, MHWN 4·2m, MLWN 2·1m

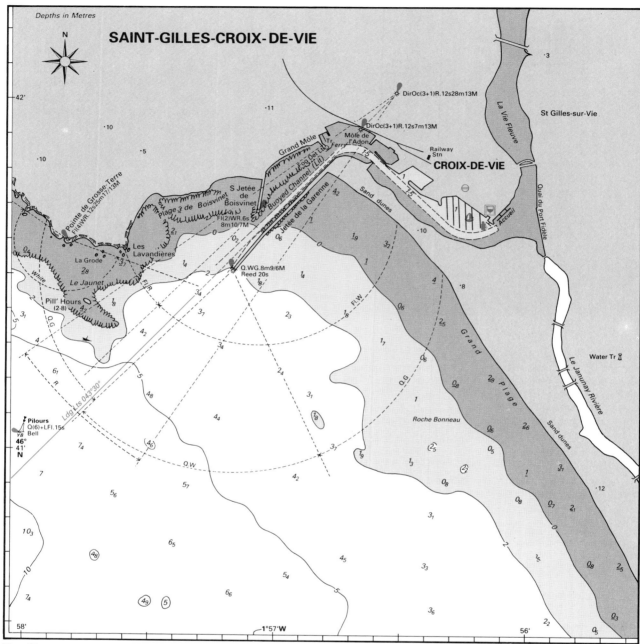

SAINT-GILLES-CROIX-DE-VIE

Plan 52

Tidal streams

The streams are weak in the offing, but strong in the harbour itself, the ebb reaching nearly 6 knots in the narrow parts. The ebb is increased and the flood reduced (it may even fail to occur) after heavy rain.

Depths

The channel is said to be dredged to 1·5m, so both fishing harbours and the yacht marina should be accessible at all states of the tide. There is, however, a serious silting problem, with continuous dredging to prevent two sand bars from forming.

Lights

1. **Pointe de Grosse Terre** 46°41'·6N 1°57'·9W
   Fl(4)WR.12s25m17/13M 290°-W-125°-R-145°
   White truncated conical tower
2. **Ldg Lts 043·5°** *Front* DirOc(3+1)R.12s7m13M
   033·5°-intens-053·5° White square tower, red top
   Rear 260m from front DirOc(3+1)R.12s28m13M
   033·5°-intens-053·5° White square tower, red top
3. **Pill-hours buoy S card** 46°41'·0N 1°58'·0W Q(6)+
   LFl.15s bell
4. **NW jetty head** 46°41'·6N 1°57'·2W Fl(2)WR.6s8m
   10/7M 045°-R-225°-W-045° Red column, white
   shelter
5. **SE jetty head** 46°41'·5N 1°57'·2W Q.WG.8m9/6M
   045°-G-335°-W-045° White support, green top Reed
   20s
6. **Lit channel buoys** in harbour, three red (port) and
   four green (starboard)

General

This harbour is formed by La Vie river; the entrance is protected by moles on either hand. The entrance faces SW, and is therefore unsuitable for entry during strong onshore winds or if there is a swell. As the ebb tide can reach 6 knots at springs, entry is impossible when a strong wind opposes this and it is safer to make both entry and exit before high water.

Within the river, there are two enclosed basins for the fishing fleet on the north side; above these lie the pontoons of the yacht marina. There are also quays further up the river at St Gilles-sur-Vie on the southeast side. Croix-de-Vie is a substantial town and the fish quays near the railway station are very busy. There is much yachting activity in the port, with 800 permanent berths and 60 for visitors. There are also mooring trots along the river opposite the marina and on up to the bridge.

Approach

In a rather featureless sandy coastline, with churches and three water towers in the background, the entrance can be located by the low rocky headland of Grosse Terre on the north side, with many houses and a lighthouse, the two church spires and the high lighthouse of Croix-de-Vie. On nearer approach the Pilours (a low reef of rocks like a small island) will be seen, marked by a pillar light buoy (S cardinal), with the entrance and the leading lighthouses beyond.

Approach should be made, preferably shortly before high water, with the leading lighthouses in transit bearing 043°. This approach leaves the Pilours buoy (S cardinal) 250m to port and, further in, the end of the Pilours reef 160m to port. Soundings fall gradually from 6m opposite the buoy to 0·7m 200m off the starboard-hand pierhead, the Jetée de la Garenne, which extends beyond the port-hand breakwater by 350m. Thence the channel should be dredged to 1·5m, but some silting may have occurred.

Entrance

The entrance lies between the two outer breakwater heads, and the transit leads on the SE side of the entrance following close to and parallel to the Jetée de la Garenne. This line is out of the dredged channel, so incoming vessels should if possible borrow to port and keep in the buoyed channel after the mole head is passed. Four lit starboard-hand buoys lead up the channel and into the sharp curve to starboard. To port are two port-hand buoys, then the old Grand Môle, with a stone tower and a ferry landing on the head. The stream runs very hard here and the buoys should be given a good berth as they are moored on the high ground beside the channel. After a 90° turn to starboard, the channel passes the fishing-boat basins to reach the reception (*accueil*) berth on the port side. Secure here to obtain a berth from the harbourmaster but beware of the strong tides passing the ends of the pontoons.

Departure should be made before high water, as the strong ebb quickly raises a sea at the entrance.

Looking east over St Gilles-Croix-de-Vie. Pointe de Grosse-Terre lighthouse left foreground, Pill-Hours rock below the extended breakwater head.

Entering St Gilles with the leading lighthouses (arrowed) in transit on 043·5°.

St Gilles. Approaching the marina, leaving the fishing basins to port.

By night

Provided weather conditions are suitable, entry is easy at night. As by day, avoid entry when a strong tide is running.

Anchorage and mooring

Anchoring in the channel is prohibited. The berths near the shore ends of the marina pontoons may dry out but the mud appears to be soft and boats remain upright. If no marina berths are available in this popular harbour there are mooring buoys on the south side of the channel opposite the marina; it may also be possible to berth below the bridge, further upstream, by the quay to starboard at St Gilles-sur-Vie, where the streams are not so strong.

Yachts which can take the ground could enquire whether a berth is available at or just off the pontoons of the sailing club, just inside the Grand Môle.

Anchorage may be possible outside in offshore winds, SE of the Jetée de la Garenne in 1·5m. There is no convenient landing place for dinghies except at the harbour moles. The ebb could set up a nasty sea for dinghy work.

Facilities

Water and electricity on the pontoons, showers and toilets at the *capitainerie*. Fuel berth by the travel-lift at the upstream end of the marina. There are shipbuilders, marine engineers and a chandlery. All shops nearby, with bank, hotels and restaurants, the best of which will be found at Boisvinet, to the west

of Croix-de-Vie. The railway station is just by the harbour. Croix-de-Vie is an important fishing port with all facilities for fishing vessels.

Rail Croix-de-Vie – Pornic – Nantes.

44. Les Sables d'Olonne

46°30'N 1°48'W

Charts

BA *2648, 2647*
Imray *C40*
SHOM *6523P, 6522P*
Navicarte *1022*

Tidal data

Tidal heights (approx)
HW −0025 Brest springs, +0015 Brest neaps
MTL 3·1m. Index 0
Heights of tide above chart datum
MHWS 5·3m, MLWS 0·8m, MHWN 4·2m, MLWN 2·1m

Tidal streams

In the offing the streams are weak, rarely exceeding ½ knot; they are rotary clockwise, N at LW Brest, S at HW Brest. In the Rade the streams are negligible and in the harbour itself they are normally weak.

Depths

The harbour is dredged to 1·5m and the marina to 2m.

Lights

1. **Les Barges** 46°29'·7N 1°50'·4W Fl(2)R.10s25m17M Grey tower, helicopter platform
2. **L'Armandèche** 46°29'·4N 1°48'·3W Fl(2+1)15s42m 24M 295°-vis-130° White hexagonal tower, red top
3. **Petite Barge S card buoy** 46°28'·9N 1°50'·6W Q(6)+LFl.15s8m7M
4. **Le Nouch S card buoy** 46°28'·6N 1°47'·3W Q(6)+LFl.15s (Note: same light char. as Petite Barge)
5. **Passe du SW Ldg Lts 033°** 46°29'·5N 1°46'·3W *Front* Iso.R.4s14m16M Metal mast *Rear* 330m from front Iso.R.4s33m16M White square masonry tower on white building shown throughout 24hrs. The above lights are displaying Iso.4s (T) 1994

6. **Jetée Saint Nicolas head** 46°29'·2N 1°47'·5W UQ(2)R.1s16m10M 143°-vis-094° Horn(2)30s White tower, red top
7. **Passe du SE Ldg Lts 320° Jetée des Sables head** 46°29'·4N 1°47'·5W *Front* Q.G.11m8M White tower, green top **Tour de la Chaume** *Rear* 465m from front Oc(2+1) 12s33m13M Large grey square tower surmounted by white turret
8. **Ldg Lts 327°** through entrance *Front* F.R.6m11M Rectangle with WRW vertical stripes over white pedestal *Rear* 65m from front DirF.R.9m11M 324°-intens-330° Rectangle with RWR vertical stripes over white tower

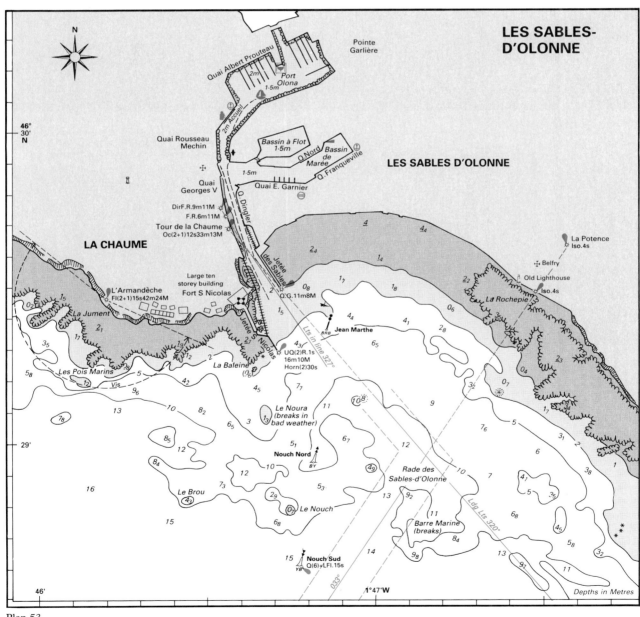

Plan 53

Les Sables d'Olonne, looking NE.

Les Sables d'Olonne from the SE. Arrowed from the left: Les Barges lighthouse, L'Armandèche lighthouse, Jetée St Nicolas head light tower, Tour de la Chaume, La Chaume church.

General

Yachts bound south for La Rochelle pass within sight of Les Sables d'Olonne, which is situated some 35 miles NW of their destination. It is a convenient staging point, although on a small-scale chart the entrance appears shallow, beset with rocks and a lee shore to the prevailing winds. With a large-scale chart, however, the approach is found to be easy, and the harbour and town provide excellent facilities. The approach is rough in strong SE, S or SW winds, especially if there is a swell, owing to the shoals. In bad weather the SE approach is the safer and, given plenty of rise of tide, fishing vessels approach and enter the harbour in severe weather.

The town of Les Sables d'Olonne on the east side of the entrance is a large sophisticated holiday resort with a casino, many hotels and restaurants facing the sands. A narrow peninsula separates this from the fishing port with its market and cafés. Visiting yachts may not lie here, but Port Olona, a large marina, has been set up in the dredged scouring basin further inland. This is a long way from the town by the ring road and the shops and restaurants of La Chaume on the west bank are more readily accessible.

Approach and entrance

The harbour lies about 1 mile to the SE of the Pointe de l'Aiguille, SE of which is the tall white lighthouse of L'Armandèche, with three tower blocks east of it and a radio mast to the north. On the east side of the harbour the hotels and other large buildings on the long curving front are also conspicuous when approaching from the south. Les Barges lighthouse, 1 mile offshore to the west, is another aid to identification of the entrance.

From the W or NW, round La Petite Barge (S cardinal) buoy, leaving it 200m or more to port, then steer 095° to identify Nouch Sud (S cardinal) buoy and leave it also to port. Proceed eastwards until the entrance has been positively identified. The white lighthouse with red top on the head of the west breakwater should be conspicuous. Behind it the tall square crenellated tower of La Chaume is partially masked by an eight-storey building but can be located to the left of the church spire. Approach the entrance with La Chaume tower in transit with the light tower on the east mole (white with a green top) bearing 320°. If entering near low water, when the west breakwater head is abeam to port alter to port to bring the WRW and RWR vertical stripe panels on the inner light structures in transit bearing 327°, and follow this transit into the channel.

Approaching at half tide or over, in ordinary weather, attention to the leading lines is unnecessary; yachts can cross over the rocks and shoals to the south and sail directly to the harbour entrance.

Approaching from the south, use the SE approach, sailing straight for the transit of the east mole head and La Chaume tower bearing 320°. This leaves all the shoals to port and the water is deep until within 400m of the harbour entrance; this approach should always be used in bad weather.

Berthing

Enter under power (sailing forbidden) past the fishing harbour to starboard, being wary of fishing boats leaving it at speed. Continue, as the channel curves to starboard, to the *accueil* pontoon of the marina on the port-hand side and check in at the *bureau du port* to obtain a berth.

Visitors may not use the fishing harbour, and the wet dock may only be entered with prior permission from the port authority.

Facilities

Water and electricity on the pontoons; showers and toilets. Fuel at the *accueil* pontoon. 28-tonne travel-lift, two slips, and all repair facilities. The marina was developing in 1988, the intention being to cater in the one complex for all the requirements of yachtsmen in the way of provisions, restaurants, chandlers, sailmakers and engineers. When it was visited again in 1992, progress in providing facilities appeared to have been limited and it was a long walk to the shops!

The nearest outside banks, shops and restaurants are those of La Chaume. Excellent communications from Les Sables d'Olonne by train, bus and air.

45. Bourgenay

46°26'N 1°41'W

Charts

BA *2648*
SHOM *6522P*
Navicarte *1022*

Tidal data

Tidal heights (approx)
HW −0025 Brest springs, +0015 Brest neaps
MTL 3·1m. Index 0
Heights of tide above chart datum
MHWS 5·3m, MLWS 0·8m, MHWN 4·2m, MLWN 2·1m

Tidal streams

3 miles offshore +0200 to +0500 Brest WNW ½ to 1½ knots; −0430 to −0000 Brest SE ½ to 1 knot.

Depths

1m in the entrance, 1m to 2m at the pontoons.

Lights

1. **Fairway buoy** 46°25'·3N 1°41'·8W Fl.10s White with red vertical stripes, fluorescent orange ● topmark

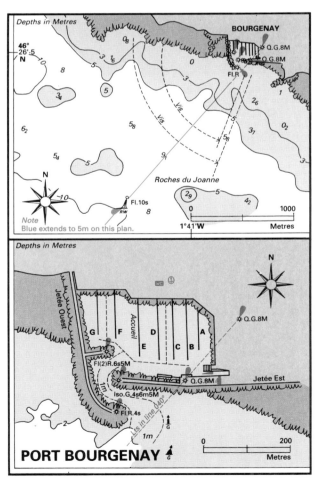

Plan 54

2. **Ldg Lts 040°** 46°26'·4N 1°40'·5W *Front* Q.G.8M 020°-vis-060° White hut on E breakwater, green rectangle mark
   Rear Q.G.8M 010°-vis-070° Tall thin white column, white rectangle, green border
3. **W breakwater head** Fl.R.4s8m9M Red structure
4. **E mole head** Iso.G.4s6m5M Not visible to seaward
5. **W breakwater elbow** Fl(2)R.6s5M Not visible to seaward

General

This large and convenient marina is situated some 6 miles SE of Les Sables d'Olonne. Behind the marina is a large holiday complex with boating lake and an old château with grey turrets which is now a convent; the conspicuous white topmark on the highest turret is in fact a statue of Notre Dame d'Esperance. The entrance is not easy to locate for the first time, with a low-lying, rocky and rather featureless coastline to the NW and a sandy beach to the SE, at the entrance to the river leading up to the town of Talmont. Entry should not be attempted in strong westerly winds, but there is complete shelter inside.

Approach and entrance

It is essential first to locate the fairway buoy situated 1 mile SW of the marina. It is a metal framework buoy with RW vertical stripes and a fluorescent orange topmark. From the buoy the buildings behind the marina will be seen, bearing 040° with the rear leading mark, a tall thin white column.

The channel has been blasted out of a rocky, gently sloping seabed, with parts exposed at LW. Keeping the white column on 040°, approach until a green beacon can be seen to the right of a white patch marking the west breakwater head. A 90° turn to port is made to enter the marina, followed by a 90° turn to starboard. Fluorescent green and red chevrons, illuminated at night, indicate the turns. The water in the entrance can be confused and dangerous during SW winds.

Berthing

The *accueil* pontoon is marked E. Visitors should secure to it unless met by a marina launch and shown to a berth. There are 110 berths for visitors; maximum length 20m.

Bourgenay entrance. The leading-light structures are in transit (arrowed) on 040°. From this distance the front structure, on the loose-rock breakwater, obscures all but the top of the rear column. The rocks forming the head of the west breakwater are painted white; the red-topped light is arrowed. On entering, turn hard to port round the west breakwater head and then hard to starboard to enter the marina.

Bourgenay, looking east.

Facilities

Electricity and water on the pontoons; showers and toilets. Fuel berth, grid, slip, 15-tonne mobile crane, chandlery and engineers. A café/bar and launderette. Some provisions are obtainable in the marina and there is a supermarket up the hill past the convent.

Taxis are available for the railway station or aerodrome.

46. Ile de Ré

St Martin-de-Ré 46°12'N 1°22'W

Charts

BA *2641, 2663*
Imray *C41*
SHOM *6521P, 6333P*
Navicarte *1022, 551*

Tidal data

Tidal heights (approx)

HW −0040 Pointe de Grave springs, HW Pointe de Grave neaps
MTL 3·6m. Index 3
Heights of tide above chart datum
MHWS 6·0m, MLWS 0·9m, MHWN 4·8m, MLWN 2·4m

Tidal streams

The streams, which are weak offshore, increase as the island is approached. The streams south of the island, in the Pertuis d'Antioche, are given under La Rochelle on page 184. North of the island, in the Pertuis Breton where the harbours are, they are as follows: Off Pointe de Lizay at the north of the island the flood runs ESE and the ebb WNW, spring rates 1½ knots. Off the mainland opposite, near the Pointe du Grouin du Crou, the turn is about half an hour after high water and low water and the rates are about half a knot higher.

Near the eastern end of the island the flood meets the north-going flood through the Rade de la Pallice, and the ebb splits similarly, leaving a zone of relatively weak streams off the NE of the island. The streams in the Rade de Pallice do not exceed 1½ knots springs.

Depths

See individual ports.

Lights

North coast

1. **Pointe du Grouin du Cou** (mainland) 46°20'·7N 1°27'·8W Fl.WRG.5s29m20-16M 034°-R-061°-W-117°-G-138°-W-034° White 8-sided tower, black lantern

2. **Les Baleineaux or Haut-Banc-du-Nord** 46°15'·8N 1°35'·2W Oc(2)6s23m11M Pink tower, red top
3. **Les Baleines** 46°14'·7N 1°33'·7W Fl(4)15s53m27M Grey 8-sided tower, red lantern RC *BN* (−···/−·) 299kHz 50M
4. **Le Fier d'Ars Ldg Lts 265°** 46°14'·1N 1°28'·6W *Front* Iso.4s5m11M White rectangle on grey framework
   Rear DirIso.G.4s13m15M Green square tower on dwelling 264°-intens-266°
5. **Ars-en-Ré Ldg Lts 232°** *Front* Q.5m9M White column, red lantern, red 'window frame' on top
   Rear Q.13m11M 142°-vis-322° Black rectangle on white framework tower, green top
6. **Le Rocha (Mouillage Extr) buoy (N card)** Q 46°14'·7N 1°20'·7
7. **St Martin de Ré SE of entrance** 46°12'·5N 1°21'·9W Oc(2)WR.6s18m10/7M Shore-W-245°-R-281°-shore White tower, red top
8. **St Martin mole head** 46°12'·6N 1°21'·9W Iso.G.4s10m6M White column, green top
9. **St Martin W end of breakwater** Fl.R.2·5s7m4M
10. **La Flotte** 46°11'·4N 1°19'·2W Fl.WG.4s10m12/9M 130°-G-205°-W-220°-G-257° Horn(3)30s White round tower, green top. Illuminated Moiré guide 212·5° operating HW −2 to HW+2

General

The island, over 13 miles long, projects seaward west of La Rochelle, which can be approached either through the Pertuis d'Antioche on the south side of the island or by entering the Pertuis Breton on the north side and proceeding on under the road bridge joining Ile de Ré and the mainland. This spectacular curving bridge, nearly two miles long, with ample clearance for masts of any height, was opened in June 1988 and immediately flooded the island with cars, coaches and their contents.

The three ports, which are all in the Pertuis Breton, are a popular destination for a weekend sail from the mainland and support substantial yachting activity of their own.

The side of the island the harbours are on is sheltered from the prevailing winds, from the S and W. This is useful to the cruising person, who can, in these winds, anchor off the harbours while waiting to enter.

The Ile de Ré is a sandy island fringed in many parts by rocks, of which the most notable are the Banc du Nord, extending from Les Baleines in the NW, and those off the Pointe de Chanchardon on the S and the Pointe de Chauveau on the SE. These are marked by light towers. The island is low and the scenery is like that in Holland, with windmills (now mostly converted into dwellings) and tall church spires rising high over the land. The houses are as tidy as Dutch ones. The island is a pleasant place in summer and much visited by holidaymakers.

Peaceful as it is today, the Ile de Ré has been the scene of much fighting; it suffered greatly from the attacks of the English, and also during the religious wars. St Martin, the capital, is a fortified town with

Vauban ramparts and a citadel, which was considerably damaged during the bombardment by the Anglo-Dutch fleet in 1696.

There are three harbours: St Martin, La Flotte, and Fier d'Ars. All the harbours are tidal but St Martin has a wet basin where yachts can lie afloat in complete shelter, in the centre of the old walled town with restaurants and shops close by.

St Martin

46°12'N 1°22'W

Depths

The near approach dries 1·6m, the inner harbour dries 1·5m. Berths at the pontoon along the NW mole have been dredged to 2·3m, of which 1·5m was soft mud in 1992, due to silting. In the wet dock there is 3m at neaps, more at springs.

General

St Martin stands rather east of halfway along the NE side of the Ile de Ré. The harbour consists of an *avant-port*, sheltered by a mole, a wooden breakwater and a jetty, connected with the drying harbour by a narrow entrance channel. From the drying harbour a channel to starboard leads through dock gates to the wet dock. There is active local yachting, as well as some fishing.

Approach and entrance

Approaching in the morning light the harbour is easily located, for the white lighthouse, the church tower and the citadel will be seen from afar. In the afternoon, with the sun in one's eyes, the walls do

Plan 55

not stand out against the dark background and trees and the first landmarks to be seen are the lighthouse and the church tower with ruined walls close to the right (see photograph).

There are extensive ledges of rock in and especially E and W of the approach, where they extend over ½ mile seaward of the land. They are not so formidable as they appear at first glance on a chart, as the ones to the west farther offshore do not dry as much as the entrance channel and the ones to the east are marked by a beacon (N cardinal).

St Martin, looking south at half tide.

St Martin church tower over the entrance, leaving the west end of the wooden breakwater to port.

The approach should be timed according to the draught of the yacht; between 3hrs before and 2hrs after high water should give 2·2m of water at the entrance on all tides. Convenient leading marks are the square church tower in transit with the lighthouse, bearing 209°, but it is not necessary to follow this line closely. When the church tower dips behind the trees, borrow to starboard and make the final approach with the church tower open of the trees and seen over the St Martin mole head light column (white column, green top[8]) on 201°. Leaving the wavebreaker close to port, alter to port and enter to leave the mole head to starboard at a distance of less than 10m. Then steer straight for the centre of the channel leading into the drying harbour. The channel to the dock gates will open up to starboard.

Approaching from the east, do not confuse the citadel, 600m E of the port, with St Martin itself; keep well to the north of the beacon (N cardinal) on the Couronneau rocks unless the tide is well up, as rocks drying up to 1m lie to the north of the beacon and the 3m contour passes nearly 600m north of it. Bring the lighthouse and church into transit and steer as described above.

By night

Make a position by Le Rocha buoy[6] and approach in the white sector of the St Martin light[7] bearing 200°. Note that the white sector extends from 090° to 245° and crosses part of the outer ledges; it is not safe simply to enter in the white sector. On close approach alter to starboard to bring the mole light[8] to bear 195° and steer so to the entrance, leaving the light Fl.R.2·5s marking the NW end of the wooden wavebreaker close to port and the mole light close to starboard.

Mooring

In the summer months a long pontoon is arranged along the Grand Môle with a section dredged to 2·3m along its length. This is said to be 16m broad to allow yachts to raft alongside the pontoon, but it quickly silts up with soft mud, into which the keels of deep-draught yachts alongside the pontoon may sink without listing. In northerly winds a swell enters round the wavebreaker, causing the pontoon to pitch.

There are quays in the drying harbour which dry 1·5m; vessels should not berth along the inner half of the west quay, where there is a large grid, white patches along the top of the wall marking the positions of the rails.

The wet dock is completely solid with yachts during the summer weekends, and the harbourmaster is magnificent at organising departure and entry when the gate is opened. To be sure of a place it is essential to arrive early. If possible, secure to the pontoon along the Grand Môle. Should there be no room, there are a number of white mooring buoys off the entrance, and the Rade de St Martin provides an anchorage, sheltered from winds from west through south to southeast, in from 1·8 to 4m, inshore of La Rocha N cardinal buoy (Mouillage Extérieur) two miles to seaward. This is a recognised anchorage for big ships; in offshore winds yachts can get closer in to anchor outside the yacht moorings, rather less than half a mile off the entrance in 2m sand and mud.

In daylight hours, near high water, the gate is opened and departure and entry are possible for at least one hour and usually one hour either side of HW, depending on the tidal coefficient. Times are posted at the *capitainerie* and a clock face on the bridge shows the opening times each tide.

Facilities

Water on the quay, showers and toilets in the *capitainerie*. Fuel berth on the E wall of the drying basin (see plan page 174). Shipyard, chandler and engineers. Slipway, grid and 9·5-tonne crane.

Bank, hotels, restaurants and all shops close by. Bicycle hire. Taxis to mainland (a bus service is likely to have been established).

St Martin is an historic town of moats, walls and gateways, with a large church which has been only partly restored. At one period Ile de Ré was independent for customs purposes and St Martin was a prosperous port carrying on a vigorous trade with America and distant parts; sailing ships loaded salt and wines and returned laden with woods, spices and other merchandise. The port now shows some signs of decay and is living in the past. The wet dock is now principally used by yachts, for which it is ideal, being clean and having every convenience at hand. The only disadvantage is that its popularity has led to overpopulation.

La Flotte

46°11'·3N 1°19'·3W

Depths

The approach and harbour dry 2m.

General

La Flotte lies about 2 miles SE of St Martin; it is easily identified and the tall square church tower is conspicuous. The harbour is formed by two jetties, protected by a long curved outer mole. The narrow entrance faces east across the shallow bay. Although there is no wet basin as at St Martin, the harbour is well sheltered, and is uncomfortable only in strong onshore winds.

A fishing port famous for lobsters, shrimps and sole, La Flotte is a compact town of short narrow streets and whitewashed houses, with a beautiful church. It is less popular and more cheerful than St Martin. Except for the trouble of drying out, some yachtsmen may prefer it; yachts will be aground for long periods on each tide.

Approach and entrance

La Flotte is easy to locate in the bay ½ mile W of Pointe des Barres. It is approached by a channel with mud and sand bottom which dries 2m and lies between ledges of rock, extending up to ½ mile seaward, covered with oyster beds marked by yellow beacons with diagonal cross topmarks.

Approach with the lighthouse bearing 215°. On this bearing (which it is not necessary to hold closely) the lighthouse will be in transit with a small belfry, not the main church tower. A beacon (N cardinal) on the rocks off Pointe des Barres will be left about 600m to port. If approaching from the east give a good berth to the beacon, as the rocks extend outside it.

Within 500m of the lighthouse, an illuminated panel with vertical black and orange stripes will be visible day and night, defining the close approach on 215·5°. This ingenious Moiré fringe system changes to an arrowhead pointing to the right if you are off course to port and to the left if you are off to starboard. If your error is great the arrowhead doubles or even triples! Change course in the direction indicated by the arrowhead and the vertical stripes will return when you are in the channel. Leave the breakwater head to starboard and steer for the narrow entrance between the jetty heads.

By night

As by day (light[10] and Moiré panel).

Mooring

The inner harbour is rectangular and dries 2m. Space for visitors is limited and it may be advisable to secure to the outer breakwater before entering and apply to the harbourmaster for a berth.

Pontoons for local boats are installed in the inner half of the basin, and visitors may dry out against

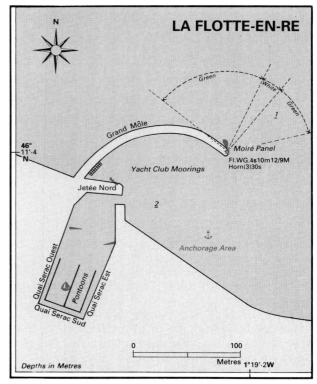

Plan 56

the inner side of the Jetée Nord. Moorings inside the Grand Môle are reserved for local boats.

It may be possible to lie alongside the breakwater and dry out in settled weather, but there is a grid at the root and fishing boats are moored with stern lines to the wall.

Outside the harbour to the west of the breakwater and inshore of the oyster beds is a line of white buoys on hard sand where vessels that can take the ground can moor. They may be reached by a close approach to the breakwater, turning to starboard inshore of the yellow beacon which marks the inner corner of the oyster beds. From here there is no problem getting ashore to the town, but the moorings are exposed to the not infrequent NW wind and the accompanying chop.

Deep-draught yachts can anchor or use the white mooring buoys some ¾ mile offshore in 2m.

Facilities

Water and electricity on the pontoons. Water taps on the quay. Showers and toilets. Two slips and a grid. Fuel in St Martin. Some hotels, restaurants and shops in the town.

Fier d'Ars

Eastern Bûcheron starboard buoy (unlit) 46°14'·38N 1°25'·9W at entrance to approach channel.

Depths

In 1992 the outer bar dried 0·4m and the outer anchorage had 2·6m. The second bar dried 1·5m and the main anchorage had 2m. The channel to the harbour of Ars-en-Ré dried out 3·4m.

Le Fier d'Ars, looking SW at LW.

Looking towards the Ars basin (gate permanently open). All the yachts as far as the entrance will take the ground. The black and white church spire is seen over the trees between the fishing boat and the van.

In July 1993 SHOM reported that the channel was being dredged as an experiment, so access may be easier in 1994. The editor would welcome reports from visitors.

General

The Mer du Fier is a lake-like expanse of water, most of which dries at low tide. The word *fier* is said to be derived from the Scandinavian *fjord*, but the resemblance is remote. It is entered from the Pertuis

The Ile de Ré road bridge.

Breton through a narrow channel some 5 miles east of Les Baleines. Though shallow, it is well sheltered and is the principal yachting centre of the island. The local boats are dinghies or of shallow draught to suit local conditions. Deep-keel yachts can lie afloat in the main anchorage off the Pointe du Fier, a delightful spot, or further out in a more exposed anchorage.

There is a proposal to construct a yacht harbour in the Mer du Fier to provide berths for 200 boats.

It is possible to go up the channel to the harbour at tide time. Entry to the inner basin, which is dredged to 2m, is through a gate (no longer closed) and over a sill. The harbour is popular and crowded with visiting yachts in season. The town is an attractive one; the local industries are, making salt by evaporating sea water in salt-pans, and cultivating oysters.

Approach and entrance

(Described as in 1992 before the channel was dredged.)

The approach is from the east. The channel lies between the ledges of rock extending from the island shore and the Banc du Bûcheron, a big sandbank extending 2 miles to the east of Pointe du Fer.

Close with the land ½ mile W of Pointe du Grouin. To the east will be seen Les Islattes tower (N cardinal), to the west the wooded Pointe du Fier and the shore north of it. The approach is with the two leading marks on the Pointe du Fier in transit, bearing 265°. These marks/lights[4] are not at all conspicuous and must not be confused with the high tower of Les Baleines lighthouse, which stands out more clearly over the trees and well to the right of the alignment. The leading marks appear in a gap in the trees. The rear mark is a green square tower on a dwelling and the front mark is a grey metal framework tower with a white square board. It is on rails so that it can be moved as the channel shifts.

Approaching on the transit, a buoy (Le Bûcheron, starboard) marking the end of the Banc de Bûcheron will be left to starboard. The Banc is tending to move southwards and a second starboard buoy close to the transit marks its present limit. This is followed by a green beacon that in 1992 was south of the transit, so that it was necessary to alter to port and, taking soundings, leave it to starboard before regaining the line.

The channel shoals midway between the buoys, where it dries 0·4m; it then deepens again, and round the beacon is a long, narrow curving hole with up to 2·6m. This is the outer anchorage. Continuing on the transit for another ½ mile, Roche Eveillon beacon (port) will be seen. Just before the yacht reaches this beacon the leading lights/marks at Ars-en-Ré[5] may be located (transit bearing 232°). They are not easy to see by day, and the conspicuous slender black-topped church spire of Ars-en-Ré makes a better mark. When the spire bears 231° steer for it, leaving Roche Eveillon beacon 200m to port, over a rocky bottom which dries 1·5m. This course will run parallel to the shoreline of the Pointe du Fier, at the inshore end of which there is a landing slip. At this point begins the second deep pool forming the main anchorage; it has 2·6m and there are usually some boats anchored there. Beware of a rocky patch, awash at LWS, towards the SE edge of the anchorage.

If proceeding to the harbour, leave the red beacon (L'Abesse) close to port and follow the buoyed channel until it enters the canalised portion leading to the harbour itself. The channel dries 3·4m and the harbour can be very crowded.

By night

Make the initial approach with St Martin light[7] showing white, bearing more than 124°. Both leading lines are lit[4, 5], but the pools will have to be found by sounding. The harbour is not accessible to strangers by night.

Anchorages

There are yacht moorings and an anchorage in 2m ½ mile E of Les Portes, which is north of Le Fier

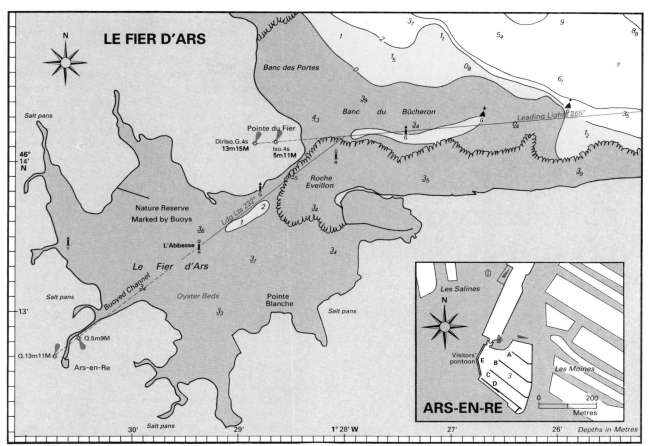

Plan 57

d'Ars. The outer anchorage in Le Fier is exposed to the N and E, but is sheltered from S and W. As it is outside the inner, shallower, bar there is more freedom to come and go, but it is a long way to the landing, with very strong tides.

The main anchorage has much better shelter, though it is somewhat exposed to the NE at high water. The tides also run hard here and the bottom is weedy. Land at the Pointe du Fier, which is a delightful strip of sand backed by woods.

The harbour is bordered by quays on each side, the width being 35m. The inner basin lies beyond a single dock gate, which is left open to help scour the channel. Visiting yachts may dry out against the starboard (western) quay after consulting the harbourmaster, or pass over the sill into the inner basin, where the visitors' pontoon lies against the west quay.

Facilities

From the anchorages by Pointe du Fier it is necessary to walk 2 miles to Les Portes to reach the shops. Restaurant and shipyard at the harbour. All shops, restaurants and buses in Ars-en-Ré, ½ mile from the harbour. Fuel from a garage (¾ mile walk) or, by arrangement, delivered by van to the quayside. The fuel symbol on the inset plan probably indicates a pump reserved for fishing boats.

Anse du Martray

46°11'·2N 1°27'·7W

This is an open anchorage on the south coast of Ile de Ré, off a sandy tourist beach, suitable in light NW to E winds.

Charts

BA *2641* or *2746*
Imray *C41*
SHOM *6521P* or *6333P*
Navicarte *551*

Approach and entrance

From a position ½ mile E of Chanchardon tower (octagonal, black with white base, Fl.RW.4s15m 11/9M), steer north to a white iron mooring buoy and thence a further ½ mile on 018° to a second white buoy. Use the church spires of Ars-en-Ré and La Couarde-sur-Mer for fixing.

Anchorage

From the second buoy, run in on about 340°, with soundings, towards the E end of the sea wall and anchor as tide and depth permit. The bottom is largely sandy, with a gentle gradient, but with a draught of 1·5m it is difficult to get within 400m of the beach.

179

Facilities

Land at the E end of the sea wall, where there is a ramp. 100m to the E there is a camp site with small supermarket, café, showers, toilets and launderette. The coast road leads W to Martray, where there are seafood shops (oysters 15F a dozen 1988) and a cycle track through the saltpans, or the road may be followed to Ars-en-Ré.

47. L'Aiguillon, La Faute-sur-Mer and Marans

For L'Aiguillon: Le Lay S cardinal buoy
46°16'·15N 1°16'·4W Q(6)+LFl.15s
For Marans: safe-water buoy off Pointe de
l'Aiguillon 46°15'·8N 1°11'·3W LFl.10s

Charts

BA *2641*
Imray *C41*
SHOM *6521P*
Navicarte *1022, 551*

Tidal data

Tidal heights (approx)
HW −0040 Pointe de Grave springs, HW Pointe de Grave neaps
MTL 3·6m. Index 3
Heights of tide above chart datum
MHWS 6·0m, MLWS 0·9m, MHWN 4·8m, MLWN 2·4m

Tidal streams

For the streams in the Pertuis Breton see page 173. In Le Lay, leading to L'Aiguillon, the currents are about 1·5 knots springs. In La Sèvre Niortaise, leading to Marans, the streams are about 4 knots springs.

Depths

Le Lay dries in parts (0m at the entrance). The approach channel to La Sèvre Niortaise dries 0·1m. The canal to Marans and the port have more than 3m, to accommodate coasters. Lights: Le Lay and Pointe de l'Aiguillon buoys are lit and there is a light on the Port du Pavé slip, but strangers should not attempt entry at night.

General

Six miles north of La Pallice and to the NE of the Ile de Ré, two rivers flow between mud flats into the Pertuis Breton. The westernmost is Le Lay, leading to the town of L'Aiguillon. The easternmost is La Sèvre Niortaise, which leads from the Anse de l'Aiguillon to a lock, from which a canal leads to

Marans. It is perverse that the town of L'Aiguillon is on a river which does not flow into the Anse de l'Aiguillon.

The entrances to both rivers, though sheltered at a distance by the Ile de Ré, are exposed to the S and W and, being shallow, are rough in winds from that quarter. Entry should only be attempted in fine weather or with offshore winds. Neither river is much visited by yachts and they provide an interesting excursion off the beaten track in suitable conditions. The scenery is similar to that of Holland or the Fens. The land is low and the rivers wind between training banks. The bird life is considerable, and with every variety of hawk in action along the poplar-lined canal to Marans one wonders how the white egrets, duck and other birds can survive.

Moorings

Some white mooring buoys are usually in position one mile SW of the Pointe de l'Aiguillon for vessels awaiting the tide for passage up to Marans or La Faute-sur-Mer.

L'Aiguillon, La Faute-sur-Mer

Cautions

1. The coast outside and the river banks are devoted to the culture of mussels. These are grown on substantial timber piles which cover at HW and are very dangerous. The areas are marked by a line of yellow buoys outside the river and withies with branching tops inside.

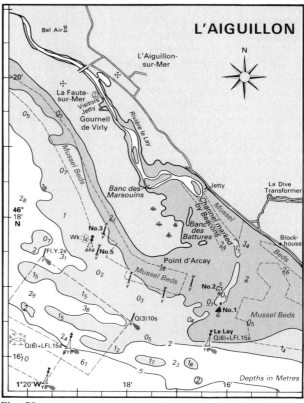

Plan 58

SHOM informed the editor that the yellow buoys are *désordonné* (disorganised) and that the positions shown on British Admiralty *2641* and SHOM *6521* are no longer accurate.

Withies with plain tops mark the oyster beds. Entering Le Lay river the channel is marked by red beacons, but in places the timber piles for the mussels extend into the channel.

2. Lying west and southwest of the Pointe d'Arçay is a rectangular shellfish-culture area, well marked by four (N, E, S and W) cardinal buoys and two yellow buoys. This area contains buoys connected by lines near the surface and should not be entered.

Entrance

The entrance to Le Lay river is not easy to locate from seaward. The low Pointe d'Arçay merges with the low shore NW of Pointe de l'Aiguillon and it is not until an incoming vessel closes with the land that the course of the river opens up. Pointe de l'Aiguillon is a long finger of sand which may be seen from a considerable distance if the sun is on it. There is a large black beacon on the extremity.

Pointe d'Arçay is low but may be identified by the belt of low trees growing on it. Some 3 miles NW of Pointe de l'Aiguillon there is a curious land formation which looks like an inland island, and is conspicuous in the absence of any other break in the low coastline. This formation is named La Dive. It is now a farm and has an electric transformer by it, adjacent to a conspicuous barn. At present the transformer is shown on charts as a mark for entry to the river. However, it is not easily identified by a stranger, and will not be shown on new editions of SHOM *6521*. The farm buildings are on the site of a pre-Christian sanctuary.

On the right-hand end of La Dive is a red-roofed house, and further to the right is a grey rectangular structure (a ruined blockhouse) which can be used as an alternative mark for entry (see photo).

From a position about 0·3M west of Le Lay buoy (S cardinal), the entrance to the river is with the transformer on La Dive bearing 035°, or the blockhouse bearing 044°. These courses leave the S cardinal buoy (YB) about 600m to starboard, No. 1 buoy (starboard) 200m to starboard and No. 2 buoy (port) 200m to port.

Thence the channel swings steadily about 60° to port between oyster and mussel beds, until the river opens up and the distant town of L'Aiguillon, with the prominent water tower of Bel Air to the NW, is seen ahead. The channel is marked by beacons; keep closer to those on the SW side but at least 15m away from beacons and withies throughout.

A low stone jetty will be passed, and there are a few buildings on the starboard bank half a mile beyond the jetty. Here the channel swings round S of W and becomes very narrow, so that it is better to proceed under power. There is a middle ground, the Banc des Marsouins, marked by beacons. The southern channel is narrow and, although it is

deeper, the northern one is to be preferred, though its deepest water is close to the middle ground and is also narrow.

Past the Banc des Marsouins the river bends 90° to starboard into a reach running NW to the bridge at L'Aiguillon-sur-Mer. All along the bank to port are wooden jetties and mooring posts for small fishing boats and yachts, which dry out on a muddy bottom.

Anchorage and mooring

On the west bank about two-thirds of the way up to the bridge at the Port de la Faute is a landing slip marked by two port beacons. Just upstream of the slip is the Association Nautique de l'Anse de Virly jetty (drying), where visitors may secure (see photo page 182.) There is a small *capitainerie* with a shower and toilet, built in 1992. Continuing up to L'Aiguillon, the river is full of fishing-boat moorings and wooden jetties line the starboard bank.

As an alternative to the La Faute jetty, it may be possible to anchor on soundings or arrange to borrow a mooring in the pool below the bridge at L'Aiguillon. Here depths are uncertain due to silting and the river can almost dry on any tide. Moorings are generally for shallow-draught fishing boats.

As the entrance dries, the editor's opinion is that it would be inadvisable to make a first visit in a vessel that cannot take the ground.

Facilities

Just below the bridge on the starboard side are a slipway and a boat yard. Water tap, shower and toilet by the La Faute yacht club jetty. No fuel at L'Aiguillon. Hotel, restaurants, shops and bus service in the town. A short walk across the peninsula leads to good bathing at La Faute.

Visitors' berth at La Faute-sur-Mer at HW. Note the Bel Air water tower (arrowed) (see plan 58, page 180).

Marans

General

The tides run very hard in La Sèvre Niortaise but it is desirable to enter well before high water to make sure of reaching the lock in time. On the Pointe de l'Aiguillon there is a large black beacon, with a topmark. Some ¾ mile to the SE of the beacon is L'Aiguillon fairway buoy (RW with solar panels and R • topmark). Leaving this buoy close to port, make good a course of 038° for the smaller RW spar buoy at the entrance to the buoyed channel leading into the river.

The Anse de l'Aiguillon is shallow, almost circular and about three miles wide. The mud flats on either side of the channel dry 4m or more and are covered with mussel beds, surrounded by piles. It is important to cross between the two RW buoys, which are nearly 2 miles apart, without deviating from the channel, and binoculars may be necessary to locate the second buoy. The channel dries 0·1m ½ mile before the second buoy and 0·0m just beyond, where the red and green channel buoys lead past the Port du Pavé slip and into the river.

The end of the slip is marked by a green beacon on a white pedestal and the channel leads between the moorings of a large fleet of mussel boats. The channel here is dredged, but silting appears to be rapid after heavy rain. In the first reach after entering the river the flats cover at HW springs, but the plan shows where the channel lies in relation to the training banks. After this there are a few buoys marking shoals on the bends; otherwise keep in the middle. About 1½ miles further up there is a landing on the starboard bank, at Le Corps de Garde, with more fishing-boat moorings.

About three miles from the river entrance the yacht will reach the lifting bridge and the Brault lock giving access to the canal leading to Marans. There are two waiting buoys on the starboard side before the bridge. Do not lie to these on a falling tide with a strong westerly wind or you will be blown onto the bank!

The bridge is operated from the lock-keeper's cabin, with TV cameras to observe the road and river traffic. During working hours, if boats are waiting, the bridge will be opened to allow the lock to be entered at high water at the lock. Departure is possible one hour before high water. The lock-keeper can be telephoned in advance (☎ 46 01 53 77).

The lock is enormous (104m long and 45m wide), with gently sloping banks. There is a short pontoon on the port-hand side to which a yacht may secure while waiting for the lock to be operated. Care must be exercised if the wind is blowing into the lock as it may be difficult to leave the pontoon. It may be simpler to remain under way, using the engine to keep in the middle of the lock. As you enter, the lock-keeper will hand you a form to record entry. At the upper end is a swing road bridge.

The pretty tree-lined canal leads straight for about 3 miles to the port of Marans. Towards the end of the canal it appears to come to a dead end, but a channel opens up to starboard, through a pair of permanently open lock gates, into the port of Marans.

Marans basin.

Anchorage and mooring

By far the best place is the port of Marans. Go past the berths used by the coasters and moor or raft alongside another yacht on the wall on the starboard side, beyond a barrage to port.

It is possible to anchor at Le Corps de Garde, where some fishing boats lie, and there is a landing with access to Charron 1½ miles away. This is quite sheltered, but the tide runs hard. Since one would only enter the river on the tide there does not seem to be much reason for stopping here rather than proceeding to Marans.

It is also possible to land at the jetty at Port du Pavé, whence Charron is a walk of 1½ miles. This anchorage is exposed to the SW at high water. However, at neaps the extensive mud flats are only

The lock at the entrance to the Marans canal.

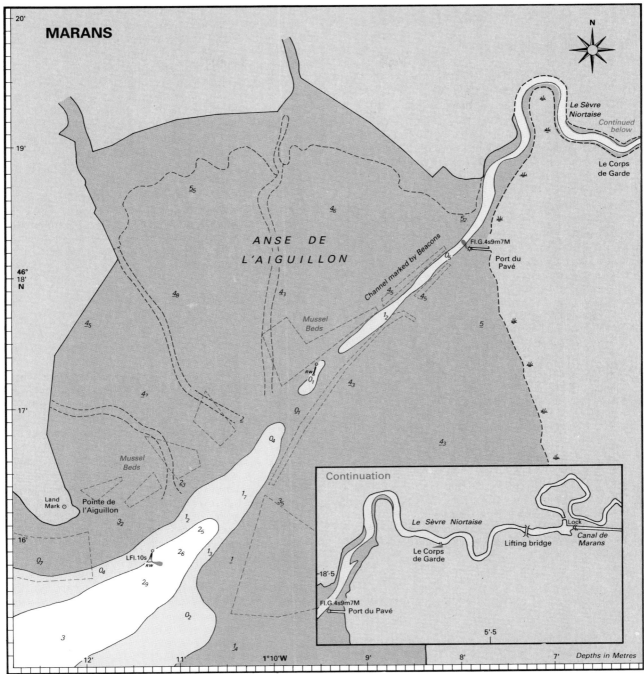

Plan 59

just covered at high water, leaving a narrow channel between them. At neaps, therefore, the shelter is better than it looks. The depth here in the channel is only 0·6m but at low water neaps there will be nearly 3m so this anchorage is possible in settled weather at neap tides.

Facilities

At Marans: Water and electricity on the quay. Fuel from the garage by the supermarket. Shipyards for repairs; crane and slip. A number of yachts winter in Marans.

Bank, hotels and a good choice of restaurants in the town, with all shops. The excellent supermarket is on the main road out of town, three minutes' walk after crossing the road bridge at the top of the port onto the north bank.

48. La Rochelle and Minimes

46°09'N 1°10'W

Charts
BA *2743, 2746, 2663*
SHOM *6334, 6468*
Navicarte *551, 552*

Tidal data

Tidal heights (approx)
HW −0035 Pte de Grave springs, +0010 Pte de Grave neaps
MTL 3·7m. Index 3
Heights of tide above chart datum
MHWS 6·1m, MLWS 1·0m, MHWN 4·9m, MLWN 2·5m

Tidal streams
For the Pertuis Breton, see under Ile de Ré, page 173. In the narrows off La Pallice the flood runs N, the ebb S, spring rates 1½ knots. In the entrance to the Pertuis d'Antioche, north of Pointe de Chassiron, the flood runs E, the ebb W, spring rates 2 knots; south of the Ile de Ré the streams turn about ½hr after HW and LW and are slightly weaker. The streams are weak in the harbour and its near approaches.

Depths
The approach carries 0·7m as far as Tour Richelieu; the buoyed channel was dredged to 0·5m in 1992 as far as the towers, but will silt. 1·3m can be found at some of the pontoons in the Bassin d'Echouage. 3m in the wet dock; 1m to 2m at the Minimes Marina pontoons.

Lights
1. **Le Lavardin** 46°08'·1N 1°14'·5W Fl(2)WG.6s14m 11/8M 160°-G-169°-W-160° Black tower, red band, two black spheres topmark
2. **Tour Richelieu** 46°08'·9N 1°10'·4W Fl(4)R.12s10m9M Siren(4)60s Red 8-sided tower RC *RE* (·−·/·) 295·5kHz 25M
3. **Ldg Lts 059°** 46°09'·4N 1°09'·1W *Front* DirQ.15m13M at night, Fl.4s by day. Red round tower, white bands
   Rear 235m from front Q.25m14M 061°-obscd-065° by St Nicolas tower. White 8-sided tower, green top
4. **Port de Minimes W mole head** 46°08'·9N 1°10'·1W Fl.G.4s9m8M White tower, green top
5. **Port de Minimes E mole head** Fl(2)R.6s6m5M 46°08'·9N 1°10'·0W White tower, red top

General
La Rochelle, halfway down the coastline of the Bay of Biscay, may be a convenient port of call for yachts bound to or from Spain or the Mediterranean via the Midi canal, or it may mark the farthest port in a cruise from England. There are few yachting centres south of it until the Gironde is entered. Beyond the Gironde, Arachon is the only port in a long, sandy, featureless coastline, and it is not accessible in strong onshore weather.

The geographical position of La Rochelle therefore makes it important to yachtsmen, and it also offers all facilities. There is a large marina at Port des Minimes, with pontoon berths for 3,000. This has lessened the congestion, but it is a long way from the shops and sights of the town. The entrance to the town harbour is shallow; inside there are wet docks where all can lie afloat, and shallow-draught yachts can lie in the Bassin d'Echouage. The entrance, between the two towers of St Nicolas on the east and La Chaine on the west, is impressive, and the historic old town is most attractive.

Water bus service from Minimes Marina to La Rochelle.

Approach and entrance
The distant approach is either through the Pertuis Breton, on the north side of Ile de Ré, and thence through the Rade de Pallice, or through the Pertuis d'Antioche on the south side.

The near approach is from a position about 1 mile S of Le Lavardin[1] isolated danger beacon tower (BRB). In most conditions the red Tour Richelieu stands out against the background of the port buildings. Coming from the south of Ile de Ré, leave Le Lavardin at least ½ mile to port, as spoil ground of varying depth lies to the SE of the tower. Coming from the Rade de Pallice, after passing under the Ile de Ré bridge, the outer breakwaters of La Pallice commercial harbour can be left to port and the coastline followed at a distance of 500m until the Tour Richelieu has been sighted.

Steer for the red Tour Richelieu and identify the church and two towers of La Rochelle. Then steer for the towers bearing about 060° until the leading lighthouses can be seen. These are just to the right of the larger, right-hand Tour St Nicolas. The front leading lighthouse is red with white bands and the rear lighthouse white with a green top. With the leading lighthouses in transit bearing 059° steer up the channel, leaving Tour Richelieu close to port.

If bound for Minimes Marina, the dredged entrance channel is marked by a W cardinal buoy and two red port-hand buoys. Keep on the 059° transit until the turn in will leave the W cardinal buoy well to port (1992), thus avoiding a shallow spit on the port side of the entrance. The position of the channel varies from year to year and many yachts ground at the entrance to Minimes.

If bound for the old port, follow the transit leaving four red channel buoys well to port. When close to the towers, bear to port and enter the harbour.

Caution
A firing danger area exists to the south of the entrance, marked by yellow buoys with × topmarks. This area is prohibited during working hours on weekdays, except public holidays.

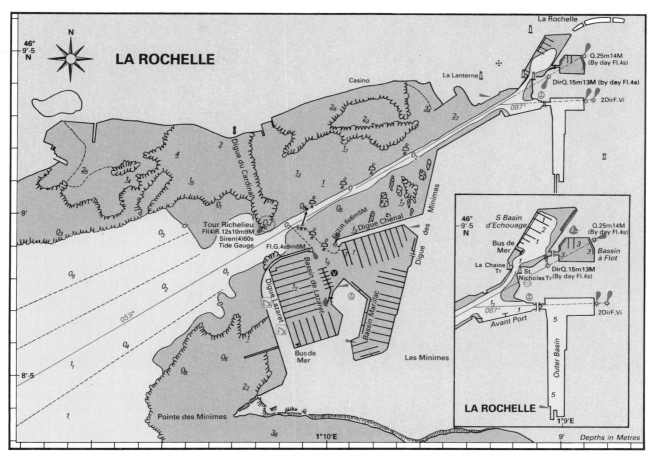

Plan 60

Looking NE into La Rochelle near LW. Tour Richelieu in centre
at the end of the long spit. The channel into La Rochelle is
narrow!

Pontoons in the Bassin d'Echouage.

By night

Entry by night is easy with the leading lights[3] in transit bearing 059°. North of the line the leading lights can be obscured by the Tour St Nicolas. To enter Minimes marina, make the turn to starboard (course 140°) 200m past Tour Richelieu. The W cardinal buoy and two port-hand buoys marking the channel are unlit.

Mooring

In Port des Minimes, lie alongside the *accueil* pontoon opposite the entrance and obtain a berth from the *capitainerie*. At present there is a charge for the first night and the second night is free.

In the old port, Bassin d'Echouage, a visitors' pontoon berth with 1m depth may be obtainable from the harbourmaster. At worst, yachts will take the ground at springs and remain upright in soft mud. Beware, however, of the open-air disco, which can continue until 0300 on a Sunday morning. There is no escape if your keel is fast in the mud!

By 1994 the new fishing harbour at Chef de Baie, just south of La Pallice, should be in operation. Fishing boats will then no longer use the old port, and the Bassin á Flot Extérieur, as well as the inner wet basin, Bassin á Flot Intérieur, should be available for yachts.

At the time of writing, daytime entry to the docks is possible from 2hrs before to ½hr after high water. At night the gates may be opened on application in advance to the *bureau du port*, ☎ 46 41 32 05. Yachts which arrive when the dock gates are closed should secure to a pontoon and visit the *bureau du port* to arrange a berth.

The quay between the dock and the Tour St Nicolas has been reserved for fishing boats and the first half of the quay beyond the dock may still be reserved for the ferries to the islands. A large scrubbing grid lies along the second half. It is possible to use this grid, but prior inspection at low water and application to the harbourmaster are essential to selecting a suitable spot in which to lie.

Facilities

Every imaginable facility is available. Banks, all kinds of shops, hotels and restaurants of every grade, yacht builders, chandlers, engineers and sailmakers. French charts can be bought at a bookshop up the street under the old clock tower.

Port des Minimes has a fuel berth at the *capitainerie*, water and electricity on the pontoons, showers and toilets, cranes and a travel-lift. Restaurants, cafés, food shops, chandlers, sailmakers and engineers are available on site, making a visit to the town for supplies unnecessary. Except at lowest tides, a *bus de mer* runs approximately hourly to the *avant-port* from the SW corner of the marina.

The town is very attractive and historically interesting. Airport and good train service.

La Pallice

This is the large modern commercial port of La Rochelle. It has no facility for yachts (which are not welcome) and no attractions for the yachtsman. No doubt it would be possible to use the port in an emergency. Entry is obvious from the large-scale charts.

49. Ile d'Aix

Lighthouse 46°00'·6N 1°10'·7W

Charts

BA *2746, 2748*
SHOM *6334*
Navicarte *551, 552*

Tidal data

Tidal heights (approx)

HW −0045 Pte de Grave springs, HW Pte de Grave neaps
MTL 3·7m. Index 3

Heights of tide above chart datum
MHWS 6·2m, MLWS 0·9m, MHWN 5·0m, MLWN 2·6m

Tidal streams

3 miles NW of the island the SE stream begins −0600 Pte de Grave and the NW begins −0030 Pte de Grave, spring rates 1 knot. 1 mile SW of the island the SE stream begins −0530 Pte de Grave and the NW begins HW Pte de Grave, spring rates 2 knots.

Depths

An open roadstead or drying beach; depths as required.

Lights

1. **Chauveau (**SE of Ile de Ré) 46°08'·1N 1°16'·3W Oc(2+1)WR.27m15/11M 057°-W-094⁵-R-104°-W-342°-R-057° White round tower, red top
2. **Fort Boyard** 46°00'·4N 1°12'·74W Q(9)15s27m round fort.
3. **Ile d'Aix** 46°00'N 1°12'·8W Fl.WR.5s24m24/20M 103°-R-118°-W-103° Two white round towers, red tops, one for the light, the other supporting the red sector screen
4. **La Charente river entrance Ldg Lts 115°** 45°58'·0N 1°04'·3W *Front* DirQ.R.8m19M White square tower, red top 113°-intens-117° *Rear* 600m from front DirQ.R.21m20M White square tower, red top

General

The Ile d'Aix lies about 8 miles south of La Rochelle and is a popular objective for a day sail; the anchorage is sufficiently sheltered for a night stop in fine weather. It is pleasanter in the evening, after the day-trippers have gone. The island is horseshoe-shaped and measures about a mile at its maximum. Within this area is built a walled and

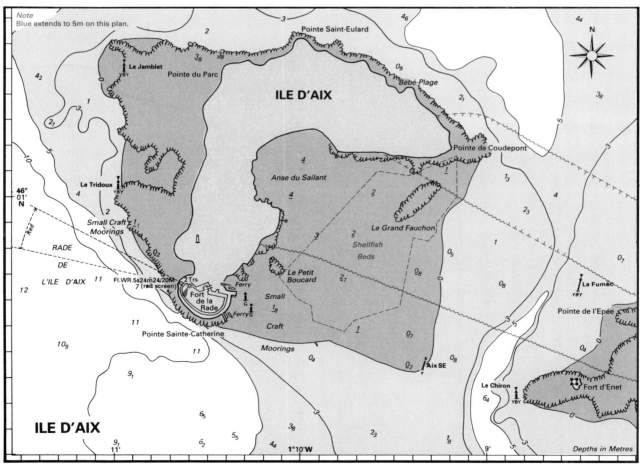

Plan 61

Looking NW over Ile d'Aix towards La Pallice. The twin light towers stand out well on Pointe St Catherine.

moated village where Napoleon was imprisoned before he was taken to St Helena in HMS *Bellerophon*.

At the east side of the island a prison still exists, but there are no restrictions elsewhere. A few fishermen live on Ile d'Aix, together with people who seek the peace of an island free of convention and so small that all parts are within earshot of the sea.

Approach

The approach is straightforward from any direction but probably easiest from the NW. Two beacons (W cardinal) mark the outlying rocks on the west side. The northern one should be given a berth of at least 500m and the southern one at least 200m. When the two white towers, one carrying the light and the other the screen for the red sector, come in transit, bearing 110°, the island can be approached. The SW side of the island is fairly clean and can be passed at a distance of 200m.

There is a narrow, deep channel to the E of the island. From the north, leave the eastern point of the island at least 500m to starboard to avoid a rocky spur and steer 195° to leave two W cardinal buoys and the conspicuous Fort d'Enet to port, passing between a W cardinal beacon to port and a yellow buoy with × topmark, marking the SE corner of the Aix oyster beds, to starboard.

By night

From the NW, keep in the white sector of the Ile d'Aix light[3] until Chauveau light[1] turns from red to white, bearing 342°; steer 162° down this boundary, passing through the red sector of Ile d'Aix light. When this turns white again, steer on the leading lights for the Charante[4] bearing 115°. When Ile d'Aix light bears N, steer 020°and anchor in 3m, or pick up a free mooring. There are liable to be yachts on moorings in this area.

Anchorage

Anchor 100m to 200m off the jetty and landing slip at Pointe Sainte Catherine, the south point of the island, going in as far as draught, tide and the need to keep clear of moorings allow. This anchorage is really sheltered only from the N and NE, but is partially sheltered from other directions by the mainland and Ile d'Oleron, so that it can be used in fine summer weather. The approaches are so well lit that there would be no difficulty in running for shelter to La Rochelle or elsewhere. The mud is very soft and the holding consequently poor.

It is also possible to anchor off the N or SW side of the island on a calm day, and several white mooring buoys may be in position for short-stay visitors. The Anse du Saillant, a sandy bay on the east side of the island, is a delightful place in which to dry out. It is advisable to observe the obstructions at low water before venturing in from the south between the oyster beds and the rocky patches off the SE side of the island.

Facilities

Those of a village: shops, PO, restaurants, hotel, *gendarmerie* and doctor, catering for the residents and holiday visitors by ferry.

50. La Charente, Rochefort

Entrance: 46°59'N 1°09'W

Charts

BA *2746, 2748*
SHOM *6334, 4333*
Navicarte *552*

Tidal data

Tidal heights (approx)

HW −0025 Pte de Grave springs, +0020 Pte de Grave neaps
MTL 3·7. Index 3

Heights of tide above chart datum
MHWS 6·4m, MLWS 1·4m, MHWN 5·1m, MLWN 2·2m

Tidal streams

Off the entrance the SE stream starts −0530 Brest and the NW starts +0130 Brest, spring rates 2 knots. In general streams in the river are about 2 knots, but where the river narrows they run up to 4 knots; they are affected by flood water. There is a bore on big spring tides which can attain 1·5m; at such times the river should be avoided. At Rochefort the streams begin about 1hr after HW and LW.

Depths

The approach is shallow (0·8m), but there is more water in the river. Without the large-scale chart, it should be treated as having 1m. Off Soubise there is 4m or more. There is commercial traffic in the river, and vessels of 5,000 tons with a draught of 5m can navigate the river at HW neaps.

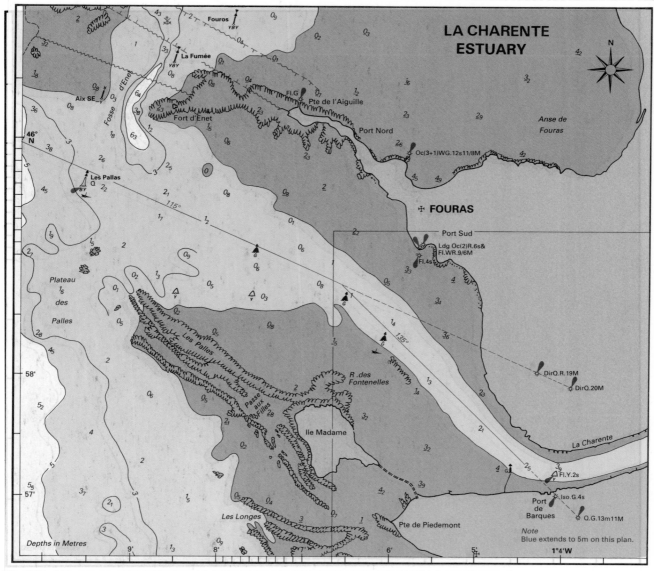

Plan 62

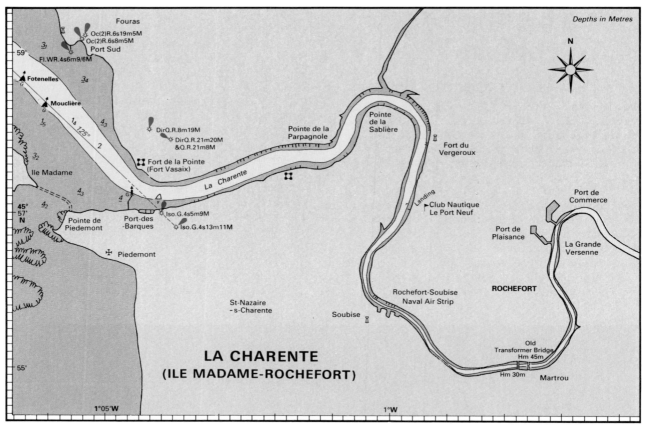

Plan 63

Lights

Two sets of leading lights (the line of starboard-hand buoys is unlit) lead into the river, after which there are no lights, so that entry by night is not advisable.

General

Suitable charts for the river are British Admiralty *2746*, for the entrance, and British Admiralty *2748*, which shows the whole river up to Rochefort. Navicarte *552* shows the entrance, SHOM *4333* shows the river to Rochefort, and SHOM *6334* shows the entrance and the river to Rochefort.

La Charante is an interesting river, away from the crowds, with a lot of bird life and some commercial traffic. The river lies between reedy banks, which have been reported to harbour mosquitoes on occasion. Rochefort is an historic town; it is an old naval base, well up the river for security from the British fleets.

Visitors in 1993 reported that Rochefort was the highlight of their cruise. The old rope-walk has been restored, and museums have been established in other buildings in the base. Upstream of the wet basin is what is claimed to be the oldest hydraulically operated dry dock in the world, constructed in 1669. The original pumping apparatus has been repaired; in 1992 the dock was operational and, sadly, occupied by a rusty fishing boat.

The wet basins have been converted into a flourishing marina. The new road bridge gives a clearance of 30m, and the old lifting bridge is permanently raised so that yachts may pass upriver without hindrance.

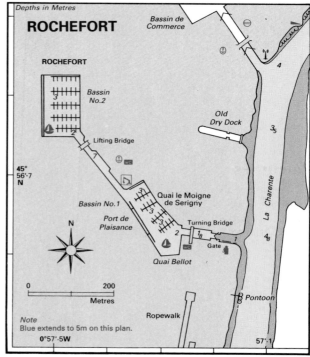

Plan 64

Masted vessels can go up to Tonnay; the river is navigable for motor yachts, and said to be very attractive, for a considerable distance upstream to Saintes.

Approach and passage upriver

The approach is straightforward at sufficient rise of tide. There are two pairs of leading lights to follow through the outer shoals, and a line of starboard-hand buoys. Oyster beds are extensive outside the channel. When the river is entered it is sufficient to keep in midstream. There are beacons on the shore, defining a succession of leading lines for the coasters. Many of the lines are marked at both ends, and the beacons for each line carry the same letter. It is better not to rely on them, as the large-scale chart shows that in some cases the intersection is in shallow water, so that it is necessary to turn off one line before the next is reached. Entrance and exit should be made on the flood or at the high water slack. As soon as the ebb starts, any sea outside produces breakers on the bar.

Anchorage

At Soubise, anchor on the S side of the river as near to the bank as possible, or arrange to borrow a mooring. The Yacht Club de Rochefort is on the north bank downstream of Soubise, and appears to be active, with landing facilities and a number of moorings along the south bank. There is a disused ferry slip at Soubise at which it is possible to land, but it is silted up with mud.

Upstream of Soubise there are sections where anchoring in the river is forbidden. Elsewhere it is not recommended, as the bottom is foul with old cables and the mud is very sticky. For a short wait on a rising tide it is preferable to stick the nose into the muddy bank.

At Rochefort the dock gate for the marina opens at HW La Rochelle, and only for a short time at neaps. While waiting it is possible to moor to the landing pontoon just downstream of the gate, or to the wall at the entrance. The docks farther upstream are strictly commercial and some commercial traffic is to be expected in the river.

Facilities

At Soubise all shops and hotel in the village, 5 minutes' walk. At Rochefort, fuel, water and toilet facilities in the marina and all the resources of a substantial town.

51. Ile d'Oléron

Charts

BA *2746* (northern part, S to Boyardville)
Imray *C41*
SHOM *6334P, 6335P*
Navicarte *552*

Tides and depths

See under the ports.

General

This island, formerly something of a backwater, looking back to the days when it was part of the realm of the kings of England, has now been connected to the mainland with a bridge. Consequently, it is developing many of the characteristics of a standard French summer resort. The *quichenotte*, a starched bonnet designed to resist the attentions of the licentious British soldiery, is not now much worn. The name is a corruption of 'kiss-not'.

There are five harbours, for four of which descriptions follow. The fifth, La Cotinière, is on the west side of the island. The west coast has a bad reputation and yachts should stand well off except in calm conditions. La Cotinière is base to a substantial fishing fleet, riding on heavy moorings against the Atlantic swell, with a recently built mole providing some shelter.

A new marina was constructed in 1989 at St Denis, at the northern tip of the island.

The marina Le Douhet, some 4½ miles down the NE coast, originally built for local boats, has been expanded to accept visiting yachts, with an improved entrance channel.

Boyardville has been up to now the main yacht harbour, with limited accommodation for visitors in the wet basin, but with a good anchorage off the beach.

Le Château d'Oléron is a small port wholly occupied with oysters, a place of historical interest whose many fishing boats, backed by the walls of the old fortifications overlooking the harbour, make a picturesque scene. Yachts are not particularly welcome in the port as they are expected to use the facilities provided for them elsewhere on the island. However, entrance to Le Château is described in this edition, since a short visit on the tide is interesting, provided that the fishermen suffer no interference.

Le Coureau d'Oléron is an interesting place to explore, rather off the beaten track. The English chart British Admiralty *2663* is of too small a scale and *2746* and *2748* each covers only part of the island. Navicarte *552* covers the area comprehensively and SHOM *6334* and *6335* overlap to cover the island and Le Coureau.

St Denis d'Oléron

46°02'·2N 01°22'W

Tidal data

Tidal heights (approx)
HW −0045 Pte de Grave springs, HW Pte de Grave neaps
MTL 3·6m. Index 3
Heights of tides above chart datum
MHWS 6·2m, MLWS 1·0m, MHWN 5·0m, MLWN 2·4m

Tidal streams
Outside SE begins −0600 Pte de Grave and NW begins −0100 Pte de Grave, spring rates 1·5 to 2 knots.

Depths
The entrance channel and sill dry 1·5m. Access across the sill for 2m draught 3 hours either side of HW. Marina dredged to 2m.

Lights
1. **Pointe de Chassiron** 46°02'·9N 1°24'·5W Fl.10s50m28M Tower b/w bands, semaphore station close to NW
2. **Rocher d'Antioche** 46°04'N 1°23'·6W Q.20m11M N cardinal beacon tower, surrounded by above-water wrecks!
3. **Dir Ldg Lt 205°** 46°01'·7N 1°21'·8W DirIso.WRG. 4s14m11·9M 190°-G-204°-W-206°-R-220° White concrete post with nacelle
4. **East breakwater head** 46°02'·1N 1°21'·9W Fl(2)WG.6s6m9/6M 205°-G-277°-W-292°-G-165° Green lantern on white square masonry shelter
5. **South breakwater head** Fl(2)R.6s3m6M Square masonry hut

Approach and entrance
The marina has been built on a point NE of the town. Approach with the church spire bearing 260°, when it should be in transit with a green beacon pole. Leaving the green beacon 100m to starboard, alter to starboard and, leaving a red beacon to port, cross the sill at the entrance.

By night
By means of the Pointe de Chassiron[1] and Rocher d'Antioche[2] lights, establish a position 2M NNE of the harbour in the white sector of the leading light[3]. Approach in the narrow white sector on 205° to

St Denis entrance.

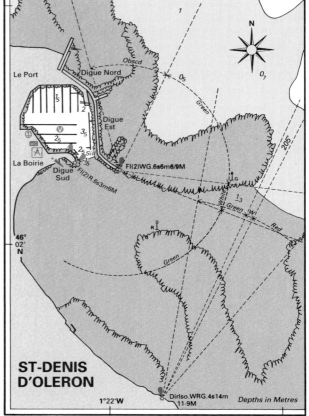

ST-DENIS D'OLERON

1°22'W   DirIso.WRG.4s14m 11·9M   *Depths in Metres*

Plan 65

enter the white sector of the E breakwater head light[4], then alter to starboard to enter the marina, leaving the E breakwater 40m to starboard to avoid an outcrop of sand and stones encroaching on the channel.

Mooring
There are three waiting buoys in 1m ENE of the entrance. In the marina, secure to the visitors' pontoon.

Facilities
When visited in 1992 the marina was not fully developed. However, there are water and electricity on the pontoons and a fuel berth near the entrance, with a depth gauge to show depth over the sill for departure. Showers and toilets at the *capitainerie*. Café/bar a short walk from the marina, and all the usual shops, with a PO and well stocked supermarket, in the town (15 minutes on foot). There are

670 berths in this marina, with 70 or 80 available to visitors. All the yachts inspected appeared to have round-headed mops instead of propellers. It is advisable to carry on board a length of plastic drainpipe with a Perspex window at one end with which to inspect the propeller so that the tight ball of Jap weed may be cleared.

Le Douhet

46°00'·1N 1°19'·00W

Tidal data

Tidal heights (approx)
HW −0045 Pte de Grave springs, HW Pte de Grave neaps
MTL 3·6m. Index 3
Heights of tide above chart datum
MHWS 6·2m, MLWS 1·0m, MHWN 5·0m, MLWN 2·4m

Tidal streams
Outside SE begins −0630 Pte de Grave and NW begins −0100 Brest, spring rates 1·5 knots.

Depths
The sill is 1·8m above datum, giving a depth of 1·5m at the pontoons. The entrance channel dries 1·5m.

Lights
At present there are no lights for entry at night.

Le Douhet, near LW.

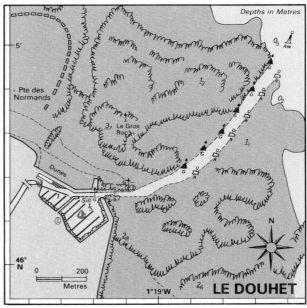

Plan 66

General
The Port du Douhet lies midway between the Pointe de Chassiron and Boyardville. It was enlarged in 1989, when an approach channel was dredged and marked and pontoons were installed to cater for 350 boats, with berths for some 30 visitors. Entrance is made across ½M of drying sand, with rocky shoals drying 2·5m or more on either side and a shifting sand bank to the south. The channel is disturbed in northerly and easterly winds and the marina must be positively identified before attempting an entrance.

Le Douhet entrance. Old mill arrowed.

Approach and entrance

Coming from the north it is advisable to keep at least 2M offshore, and at this distance the marina is not easy to identify. If a W cardinal spar buoy can be located, yacht masts can be seen in the marina, with a white red-roofed building with a gable on the north end in the trees behind them, bearing 225°. The entrance is in front of a gap in the tree line, with an old mill with a conical roof on the edge of the trees, to the north of the building. The final approach should be made with the old mill bearing 255° to pick up the line of small channel buoys.

The ends of the submerged loose-rock breakwaters are marked by a green starboard and a red port beacon. There is a second green beacon 300m north of the entrance beacon, marking Le Gros Roc, which dries 3·7m.

After entering the channel, a turn to port just inside the entrance will lead over the sill to the visitors' pontoon (see plan page 193).

Facilities

Water and electricity on the pontoons. Showers, toilets, launderette, restaurant, no fuel berth. Drying hard with concrete scrubbing platform, for 2·9m draught, in N part of harbour. Nearest shops at La Brée les Bains (3km) or St Georges d'Oléron (4km).

Boyardville (La Perrotine)

45°58'·2N 1°13'·8W

Tidal data

Tidal heights (approx)
HW −0040 Pte de Grave springs, +0010 Pte de Grave neaps
MTL 3·6m. Index 3
Heights of tide above chart datum
MHWS 6·1m, MLWS 0·8m, MHWN 4·9m, MLWN 2·3m

Tidal streams

Outside SE begins −0530 Pte de Grave, NW begins +0030 Pte de Grave, spring rates 2 knots. There can be 2 knots in the channel at maximum flow.

Depths

The bar dries 2m. Yachts take the ground inside, but the channel does not completely dry. The wet basin has 2m.

Light

1. **La Perrotine mole head** Fl(2)R.6s8m5M White metal framework, red top

General

The small port is on a tidal river, La Perrotine, with a bar at the entrance, which dries. There is a long stone mole on the SE side of the entrance. Outside the wet dock there are only a few berths suitable for yachts which cannot take the ground.

Approach

The entrance lies about 2 miles (200°) from the conspicuous Fort Boyard. A green (starboard) buoy lies in 11m, 800m NE of the mole head. 150m inside the buoy the bottom shoals almost vertically to the sand bank, which dries 2m. The channel across the sand shifts. In July 1988 and June 1992 a bulldozer was moving sand out of the channel inside the mole. Between the mole head and the buoy the direction of the channel is unpredictable. With sufficient water, steer for the mole head from the buoy and (with soundings) leave the mole head about 40m to port. Thence keep close to the mole, say 10m off, until the side begins to slope as the river is entered. From here, cross over to steer starboard of midchannel, and be prepared for a sharp turn to starboard to enter the wet basin.

By night

It is not really practicable for a stranger to enter by night, unless there is very bright moonlight. See below for offshore moorings.

Mooring

The entrance to the wet dock is at its E corner; the gates open and close automatically about two hours either side of high water, a warning light indicating their movement. Visitors must be prepared to berth against the NE wall, which is piled so that a plank is useful. In 1989 the number of visitors' berths was increased from 40 to 60. There is little room to manoeuvre in the dock.

Boyardville, photographed in 1993 at LW. The curious bank formation may not be there in 1994!

Entrance to Boyardville.

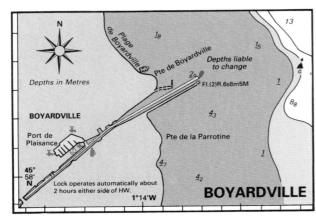

Plan 67

Yachts can lie in the river against quays above the marina entrance, the second from the sea end being recommended, or they can take the ground between the last quay and the bridge. The harbourmaster's office is on the wet dock quay. He is most obliging and his help should be sought. Yachts take the ground but do not dry out completely. The bottom is not level everywhere, so care is needed.

¾ mile north of the mole is a line of visitors' moorings, and one can anchor nearby in from 8m to 12m, with due regard to the rapidly shoaling bottom.

Facilities

Water and electricity on the pontoons. Yacht yard, chandlery and fuel berth on the port hand entering the river. Showers and toilets in the *capitainerie*. Supermarket upstream, past the square and restaurants on the quayside. Some shops in the small town, with a laundry which will do washing, drying and folding for a reasonable fee. Excellent bathing beach; small clams can be collected at low water.

Ferry to Ile d'Aix, connecting to La Rochelle, is convenient for foot passengers.

Le Château d'Oléron

46°53'·0N 1°11'·3W

Tidal data

Tidal heights (approx)
HW −0010 Pte de Grave springs, +0010 Pte de Grave neaps
MTL 3·5m. Index 2
Heights of tide above chart datum
MHWS 5·9m, MLWS 1·1m, MHWN 4·6m, MLWN 2·8m

Tidal streams
North of Le Château the streams reach 2 knots, SSE on the flood and NNW on the ebb. South of the road bridge, under which the streams can reach 4 knots, the streams reach up to 3 knots NE of the Pertuis de Maumusson, the flood running N and the ebb S. Off the entrance to Le Château the streams are weak. The SSE stream begins −0330 Pte de Grave, the NNW at +0030 Pte de Grave. There is no stream in the harbour.

Depths
The approach has a depth of 0·6m; the harbour dries 1·6m.

Lights
1. **Ldg Lts 319°** 45°53'·1N 1°11'·4W
   Front Q.R.11m7M 191°-vis-087° Red rectangle on low white tower
   Rear 240m from front Q.R.24m7M White tower, red top

General
There is no yachting activity in this small but busy oyster-fishing port. However, Le Château has the facilities of a holiday town, with the historical interest of the old fortifications.

Approach
The approach is made in the Coureau d'Oléron.

To explore this area, SHOM *6335* or a recently updated Navicarte *552* is recommended.

From the north
The shallows in the southern half of the Coureau are entirely covered by oyster beds. The channels are narrow and winding. Buoy-hopping is the order of the day, with a careful lookout for withies and the beacons which are often located well into the shallows. Read the name on the buoy to confirm your position before proceeding.

From a position midway between Ile d'Aix and Fort Boyard, a course of 155° should lead nearly 5 miles to the west cardinal buoy Chenal EN (the northern buoy at the entrance to the east channel) and will clear the dangers off the mouth of the Charente. Leaving Chenal EN close to port, continue on 155° for 1·5 miles to leave Chenal ES E cardinal buoy (in transit with the conspicuous tower of Marennes church on 167°) to starboard and Brouage red (port) buoy (lit) close to port. From here on port-hand beacons should be left to starboard, as the channel is marked for entry from the south. A course of 210° leads clear of Banc Lamouroux. The Banc de Charret beacon (black ■ topmark), well into the mud flats to port, and a red beacon and the green buoy Agnas to starboard should be located.

Steer for Agnas, leaving her close to port, then leave two red beacons on the Grande Mortanne to starboard and make for the Mortanne Sud S cardinal beacon, marking the entrance of the channel to Le Château d'Oléron.

Looking north over the Château d'Oléron at LW.

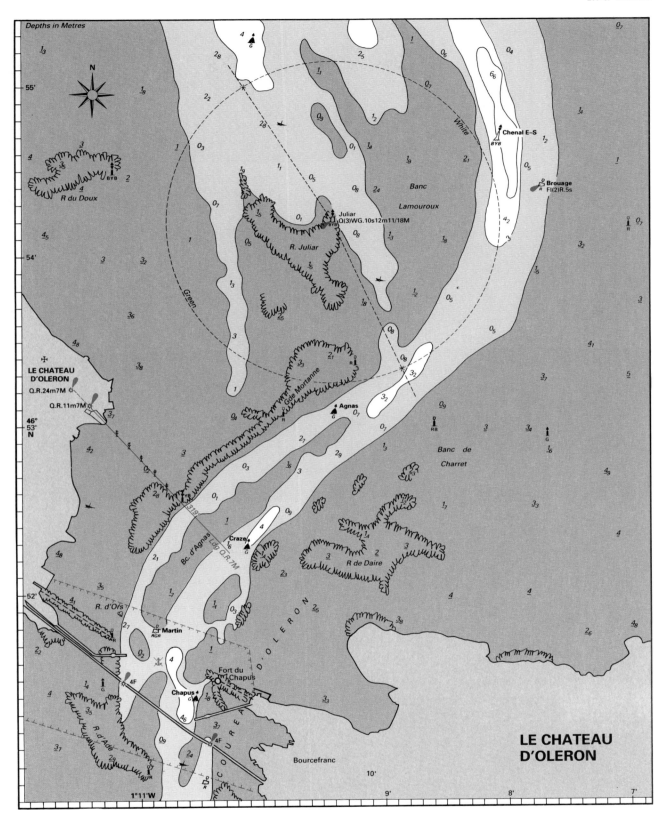

Depths in Metres

LE CHATEAU
D'OLERON

Plan 68

Entering Le Château through the narrow channel slightly left of the transit of the church spire and the two light towers. The starboard side of the channel is marked by withies.

Looking out of Le Château. *Capelan* is occupying the visitors' berth. The red board on the right is the front leading mark for the channel.

From the south

The channels look rather intricate and are subject to change. At low water an up-to-date chart is the best guide. If the rise of tide is sufficient to enter the harbour, it will be possible to pass safely over the shoals in midstream; note that the Banc d'Agnas dries up to 2m.

Entrance

Keep the Mortanne Sud S cardinal beacon close-to to starboard. Steer straight for the leading light structures. The front mark is a tubby white cylindrical tank with a red board above it, the rear mark is an ordinary white light tower with a red top. The starboard side of the entrance channel is marked by a line of withies; leave these about 10m to starboard. The channel is 10m wide and has been dredged to a depth of 0·8m, but is subject to silting. Do not obstruct the passage of the fishing boats and oyster barges, which are working to beat the tide.

By night

A stranger would not be able to navigate the Coureau d'Oléron by night. If he has reached the entrance channel by nightfall, the leading lights[1] will take him up to the harbour.

Harbour

The best water is at the quay on the port side of the outer harbour, drying 1·6m. The bottom is soft mud. Here a yacht will be very much in the way of fishing vessels and must take advice. The quay on the starboard side dries about 3m (bottom soft mud) near the seaward end, getting shallower near the shore. Here the yacht will be out of the way, so this is the place to go. There are plenty of ladders and mooring rings.

There is an inner harbour. It has a serviceable dock gate, but this is not used. The inner harbour is therefore shallower, and it is absolutely packed with fishing boats.

Facilities

Petrol and diesel on the quay, but fuel may not be available to pleasure craft. No visible signs of water. Chandlers near the harbour. All shops and restaurants in the town, about 10 minutes' walk. Municipal showers at the far end of the town. This is an interesting little harbour; the only difficulty is finding enough space without inconveniencing the busy fishermen.

Le Port de St Trojan

46°50'·9N 1°12'·3W

Moorings

The drying moorings off St Trojan les Bains at the south of the island below the bridge were recommended by a French yachtsman in Rochefort. There appears to be much yachting activity here, but a visit by land indicated that the area was not really suitable for visitors.

A French chart should be used to avoid the oyster beds when visiting St Trojan.

52. La Seudre

Charts

Imray *C41*
SHOM *6335*
Navicarte *552*

Tidal data

Tidal heights (approx)

HW −0010 Pte de Grave springs, +0010 Pte de Grave neaps
MTL 3·5m. Index 2
Heights of tide above chart datum
MHWS 5·8m, MLWS 1·2m, MHWN 4·7m, MLWN 2·4m

Tidal streams

In the Coureau d'Oléron the tides vary considerably from point to point but typically run at up to 2 knots springs, except under the Oléron-to-mainland road bridge and in La Seudre river, where they can reach 4 knots.

Depths

The channels of approach are shallow, one carrying 1·1m and the other drying 1m. The river is deep, typically about 7m. The canals to Marennes and Tremblade can be assumed to dry 2·5m.

Lights

Except for those on the bridges, the area cannot be considered to be lit.

General

La Seudre offers an anchorage in fair conditions near the southern end of the Coureau d'Oléron. When it was visited in 1988 conditions were good and it was possible to proceed up the canal to Marennes for a two-night stay in the wet basin. In 1992, with a steady NW wind of force 5 to 6, there was not enough water to proceed up the canal, and a combination of strong wind and flood tide would have made a night at anchor in the river unpleasant.

The entrance to the river is shallow and should not be taken near low water, but once inside the river is deep. The scenery is not exciting, as old saltpans lie for some distance behind either bank; in these an extensive and intensive oyster culture is carried on. Both La Tremblade and Marennes are pleasant towns in the season; the latter is farther from both the river and the inner end of its canal.

Approach and entrance

There are two entrance channels, La Soumaille to the north and La Garrigue to the south. Both channels are narrow, and the stranger should take frequent soundings to ensure that he is keeping in the deep water.

An up-to-date French chart should be used, as the configuration of the banks and positions of the buoys change. At present there is no large-scale English chart available.

Chenal de la Soumaille

In 1992 the simplest way to enter this channel was across part of the Banc Bourgeois, drying 1m. Coming from the north it is first necessary to pass under the road bridge joining Oléron to the mainland. 400m S of the bridge in midchannel is a wreck, which may be marked by a red beacon. The channel is buoyed for entry from the south and it is advisable to check the buoys' names as they are passed. The preferred arches for passage under the bridge are south of the old ferry piers on either side of the channel and are marked by white squares with a red square or a green triangle. Local fishing boats ignore these and pass under the central arches.

To make use of the SE preferred arch, leave a green (starboard-hand) buoy to port and round the head of the old ferry pier on the mainland bank. Leave a red (port-hand) buoy (if it is in position) to starboard and pass under the marked arch of the bridge to leave the next red buoy close to starboard. The next buoy to steer for, bearing 198°, is the green (starboard) Meule NW, to be left close to port. Meule SE (150°) is the next green buoy to leave to port, followed by a red (port) buoy, Trompe de Sot (210°). Leave this and La Palette (port) to starboard and approach Bry NE green (starboard) buoy closely enough to read its name without passing it, as it will be left to starboard.

From Bry NE buoy, the red buoy (port), Soumaille NW, marking the beginning of the Soumaille channel bears 113°. Steer to leave this buoy to port, as you will now be passing up the channel. The southern end of Banc Bourgeois (drying 1m) will be crossed. After Soumaille NW, the channel, which is narrow and steep-to on its northern side, deepens to 2m and shortly after to 4·5m. The Seudre road bridge (clearance 18m) will be seen ahead. Leave Soumaille SE buoy (port) and Le Jéac beacon (port) to port, and Saut de Barat E cardinal buoy to starboard, before passing under the marked arch of the bridge.

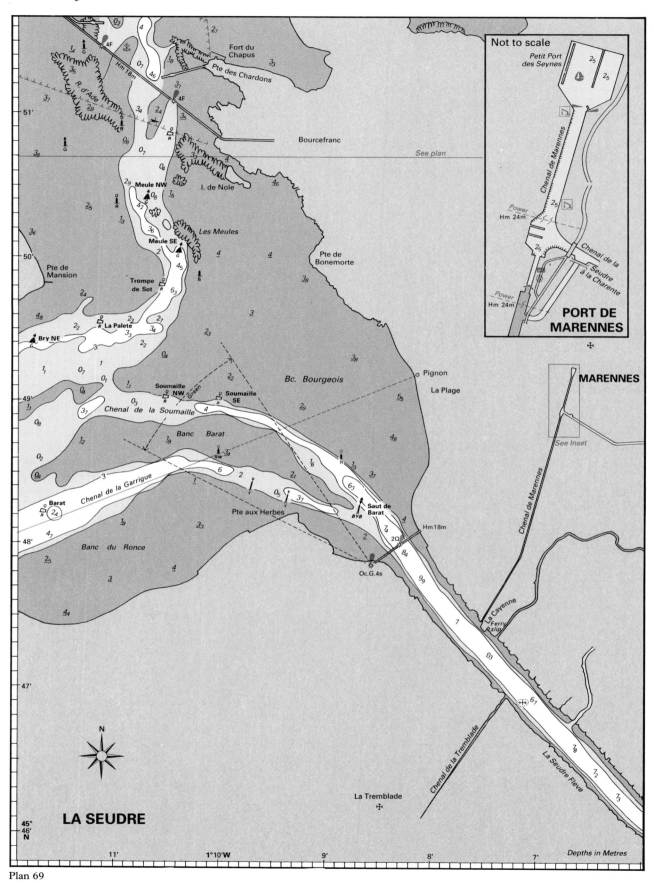

Not to scale

Petit Port
des Seynes

2₅

2₅

Chenal de Marennes

Power
Hm 24m

2₅

2₅

Chenal de la

Seudre
à la Charente

2₅

Power
Hm 24m

**PORT DE
MARENNES**

MARENNES

See Inset

O₂

4F

4
Hm 18m

O₁
4₆
1₈

Fort du
Chapus

Pte des Chardons

3₃

4F
3₇

Bourcefranc

See plan

R. d'Ade

3₇

3₄
2₄
3₅

O₈
R

51'

G

3₈

O₇

Meule NW
O₈
4₂
G
1₅
1₃

I. de Nole

4₆

2₉

Les Meules

2₅

3₆

3₆

50'

Pte de
Mansion

Meule SE
G

2

4

4

Pte de
Bonemorte

3₈

Trompe
de Sot
R

6₃

4₅

B

2₄

4₈

La Palete
2₃
2₇
3₄

3

La Plage

Bry NE

2₂

3₃

2₂

3

1₁

O₇

1

O₄

3

Bc. Bourgeois

Pignon

5₅

1₁

O₄

Soumaille
NW
R

Green

Soumaille
SE
R

2₂

49'

1₁

O₃

3₇

Chenal de la Soumaille

4

2₉

4₈

O₈

Banc   Barat

1₂

1₉

RW
3₄

1₃

O₈

O₂

3

Chenal de la Garrigue

6

2

2₁

1₆

6₃

3₇

Barat
R
2₄

1

O₅

3₇

Saut de
Barat
BYB

7₄

Hm 18m

Pte aux Herbes

2

2Q

O₄

1₉

3₃

2

8₄

48'

4₇

Banc   du   Ronce

4

Oc.G.4s

9₉

2₅

3

Chenal de Marennes

7

La Cavenne

4₄

Ferry
slip

8₃

47'

6₁

N

La Seudre Fleve

7₈

Chenal de la Tremblade

7₂

La Tremblade

7₃

45°
46'
N

LA SEUDRE

Entrance to the Marennes canal.

Chenal de la Garrigue

The outer section of this channel, which leads in from the Pertuis de Maumusson, is well buoyed on the port side; the first buoy is Galon d'Or (RW fairway buoy), inside the Pertuis de Maumusson at the southern end of Ile d'Oléron. It is followed by three port-hand buoys. From the last of these, Barat, with extensive oyster beds to starboard, the channel continues towards the Barat beacon (red with • topmark) 1½ miles away (070°). Steer to keep a white wall beacon on the shore in transit with Barat beacon, bearing 067°. About 400m from the Barat beacon the channel turns to starboard. Steer to keep the Saut de Barat buoy (E cardinal) bearing 107°. ½ mile before Saut de Barat the channel narrows and soundings are necessary to avoid straying into the shallows. The depth here should be 5m, but reduces to 0·8m abreast of the buoy, shortly after increasing to 7m or more below the bridge.

Anchorage and mooring

The best anchorages are near the disused ferry slips for Marennes (north bank) and La Tremblade (south bank). The former is called La Cayenne and is about ½ mile downstream of the latter. Anchor near the side of the river and land on the ferry slip, carrying the dinghy ashore clear of the slip.

There are canals, which should be treated as drying 2·5m, leading to the villages of Marennes and La Tremblade. To get this depth it is essential to keep exactly in the middle of the channel. The canals are lined on each side by the boats and other apparatus for oyster culture.

At La Tremblade it is possible to berth alongside the stone quay to starboard just round the bend at the top end of the canal. Once round the bend the best water is on the starboard side; the bottom is soft mud. The water shoals rapidly once the far end of the quay is reached. There is not much room, but visitors may be helped to find a berth. Although some yachts are based at the top of the canal, it is really better for a dinghy excursion, which is worth while if only to have it brought home how many oysters there are.

At the entrance to the Marennes canal, which lies just downstream of the ferry pier, there is a slight bend to starboard. The perches are high on the mud, but the best water lies roughly halfway between them. At the upper end of the canal is a wet dock with 2·5m depth, the gates of which are open about one hour each side of high water. A power line with 16m clearance crosses the canal below the gate and another with 24m clearance crosses the dock. The dock is used by some 70 yachts and provides a convenient and pleasant berth if there is room. The oyster culture, though notable, is not quite on the scale of that at La Tremblade.

Facilities

At La Tremblade all shops and restaurants. Marine engineer and outboard specialist. At Marennes there are shops, cafés and a large hypermarket, which sells everything, at the rear of the post office, reached by a few minutes' walk through pretty municipal gardens. There is a yacht builder at the wet dock, as well as a 6-tonne crane, toilets and 1 cold and 1 hot shower, with a water tap and electricity on the quay.

53. Pertuis de Maumusson

Note The information for this chapter, which has not been altered from the 4th edition, comes principally from Mrs Tew, Mr Ian Tew and Mr P.C. Hordern.
Fairway buoy 45°47'·0N 1°17'·8W

Charts

Imray *C41*
SHOM *6335P*
Navicarte *552*

Tidal data

Tidal heights (approx)
HW −0010 Pte de Grave springs, +0010 Pte de Grave neaps
MTL 3·4m. Index 1
Heights of tide above chart datum
MHWS 5·5m, MLWS 1·3m, MHWN 4·5m, MLWN 2·4m

Looking over the Pertuis de Maumusson to the entrance to La Seudre river in 1993.

Tidal streams

The flood begins at about +0600 Pte de Grave and the ebb at about −0100 Pte de Grave; spring rates 3 knots.

Depths

Variable, but sufficient for yachts near high water.

General

The Pertuis de Maumusson, between the southern end of Ile d'Oléron and the mainland, has such a bad reputation that many people say that it cannot be used by yachts in any circumstances. Twenty-five years ago, discussions with local fishermen, and the experience of at least one yachtsman who used it, suggested that this was not true. Mrs Tew told the present editor that her husband went out through the Pertuis in a local fishing boat to reconnoitre and that when they attempted the passage in their yacht they missed the tide by 15 minutes. The rapid formation of the breakers made it essential for them to turn back.

Mrs Tew's advice today is that the passage should only be attempted in a well-found boat with a strong keel and that arrangements should be made to follow a local fishing boat known to have a greater draught.

The passage is completely exposed to the Atlantic, and if there is any onshore wind or swell the shallow and uneven bottom causes breakers to form right across as soon as the flood tide stops. The passage must therefore be made on the last of the flood, and at that only in calm weather or with an offshore wind, and in the absence of swell.

The bottom is sand, so the channel shifts and is said to be tending to get shallower. The buoys are not moved to follow all these shifts, though normally they indicate a line which will give enough

water for a yacht at high water in smooth conditions. Only the local people know the current position of the deepest water in relation to the buoys; hence the need to follow a local fishing boat.

For the outward passage there is the opportunity to inspect the channel near low water if one arrives in good time, to see the state of the sea, and if necessary to turn back with a favourable tide, since the passage should be taken before high water.

The inward passage must contain an unacceptable element of risk except in very good weather. The breakers, if they exist, cannot always be seen clearly from seaward, it is more difficult to identify the run of the channel, and if one gets into difficulty it will be hard to retreat to sea with the tide carrying one in. It is the opinion of Colonel J. Tisserand, Président de la Station de Sauvetage de Royan, that a modern yacht should not attempt entry whatever the conditions.

Finally, it must be emphasised that this passage is very SEVERE, only to be attempted in very good weather by those who have experience of tidal race conditions and a robust boat. Adequate and reliable power is essential. The speed at which the breakers begin near high water is dramatic.

54. Royan and the Gironde

BXA light buoy 45°37'·6N 1°28'·6W

Charts

BA *2910, 2916, 2664*
Imray *C41*
SHOM *7028P, 7029P*
Navicarte *553, 554*

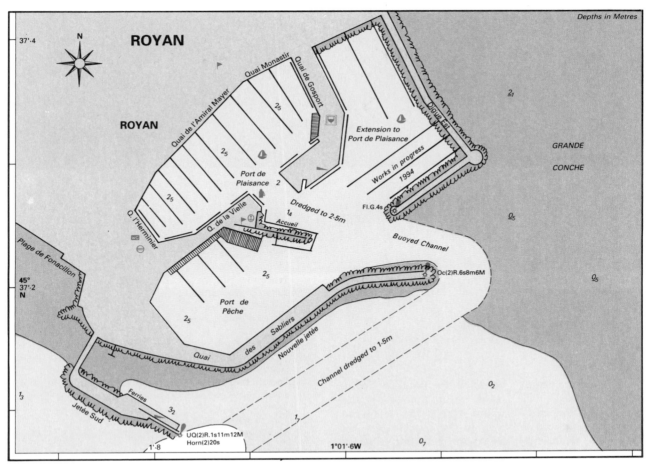

Depths in Metres

ROYAN

37'·4

N

ROYAN

Quai de l'Amiral Mayer

Quai Monastir

Quai de Gosport

2₅

2₅

Extension to
Port de Plaisance

Works in progress

1994

Digue Est

GRANDE

CONCHE

2₁

2₅

Port de
Plaisance   2

Q. l'Herminier

Q. de la Vielle

Accueil

Dredged to 2·5m

1₄

Fl.G.4s

0₅

Plage de Fonacillon

45°
37'·2
N

2₅

Port   de
Pêche

2₅

Buoyed Channel

Oc(2)R.6s8m6M

0₅

0₅

Quai   des   Sabliers

Nouvelle jetée

Channel dredged to 1·5m

1₇

0₂

1₃

Ferries

3₂

Jetée Sud

UQ(2)R.1s11m12M
Horn(2)20s

1'·8

1°01'·6W

0₇

Plan 70

Looking NW over Royan harbour. The pontoons in the new
basin were not in position in 1993. Cathedral arrowed.

Approaching Royan in 1988, before the new basin was constructed. The curved roof of the cathedral is a good mark.

Tidal data

Tidal heights (approx)
HW −0005 Pte de Grave springs, HW Pte de Grave neaps
MTL 3·0m. Index 0
Heights of tide above chart datum
MHWS 5·1m, MLWS 0·9m, MHWN 4·1m, MLWN 1·9m

Tidal streams

In the main entrance channel the flood E begins about −0530 Pte de Grave, spring rate about 3½ knots, and the ebb W about +0100 Pte de Grave, spring rates about 4 knots. In the bay close to the port there is an eddy; the stream runs continuously southward, 1 knot during the flood, 2 knots during the ebb.

Depths

The estuary channel is deep. There is 1m or less at the entrance to Royan harbour. The marina is dredged to 2·5m.

Lights

1. **BXA light buoy** 45°37'·6N 1°28'·6W Iso.4s8m8M Whis
2. **La Coubre** 45°41'·8N 1°14'·0W Fl(2)10s64m28M White tower, red top
   Auxiliary light F.RG.42m12/10M 030°-R-043°-G-060°-R-110° On same support
   RC *LK* (·−··/−·−) 292kHz 100M
3. **Cordouan** 43°35'·2N 1°10'·4W Oc(2+1)WRG.12s 60m22-18M 014°-W-126°-G-178·5°-W-250°-W(unintens)-267°-R(unintens)-294·5°-R-014° White conical tower, dark grey band and top, dark grey base
4. **Palmyre Ldg Lts 081·5°** 45°39'·6N 1°08'·7W *Front* DirIso.4s21m22M 080·5°-intens-082·5° White frame structure
   Auxiliary Q(2)5s10m3M same structure
5. *Rear for 4* DirQ.57m27M 080·5°-intens-082·5° White radar tower
   Rear for 6 DirF.R.57m17M 325·5°-intens-328·5° Same structure
6. **Terre Nègre Ldg Lts 327°** 45°38'·8N 1°06'·4W *Front* Oc(3)WRG.12s39m18-14M 304°-R-319°-W-327°-G-000°-W-004°-G-097°-W-104°-R-116° White tower, red top on W side

7. **The channel buoys** are port: red, flashing or occulting, starboard: green, flashing, occulting or isophase, except for No. 7, N card, Q
   Note that No. 7a (Fl.G.4s) and No. 9 (Fl(2)G.6s) are north of the leading line
Royan entrance (Lights may be altered from 1994.)
8. **R1 starboard wreck buoy** 45°36'·7N 1°01'·8W Iso.G.4s
9. **South jetty head** 45°37'·1N 1°01'·7W UQ(2)R.1s 11m12M Horn (2) 20s. White tower, red brick base Klaxon(2)20s by day from HW−2½ to HW+2
10. **New jetty, 20m from head** Oc(2)R.6s8m6M White mast, red top. Extinguished while work in progress 1993
11. **North mole spur** Iso.4s strip light
12. **East jetty head** Fl.G.4s2m6M 311°-vis-151° White post, green top

Leading marks for entry to the Gironde. La Palmyre lighthouse is the rear mark. The front mark is on rails so that it can be moved left or right as the channel changes.

General

In the 1939–45 war, according to information in the modern church of Notre Dame, the town of Royan was thought by the Allies to be a German base and was consequently bombed, with heavy loss of life to the inhabitants. The buildings are all new and the asymmetrical spire of the church stands up above the town as a landmark. Royan is now a holiday centre with a yacht harbour; it is twinned with Gosport. The marina was extended in 1993 and makes an excellent staging point for those entering or leaving the Gironde on the way to or from the Canal du Midi. Out of 1,000 berths, 100 are reserved for visitors. The harbourmaster is most helpful and will do his best to find a berth for a short stay in the busy season.

Approach

Entry to the Gironde should not be attempted in heavy weather, or in bad visibility. The shoals extend a long way seaward and the strong tides can make bad seas. A recently corrected chart is essential; the banks shift, and this entails frequent movement not only of the buoys, but also of the leading lights. In 1992 the starboard-hand channel buoys Nos 7a and 9 were north of the leading line of 081·5°, although there was still sufficient water (6m) for a yacht if she kept to the line.

The Banc de la Mauvaise/Banc de la Coubre has an evil reputation which is well merited. Coming from the north, keep at least 5 miles offshore. It is convenient to enter the channel two hours before high water and so to arrive at Royan before the tide turns. Make a position ½ mile west of the first two channel buoys, Nos 1 and 2, and turn in onto 081° to steer between the buoys and pick up the leading line. The deep-water channel is narrow for 3 miles and a yacht may prefer to sail a parallel course, keeping south of the port-hand buoy No. 6. After No. 7 (N card) it is wide and there is no problem in following the buoyed channel to Royan.

The town of Royan, with its white buildings and modern church, will be easily identified. The shore should be given a berth of 400m; on reaching Pointe du Chay, steer for the red and white light tower on the south jetty head, where the ferry berths.

From the SE, pass outside Banc de St Georges, leaving to starboard No. 12 (port-hand) buoy at its NW end, or cutting the corner if tide and conditions allow. An alternative daylight course inside the Banc passes about 500m off Pointe de Susac and Pointe de Vallières; thence continue on 330° for the south jetty head, avoiding the wrecks, over which there is 3m, marked by a starboard buoy.

By night

The outer approach is as by day, remembering that buoys Nos 7a and 9 (starboard) are north of the leading line. On passing No. 11 buoy (starboard, Iso.G.4s), alter to starboard to follow the curve of the channel.

Entrance

On close approach leave to port the south jetty and the outer harbour mole. The marina entrance then opens up, the straight approach on a NW course leaving 3 mole heads to port and two to starboard. There is only 1m outside, but the marina is dredged to 2·5m.

By night

Pick up the harbour lights[9, 10, 11, 12] and leave to starboard a buoy[8] (Iso.G.4s) marking a wreck.

Mooring

On arrival, secure to the *accueil* pontoon on the port-hand side in the entrance. Visit the *capitainerie* to obtain a berth. If possible do not remain on the *accueil* pontoon, as the excursion boats sometimes have trouble with their departure manoeuvres.

Facilities

All the facilities of a sophisticated holiday town. Water and electricity on the pontoons; showers and toilets in the *capitainerie* and elsewhere. Fuel berth below the *capitainerie*. Slipway, grid, crane (which could be used for dismasting if proceeding into the Canal du Midi), 26-tonne travel-lift. All shops, chandlers, restaurants, banks and hotels close by, many in the arcade overlooking the marina. Railway station and aerodrome. A ferry runs from the south jetty to Port Bloc.

The Gironde

Although this area is outside the scope of this book, the following notes may be helpful. There is a well marked ship channel to Bordeaux. The tide runs so hard that a yacht with a reasonable turn of speed can make Bordeaux on a single tide.

It is also possible to stop at a number of places, such as the new yacht harbour at Meschers-sur-Gironde, some five miles upstream of Royan (avoiding the Banc de St Georges), Pauillac and Blaye, on the way up. At Bordeaux there is a marina to starboard just above the suspension bridge, and it is also possible to enter the docks, a little further up to starboard, from 2hrs before HW until HW. There are cranes for dismasting both at the marina and at the docks.

Meschers new marina (1993), 5 miles upstream of Royan, at LW.

55. Port Bloc

Estacarde Nord (landing stage) light
45°34'·2N 1°03'·7W

Charts

BA *2910, 2916, 2664*
Imray *C41*
SHOM *7028P*
Navicarte *553, 554*

Tidal data

Tidal heights (approx)
HW HW Pte de Grave
MTL 3·2m. Index 0
Heights of tide above chart datum
MHWS 5·3m, MLWS 1·0m, MHWN 4·3m, MLWN 2·1m

Tidal streams

The SE stream begins at −0530 Pte de Grave, the NW at +0100 Pte de Grave; spring rates 3¾ knots.

Depths

The approaches are deep. There is 2m to 2·5m in the harbour.

Lights

1. **Pointe de Grave** 45°34'·2N 1°03'·9W Oc.WRG.4s 26m19-15M 033°-W(unintens)-054°-W-233·5°-R-303°-W-312°-G-330°-W-341°-W(unintens)-025° White square tower, black corners and top
2. **Buoy 13B (starboard)** Oc.G.4s7m5M
3. **N exterior mole head** Q.6m2M N card beacon
4. **N landing stage** Fl.G.4s9m3M White metal framework tower, green top. Lit by day in poor visibility
5. **S landing stage** Iso.R.4s8m6M White tower, red top, lit by day in poor visibility

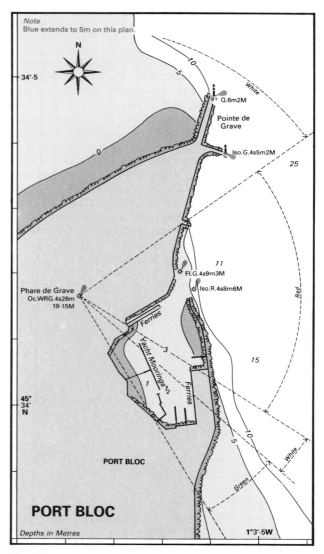

Plan 71

Entrance to Port Bloc.

General

Port Bloc, a small harbour just behind Pointe de Grave, is a convenient passage harbour. It is used by the ferries to Royan and by the buoy-maintenance vessels, but is otherwise a long way from anywhere. Pleasantly situated among the pine trees, it is reasonably sheltered, though some swell is said to enter in bad weather.

Approach and entrance

For the outer approach, and notes on the Gironde, see the previous chapter. By night the final entry into the river can be made with La Palmyre red light in transit with Terre Nègre light astern, bearing 327°.

The main problem in the final approach is not to be set onto the mole off Pointe de Grave, or swept up the river, depending on the tide. The harbour entrance faces NE, nearly parallel with the shore. The entrance is not very easily made out until it is close to, but it is only about 600m to the south of the extreme tip of the Pointe de Grave.

Approach on a SW course from buoy No. 13B (starboard), and enter between the light structures, white with red top to port and white with green top to starboard. The ferries occupy the whole of the entrance, so if one is on the move stand off until the entrance is clear.

Anchorage and mooring

There is a long pontoon for local boats running down the centre of the harbour in a north/south direction, with a line of mooring buoys inside. The eastern or seaward side of the harbour is for the use of the ferries, the buoy vessels and the lifeboat. Visiting yachts may berth between the mooring buoys in 2m or less, or, if a berth is available, at the pontoon. There is little space for visitors. The depth between the moorings and the shore to the west is given as 0m and it may be possible, if uncomfortable, for shallow-draught vessels to anchor well south of the ferry slip.

Facilities

Water, showers and toilets, scrubbing slip. Not much else at present. There is a café and there are frequent ferries to Royan. There is also a railway with train services to Bordeaux.

Appendix

III. CONVERSION TABLES

Feet	Metres	Metres	Feet	Nautical miles	Kilo- metres	Gallons	Litres	Pounds	Kilograms
1	0·3	1	3·3	1	1·9	1	4·5	1	0·4
2	0·6	2	6·6	2	3·7	2	9·1	2	0·9
3	0·9	3	9·8	3	5·6	3	13·6	3	1·4
4	1·2	4	13·1	4	7·4	4	18·2	4	1·8
5	1·5	5	16·4	5	9·3	5	22·7	5	2·3
6	1·8	6	19·7	6	11·1	6	27·3	6	2·7
7	2·1	7	23·0	7	13·0	7	31·8	7	3·2
8	2·4	8	26·2	8	14·8	8	36·4	8	3·6
9	2·7	9	29·5	9	16·7	9	40·9	9	4·1
10	3·0	10	32·8	10	18·5	10	45·5	10	4·5
20	6·1	20	65·6	20	37·1	20	90·9	20	9·1
30	9·1	30	98·4	30	55·6	30	136·4	30	13·6
40	12·1	40	131·2	40	74·1	40	181·8	40	18·2
50	15·2	50	164·0	50	92·6	50	227·3	50	22·7
100	30·5	100	328·1	100	185·3	100	454·6	100	45·4

Conversion tables

An approximate method of converting metres to feet
is to multiply by 10 and then divide by 3. The
answer will be too great, but only by one part in 60,
which can usually be neglected.

Index